QUESTIONING ETHICS

Questioning Ethics: Contemporary debates in philosophy is a major discussion by some of the world's leading thinkers of crucial ethical issues confronting us today.

Original contributions by Habermas, Derrida, MacIntyre, Ricoeur, Kristeva and other major philosophers are organized around five sections: hermeneutics, deconstruction, critical theory, psychoanalysis and applications of ethics. Topics considered in these sections include the nature of politics, women's rights, lying, repressed memory, historical debt and forgiveness, the self and responsibility, revisionism, bioethics and multiculturalism. Each section engages with the critical implications of these problems for philosophy.

A key feature of this book is an interview with Jacques Derrida, which makes available the most accessible insight into his thinking for many years. There is also an interview with Paul Ricoeur, which offers a very useful introduction to some of the key themes in his work.

Contributors: *Hermeneutics:* Paul Ricoeur; Richard Kearney; Jeffrey Barash; Jean Greisch. *Deconstruction:* Jacques Derrida; John D. Caputo; David Wood; Simon Glendinning. *Critical Theory:* Jürgen Habermas; Karl-Otto Apel; Thomas McCarthy; David M. Rasmussen. *Psychoanalysis:* William J. Richardson; Julia Kristeva; Simon Critchley. *Applications:* Alasdair MacIntyre; Maeve Cooke; Peter Kemp.

The Editors: Richard Kearney is Professor of Philosophy at University College Dublin and Boston College. He is the author of *The Wake of Imagination, Poetics of Imagining, Postnationalist Ireland*, editor of *Continental Philosophy in the Twentieth Century* and co-editor of *The Continental Philosophy Reader*, all published by Routledge. Mark Dooley is Lecturer in Philosophy at University College Dublin, and at the National University of Ireland, Maynooth. He has published numerous articles in the area of continental philosophy, and has a book forthcoming on Kierkegaard, Derrida, and postmodern ethics.

QUESTIONING ETHICS

Contemporary debates in philosophy

*Edited by Richard Kearney
and Mark Dooley*

London and New York

First published 1999
by Routledge
11 New Fetter Lane, London EC4P 4EE

Simultaneously published in the USA and Canada
by Routledge
29 West 35th Street, New York, NY 10001

The editor and publisher wish to thank the following for permission
to reprint previously published material: Chapter 12: Thomas McCarthy (1995)
'Enlightenment and the Idea of Public Reason' in *The European Journal
of Philosophy*, 3, (1995) 242–256. Reprinted with permission
from Blackwell Publishers Ltd.

Typeset in Sabon by
BC Typesetting, Bristol
Printed and bound in Great Britain by
TJ International Ltd, Padstow, Cornwall

British Library Cataloguing in Publication Data
A catalogue record for this book is available from the British Library

Library of Congress Cataloging in Publication Data
Questioning ethics: debates in contemporary philosophy/edited by
Richard Kearney and Mark Dooley.
p.   cm.
1. Ethics, Modern–20th century.   I. Kearney, Richard.
II. Dooley, Mark.
BJ319.Q47   1999
170–dc21   98-8544
CIP

ISBN 0–415–18034–1 (hbk)
ISBN 0–415–18035–X (pbk)

This book is dedicated to the memory of
Míceál O'Regan
and
John Kevin Tierney

CONTENTS

CONTENTS

CONTRIBUTORS

Karl-Otto Apel is Emeritus Professor of Philosophy at the Johann Wolfgang Goethe University, Frankfurt.

Jeffrey Barash is Professor of Philosophy at the University of Amiens.

John D. Caputo is David R. Cook Professor of Philosophy at Villanova University.

Maeve Cooke is Lecturer in German at University College Dublin.

Simon Critchley is Reader in Philosophy at the University of Essex.

Jacques Derrida is Director of Studies at the Ecole des Hautes Etudes en Sciences Sociales, Paris.

Simon Glendinning is Lecturer in Philosophy at the University of Reading.

Jean Greisch is Dean of the Faculty of Philosophy at the Institut Catholique de Paris.

Jürgen Habermas is Professor of Philosophy at the Johann Wolfgang Goethe University, Frankfurt.

Peter Kemp is Director of the Centre for Ethics and Law, Copenhagen.

Julia Kristeva is Professor of Linguistics at the University of Paris VII.

Alasdair MacIntyre is Professor of Philosophy at Duke University.

Thomas McCarthy is Professor of Philosophy at Northwestern University.

David M. Rasmussen is Professor of Philosophy at Boston College.

William J. Richardson is Professor of Philosophy at Boston College.

Paul Ricoeur is Emeritus Professor of Philosophy at the Universities of Nanterre and Chicago.

David Wood is Professor of Philosophy at Vanderbilt University.

INTRODUCTION

Richard Kearney and Mark Dooley

One of the key Continental thinkers of this century, Emmanuel Levinas, declared that 'ethics is first philosophy'. Whether one agrees with this challenging claim or not it is certain that no philosophy can do without ethics. This book brings together some of the most recent debates on this subject in contemporary European thought.

Opening with a series of critical exchanges on the moral significance of memory, history and value (Ricoeur, Kearney, Barash, Greisch), the volume proceeds to the question of the role of responsibility and justice in deconstruction (Derrida, Caputo, Wood, Glendinning). The third section of the book comprises some of the most innovative thinkers in critical theory, debating such controversial issues as democracy (Habermas), multi-culturalism (Apel) and public reason (McCarthy, Rasmussen). The fourth part features three pioneering theorists of current controversies in the ethics and politics of psychoanalysis (Richardson, Kristeva, Critchley). A final section deals with three applications of these theories to the moral challenges of post-Enlightenment reason (MacIntyre), feminism (Cooke), and bioethics (Kemp).

We speak of 'contemporary European ethics' in the broadest sense to cover a generous range of philosophies running from phenomenology to theories of communicative action. The contributions to this volume include references to diverse thinkers, from Husserl to Wittgenstein, Kant to Marx, Foucault to Taylor, Heidegger to Freud. Our contributors themselves hail from different continents and cultures, and we are grateful to our translators who have made several of the foreign-language essays available in English for the first time.

It has been said that ethics is one of modern Continental thought's forgotten subjects. We would hope that the current collection serves to revise such an opinion. It may even be argued that questioning ethics – as both a questioning of ethics and an ethics of questioning – is now a pivotal preoccupation for many of the leading figures working in contemporary European philosophy. In our post-Heideggerian, post-metaphysical, climate we are beginning to realize that to poetically dwell requires us also to

1

ethically dwell. No amount of neo-Nietzschean aestheticizing can dispense with the need for moral and political vigilance.

In conclusion, we want to gratefully acknowledge the help and encouragement of our colleagues in the Department of Philosophy at University College Dublin, and of Professor Fergus D'Arcy, Dean of Arts, who provided support for this volume. We wish to express our gratitude also to the German and French embassies for having made it possible for many of our contributors to visit UCD. Finally, a special word of appreciation is owed to Brian O'Connor and Tim Mooney for their help in organizing the recently formed Graduate Programme in Contemporary European Philosophy, and also to Eileen Brennan, Eoin O'Connell, Brian Garvey and John Gorman for their invaluable assistance in the preparation of this text.

Part I

HERMENEUTICS

1

MEMORY AND FORGETTING

Paul Ricoeur

To reflect upon the ethics of memory is, at first sight, a puzzling task. This is so because memory is not in the first instance an action, but a kind of knowledge like perception, imagination and understanding. Memory constitutes a knowledge of past events, or of the pastness of past events. In that sense it is committed to truth, even if it is not a truthful relationship to the past; that is, precisely because it has a truth-claim, memory can be accused of being unfaithful to this claim.

So how is it possible to speak of an ethics of memory? It is possible because memory has two kinds of relation to the past, the first of which, as I have already mentioned, is a relation of *knowledge*, while the second is a relation of *action*. This is so because remembering is a way of *doing* things, not only with words, but with our minds; in remembering or re-collecting we are exercising our memory, which is a kind of action. It is because memory is an exercise that we can talk of the *use* of memory, which in turn permits us to speak of the *abuses* of memory. The ethical problems will arise once we begin to reflect on this connection between *use* and *abuse* of memory.

This approach to memory as a kind of doing things with the mind, or as an exercise, has a long trajectory in the history of philosophy. In the *Sophist*, for example, Plato speaks of 'the art' of imitating (*mimetike techne*). In this context, he makes a distinction between *phantastike techne*, which is unreliable, and *eikastike techne*, deriving from the Greek *eikon* or image, which may be true. There are, therefore, these two possibilities of imitating or of evoking: *phantastike techne*, which is fallible and unreliable, and *eikastike techne*, which *could be* reliable.

Beyond this we have the long history of the *ars memoria*, the art of memory, which is a kind of education of the act of memorising the past. And at the end of this tradition of treating memory as an art stands Nietzsche in the second of the famous *Untimely Meditations* (*Unzeitgemasse Betrachtung*), entitled 'On the Advantage and Disadvantage of History for Life'. This is interesting because the title itself is about 'use', not the use of memory itself, but of the philosophy of history in the

5

Hegelian sense of treating the practice of history as a science. In this meditation, Nietzsche speaks precisely of the abuses and burdens of historical consciousness, after which he makes a plea for being unhistorical. There is in this context, therefore, a kind of suspiciousness of memory, or an approach to memory or history treated as a disease.

So it is through this approach to memory as a kind of action that we can best broach the problem of the ethics of memory. Before doing that, however, I wish to construe a framework of thought which will permit me to place ethics within a broader context. I will consider three levels in this practical approach: first, the *pathological–therapeutic* level; second, the *pragmatic* level; and finally, the properly *ethical–political* approach to the act of memory.

I

The first level demands close attention, because it is here that abuses are rooted in something that we could call the wounds and scars of memory. We have a good example in the present state of Europe: in some places we could say that there is too much memory, but in other places not enough. Likewise, there is sometimes not enough forgetting, and at other times too much forgetting. How is it possible to graft these misuses upon the capacity to memorise?

To support my claim concerning this pathological–therapeutic level, I shall evoke two short essays by Freud from 1914, belonging to the collection *Metapsychology*. The first essay is entitled 'Remembering, Repetition, and Working Through [*Durcharbeiten*]'. The starting-point of this essay is an incident or an accident in the progression of the psychoanalytic cure, when the patient keeps repeating the symptoms and is barred from any progress towards recollection, or towards a reconstruction of an acceptable and understandable past. This first stage is linked, thus, to the problems of resistance and repression in psychoanalysis. It is interesting that at the beginning of the essay Freud says that the patient repeats instead of remembering. Repetition, therefore, is an obstacle to remembering. At that same stage in the essay, Freud says that both the doctor and the patient must have patience; that is, they must be patient concerning the symptoms, which in turn allows them to be reconciled with the impossibility of going directly to the truth – if there is any truth concerning the past. But also the patient has to accept his illness in order to anticipate a time when he could be reconciled with his own past. The way towards reconciliation with oneself is precisely what, in the title, is called 'working through' (*Durcharbeiten*). It is also on this occasion that Freud introduces the important term 'memory as work' (*Erinnerungarbite*). So memory for Freud is work, what we might call a *travail*. Let us keep in mind, therefore, this concept of the 'work of memory', or memory as work.

The second essay, which I will try to put side by side with the first one, concerns 'mourning' – the title is 'Mourning and Melancholia' – and contains the well-known account of Freud's struggle to distinguish mourning from melancholia. It is here that he speaks also of the 'work' of mourning. I will attempt, therefore, to bring together these two expressions: 'the work of memory' and 'the work of mourning', because it is quite possible that the work of memory *is* a kind of mourning, and also that mourning is a painful exercise in memory.

But what is mourning? Mourning is a reconciliation. With what? With the loss of some objects of love; objects of love may be persons of course, but also, as Freud says, abstractions like fatherland, freedom – ideals of all kinds. What is preserved in mourning and lost in melancholia is self-esteem, or the sense of one's self. This is so because in melancholia there is a despair and a longing to be reconciled with the loved object which is lost without the hope of reconciliation. In the commentary concerning mourning, Freud says that the task of the 'patient' is to renounce all the ties which linked him with the object of love, or to break off all the ties that connect the conscious and the unconscious to this lost object. At this point, mourning protects me from the trend towards melancholia when there is what he calls 'the interiorisation of the object of love', which becomes a part of the soul. But the price to pay is very high because the patient has to realise, step by step, degree by degree, the orders dictated by reality. It is the principle of reality against the principle of pleasure. So melancholia, in a sense, would be the permanent claim of the pleasure principle. This essay allows us, therefore, to bring together the two expressions: work of memory and work of mourning, work of memory versus repetition, work of mourning versus melancholia.

Let us at this point return to our examples from the political sphere, which I spoke of in terms of an excess of memory in some places and a lack of memory in others. In a sense, both are on the same side: they are on the side of repetition and melancholia. It is the wounds and scars of history which are repeated in this state of melancholia. Hence, mourning and 'working through' are to be brought together in the fight for the acceptability of memories: memories have not only to be understandable, they have to be acceptable, and it is this acceptability which is at stake in the work of memory and mourning. Both are types of reconciliation.

II

From this we can move to a second level where abuses are more conspicuous. I will characterise this level as 'pragmatic', because it is here that we have a *praxis* of memory. Let us ask at this juncture why memory is subject to abuses. I suggest it is because of its links to the problem of identity. In fact, the diseases of memory are basically diseases of identity.

This is so because identity, whether personal or collective, is always only presumed, claimed, reclaimed; and because the question which is behind the problematics of identity is '*who* am I?' We tend to provide responses in terms of *what* we are. We try, that is, to saturate, or to exhaust, the questions beginning with 'who' by answers in the register of 'what'. It is the fragility of all the answers in terms of 'what' to the question in terms of 'who' which is the source of the abuses of which I shall speak.

Why are the answers to this question so inappropriate and so fragile? First, we have to face the difficulty of preserving identity through time. This is the approach which I developed in my recent work *Time and Narrative*, but from the point of view of narration, not of memory. So the first problem I now evoke – how to preserve my identity through time – is a problem raised through both narrative and memory. Why? Because we oscillate always between two models of identity. In *Oneself as Another*, I tried to introduce two Latin words to support my analysis: *idem* identity and *ipse* identity. *Idem* identity connotes sameness; sameness is a claim not to change in spite of the course of time and in spite of the change of events around me and within me. What I call my 'character' is a possible example of this type of identity or this level of sameness. But in the course of personal life, I need a kind of flexibility, or a kind of dual identity, the model of which would be for me the promise, i.e. the capacity to keep one's own word. This is not the same as remaining inflexible or unchanged through time. On the contrary, it is a way of dealing with change, not denying it. This I call *ipse* identity. The difficulty of being able to deal with changes through time is one reason why identity is so fragile.

Second, we have to face the problem of *the other*. Otherness, as I also argue in *Oneself as Another*, is met, first, as a threat to myself. It is true that people feel threatened by the mere fact that there are other people who live according to standards of life which conflict with their own standards. Humiliations, real or imaginary, are linked to this threat, when this threat is felt as a wound which leaves scars. The tendency to reject, to exclude, is a response to this threat coming from the other.

I would like to add a third component in explication of this difficulty of preserving one's identity through time, and of preserving one's selfhood in face of the other, and that is the violence which is a permanent component of human relationships and interactions. Let us recall that most events to do with the founding of any community are acts and events of violence. So we could say that collective identity is rooted in founding events which are violent events. In a sense, collective memory is a kind of storage of such violent blows, wounds and scars.

With this reflection we arrive at the problem of an *ethics* of memory. It is precisely through narratives that a certain education of memory has to start. Here we can introduce the connection between memory and forgetting, because the best use of forgetting is precisely in the construction of plots, in the elaboration of narratives concerning personal identity or collective identity; that is, we cannot tell a story without eliminating or dropping some important event according to the kind of plot we intend to build. Narratives, therefore, are at the same time the occasion for manipulation through reading and directing narratives, but also the place where a certain healing of memory may begin. Speaking of 'abuses', I would underline the excesses of certain commemorations, and their rituals, their festivals, their myths which attempt to fix the memories in a kind of reverential relationship to the past. Here we may say that the abuse of commemorative festivals is an opportunity for the abuse of memory. There is, however, an ethics of memory precisely in the good use of commemorative acts against the abuses of ritualised commemoration.

Why are narratives helpful in this ethical respect? Because it is always possible to tell in another way. This exercise of memory is here an exercise in *telling otherwise*, and also in letting others tell their own history, especially the founding events which are the ground of a collective memory. It is very important to remember that what is considered a founding event in our collective memory may be a wound in the memory of the other. There are different ways of dealing with humiliating memories: either we repeat them in Freud's sense or, as Todorov suggests, we may try to extract the 'exemplarity' of the event rather than the factuality (for exemplarity is directed towards the future: it is a lesson to be told to following generations). So whereas the traumatic character of past humiliations brings us back permanently towards the past, the exemplary dimension of the same events is directed towards the future and regulated, 'towards justice', to quote Todorov. It is the power of justice to be just regarding victims, just also regarding victors, and just towards new institutions by means of which we may prevent the same events from recurring in the future.

So we have here a work on memory which reverts from past to future, and this revision from past to future is by way of drawing out the exemplary significance of past events.

III

In the final phase of my analysis, I wish to say something about what I call the 'ethico-political' level of the problem. To what extent may we say that there is a 'duty to remember' (*devoir de memoir*)? This is an ethico-political problem because it has to do with the construction of the future: that is, the duty to remember consists not only in having a deep concern for the past, but in transmitting the meaning of past events to the next generation.

The duty, therefore, is one which concerns the future; it is an imperative directed towards the future, which is exactly the opposite side of the traumatic character of the humiliations and wounds of history. It is a duty, thus, to tell. An example of what is at issue here can be found in Deuteronomy, when the author says 'you will tell your children, you will tell them, you will tell them!'

The first reason why it is a duty to tell is surely as a means of fighting against the erosion of traces; we must keep traces, traces of events, because there is a general trend to destroy. There is a famous text by Aristotle in *Physics* Book 4, Chapter 11, where he says that time destroys more than it constructs. In this context, Aristotle appropriates one of his ontological categories, that of 'destruction'. This is an intriguing text because it is true that there is a kind of erosion which strives to bring everything to ruins, to ashes. In a sense, all human activity is a kind of counter-trend which endeavours to see that growth prevails over destruction, and that traces and archives are preserved and kept alive.

There is, however, a second and more specifically ethical reason to cherish this duty to remember. Allow me to refer here to Hannah Arendt in Chapter 5 of *The Human Condition*, entitled 'Action'. Here she asks how it is possible that there be a continuation of action in spite of death, in spite of the erosion of traces. In response, she brings together two conditions for what she calls continuation of action: forgiving and promising. To forgive is basically to be liberated from the burden of the past, to be untied or unbound, while promising enjoins the capacity to be bound by one's own word. Arendt argues that only a human being is capable of being unbound through forgiveness and bound through promising. This is a very powerful *rapprochement*, forgiving and promising, untying and tying.

I would advance a third reason for cherishing this duty to remember. In preserving the relation of the present to the past, we become heirs of the past. So the notion of 'heritage' is privileged here. Heidegger developed this aspect of the problem under the notion of *Schuld*, which he renders both as 'guilt' and as 'debt' in the sense that we are 'indebted to' the past. I too developed this theme in my work *Ideology and Utopia* when I argued that all utopias would be empty were it not for the reactivation of unkept promises.

Finally, I would say that a basic reason for cherishing the duty to remember is to keep alive the memory of suffering over against the general tendency of history to celebrate the victors. We could say that the whole philosophy of history, especially in the Hegelian sense of this expression, is concerned with the cumulation of advantage, progress and victory. All that is left behind is lost. We need, therefore, a kind of parallel history of, let us say, victimisation, which would counter the history of success and victory. To memorise the victims of history – the sufferers, the humiliated, the forgotten – should be a task for all of us at the end of this century.

I will finish by raising what I believe to be an intriguing question: Is there a duty to forget? Are we allowed to add to the duty to remember a duty to forget? We have good examples of this in the history of classical Greece, where most cities at regular intervals elaborated *amnesty* as an institution. In one of these Greek cities there was even a law proclaiming that citizens should not evoke the memory of evil, or what was considered bad. In this case, the citizens had to promise not to recall such an event. We see here the function of amnesty. In fact, amnesty is present in all our institutions, because when somebody has reached the end of his punishment all his civic rights are re-established. This signals the end of the punishment. We see, therefore, that there can be an institution of *amnesty*, which does not mean *amnesia*. I would say that there is no symmetry between the duty to remember and the duty to forget, because the duty to remember is a duty to teach, whereas the duty to forget is a duty to go beyond anger and hatred. The two aims are not comparable.

Both memory and forgetting do, however, contribute in their respective ways to what Hannah Arendt called the continuation of action. It is necessary for the continuation of action that we retain the traces of events, that we be reconciled with the past, and that we divest ourselves of anger and hatred. Once again, justice is the horizon of both processes. Let us conclude by saying that at this point in our history we have to deal with the problem of evolving a culture of *just memory*.

Bibliography

Hannah Arendt, *The Human Condition*, Chicago: Chicago University Press, 1992.
Paul Ricoeur, *Lectures on Ideology and Utopia*, New York: Columbia University Press, 1986.
Paul Ricoeur, *Oneself As Another*, Chicago: Chicago University Press, 1992.
Paul Ricoeur, *Time and Narrative*, 3 vols., Chicago: Chicago University Press, 1984–1987.

2

IMAGINATION, TESTIMONY
AND TRUST

A dialogue[1] with Paul Ricoeur

Q: I am sure that Professor Ricoeur realises that in a country like Ireland we have a particular interest in the idea of obsessive memorisation, and of repetition and ritual in political terms, so that if we could retell stories, if we could re-create a narrative and liberate ourselves from this, we would be looking to a better future. But the problem of retelling the narrative is that it is told and retold, so that you get not one agreed narrative but two narratives, and the competing narratives simply duplicate the conflicting ideologies from which they come. How, in this country, can you get to a shared narrative about identity?

PR: This problem of a common narrative calls for an ethics of discussion. In so-called discourse ethics, developed by people like Habermas and Apel, we argue one against the other, but we understand the argument of the other without assuming it. This is what John Rawls calls 'reasonable disagreements'. I take the example of the relationship between Europe and the Islamic world, where we distinguish between those Islamic speakers with whom we can discuss and others with whom we cannot. We make the difference between reasonable disagreement and intractable disagreement. A common or identical history cannot be reached – and should not be attempted – because it is a part of life that there are conflicts. The challenge is to bring conflicts to the level of discourse and not let them degenerate into violence; to accept that they tell history in their own words as we tell our history in our own words, and that these histories compete against each other in a kind of competition of discourse, what Karl Jaspers called a loving conflict. But sometimes consensus is a dangerous game, and if we miss consensus we think that we have failed. To assume and live conflicts is a kind of practical wisdom.

Q: You speak, in relation to Freud, of repetition as an obstruction to memory. But might it not also be, in certain instances, a way of constructing a memory one could be comfortable with?

PR: This is why Freud speaks of patience. The work of memory is a slow transformation of compulsive repetition into a talking cure, a liberation from pathological obsession into words as free association. Freud provides some historical examples where repressed feelings and memories were allowed to be brought to the surface; and it is quite possible that the positive side of commemoration has, in a sense, to do with this 'acting out' which is a form of substitution allowing for healthy memory. This sort of patience is very important: to let time do its own work, which is not destruction but a diluting resistance.

Q: I'd like to raise the question of historical retrieval.

PR: Let me cite a situation where there are several different interpretations of the same past event. I take the case of the French Revolution since, over nearly two centuries, it has been a bone of contention among French historians. We have many stories of the French Revolution, and it is the competition between these stories that makes for historical education. There are two extreme approaches. That of claiming the event as the beginning of everything, a new creation of a new human being; some of the revolutionary leaders even tried to invent a new calendar with a new way of dividing times and years and months and weeks (a week of ten days and so on). So it claimed to be the master of time and history. The opposite interpretation claims the French Revolution to have been only an acceleration of the centralising trend of the monarchy, or a mere prefiguration of the Bolshevik Revolution. Here the French Revolution is not seen as a unique event but a mere variation on a larger historical movement. By acknowledging that the history of an event involves a conflict of several interpretations and memories, we in turn open up the future. And this retrieval–projection of history has ethical and political implications. Different political projects concerning the future invariably presuppose different interpretations of the past. Utopian projects, for instance, are about unkept promises of the historical past being re-projected, reanimated in terms of a better future which might realise such lost opportunities or unfulfilled, betrayed, possibilities. So here we have to connect past and future in an exchange between memory and expectation. The German historian Rheinhart Kosselek put this past–future relation well in saying that there is a permanent tension between what he calls the space of experience (*Erfahrungsfeld*) and the horizon of expectation. This critical exchange between memory and expectation is, I believe, fundamental.

Q: You say utopias are places where we reactivate unkept promises of the past. Does that mean there are no *new* dreams to dream? That the future is just a recollection of past historical movements, fulfilled or unfulfilled?

PR: The epistemic status of utopia is very complex. I tried to explore this issue in my book *Lectures on Ideology and Utopia*. There I argued that ideology usually reasserts the historical field of past experience in a gesture of reassurance; utopia, by contrast, attempts a kind of excursion out of time, a radical break into the future. There is a moment of madness in utopia which is irreducible to mere repetition. Utopia claims to be imagination of the new, of a pure beginning. But the opposition is not so simple. No historical period ever exhausted its own dreams. What happened in the past is only a partial realisation of what had been projected. We may say this of the Greek city which failed, of the Roman Empire which was rescued by the Catholic Church as the Holy Roman Empire, before it collapsed again. The promise of an historical event is always more than what was actually realised. There is more in the past than what happened. And so we have to find the *future of the past*, the unfulfilled potential of the past. That is why Raymond Aron argues that one of the tasks of the historian is to return to the moment of time when the actors did not know what would happen later, and therefore to assume the state of uncertainty in which these actors were positioned, exploring the multiplicity of their expectations, few of which were ever fulfilled. Even Habermas approaches the Enlightenment in this way, as a still unfulfilled project. There is something still unfulfilled in the Greek heritage, in the Christian heritage, in the Enlightenment heritage, in the Romantic heritage. There is never pure rupture. There is always reactualisation to some degree or another.

Q: In Ireland we have a saying: if you want to know what happened ask your father, and if you want to know what people say happened ask your mother. There is this double attitude to the history of the past – what actually happened (history) and the way in which people interpreted what happened (story). Do we not always select and edit memories? Is it not true that to remember everything, as the Irish playwright Brian Friel says, is a form of madness?

Q: Following on from the previous question, if you allow many different interpretations of your own memory and of the memories of the nation, and if you claim that the healthy thing is a conflict of interpretations which disallows any final consensus – since there is no one who has the perspective from which to say what *really* happened – how can you talk of the *abuse* of memory, either on a personal level or on the level of the nation? If there are only competing interpretations, each with a claim on truth, how can we speak of truth or untruth in history? To speak of abuse assumes you have some perspective from which you can judge that someone is making a proper use of memory, and that someone is making an improper use of memory.

PR: In relation to both questions, allow me to refer to my essay 'Memory and Forgetting', in which I spoke of the truth-claim of memory. This should not be forgotten. There could be no *good* use of memory if there were no aspect of truth. So in a sense what 'really happened' must keep concerning us. And here I am faithful to the German school of historians of the nineteenth century in saying that we have to tell things as they really happened (*wie es eigentlich gewesen*). This is a very difficult problem because we have two ways of speaking of the past. The past is something that is no longer there but which has been there, which once was there. So the grammar of the past is a two-fold grammar. It is no longer and yet it *has been*. In a sense we are summoned by what was beyond the loss of what is no longer to be faithful to what happened. Here we confront problems of historical representation and reference to the past, but we must never eliminate the truth-claim of what has been. This is so for ethical as well as epistemological reasons.

Q: You are not saying that history is a matter of a pure relativism of interpretations where anything goes?

PR: No. This crucial issue brings us to the borderline between imagination and memory. In his book on imagination – *The Psychology of Imagination* – Sartre said that imagination is about the unreal and memory is about the (past) real. So there is a positing act in memory whereas there is an unrealising of history in imagination. It is very difficult to maintain the distinction; but it must be kept at least as a basic recognition of two opposite claims about the past, as *unreal* and *real*. In that sense, memory is on the side of perception whereas imagination is on the side of fiction. But they often intersect. What we call 'Revisionist' historians, those who like Faurrison deny the existence of extermination camps, ignore this problem of 'factual' truth. This is why historical memory needs to be supplemented by documentary and archival evidence. The Popperian criterion of falsifiability must be observed. This is not to ignore the fact that sometimes fictions come closer to what really happened than do mere historical narratives, where fictions go directly to the *meaning* beyond or beneath the facts. It is puzzling. But, finally, we have to return to a body count. You have to accurately *count* the corpses in the death camps as well as offering vivid narrative *accounts* that people will remember.

Q: Is it possible to get a balance between the two approaches, between a narrative retelling (which evokes in us the feeling of the horror of what happened) and a critical, scientific, objective distance (which informs us of the 'facts' of what happened). Is this not a paradox?

PR: I would say that the paradox is not on the side of memory but of imagination. This is the case because imagination has two functions: one is to bring us outside of the real world – into unreal or possible worlds – but it has a second function which is to put memories *before our eyes*. Bergson touches on this in the second chapter of *Matter and Memory*. He says that pure memory is virtual and has to be brought back into the field of consciousness *as* an image. This is why writing history as memory is so difficult. We are dealing with memory-images where imagination serves as a kind of *mise-en-scène* of the past. The reality of history is made 'visible' again through images; and this makes memory a reproduction, a sort of second production. Yet, at the same time, the difference *remains* between the unreal and the real. So the paradox of imagination-memory is very puzzling indeed. Many philosophers, such as Spinoza, have treated memory as a province of imagination. And we also have the view, expressed by Pascal and Montaigne, that memory is a form of imagination which is to be guarded against. This is why I stress so strongly the reality claims of memory to remain faithful to our *debt* to the past, to the pastness of the past. Which brings me finally to the indispensable issue of *testimony*. Testimony is the ultimate link between imagination and memory, because the witness says 'I was part of the story. I was there.' At the same time, the witness tells a story that is a living presentation, and therefore deploys the capacity of imagination to place the events before our eyes, as if we were there. Testimony would be a way of bringing memory and imagination together. It is very difficult of course. I am struggling with this difficulty at present. Maybe it has to do with the two meanings of pastness, no longer there and still there, absent and present (or quasi-present). How do we make the past visible, as if it were present, while acknowledging our *debt* to the past as it actually happened? That is my main ethical question of memory.

Q: Is it not the case that testimonies can be manipulated and distorted to serve certain interests? If so, what critical tools must we avail ourselves of to unmask such manipulation?

PR: In order to anwer this we must refer to the epistemological structure of historical knowledge. The fundamental objective of the *good* historian is to enlarge the sphere of archives; that is, the conscientious historian must open up the archive by retrieving traces which the dominant ideological forces attempted to suppress. In admitting what was originally excluded from the archive the historian initiates a critique of power. He gives expression to the voices of those who have been abused, the victims of intentional exclusion. The historian opposes the manipulation of narratives by telling the story differently and by providing a space for the confrontation between opposing testimonies. We must remember, however, that the historian is also embedded in history, he belongs to his own field of research. The historian is an actor in the plot. Our condition dictates that we can never be in a state of pure indifference. The historian's testimony is therefore not completely neutral, it is a selective activity. It is, however, far less selective than the testimony of the dominant class. Here we should invoke what John Rawls calls 'reflective equilibrium'. He speaks of the need for reflective equilibrium between predominantly held beliefs and the findings of critical minds represented by professional people such as historians. Such a mechanism helps us to distinguish good from bad history. In the final analysis, however, we must emphasise the role of 'trust'. When I testify to something I am asking the other to trust that what I am saying is true. To share a testimony is an exchange of trust. Beyond this we cannot go. Most institutions rely fundamentally on the trust they place in the word of the other.

Q: How do you reconcile the emphasis which you place on the role of 'trust' with what you call 'the hermeneutics of suspicion'?

PR: The hermeneutics of suspicion functions against systems of power which seek to prevent a confrontation between competing arguments at the level of genuine discourse. In such discourse we bring together diverse and opposing interests with the hope that they will engage at the level of rigorous argumentation. Habermas sees in such a strategy an 'ethics of discussion'. Such an ethics of discourse obliges me to give my best argument to my enemy, in the hope that he will in turn articulate his resentment and aggression in the form of an equally plausible argument. It is through discussion of this sort that suspicion between opposing interests gives way to trust and a certain level of consensus.

Q: How can an 'ethics of discussion' help us to forgive and forget?

PR: It is always better to give expression to anger or hatred than to repress it. It is good that the wounds of history remain open to thought. There is indeed something healthy in the expression of anger. To repress grievances is certainly bad. Expression and discussion are ways of healing. Psychoanalysis relies precisely on this expressive function of language. To hear the anger of other people forces us to confront our wrong-doings, which is the first step towards forgiveness. We must have trust in language as a weapon against violence, indeed the best weapon there is against violence.

Note

1 Our thanks to the following for contributing to this dialogue: Brian Cosgrave, Gayle Freyne, David Scott, Imelda McCarthy, Redmond O'Hanlon, Brian Garvey, John Cleary, Margaret Kelleher, Dermot Moran and Maeve Cooke.

3

NARRATIVE AND THE ETHICS
OF REMEMBRANCE

Richard Kearney

To tell or not to tell? That is the question I propose to explore in this essay. How much of the past should be remembered and recounted? How much forgotten and forgiven? How do we respect the summons of history – personal or communal – to be recollected again and again, so that our debt to the past be honoured, without succumbing to resentment and revenge? And, finally, how does memory itself negotiate a passage between its opposing fidelities to imagination and reality?

I will attempt to answer these questions in respect of both literary memory and literal (lived) memory. And, in each case, I will weigh the poetic right to recreate against the ethical duty to represent the past as it actually happened (*wie es eigentlich gewesen*).

I

I begin with the literary example of *Hamlet* – a play which begins and ends with the question of memory.

'Remember me' says King Hamlet to his son. Tell my story. Carry my memory, my legacy, my legitimacy, into the next generation, to my people, to my children and grandchildren. And why not? Should not every son remember his father? Especially when he was a glorious King, the sun of all the firmament, cut down while still in his prime? Is it not mandatory for any king – and certainly those in Shakespeare plays – to end their days confiding their secret stories to their sons, transferred with their benediction and their birthright? Of course. And was not young Hamlet born for this indeed, to tell his father's story to the people of the Union: the Union of two nations, Denmark and Norway, sealed by the pearl won by his father in the famous duel with Fortinbras the Elder on the day (lest we forget) of the younger Hamlet's birth? Was not Prince Hamlet born to carry on his father's history and avenge his crime? Of course.

18

But there's a rub. First, we can't be sure who speaks. Hamlet's friend Horatio, scholar returned from Wittenburg, says ''tis but a fantasy' – or worse 'a guilty thing' – that speaks to Hamlet. At best a ghost, one moment there, one moment gone, there and not there, present and absent, the past-as-present. And when the ghostly, guilt-ridden, spirit finally speaks, after much coaxing, he claims he is a creature come back, not from heaven but from hell: from 'sulphrous and tormenting flames'. He is indeed a 'questionable shape'.

And there's another rub. If we can't be sure *who* the ghost is, we can't be sure *what* he is saying either. He tells his son, 'remember!' Yes. *But what is he to remember?* His father's glories as illustrious monarch, faithful to his people, spouse and son? No. The irony is that the first thing father tells son is *what he cannot tell him*.

> I am thy father's spirit,
> Doomed for a certain term to walk the night
> And for the days confined to fast in fires
> Till the foul crimes done in my days of nature
> Are burnt and purged away. But that I am forbid
> To tell the secrets of my prison house,
> I could a tale unfold whose lightest word
> Would harrow up thy soul . . .
>
> (*Hamlet*, Act 1, sc. v)

The second thing King Hamlet tells his son is to prevent the 'royal bed of Denmark' from being 'a couch . . . of damned incest'; but here again there are problems, for he adds: 'do not contrive against thy mother aught' – in other words, another double injunction. First: remember me– remember me not. Second: intervene–don't intervene.

Freud, as we know from his famous reading of the play in the *Interpretation of Dreams* (1900), sees these paradoxes as the betrayal (in both senses of the term) of Hamlet's Oedipus complex – the repressed desire to vilify the father and possess the mother. Lacan (1982) sees the double injunction as a 'tragedy of desire', while Nicolas Abraham (1988) reads it as a symptom of the gap left in us by the untold secrets of others who came before us. King Hamlet's 'Remember me!' is an injunction *both* to commemorate the ghost's memory by honouring his summons to avenge *and* to recall what the ghost–King actually did if he could only say it (which alas he is 'forbid'). This contradictory summons represents what might be described as a *tragedy of narrative*. We have a story to tell but can't tell it. Or, as the narrator of Beckett's *Molloy* puts it, 'I can't go on [telling stories], I'll go on'.

Hamlet, on this reading, is a story about the simultaneous necessity and impossibility of stories. Ophelia cannot tell her story until she goes mad (when she tells everything but is no longer herself: 'Here's rosemary for remembrance'); Claudius cannot tell his story, even in the confessional, until it is forced from him by the play within the play; Gertrude cannot tell her story because she is ignorant of it (she does not know that Claudius killed the King); Polonius and his fellow courtiers, Rosencrantz and Guildenstern and Osric, cannot tell their stories since they say only what pleases or deceives. Even Prince Hamlet cannot tell his story for as long as conscience makes a coward of him: not until, dying of a fatal wound, he begs his friend Horatio: 'absent thee from felicity awhile to tell my story'. Which means that this is a play where no one actually tells their story, no one truly remembers, until Prince Fortinbras arrives too late on the scene, and announces: 'I have some rights of *memory* in this kingdom/ Which now to claim my vantage doth invite me' (V, ii).

What exactly these rights of 'memory' are no one tells us. And, if they could, one has good reason to suspect the play would not have survived the first act. In other words, the play is about a cover-up, a concealment of a crime (or crimes) which the hero Hamlet is trying to uncover and reveal. Numerous psychoanalysts over the years – drawn to the play like kittens to a ball of wool – have read between the lines and dared to tell the untold tale: namely, as André Green and Nicolas Abraham would have it, that King Hamlet has done to King Fortinbras what Claudius does to Hamlet (King and Prince) – poison him to secure the rights of kingship. The 'rights of memory' restored by the young Fortinbras in the last act would refer, on this reading, to the final righting of the wrong committed against Fortinbras' own father by Hamlet's father. That King Hamlet's 'foul crime' occurred on Hamlet's birthday is surely no accident, as suggested by the Prince's opening invocation of the 'dram of evil' – that 'vicious mole of nature in (particular men),/ As in their birth, wherein they are not guilty,/ (Since nature cannot choose his origin) . . .' (I, iv).

The ethics of remembrance, Shakespeare reminds us, proves more complex than it seems. Indeed, one wonders if, were it *less* complex, Shakespeare would have spun his marvellous play at all in the first place. It is true: 'the play's the thing in which we'll catch the conscience of the king'. But of which king are we speaking? King Hamlet? King Claudius? Hamlet pretender to the throne? Or King Fortinbras who, too, to his grave was untimely sent?

It is because there is no quick answer to this question that *Hamlet* the play survives to this day and Hamlet the prince is the most written about person in Western culture after Jesus and Napoleon!

So what's the story? Tell–don't tell! The double injunction that makes us human: the essence of tragedy in literature and life. But there is a difference between literature and life and, I will argue, it is a significant one. In the face of certain current views that the imaginary and the real are one and the same, I submit that what is good for literature is by no means always good for life. If at the epistemological level it is often extremely difficult to establish clear referential relations between narrative and world, this does not mean, especially from an ethical point of view, that there is no distinction whatsoever.

Most writers respond to the double injunction of all poetics – tell it, but do not tell it as it was. This double exigency can be interpreted in different ways, of course. On the one hand, there is the Beckettian view that 'silence is our mother tongue'; and that all forms of remembering (apart from involuntary memory *à la* Proust) are distortions, stories we invent to ward off the 'suffering of being'. Hence Beckett's resolve to dismantle the narrative form, paring down his stories until they become 'residua' or 'no-texts' – anti-novels. Seamus Heaney offers a recent and ironic variation on this same tune when he writes: 'Whatever you say say nothing'. The best stories are the stories *never told* – hence Heaney's correlative counsel to 'govern the tongue', to write poetry rather than fiction.

Against this, there is the Joycean tradition that says: tell everything! – a tradition that produced *Finnegan's Wake* (the text of 'allmen') rather than Beckett's *No's Knife* (the text of 'noman'). This Joycean impulse celebrates the fictional re-creation of history in its entirety, working to the refrain of the garrulous washerwomen by the Liffey: 'mememormee, mememormee!'

So while the former poetic exigency may be expressed as *tell nothing whatever you tell*, the latter translates as *tell everything you can tell*.

II

This is fine for literature. When it comes to history, however, it is another matter. Here the double injunction – tell–don't tell – may have very different consequences, especially at the existential and ethical levels. It is this contrast between fictional and historical remembrance that I wish to explore in the remainder of this essay. If fiction is entirely free to recreate the past *as it might have been*, history has a duty to recount the past *as it actually was (wie es eigentlich gewesen ist)*. For if it is true, as Ricoeur claims, that 'l'imaginaire ne connaît pas de censure', the same cannot be said of historical narrative. The difference is crucial, though not always self-evident.

To illustrate this contrast between literary and non-literary forms of narrative memory, I will concentrate on some controversial 'case histories' in psychotherapy, before briefly touching on the more general debate about the role of narrative in the recounting of public historical events.

In psychotherapy the double injunction – tell–do not tell – would seem to be resolved. A cure happens when one gets to the bottom of things, when the suffering subject manages to remember and recount the *whole story*, or at least as much of it as is recoverable and utterable given the lapses of time between the events of trauma and the recalling of those events.

This at least seems to be Freud's view in the famous case of Dora. Here Freud believed he could cure his patient's hysteria if only he could reconstitute the 'missing pieces' in Dora's fragmented narrative. Freud's theory was that hysterics suffer from blockages of memory which result in 'hysterical conversion symptoms' such as (in Dora's case) insomnia, depression, coughing fits and so on. The psychoanalytic hypothesis was, accordingly, that Dora would be cured once her repressed desires and traumas were recovered in and through narrative – that is, once she succeeded in telling her *full* story: in this instance, her secret desire to marry Herr K. The therapy would therefore comprise a 'talking cure' made possible by the recovery of repressed desire through analytic discourse and transference.

The same applies to Freud's other case histories – Little Hans, the Ratman, the Wolfman, Schneider – a telling concession being that the decisive evidence is revealed more as 'creative narrative' than as 'scientific fact'. But there is an immediate problem, is there not? How are we to know whether the narrative is 'true'? It was precisely the difficulty of responding to this question that provoked the controversy surrounding Freud's changing views on the seduction theory – at one time suggesting that childhood memories of abuse were real, at other times claiming they were fantasy.

I do not propose to go into the history of this well-rehearsed controversy here. Suffice it to say that from an ethical and a juridical standpoint (and irrespective of the complex epistemological issues of how we can ever *know* the past as past), it *does* and *should* matter whether or not a recovered memory relates to things which actually happened. And this mattering pertains both to the person allegedly abused and to the person who allegedly perpetrated the abuse.

Let me give some examples. We have seen recently, particularly in the United States, a widespread debate on the so-called 'false memory syndrome'. This has been documented in a number of highly publicised books, such as Michael Yapko's *Suggestions of Abuse: True and False Memories of Childhood Sexual Trauma*, Lenore Terr's *Unchained Memories: True Stories of Traumatic Memories*, Lawrence Wright's *Remembering Satan* and Mark Prendergast's *Victims of Memory*. Even if none of these authors wish to contest the veracity of the 'persistent' memory of infantile sexual abuse, some of them cast serious doubt on the use of 'suggestion' and 'trancework' techniques in cases of 'long-term recovered memory'. Wright, for instance, cites the case of a Mr Ingram accused by his daughter of performing sexual abuse rites on her after she had recovered a long-repressed memory thanks to her reading of some recent literature on Satanic rituals and a number of trancework sessions with 'abuse experts'. The accused himself confessed to the crimes, after sustained interrogations by police and psychologists during which he was assured that the more he acknowledged the abuse the more clearly his own (repressed) memories of such events would be recovered. As Paul Ingram admitted: 'My memory is becoming clearer as I go through all this. . . . It's getting clearer as more things come out.' The basic 'suggestibility' premiss of the interrogators was: if you have the *feeling* that such abuse occurred, even if not actually the cognitive awareness, then it did occur. Mr Ingram was sentenced to twenty years of imprisonment before the case was contested and re-opened. (One can think of more notorious cases of such suggestion-confession, running from the Salem witch trials, so brilliantly captured by Arthur Miller's *The Crucible*, to the recent investigations of alleged Satanic abuse of children in the Orkney Islands off Scotland.)

As a result of certain abuses of the memory of abuse (even if such be the exceptions rather than the rule), the whole notion of psychological memory may be put in doubt. As Walter Reich argues in his essay 'The Monster in the Mist: Are Long-Buried Memories of Child Abuse Reliable?':

> Given memory's indispensability and frailty, it's striking that so many of us are ready to play so fast and loose with it. When we uncritically embrace reports of recovered memories of sexual abuse, and when we nonchalantly assume that they must be as good as our ordinary memories, we debase the coinage of memory altogether. What we *should* do is shore up the legitimacy of an imperfect but precious human capacity – the capacity to attest to events that we have always remembered – by resisting the creation of a new category of memory whose products are so often mere inventions conjured by the ministrations of recovery specialists. Instead, too many of us undermine that legitimacy by according to recovered memories, even the most bizarre ones, the same status – psychologically as well as legally – that we accord to traditional forms of memory.
>
> (1994: 38)

The undermining of testimonial memory in this way does a grave disservice not only to those falsely accused of abuse but to those many victims of real abuse. The question of the *veracity* of narratives of childhood abuse – recovered or persistent – is of capital importance (especially, I repeat, from an ethical–judicial point of view).

Let me return for a moment here to the famous case of Dora. The possibility of the influence of 'suggestion' is far from absent in this controversial case history – which itself comprises a history of revisions and controversies. As several of Freud's contemporaries and successors noted, the 'talking cure' did not actually work for Dora for the probable reason that Freud constructed her story according to his own unconscious identifications – in particular with the virile Herr K. whom Freud believed Dora secretly wished to marry. Freud's remarks about Dora's resistance to his hypothetical interpretation of her hysterical symptoms may thus actually betray a *counter-transference* of his own desires onto his analysand – a complex psychoanalytic phenomenon which Freud himself had not at that time come to fully appreciate, as Lacan and others observed. But Freud did, in fairness, have the professional honesty to call this case history a 'fragment', thereby acknowledging, at least implicitly, that the 'missing pieces' of Dora's story were never fully filled in or completed by Dora herself.

The question raised by this fragmentary narrative is therefore: *whose story is it anyway?* Dora's, or Freud's? Certain commentators, most notably Claire Kahane in *In Dora's Case*, construe the oblique, truncated and unfinished character of Dora's story as itself a signal of its authenticity. Hysteria, this argument goes, is by its very nature an experience of fragmentation, and its truthfulness derives from its uncompromising resistance to attempts by omnipotent father-figures to fill in the fissures of her story in order to sign off a 'total account'. Dora's narrative has thus become in certain feminist circles a *cas célèbre* of genuine feminine resistance – hysterical or otherwise – to the phallocentric exigency to 'tell everything'. According to this view, it is precisely the covert, oblique and obscure elements in Dora's version which constitute a necessary female refuge from the male imperative to know and appropriate anything alien to it.

This reading is persuasively developed by Jane Gallop who argues that hysterical discourse is a paradigm of 'woman's story' ('Keys to Dora'). And it is invoked also by Stephen Marcus in his literary–psychological account, 'Freud and Dora: Story, History, Case History', where he cites Dora's narrative as an exemplary instance of modernist fiction, displaying four central common features:

1 the impossibility of access to truth;
2 the dissolution of linear narration and its explosion into multiple, often competing, perspectives;
3 the existence of an unreliable narrator (Freud); and
4 the undecidable relation between fiction and reality, both inside and outside of the discourse.

What some of these commentators seem to ignore, however, is that if it is true that at the *aesthetic* level it matters little whether there is an accurate correspondence between narrative and reality, it matters hugely at the *ethical* level. It certainly mattered to Dora – who got worse rather than better thanks to Freud's counter-transferential account – and to all those other victims of abuse. What is good for the modernist or postmodernist novel is not necessarily good for life. There is, after all, a need to discriminate (as best we can) between the pure story-line of case histories and their historical element as reference to the past 'as it actually happened'. The two strands – fiction and fact – are, of course, always intimately interwoven in the narrative text (oral or written), but that does not mean that the strands can never be, at least partially, disentangled and distinguished. Consequently, while I would not for a moment deny that literary analogies between Freudian case histories and modernist fiction can teach us much about the subtle and sophisticated uses of narrative, such analogies do not do justice to the ethical significance of memories of *real* suffering – memories which the sufferers who recount them wish to have *recognised as true*, that is, as referring to events which did happen.

The moral implications of such an imaginary–real distinction in the operation of narrative memory are crucial not only for psychological cases of abuse but also for the more public and collective cases of historical crime. The instances of revisionism and negationism with regard to the Holocaust and other genocides in history are timely reminders of the fundamental stakes involved. The whole nature of memory as historical witness is at issue here. While revisionist historians like Faurisson and Irving deny the existence of gas chambers, anti-revisionists like Lawrence Langer in *Holocaust Testimonies: The Ruins of Memory* recall just how indispensable the role of fragile testimonial memory is. Indeed, Langer's scrupulous distinctions between 'deep memory' and other variant categories of remembering – 'anguished', 'humiliated', 'tainted' and 'unheroic' – represents just the kind of typological work that is necessary to answer those who would discredit the legitimacy of personal historical remembrance. As Walter Reich aptly reminds us:

> The institution of memory deserves the respect and protection it can get. One indication of just how vulnerable to manipulation it already is can be appreciated from the fact that Holocaust deniers have managed to receive, in recent years, a respectful hearing on college campuses and elsewhere, despite the existence of mountains of firsthand and corroborated traumatic memories of the Holocaust provided by many thousands of survivors – memories that don't have to be recovered because they are all too vividly, and all too persistently, remembered. Holocaust deniers began to achieve their victory over memory even before efforts were made to establish the new category of recovered memory. If recovered memory continues to remain unchallenged as a new form of memory, then one can only guess how much more vulnerable to doubt and manipulation legitimate memory will become. Memory is one of our most precious human assets. It needs protection

from those who, by debasing it, diminish its integrity, even as victims of sexual abuse need protection from those who, by abusing them, diminish their humanity.

(Reich 1994: 38)

III

In this third and final section, I propose to explore further some of the specifically ethical implications of this rapport between narrative and collective historical memory.

Historical communities are constituted by the stories they recount to themselves and to others. Hence the importance of the rectifications that contemporary historians bring to the historical accounts of their predecessors. This is as true of the revisionist controversies in Irish history (the Famine, 1916, 1969) as it is of the French debates on the meaning of the French Revolution, or the German *Historiestreit* on the Second World War. It is also true of the classic case of biblical Israel – an historical spiritual community formed on the basis of foundational narratives (especially the books of Genesis and Exodus) which successive generations recount and reinterpret. This explains why Judaism is the 'culture of the book' *par excellence*. Moreover, it is precisely because stories proceed from stories in this manner that historical communities are ultimately responsible for the formation and reformation of their own identities. One cannot remain constant over the passage of historical time – and therefore remain faithful to one's promises and covenants – unless one has some minimal remembrance of where one comes from, of how one came to be what one is. In this sense, identity is memory; or, as Hegel put it, *das Wesen is das Gewesene.*

But with this ethic of responsibility comes an attendant ethic of flexibility. Once one recognises that one's identity is fundamentally narrative in character, one discovers an ineradicable openness and indeterminacy at the root of one's collective memory. Each nation, state or *societas* discovers that it is at heart an 'imagined community' (in Benedict Anderson's phrase), that is, a narrative construction to be reinvented and reconstructed again and again. After such discovery of one's narrative identity, it is more difficult to make the mistake of taking oneself *literally*, of assuming that one's collective identity *goes without saying*. This is why, at least in principle, the tendency of a nation towards xenophobic or insular nationalism can be resisted by its own narrative resources to imagine itself otherwise – either through its own eyes or those of others.

Fundamentalism arises when a nation forgets its own narrative origins, bearing out Adorno's adage that 'all reification is forgetting'. That is why the solution to the problem of Northern Ireland may well reside in the willingness of both British and Irish nationalists to exchange narrative memories – which found their respective national identities – thereby learning to see each other through alter-native eyes. The same goes for Israel and Palestine, of course, where an acknowledgement of the narrative basis of their respective identities might lead to a greater willingness by each to re-imagine the identity of the historic enemy. In that way, reified memory (expressing itself in compulsive repetition and resentment) may find its best antidote in alternative memory – liberating one's historical consciousness by remembering *oneself-as-another*. It is by means only of the latter kind of memory that pardon may release the historical past into a different, freer, future. For genuine anmesty does not and cannot come from blind forgetfulness (amnesia), but only from a remembering which is prepared to forgive the past by emancipating it from the deterministic stranglehold of violent obsession and revenge. Genuine pardon, as Ricoeur observes, does not involve a forgetting of the events themselves but a different way of *signifying* a debt to the dead which paralyses memory – and, by implication, our capacity to recreate ourselves in a new future. The proper task of amnesty is not to efface the memory of crimes but, contrariwise, to dissolve the debt which they have accrued. 'Forgiveness is a sort of healing of memory, the completion of its mourning period. Delivered from the weight of debt, memory is liberated for great projects. Forgiveness gives memory a future' (Ricoeur 1995: 12–13). Ricoeur claims accordingly that it is not a contradiction to say that amnesty-forgetfulness is the strict corollary of 'critical memory' even as it is the strict contrary of 'repetition memory' (*ibid.*: 23).

Critical caution is clearly called for here. Narrative memory is never innocent. It is an ongoing conflict of interpretations. A battlefield of competing meanings. Every history is told from a certain perspective and in the light of specific prejudice (at least in Gadamer's sense). Memory, as suggested above, is not always on the side of the angels. It can as easily lead to false consciousness and ideological closure as to openness and tolerance. This distorting power is sometimes ignored by contemporary advocates of narrative ethics – MacIntyre, Nussbaum, Booth – who tend to downplay the need for a hermeneutic of critical suspicion (*à la* Ricoeur or Habermas). Nor is it properly appreciated by those disciples of Nietzsche's *Second Untimely Considerations* who believe it is sufficient to 'actively forget the past' in order to have done with it. Those who think they can dispense with historical memory by fiat will ultimately be dispensed with by it.

The better to adjudicate the critical stakes involved in such debates, let me take the example of the Holocaust.

The first-hand narratives of Lawrence Langer's *Holocaust Testimonies*, no less than the literary witness of authors like Primo Levi, Milena or Elie Wiesel, are reminders of just how indispensable narrative memory is for the ethical remembrance of genocide. For Primo Levi the need to recount his memoirs was the ethical duty to have others participate in the events which might otherwise be forgotten and, by being forgotten, repeat themselves. For Wiesel the reason for telling and retelling these narratives is to give the victims 'the voice that was denied them' by history. Or as one of his characters puts it, searching for a former Holocaust survivor in a New York psychiatric hospital: 'Perhaps it is not given to humans to efface evil, but they may become the consciousness of evil.' Recounting is a way of becoming such an ethical consciousness. For just as the Greeks knew that virtues were best transmitted by remembering and retelling the admirable deeds of the heroes, so too the horror of moral evil must be retrieved from oblivion by means of narrative memory (see Ricoeur 1995: 290).

Similar scruples attach to cinematic narrations of the Holocaust, though here the tension between ethical and aesthetic fidelities to historical memory have proved more evident. I am thinking particularly of the controversy surrounding the recent films of Spielberg and Lanzmann. In a hard-hitting essay entitled, 'Holocaust: The Impossible Representation' (1994), Lanzmann – himself the maker of a powerful film of the Holocaust, *Shoah* – delivered an emphatic critique of Spielberg's attempt to transpose the unique and ultimately 'irrepresentable' event of Auschwitz into dramatised images. According to Lanzmann, *Schindler's List* is guilty of a distortion of historical truth, for in this fictional re-creation of the Holocaust everyone communicates with everyone, even the Jewish victims with their Nazi persecutors, whereas in reality Auschwitz was the absence of human language *par excellence*. By contrast, writes Lanzmann, *Shoah* is a film where 'nobody meets anybody'; and he adds that this is for him an 'ethical position'. Lanzmann's quarrel is not with Spielberg's respect for 'historical detail' per se, or indeed with Thomas Keneally who wrote the book on which the film was based; he fully respects the integrity of their intentions in this regard. His quarrel is with the manner in which such details and facts are *portrayed* – that is, *represented through narrative*. For Lanzmann, *Schindler's List* is a 'kitsch melodrama' which trivialises the unique character of the Holocaust. It transgresses by fictionalising it. In this it resembles other sensational dramatisations of this event such as the TV series 'Holocaust' or Caviani's *The Night Porter*.

Auschwitz prohibits representation through images, not just for biblical reasons ('Thou shalt have no graven images') but for moral reasons.

> The Holocaust is first and foremost unique in that it builds around itself, in a circle of flames, the limit not to be crossed, because a certain absolute of horror is uncommunicable: to pretend crossing it is to become guilty of the most serious transgression. Fiction is a transgression, I feel deeply that there is a prohibition of representation.
>
> (Lanzmann 1994)

In short, while Spielberg offers an 'illustrated *Shoah*' where we, the spectators, are invited to participate emotionally in the story and identify with the hero (Schindler) and the victims (the Jews), Lanzmann refuses to deploy conventional narrative techniques. Spielberg puts images where there are none in *Shoah,* observes Lanzmann, and 'images kill imagination'.

But what kind of 'imagination' is Lanzmann talking of here? A narrative imagination to be sure – for the many real-life survivors who bear witness in the eight-and-a-half-hour running time of *Shoah* do so in terms of to-camera testimonies – but narrative with a difference. The witnesses speak not for themselves, not in the first person, but for others, for those who have been deprived of a voice. None of the survivors say 'I'; none tells a personal story – even the haircutter who survived Treblinka after three months of captivity does not explain how he did it. It is not that which interests him (the first-hand narrator), or indeed Lanzmann (the second-hand narrator). What interests him is the voice of the voiceless, the remembering of what has been forgotten precisely as forgotten. 'He says "we", he speaks for the dead, he is their voice' (Lanzmann 1994). Where Spielberg portrays the extermination as a backdrop, Lanzmann seeks to confront the 'blinding black sun' of the Holocaust, that blind spot of horror and evil which can never be adequately conveyed by conventional 'comparative' or 'comforting' identifications. There is no consolation in Lanzmann's narratives. There are no tears to feel with, no sensations to orient oneself, no ecstasy, no catharsis, no purgation. There is, as Lanzmann admits, 'no possibility of crying'. By refusing the temptation of a happy ending, by eschewing redemptive or reconciliatory conclusion (*à la Schindler's List*), Lanzmann opts for a form of narrative memory which testifies, first and last, to the need to recall our own forgetfulness.

How does he do this? By showing us witnesses who testify to the impossibility of representing what happened in Auschwitz, by letting a faltering voice or broken anecdote or failed retelling betray what no shot (fictional or documentary) of dead bodies could tell us. Namely, the impossibility of representing in images what these survivors saw with their own eyes. As Lyotard puts it:

> *Shoah* resists the use of representation in images and music . . .
> and hardly offers a single testimony where the unrepresentable
> character of the extermination is not indicated, even momentarily,
> by the alteration of voice, a tightening of throat, a tear, a sob, the
> disparition of a witness out of frame, an upset in the tone of the
> narrative, some uncontrolled gesture.
>
> (Lyotard 1988: 51)

There is, quite literally, no way in which this past can ever be retrieved or relived as a compensating, salving, presence. What is required here is narrative memory without images. Remembrance without re-presentation.

It is clear that the history of victims calls for a mode of remembering different from the ritualistic commemoration of heroes and gods. The 'little narratives' of the vanquished as opposed to the 'Grand Narratives' of the victors. But moralists of narrative memory such as Lanzmann and Lyotard fail, it seems to me, to fully appreciate that reminiscence of suffering has just as much need to be *felt* as rememoration of glory. Historical horror requires to be served by an aesthetic (*aisthesis*-sensation) quite as powerful and moving as historical triumph – perhaps even *more* powerful if it is to compete for the attention of the public at large. It is not enough that a film like *Shoah* be shown in elite art-house cinemas or as late-night highbrow TV specials on Arte or C4 or PBS. The story of the Holocaust demands to be heard and seen by as many people as possible in each new generation. And this is at bottom an ethical demand. Hence the importance of the decision by national public television in the US, in March 1997, to screen a vivid reminder of the Holocaust which, it was legitimately feared, a whole new generation of young Americans ignored. The film which was chosen, and which provoked widespread debate throughout the schools and media networks of the entire continent, was *Schindler's List*. A phenomenon which should give some pause to the moralising elitism (however well intentioned) of Lanzmann and his fellow avant-gardists.

Sometimes an ethic of memory is obliged to resort to an aesthetic of representation. Viewers need not be made only intellectually aware – *à la* Brecht and Lanzmann – of the horrors of history; they need to experience the horror of that suffering *as if* they were actually there. 'Fiction gives eyes to the horrified narrator. Eyes to see and to weep. The present state of literature on the Holocaust provides ample proof of this . . . one counts the cadavers or one tells the story of the victims' (Ricoeur 1988: 188). Memory not only illuminates, it illustrates; and part of this illustration is its use of images to *strike* us – in the sense of striking home the horror of evil and the charism of goodness.

A key function of narrative memory is empathy. And empathy is not always escapism. It is, as Kant noted in his account of 'representative thinking', a way of identifying with as many fellow-humans as possible – actors and sufferers alike – in order to participate in a common moral sense (*sensis communis*). In this manner, narrative imagination can assist a certain *universalisation* of remembrance, where our own memories – personal and communal – can be shared and exchanged with others' of very different times and places, where the familiar and the foreign can change hands. This is what Ricoeur means when he states that the 'horror attaches to events that must never be forgotten. It constitutes the ultimate ethical motivation for the history of victims. The victims of Auschwitz are, *par excellence*, the representatives for the history of all history's victims' (Ricoeur 1988: 186).

We may say, in summary, then that if Lanzmann and Lyotard are correct in stressing memory's ability to attest to the incomparable *singularity* of a unique event like Auschwitz, Spielberg and Ricoeur are right to counterbalance this by emphasising its testimony to the representative *universality* of good and evil. The truth is no doubt to be found in some kind of Aristotelian mean which combines both ethical impulses in a delicate complementary tension. That is no doubt what a practical wisdom (*phronesis*) of historical narrative requires is this age of easy forgetfulness – a proper balance between the dual fidelities of memory to the *uniqueness* and *communicability* of past events.

Sometimes, some places – Northern Ireland, Bosnia, Rwanda – it is important to let go of history, to heed Nietzsche's counsel to 'actively forget' the past in order to surmount the instincts of resentment and revenge. Other times, other places – Auschwitz being the time and place *par excellence* – it is essential to *remember* the past in order to honour our 'debt to the dead' and to ensure it never happens again.

> We must remember because remembering is a *moral duty*. We owe a *debt* to the victims. And the tiniest way of paying our debt is to tell and retell what happened at Auschwitz. . . . By remembering and telling, we not only prevent forgetfulness from killing the victims twice; we also prevent their life stories from becoming banal . . . and the events from appearing as necessary.
>
> (Ricoeur 1995: 290)

Narrative remembrance can serve two functions: it can help us represent the past as it really was *or* reinvent it as it might have been. In fiction, the role of reinvention is what matters most – even in historical novels like *War and Peace*. In psychotherapeutic and historical testimony, the function of veridical recall claims primacy.

Distinguishing between these two separate, if often overlapping, functions is, I submit, of crucial ethical import. As is discerning *when* it is right to remember and *when* it is better to forget. Or, indeed, *how much* we should remember and forget.

These are critical hermeneutic tasks requiring far more detailed analysis than I can provide here. For if the matter is crucial, it is also extraordinarily complex. To be reminded of this we need only recall the difficulty that arises when one is asked, like Hamlet, to *remember and forget* at the same time. Such a double injunction can lead to good literature – but not always to a good life. Hamlet, the suffering Prince, paid the price with his own life – as have many before and since.

RICHARD KEARNEY

References

Abraham, N., 'The Phantom of Hamlet', *Diacritics*, Vol. 18 No. 4 (1988).
Freud, S., *The Interpretation of Dreams* (Pelican, New York, 1983).
Gallop, J., 'Keys to Dora' and Stephen Marcus, 'Freud and Dora: Story, history, case-history', in *In Dora's Case*, ed. C. Kahane and C. Bernheimer (University of Columbia Press, New York, 1990).
Green, A., *Hamlet et Hamlet* (Balland, Paris, 1982).
Lacan, J., 'Desire and the Interpretation of Desire', in *Literature and Psychoanalysis*, ed. S. Felman (Johns Hopkins University Press, Baltimore, 1982).
Langer, L., *Holocaust Testimonies: The Ruins of Memory* (Yale University Press, New Haven, 1991).
Lanzmann, C., 'Holocaust, la représentation impossible', in *Le Monde* (February 1994).
Levi, P., *Si c'est un homme?* (Julliard, Paris, 1987).
Lyotard, J.-F., *Heidegger et les 'juifs'* (Editions Galilée, Paris, 1988).
Nussbaum, M., 'Narrative Emotions', in *Love's Knowledge* (Oxford University Press, Oxford, 1990).
Reich, W., 'The Monster in the Mist: Are Long-Buried Memories of Child Abuse Reliable?'(a critical review essay of books by M. Yapko, L. Terr and L. Wright), *The New York Times Review of Books* (May 15, 1994).
Ricoeur, P., *Time and Narrative III* (University of Chicago Press, 1988).
—— 'Memory–Forgetfulness–History', *ZIF*, vol. 2 (Universitat Bielefeld, 1995).
—— 'The Memory of Suffering', in *Figuring the Sacred: Religion, Narrative and Imagination* (Fortress Press, Minneapolis, 1995).
Shakespeare, W., *Hamlet* (Signet Classics, New York, 1963).
Wright, L., *Remembering Satan* (A. Knopf, New York, 1994).

4

THE POLITICS OF MEMORY

Reflections on practical wisdom and political identity

Jeffrey Barash

I take as the starting-point for my reflection, in the pages that follow, the ethico-political thought of Paul Ricoeur, as elaborated both in and following the work *Oneself as Another*. I will focus on Ricoeur's notion of practical wisdom – *la sagesse pratique* – in its application to the theme of political identity. My analysis will concern primarily a difficulty to which the phenomenon of identity, in its political and therefore *plural* dimension, gives rise: that of comprehending the precise contours of this phenomenon as it extends beyond oneself and the other as individual persons to encompass identity in its 'collective' dimension. It is to the task of analyzing this politically charged notion of 'collective' identity that, in what follows, I will apply the concept of practical wisdom that Paul Ricoeur has placed at the center of his most recent philosophical investigations. Before examining the specific manner in which I will delimit this task, however, I will recall, by way of introduction, Ricoeur's interpretation of the phenomenon of 'collective' or plural identity in the work *Oneself as Another*.

In *Oneself as Another*, the phenomenon of plural identity is brought to light in relation to what Ricoeur terms the 'cohesion of life in common'. In its optimal sense, this cohesion of life in common assumes an intermediary configuration between two extremes: between the attempt, on the one hand, to construct life in common in terms of atomized individuals, after the fashion of classic liberalism as exemplified in the philosophy of John Locke; and the assumption, on the other hand, that life in common might be welded together in terms of the spirit of peoples, invoking the existence of an autonomous socio-political entity above and beyond the individuals constituting it. Ricoeur traces this assumption back to the philosophy of Hegel. The question thus arises concerning the way of formulating a principle of cohesion of plural existence – of the *res publica* in its original sense – capable of avoiding the two opposing tendencies which have continually haunted ethico-political theory in the modern world: at the one end, the Scylla of atomized private interests out of which collective cohesion is supposed to spontaneously spring; at the other end, the Charybdis of the crushing domination by the organic State, conceived as a *Volksgeist* or, to speak the twentieth-century totalitarian language which distorted Hegel's thinking, as 'substantial homogeneity'. It is precisely in relation to this problem that Paul Ricoeur has revivified, in the context of his reflection, the ancient notion of practical wisdom, or what he elsewhere terms 'circumspect moral judgement' (*le jugement moral circonstancié*),[1] as a theoretical tool for situating the cohesion of life in common in an intermediary sphere between these extremities.

My interest in this concept of practical wisdom will not be limited, however, to an examination of Ricoeur's creative adaptation of the Aristotelian notion of practical wisdom to the socio-political sphere in *Oneself as Another*, as in other more recent writings. In accompanying him along the way he has marked out, I will attempt to extend his analysis of the cohesion of plural identity into an area that has directly concerned him in his most recent work in relation to the theme of 'memory and history'. In this area, we encounter a problem analogous to that examined in relation to individual and plural identity in the ethico-political domain, involving the configuration of *memory* as a source of the link between individual and plural identity. Here too, as we can note from his most recent articles, Ricoeur attempts to locate an intermediary zone between a conception of memory limited to the sphere of personal identity and collective memory extended to a group identity that takes the form of a substantial autonomous reality. This intrinsic relation between memory and identity, at once individual and collective, leads me then to delimit more precisely the question I raised at the outset: might the notion of practical wisdom, employed to clarify the contours of plural identity in the ethico-political domain, guide us in the attempt to uncover the sources of plural identity constituted by collective memory? In extending the analyses of Paul Ricoeur in this direction, I will examine the implications of an interpretation of practical wisdom on the basis of Ricoeur's ethico-political reflections for a theory of memory as I myself conceive of it.

In the first part of my analysis, I examine more closely those aspects of Ricoeur's notion of 'practical wisdom', as presented in the work *Oneself as Another*, which are most pertinent to the investigation of the political contours of plural identity. Following this, I examine the implications of this theory of practical wisdom in relating the problem of the cohesion of collective identity to that of collective memory.

I

Let us begin with a closer examination of the notion of 'practical wisdom'. We recall the definition proposed by Aristotle in Book VI of the *Nicomachean*

Ethics, in which practical wisdom – prudence, or *phronesis* – figures among the intellectual virtues. Whereas theoretical wisdom, *sophia*, aims toward eternal and immutable being, practical wisdom takes the contingent and the variable as its object. Given the essential contingency of human action, of *praxis*, due to the unforeseeable character of its consequences, the virtue of practical wisdom applies most directly to the domain of human affairs. Without entering into a detailed description of this idea, which would reach beyond the purpose of our present analysis, I will insist above all on the remarkable way in which Aristotle's theory of *phronesis* establishes a framework for individual action presupposing life in common as the necessary foundation for such action. As Aristotle wrote in Book VI of the *Nicomachean Ethics* (1142a):

> For people seek their own good, and suppose that it is right to do so. Hence this belief has caused the word 'prudent' to mean those who are wise in their own interest. Yet probably as a matter of fact a man cannot pursue his own welfare without Domestic Economy and even Politics.[2]

And, since private interest is so essentially related to public affairs, prudence, practical wisdom, is primarily defined as a political virtue.

One further aspect of Aristotle's theory of practical wisdom is particularly important for understanding Paul Ricoeur's development of this notion: if, for Aristotle, practical wisdom is a virtue, this is precisely because of its *ethico*-political significance, distinguishing it, for example, from a simple ruse or calculation, which might indeed be applied toward unwholesome designs. From this *ethico*-political perspective, practical wisdom depends upon an ethos, upon a whole series of dispositions, as a basis of prudent choice. As opposed to simple calculation, the employment of practical wisdom draws upon good counsel (*euboulia*) oriented toward the realization of the good life – which always essentially involves the good life in common.

If practical wisdom deliberates on a course of action to follow in a particular context, its application necessarily varies in relation to the different situations in which it is engaged. As Aristotle explained in the *Politics*, the rules of practical wisdom vary in relation to their application to the different political forms of democracy, aristocracy, and monarchy. What, however, constitutes the precise difference between these diverse political forms in terms of which practical wisdom must orient its choices? It is of particular importance for my analysis to underline the fact that, for Aristotle, this principle of differentiation, corresponding to the specific identity of a people, arises essentially in its *politeia* – in its mode of *political* organization. Its cohesion is rooted in this principle. According to the Aristotelian theory, this unity is more than the simple sum of individual interests but, given its essentially *political* basis, it shares no affinity with modern conceptions of organic principles of cohesion – whether posited in terms of the Spirit or of its bleak reflection in the notion of substantial homogeneity.

The aspect of Ricoeur's theory of collective identity in *Oneself as Another* that I draw upon here concerns above all his reinterpretation of Aristotelian practical wisdom as a means of reorienting the Hegelian idea of the ethical order – of *Sittlichkeit*. Hegel, as Ricoeur explains, sought to relate ethical criteria to a concrete historical context in order to overcome the abstraction of Kantian moral philosophy. Kant's philosophy, we recall, had set aside any consideration of the context of elaboration of the moral norm in the name of the universality and necessity of pure practical reason operating beyond contextual particularity and contingency. As we note in Kant's essays 'Theory and Practice' and 'On Perpetual Peace', practical wisdom or 'prudence' in the Aristotelian sense, with its emphasis on the singularity of the context of elaboration and application of ethical aims, constituted one of the principal orientations that Kant's idea of the universality of the practical norm sought to place in question. And it is precisely in order to reaccount for this singularity of context, albeit in a manner different than for Aristotle, that the Hegelian interpretation of *Sittlichkeit* opposes the Kantian philosophy of practical reason. Drawing less immediately on the Aristotelian heritage of practical wisdom than on the modern theory of historicity of the Spirit bequeathed by Herder, Hegel, beginning with *The Phenomenology of the Spirit*, posited the singular context of elaboration of political action in terms of the Spirit of a people, or *Volksgeist*. As Ricoeur notes in *Oneself as Another*, we encounter here a first model of the theory of organic politics, according to which the State, beyond the will of the individuals who comprise it, establishes a principle of absolute legitimacy. It is hardly necessary to recall in detail how this interpretation, well beyond Hegel's own intentions, was deformed over the course of the twentieth century. I call attention only to the somber reemergence of this tendency in our contemporary world, where once again, in accord with the principle of substantial homogeneity initially elaborated by authors like Carl Schmitt, a substantial principle of unity – such as race – occupies the place previously accorded to the *Geist*, for example in the recrudescence of neo-fascist theories in present-day Europe.

The originality of Ricoeur's interpretation of the Hegelian theory of *Sittlichkeit*, in light of Aristotelian practical wisdom and good deliberation, resides to my mind in the following innovation: the resolute affirmation of the ideal of democratic pluralism at the foundation of our modern societies, necessitating the application of the good counsel of practical wisdom, not only to the ideal of the good life as the purpose of the city, but above all to the reconciliation of a plurality of conceptions of the good life within a single community (given its modern complexity and diversity), which inevitably run up against situations of competition and of conflict. Beyond the Aristotelian source of inspiration, Ricoeur admits, in accord with this pluralist ideal, the fundamental indeterminacy of modern democracy in its capacity to conceive of any single ultimate purpose. At the same time, in order to avoid the danger both of a diluted eclecticism and of a relativism of values – which is the risk accompanying such an appeal to open-ended pluralism – the ethical aim must ultimately submit itself to the practical universality of the moral norm bequeathed by Kant, which it cannot be permitted to ignore, above all in a situation of conflict.

At this point, I would like to scrutinize Ricoeur's theory more closely, in relation to the question raised at the outset: how might we determine a principle of plural cohesion once we abandon any hope of identifying an ultimate common purpose, thus admitting the coexistence of a number of possible competing or even conflicting purposes among different social groups? Once we have demystified the ideology of the organic State derived from the perversion of the Hegelian notion of *Sittlichkeit*, how might we avoid the danger of social atomization which, as a byproduct of unrestrained liberalism, threatens our contemporary societies? This problem stands at the heart of what Ricoeur terms, in Chapter 8 of *Oneself as Another*, the 'crisis of legitimization' faced by modern democracies.

Here we appreciate the pertinence of the Aristotelian assumption according to which the unity of a polis depends primarily upon its mode of *political* organization. The principle of cohesion of life in common, as Ricoeur himself interprets it, might therefore find its most solid roots in the consensus concerning the primary value of democracy as such, however radical all other points of discord arising from the pluralism intrinsic to democracy might prove. Inversely, the problem of plural cohesion presents itself in all its acuity in those situations where the consensus concerning the fundamental worth of democracy collapses. What, however, permits us to maintain this consensus, which the anomie of social atomism and the tyrannical tendencies inherent in social organicism threaten to undermine?

It would reach beyond the framework of my present theme to attempt to provide a detailed response to this question, as raised by Paul Ricoeur in the work *Oneself as Another*. In relation to the present topic of analysis, I will emphasize only one particular passage in this work which situates the role of memory in this overall investigation. As Ricoeur writes in Chapter 9 of *Oneself as Another*, entitled 'The Self and Practical Wisdom', in relation to the crisis of legitimization which threatens to undermine the consensus concerning democracy:

> There is nothing better to offer, in response to the crisis of legitimation . . . than reminiscence [*réminiscence*] and mutual inter-relation in the public space of emergence of the traditions allowing for tolerance and pluralism, not through concessions made to

external pressure, but through internal conviction, however recent it might be. It is in conferring a memory to all of the beginnings and re-commencements, and to all of the traditions sedimented on their foundations, that 'good counsel' can meet the challenge presented by the crisis of legitimization. If, insofar as this 'good counsel' prevails, Hegelian *Sittlichkeit* – which itself is at the same time rooted in *Sitten*, in 'mores' [*moeurs*] – proves to be the equivalent of the Aristotelian *phronesis*: a plural, or rather public *phronesis*, just like the debate itself.

II

Having accompanied Paul Ricoeur up to this point, the reference in *Oneself as Another* to the ethico-political task of remembrance will provide me with the occasion to extend this reflection in another direction.

The theme of memory as Ricoeur conceives of it, not only in *Oneself as Another*, but still more directly in a recent article entitled 'Memory–Forgetfulness–History', concerns the problem of plural cohesiveness. As the source of both personal and collective identity, memory is situated at the very heart of this problem which practical wisdom seeks to comprehend. Here, indeed, the search for an intermediary sphere between atomized individuals and the organic State, the latter claiming an existence independent of its members, calls for a conception of group identity, drawing in turn on a correlative theory of memory: memory situated between the strictly private sphere, on the one hand, and the organic group, on the other, for which the notion of collective reminiscence presents itself as an ideological buttress reinforcing the claim to homogeneity of a national substance. It is the intrinsic role of practical wisdom in delineating this intermediary sphere that I now examine in terms of the following question: In what manner does the cohesiveness of purposeful life in common depend on – indeed, *should* it depend on – a long common experience rooted in memory?

Any attempt to answer this question assumes that we already know precisely what *memory* is, not only personal memory, but collective memory or, to adopt a phrase of Paul Ricoeur, 'an anthology of the traces left by events which have affected the course of history of the groups concerned'.[3] By focusing more closely on the idea of collective memory, we will investigate the level at which it should be situated.

As I see the matter, it is possible to identify several aspects of collective memory. I would name the most rudimentary of them 'reiterative memory'. This first aspect of memory corresponds, at the collective level, to one of the two types of personal memory described by Henri Bergson in *Matter and Memory*, and which he termed 'habit-memory' (*mémoire-*

38

habitude). Taken in this sense, reiterative memory is memory governing habitual action in its public and collective expression: the rhythm of the days of the week, of the market days and their rush hours, of summer vacation days; the psychological and physical abilities corresponding to the practice of given professions or sports, or of an occupation typical of a given region. Reiterative memory concerns the rhythms and dispositions of collective life as carried out in habitual everyday experience.

It is clear that this rudimentary aspect of collective memory can hardly comprehend the reliefs of collective identity. A second aspect of collective memory comes to light in relation to the *singularity* of momentous events of public significance, events which are recounted by historians and become an object of commemoration. This second aspect of collective memory – which we might term 'commemorative recollection' – retrieves at the collective level the principal sense of what Bergson, in relation to personal memory, qualified as the memory-image (*souvenir-image*): the image of memory in its singularity. Nonetheless, at the collective level the problem of the initial experience at the source of memory must not be confused with the memory-image as a trace of individual experience. I have a vivid recollection of the day of President Kennedy's assassination in 1963, even if I was not an eye-witness to this event or to those that immediately followed it. And yet, along with millions of other individuals, I in a certain sense participated in this event, which left a deep trace on public memory in its wake.

Since Antiquity, the historian's monumental narrative has carefully attempted to conserve the trace of great events, endowed with public significance, in order to prevent them from falling into oblivion. Since the practice of ancient historiography, we recognize the crucial importance of historical narratives and monuments, like the commemorations that accompany them, for the constitution and continuity of a collective identity.

The significance of commemorative recollection as a source of social cohesiveness appears in a particularly clear light through an example which is especially pertinent to my present theme: the interpretation of memory provided by Ernest Renan in his essay 'What is a Nation?' which was initially presented as a speech at the Sorbonne in 1882. In this essay Renan attempted to identify the principle of cohesion capable of transforming a collectivity into a nation. Renan's theory demonstrates a profound affinity with Aristotelian philosophy when he explains that the mere sum of individual interests cannot possess the force to weld together a national identity. And, after rejecting two other commonly held modern theories of national unity, those based on language and on race, Renan arrived at a conclusion that is highly significant for any discussion of national identity. He wrote:

39

A nation is a soul, a spiritual principle. Two things, which are in truth the same, constitute this soul, this spiritual principle. One is situated in the past, the other in the present. One consists of the common possession of a rich heritage of memories; the other of present consent, the desire to live together, the will to continue to accredit the heritage that one has received undivided. . . .

[. . .] To have common past glory, a present common will: to have done great things together and to want to accomplish still other great things, these are the essential conditions that make up a people.[4]

Renan's interpretation of collective memory continues to play a decisive role for the articulation of the idea of the nation in the twentieth century. However, in considering it alongside the notion of reiterative memory, have we accounted for all of the possibilities of collective memory? In the case of each of these aspects of collective memory, we are concerned with an *explicit* memory or, at least in the case of commemorative recall, with a memory which aims to keep traces of public experience from falling into oblivion. And yet would it be legitimate to attribute to collective memory an implicit facet which, although intimately intertwined with these two aspects of public memory, is only rarely an object of explicit recall? I am referring above all to tacit memories rooted in a long collective experience, in terms of which the most profound attitudes of a people are sedimented. The tacit memories, which are generative of the deep attitudes that predominate among a people, fluctuate between the most diverse kinds of experience: at one extremity, tacit collective memories that mark life in common following terrible and traumatic experiences which are particularly difficult to assimilate, and which influence the deeper attitudes of a people over a long course of time, even when they are not explicitly recalled. At the other extremity, it is possible to identify also those latent memories which, rooted in an experience of political equipoise and stability, orient the profound dispositions of an entire people. It is said, and rightly so, that one of the chief sources of the stability of democracies lies in a long democratic experience.

But are we really dealing in such cases with the phenomenon of *memory*? Is it not rather a question here of a vague notion in relation to which we attempt to lump together the most heterogeneous of phenomena?

The task I set out to accomplish at the outset was to delineate a sphere of collective memory situated between the two extremes of personal memory and group memory conceived in terms of a substantial entity. To my mind, this intermediary theory of memory comes to light if, for the purposes of our interpretation, we pursue more closely an idea elicited at the outset: that of the *ethos* in the Aristotelian sense of the term. The *ethos*, as we have seen with Paul Ricoeur, is configured in relation to an entire series of dispositions that characterize the specific context of collective life. As I apply them to the theory of collective memory, these dispositions are not so much concerned with explicit and habitually performed actions – even where implicit memory draws upon such actions – as it is with the *singular* modes of life in common.[5] And, if commemorative recall can at the same time elicit certain aspects of this tacit memory, its reservoirs are at once too vast and too multiform for explicit recall to encompass. Beyond reiterative memory and commemorative recall, the interpretation of collective memory proves especially fruitful where, guided by the Aristotelian notion of the *ethos*, it is grounded in an essentially *political* conception of experience constitutive of the lines of social cohesion.

I would like to clarify this unusual application of the Aristotelian concept of *ethos* by referring to a passage of Aristotle's *Politics* dealing with this theme. In Book II, Chapter 8, of the *Politics*, Aristotle wrote the following passage in response to the question concerning whether, in a given State, it is desirable to change the laws, much as, for example, in medicine or in the various arts a change in practice occasionally becomes necessary. Aristotle responded to this question in the following way (1269a):

> These considerations then do seem to show that it is proper for some laws sometimes to be altered. But if we consider the matter in another way, it would seem to be a thing that needs much caution. For in cases when the improvement would be small, while it is a bad thing to accustom [*ethesein*] men to repeal the laws lightly, it is clear that some mistakes both of the legislator and of the magistrate should be passed over; for the people will not be as much benefited by making an alteration as they will be harmed by becoming accustomed to distrust their rulers. Also the example from the case of the arts is fallacious, as to change the practice of an art is a different thing from altering a law; for the law has no power to compel obedience beside the force of custom [*ethos*], and custom only grows up in long lapse of time, so that lightly to change from the existing laws to other new laws is to weaken the power of the law.[6]

This example clearly illustrates in what sense a system of laws – built upon the 'force of custom' – differs from a simple habit governing everyday activity. Legal systems in this sense are rooted in a specific *ethos* – a mode of life in common – constituted over a long period of time and, I would add, incarnating a network of tacit significations that draw on implicit collective memory. Where it is conceived as an argument in favor of resistance to change, this example might seem to justify political conservatism. My purpose, however, is quite different: in insisting on the temporal dimension of the constitution of collective identities, my argument, far from concerning the danger or necessity of change, has to do with the *particularity* of the context that plural identity configures over time. And, in my opinion, implicit collective memory designates an underlying source of cohesiveness through which such particularity – involving whole networks of gestures and symbolic structures – comes to predominance.

I will conclude by taking up again the theme of practical wisdom with which I began. Practical wisdom, as we have seen, refers to action undertaken in a singular political context. And it must account for the contingency that characterizes human action within this context. In thus insisting on the notion of singularity, I in no way deny the possibility of invoking universal rules of practice, but seek to argue for a certain kind of prudence in the theoretical domain. Oriented toward the singularity of collective identities, the idea of practical wisdom seems to me to provide insight into the profound difficulties which societies face in their attempts to overcome the effects of traumatic experiences of the past. This has been one of the themes of Paul Ricoeur's reflection in his recent article 'Memory–Forgetfulness–History'.

For my part, I would insist on the idea of the particularity of collective identities and of collective memory between personal recollection and the reified memory used to reinforce the latter-day ideologies of the organic State, in order to exhibit the limits inherent in a number of comparative models that have become current in contemporary political theory. The exaggeration of comparative methods overlooks the danger of reducing the complex socio-political systems of modern states to identical explanatory types, while ignoring the profound temporal dimension through which the particularities intrinsic to their respective identities have emerged. In this sense, totalitarianism, fascism, or communism have become labels which, when applied according to broad comparative models, too often mask the specific phenomena underlying collective experience. This seems to me to be an especially important application of the concept of practical wisdom, drawing on the theme of memory, which will provide material for later reflection.

Notes

1 Paul Ricoeur, 'Le concept de responsabilité', in *Le Juste* (Paris: Esprit, 1995), p. 69.
2 Aristotle, *Nicomachean Ethics*, trans. H. Rackham (Cambridge, Mass.: Loeb Classics, 1982), p. 349.
3 Paul Ricoeur, 'Memory–Forgetfulness–History', in *History, Memory, and Action. The Israel Academy of Sciences and Humanities, 13–24 Iyyun, The Jerusalem Philosophical Quarterly*, 45 (juillet, 1996), p. 15.

4 Ernest Renan, 'Qu'est-ce qu'une nation?', in *Oeuvres Complètes* (Paris: Cal-mann-Lévy, 1947), pp. 903–14.
5 In Aristotle's vocabulary, as more generally, the notion of disposition (*hexis*) which is constitutive of an *ethos* may be understood in a number of senses, encompassing both simple habits and specific modes of life in common. I relate the notion of collective implicit memory to this latter connotation, the modes of life in common, thus distinguishing it from the more explicit sphere of reiterative memory, resulting from the performance of habitual acts.
6 Aristotle, *Politics*, trans. H. Rackham (Cambridge, Mass.: Loeb Classics, 1977), p. 131.

Bibliography

Immanuel Kant, 'On the common saying: "This May Be True in Theory But It Does Not Apply in Practice"', in *Kant's Political Writings*, ed. Hans Reiss, Cambridge: Cambridge University Press, 1989.
Immanuel Kant, 'To Perpetual Peace: A Philosophical Sketch', in *Perpetual Peace and Other Essays on Politics, History, and Morals*, trans. Ted Humphrey, Hackett, 1983.
Paul Ricoeur, *Oneself As Another*, Chicago: Chicago University Press, 1992.

5

ETHICS AND LIFEWORLDS*1

Jean Greisch

There are certain passages where a thinker – often under the pressure of constraints or of external threats – succeeds in compressing a fundamental intuition into a few questions or propositions. In respect of ethics, two short texts immediately spring to mind. The first was written in the trenches of the First World War, part of it on the Carpathian Front. It was recorded (dated 5.7.16) in the war-time diaries of Ludwig Wittgenstein, then attached to a garrison artillery regiment of the Austrian army:

> What do I know about God and the purpose of life?
> I know that this world exists.
> That I am placed in it like my eye in its visual field.
> That something about it is problematic, which we call its meaning.
>   That this meaning does not lie in it but outside it.
> That life is the world.
> That my will penetrates the world.
> That my will is good or evil.
> Therefore that good and evil are somehow connected with the meaning of the world.
> The meaning of life, i.e. the meaning of the world, we can call God.
> And connect with this the comparison of God to a father.
> To pray is to think about the meaning of life. . . .2

The second text is of a more classically academic construction and is not so strongly expressed in terms of existential stakes. It was published, together with other material, as an appendix to Husserl's *Lectures on Ethics*. Husserl's editors estimate that it was written *c.* 1902, shortly after the publication of the *Logical Investigations*. It offers a summary of the main questions that Husserl had to confront in attempting to characterize a phenomenological approach to ethics:

* Translated by Eileen Brennan.

44

1 Whether there might be any ethics without the presupposition of emotion as a fundamental function of consciousness. Whether ethics would be possible and meaningful apart from the faculty of feeling (*Gefühlsvermögen*), whether ethics would be possible and meaningful apart from the faculty of reason.

2 Whether the difference between virtue and vice has its source in distinct emotions or whether it originates from elsewhere, and following from this, whether this difference could still subsist whether there were no emotions.

3 Whether reason can discover what is virtue or vice in a particular case, what is to be done or not done, and what is to be found or abhorred.

4 Whether morals, value and non-value, can be discovered *a posteriori* or *a priori* in facts and 'objective' states of affairs, thus whether they are 'in the nature of things', where the nature of things is taken totally in itself and independently of the emotions which are attached to it.

5 Whether the addition of emotions to certain states of affairs is an empirical fact which exhausts the object of value or whether, on the contrary, the affective conception (*Gefühlauffassung*) of the state of affairs forms an *a priori* connection which forms part of the general essence of affective consciousness so that this affective conception is possible over and against states of affairs of this type and its opposite is impossible, whilst one of them is necessarily justified (approval–disapproval); necessary then means: one of them is compatible (in the case of the *adiaphora*, of the states of affairs which are not submitted to any ethical judgement, neither of them is compatible).

6 Whether, in general, there is apriority in the affective domain, and whether it is an apriority or whether an apriority is given which being independent of the matter of emotion concerns the simple form of affective-desiring consciousness.

7 Whether, in this respect, the notions of understanding and reason do not have, in spite of everything, a meaning which goes beyond that of Hume. The intellectual laws of consciousness – the purely logical laws – the practical laws of consciousness – the pure laws of values. Theoretical consciousness discovers all the laws. Thus the understanding discovers its pure laws, the purely logical laws and the purely practical ones.[3]

It was at first by a simple matter of association that I thought of grouping together these two testimonies and these two distinct philosophers' voices. But if I had to give a reason for making this comparison I would be tempted to read the first text as a Wittgensteinian variation on the three principal questions which in Kant's eyes summarize the fundamental interests of reason: *What can I know? What should I do? For what ought I to hope?* Reduced to its simplest expression, ethics – essentially a matter

45

of good and bad will which, in either case, has the power to change the meaning of the world – appears in this instance as a link between the onto-logical question of the meaning of the world and the religious question of the meaning of life, i.e. of the purpose of the world.

The second text raises a question which has become the standard ques-tion in ethics since the time of Hume and Kant, namely, the role of affects and of reason in the realization of the good life. At the same time, the text also attempts to define a perfect equilibrium between the *a priori* and the *a posteriori* dimensions of moral philosophy. Both questions are crucial for phenomenology which, in ethical matters as in other matters, is defined as a 'transcendental empiricism'.

The 'world in which we live' and its ethical stakes

These early reflections of Wittgenstein, the founder of analytical phil-osophy, and Husserl, the founder of transcendental phenomenology, informed their respective later philosophies. As we know, the later Witt-genstein developed the theory of the irreducible plurality of language games anchored in 'forms of life' – including ethics and religion – a theory pivotal to the conception of language developed in the *Philosophical Investigations*. The later Husserl, author of *The Crisis* and *Experience and Judgment*, works with the notion of the 'lifeworld' (*Lebenswelt*) in an attempt to reconcile the poles of *a priori* and *a posteriori*, reason and pre-reflective lived experience, the transcendental and the empirical – a task conceived as an ethical responsibility. There is a crucial difference between these two developments, however: where Wittgenstein sought to resolve the difficult question of values in terms of *plurality*, Husserl strove towards some kind of teleological *unity*.[4]

I have tried elsewhere to compare Wittgenstein's 'forms of life' with Husserl's 'lifeworld'. I should like to repeat that comparison here but, in a more specifically ethical perspective, asking myself:

1   what is the ethical significance of the plurality of worlds in which we develop and of the diversity of corresponding language games? and
2   is it possible to discover any unity which traverses this plurality?[5]

To this end, I should like to prepare the ground for a dialogue with, first, the conception of ethics developed by Peter Kemp in his *Das Unersetzliche* (*The Irreplaceable*),[6] a work in which the Danish philosopher sets out his ethics of technology, and, second, with the German phenomenologist Werner Marx (in his *Ethics and Lifeworld*). Kemp's *The Irreplaceable* observes the author's plan to reconcile a philosophy of action (which finds its key concept in commitment) with philosophies of perception within an ethical phenomenology which is in the first instance a pathos.[7]

46

In Kemp's initial conception, the theory of commitment presented itself in the form of a diptych. At first, it established a strong connection between the existential sense of commitment and the 'existential pathos' described by Kierkegaard. But the objective description of the foundation of commitment and of its actual forms ends in aporias which pathos by itself proves incapable of resolving. Thus the pathos of commitment needs to open up to a poetics of commitment. As Kemp presents it, this poetics of commitment takes the form of a fundamental theology in which the 'Poem of Christ' plays a central role.

The same fundamental oscillation between a pathetic and a poetic pole is found in the author's more recent works on biomedical ethics[8] and the ethics of technology. Commitment is now expressed in the concern to surmount the dreadful chasm between the problems raised by contemporary technologies and the ethical reflection on the good life. At the same time, Kemp retains the central intuition of his poetics of commitment which now finds its expression in the concern to exploit the resources of narrative discourse in order to give concrete expression to those problems and solutions which an ethics of the good life must face today. I agree entirely with the conviction expressed by Kemp when he writes: 'Modern society does not only need science and technology, it also needs ethics in the form of a practical wisdom of the good life with and for others'.[9] But precisely because our society needs such an ethics we cannot resign ourselves to contrasting the ethical order (applicable to the world of everyday life) with the artificial world of technology. Somehow or other ethics must bring these two into contact with one another.[10] And it is precisely this that Kemp tries to do in his inquiry into the 'irreplaceable'.

Refusing to withdraw too quickly to a meta-ethics, Kemp starts from the conviction that 'we must know in which world we live before we are able to ask what is the role of language, of thought, and of the creative imagination in the ideas and the representations to which we attach a validity in our practical life'.[11]

Can there be an ethical measure in a postmetaphysical world?

Before we are able to propose an ethics, we must first find a convincing reply to the question of 'knowing in which world we live'. When we speak here of a convincing reply, we mean one which is respectful of the phenomena as they actually give themselves. *Sôzein ta phainomena* or 'Save the phenomena': it is at this level that the phenomenological method first becomes interesting. But in what way? I shall try to answer this question by turning to the exemplary work of Werner Marx. It was, incidentally, the aforementioned inquiry into phenomenology's contribution to the renewal of moral philosophy which led me to him. A disciple of both

Husserl and Heidegger, Marx tried to find a phenomenological solution to the problem posed by the unity and plurality of lived worlds (*mondes vécus*), endeavouring in particular to draw out their ethical stakes.

Marx's ideas are set out in two important works which were published in the 1980s. The dominant theme of both studies is drawn from Hölderlin's poem, *In lieblicher Bläue* (*In Adorable Blue*). It is: *Gibt es auf Erden ein Maß?* or 'Is there a measure on earth?'[12] Hölderlin's reply is 'no', while Marx answers 'yes'. Be that as it may, the author's formulation of the question tells us that it is addressed to a generation for whom the gods have fled and metaphysical certainties have become questionable. In some ways the very wording of the question presupposes that we subscribe to the Heideggerian critique of metaphysics. Heidegger criticized metaphysical reason or 'ontotheology' for thinking of being as substance and for understanding the subject from the stance of a rational animal whose highest expression of value is freedom. But what are we to do when that double presupposition becomes problematical and when, at the same time, traditional religion-based ethics is no longer ratified by many? In such circumstances the question arises as to the possibility of a postmetaphysical ethics. Like Hans Jonas at the beginning of his *The Imperative of Responsibility*, Marx believes that we cannot allow an ethical vacuum to establish itself around us, and that the candyfloss of finer feelings must give way to the soundness of well-constructed ethical concepts.

I attempt in what follows to characterize the general aspect of Marx's ethics, taking as my reference his second work *Ethos und Lebenswelt*. The 'ethos' of Marx's title has a very precise but ultimately quite simple meaning. In the absence of fully developed moral codes the phenomenologist's rather modest task is that of describing the ethos or manner of living in the world which harmonizes with the new situation in which we find ourselves today. Marx's principal question is the following: how can man be led to accept a maximum amount of responsibility and to practise the virtue of compassion on the simple basis of his mortality and social being? Marx delivers a threefold response:

1   he claims that the sought-after ethics will have to assume the form of an ethics of responsibility;
2   he introduces a 'compassion principle' which is to be distinguished from Jonas' 'responsibility principle'; and
3   he structures this principle around a theory of the virtues, identifying his task as that of legitimizing anew the 'givens of the ancient virtues'.[13]

Clearly this triple presupposition places us at some remove from the ethics of discussion which in Habermas and Apel's versions favours the formality of argumentative reason and refuses to propose a theory of virtue. In contrast, it is a fundamental assumption of Marx's ethics that affects or moods (*Stimmungen*) play a role in the ethical life which is at least as important as that played by rationality proper.[14] (We find an equivalent assumption in the writings of Peter Kemp already mentioned.[15])

For Marx, the key word determining the orientation of ethics is 'compassion' or 'being able to sympathize' (*Mit-Leiden-können*). Therefore the ethics which he is attempting to construct will have to be an ethics of compassion. To that end he will have to wager on 'the possibility that the experience of his own mortality can transform man to the point of making him discover the measure of compassion [*Maß des Mit-Leiden-können*] as a force capable of producing the virtues of mercy, recognition and love of one's neighbour'.[16] As a phenomenologist, Marx is not required to examine the different philosophical theories of compassion from Rousseau to Schopenhauer: his task is to describe the *genesis* of these virtues in our actual experience. The critical question, then, will be that of knowing if it is possible to show that 'being able to sympathize' is a central moment of the existential constitution of *Dasein* even if this phenomenon is veiled – something rarely encountered in the open. Subsequently, it will be a matter of establishing within this fundamental structure the existence of a necessary connection between what we might term the 'cardinal virtues' of recognition, mercy and love of one's neighbour. Thus a path is outlined whose general course can be summarized in three stages:

1 identification of the fundamental existential structures which under certain conditions are capable of receiving an ethical sense;
2 description of the transformation which gives rise to this ethical sense where the latter is seen as a *possibility* inscribed in experience;
3 demonstration of the conditions under which this possibility becomes a force, i.e. a value which presents three faces in turn: recognition, mercy, love of one's neighbour.

The author's analysis comes down to three basic theses.

1 By describing the structures of meaning inscribed in life itself, and trusting in what manifests itself in affects, we can show that at the individual level (an ethics of the neighbour) as well as at the social level (social ethos), being-able-to-sympathize is the sole measure which provides a foundation for moral action.[17]
2 The second thesis postulates that we cannot do justice to the complexity of our relationships with the world unless we assume an irreducible plurality of lived worlds (*mondes vécus*) whose inner richness emerges through the complexity of the moods and experiences of meaning which characterize the lifeworld. The notion of 'lifeworld'

(*Lebenswelt*) thus forms a *plurale tantum* which has to be described as such. This second thesis seems to me to represent a phenomenological counterpart to the Wittgensteinian thesis of the irreducible plurality of language games and forms of life.

3   Does this mean that the last word must go to a complete dissemination, precluding every form of unity? Marx denies that this is the case in his third thesis: if we know how to recognize the richness and complexity of the heterogeneous worlds in which we develop, we are obliged to look for a unifying principle. And this principle can only be ethical: 'The ethical element, the ethos anchored in the value of being able to sympathize, does not itself designate a world alongside numerous other worlds, but – similar in that to the religious and the aesthetic – it represents something which permeates all of the worlds and all the contexts of meaning'.[18] It follows that the ethos in question will have to be conceived as 'an active power which in spite of everything is capable of linking up with numerous worlds'.[19]

Having presented the author's problematic in general terms let us now examine these three theses in a more precise manner, taking them in sequence and asking ourselves in what sense they intersect the reflections of Wittgenstein and Husserl, presented at the start of this essay.

The possibility of a fundamental ethics: the force of sympathizing

Maß für verantwortungsvolles Handeln – 'measure of acting responsibly': it is this emblematic formula which summarizes Marx's research. The translator is faced with an immediate problem here of interpretation: how is he/she to render *Maß*, a term borrowed from Hölderlin? In French we think of the measure of metre, or of the contrast measure – excessiveness. As it is employed by Marx, the term acts as a substitute for notions of order and law which he sees as belonging either to the metaphysical tradition or to the religious tradition and frequently to both at the same time. And, as I have already pointed out, the critical question for him is precisely that of the 'measure' of ethical action which is able to impose itself in an incontestable manner upon a humanity for whom the fundamental postulates of metaphysics have become problematical and from whom the gods have fled. Quite often Marx glosses the term *Maß* with the word *Verbindlichkeit*. The latter expresses an obligation which has the form neither of a law nor of an imperative. In spite of the rupture with metaphysics the sought-after criterion or measure will have to share the character of 'absolute certainty' with the ancient notions.[20]

But can there still be 'absolute certainties' if, for a great number of our contemporaries, religion seems to have become incredible and metaphysics unworkable? The reply that Marx gives is similar to that of Heidegger: the apodictic certitude of the Cartesian *cogito, sum, existo* draws its existential sense from the irrevocable *sum moribundus*.[21] Thus the entire question will be that of knowing what kind of ethical certainty we can draw from the fundamental existential certainty of our being-towards-death.

Marx first recalls that this certainty is inseparable from an affection and a mood (*Befindlichkeit, Gestimmtsein*) which bestows an existential sense on these notions, as Heidegger had done in *Sein und Zeit*. But more so than Heidegger, Marx thinks about the transforming power of affects. While Heidegger is interested above all else in the self's becoming authentic through the fundamental mood (*Grundstimmung*) of anguish – itself inseparable from the fundamental existential of care – Marx tries to identify an affect which has a power of reversal such that its fruits are the virtues of love, compassion and justice.

For him it is terror (*Entsetzen*) which is the sought-after affection. This term must be taken here in the ecstatic sense of a wrench which has just shaken up all the plans and projects of the subject. Terror (an affect which for Heidegger is only a more intense variant of fear[22]) and its effects – the feeling of abandonment and distress – brings about the conversion from the feeling of indifference which dominated until then. Its transforming power is such that others who bring aid to me, and to whom I must bring aid, are made to appear as 'the other of myself' (*anderes meiner selbst*), according to Hegel's formulation in the *Phänomenologie des Geistes*. Equally, we could say with Ricoeur that terror alone discovers 'myself as another'.[23] In terror, the other becomes one who brings aid, a *Nothelfer*, in the most basic sense 'a helper in times of distress'.

Unlike Levinas, Marx does not introduce the dimension of listening to and questioning others straightaway.[24] It is only after having concretely experienced in my own flesh the meaning of 'assistance to someone in danger' that I become capable of bringing aid to others and of making them my neighbours. Despite this considerable difference of emphasis between Marx and Levinas, the two thinkers share a sense of wonder before the miracle of compassion: 'On this unique planet, in this heartless universe [*in diesem gefühllosen Weltraum*], there is a being who bears within himself the possibility of being able to sympathize.'[25]

I remember a train journey (from Liège to Paris) with Levinas during which, over a period of some hours, he told me about his sense of wonder before the miracle of kindness. From his point of view kindness is infinitely more wonderful than the simple fact that there is something rather than nothing. That day, it seemed to me that the wonder of human kindness is the fundamental intuition which underlies all of Levinas' thought. I find a similar intuition in Marx. In the shocking experience of terror before our own fragility, the simple possibility of sympathizing becomes a force in the sphere of action, i.e. a 'virtue' in the ancient sense of this word. Conversely, the fundamental virtues of recognition, mercy and love of one's neighbour would be nothing outside of the ability to sympathize which defines a measure more original than the maxims, rules, imperatives and standards of deontological morals.

In regard to the forms of relationship with others, Marx suggests replacing the Heideggerian ontological lexicon (*Mitsein*, being-with) with the notion of *gestimmte Gemeinsamkeit* or *gestimmte Intersubjektivität*. To be brought together with others, or a harmonious intersubjectivity: this displacement exploits (the) being-*for*-others (*Anteilnahme*) or concern. It alone is capable of founding an authentic intersubjectivity[26] which has its strongest expression in love of one's neighbour. It is a revealing trait of this approach that it lends a specific attention to melancholy, while it thinks of the fundamental virtues in terms of safety and healing.[27]

Even if under the triple expression of the fundamental virtues 'measure' does not amount to a simple imperative, it does echo distinctive traits of metaphysical measure: absoluteness, certainty, obligation (*Verbindlichkeit*).[28] But it must not be forgotten that compassion is a mere possibility. It therefore does not have a guarantee other than the testimony of those who actually put the corresponding virtues into practice. Their certainty is anchored in the phenomenon of attestation.

Marx is anxious to defend his conception of ethics against the charge that it is a withdrawal into the private sphere of the individual; and to this end he endeavours to show that it holds just as well for the social ethos. In critical debate with the two authors of the speculative tradition, Hegel and Schelling, he introduces a double *a priori*. Formal in the first instance, it is formed by the idea of belonging, an idea which is inseparable from the notion of the lived social world, in the sense understood by Husserl and Alfred Schütz. In its formality the 'lived world' appears as a complex system of belongings of every order. Marx's double *a priori* is not only formal but material. The material *a priori* is formed by the idea of dwelling and its numerous modifications. There are several possible ways of dwelling in the world, and even an uninhabitable world is a world habitable by default. It is here that the notion of ethos as something preceding ethics has its roots.

As he has done for the experience of mortality, Marx tries to identify the affection and mood corresponding to this double *a priori* structure. His thesis is 'that in every aspect, our material belonging to the social world holds together in the mood of a disinterested indifference unless we have an attitude of refusal towards our society – unless we are "alienated" from it or, conversely, are committed to it'.[29] Is it the phenomenologist concerned with describing the forms of social being (*l'être-ensemble social*) who speaks here? Or is it the moralist who will not support the indifference which seems to be characteristic of the functioning of our societies? Obviously, it is the latter. All that remains is to interpret this indifference as a 'lack' and ask oneself the question: in what circumstances can this belonging by default, or this purely possible belonging, be overcome?

We might well call to mind here extreme situations – such as natural disasters, when solidarity or even heroism is suddenly awakened (for example, among the fire brigade at Chernobyl) – but which have been buried away or forgotten until now. Here, again, Marx appeals to the feeling of terror which is aroused by all-out war or nuclear catastrophe in order to describe a transformation which takes the double form of the universalization *and* the internalization of cries for help. But there remains the problem of knowing how what is experienced in the terror provoked by exceptional situations can become a lasting intuition, giving birth to the virtues of social justice and social compassion.[30] Marx does not seem to have any doubts on the subject, because he even engages in a sort of transcendental deduction of the forms of social organization which correspond to this transformation.[31]

The unity of the world in question: the *plurale tantum* of lifeworlds

Let us turn now to an examination of the second thesis. It has for its backdrop the idea of 'world' as it functions in Western metaphysics, an echo of which we find still in Kant's transcendental dialectic. In this context, the idea of world takes on three basic functions: unity; totality; and order. The question which arises is one of knowing what these functions become once we detach them from a metaphysical concept of the world and instead refer them to a phenomenological one. In other words, what becomes of the functions of unity, totality and order if we take into account the 'natural concept of world', as described by Husserl and Heidegger (with, of course, their respective and significant differences of emphasis). Marx first defines the phenomenon 'world' through four 'formal' traits: (i) spatiality (*Umwelt*, the surrounding world); (ii) temporality (which, in Heidegger, takes on the form of care and *Bekümmerung*, thus echoing the Augustinian *cura*); (iii) alteration and change; and (iv) universality (the world is everyone's world). From this fourfold perspective the world does not present itself as a chaos, but as a meaningful world (*un monde sensé*) endowed with a certain order.

The entire question is one of knowing what relationships this prelogical order maintains with the logical notions of unity and totality. It seems to me that Marx's use of *Lebenswelt* is closer to the Heideggerian concept of 'everyday world' than it is to that of Husserl. Marx remains more faithful to hermeneutic phenomenology than he is to transcendental phenomenology. That leads him to contrast in a slightly artificial way 'experience of sense' and 'giving of sense'.[32]

Taken in the logical sense the concept of unity excludes plurality, while totality includes it, because where there is a whole there are also parts. As long as we confine ourselves to the formal concept of natural world the question of knowing whether the world forms a unity or a totality remains undecidable. But this concept makes sense only if it is related to material contents: customs, habits, practices, convictions, etc., which form what Husserl calls a *Glaubensboden*, 'a ground of belief'. As soon as we introduce this dimension there can be no doubt that the prelogical relationship to the lifeworld has the structure neither of unity nor of totality.[33] On the contrary, the way in which we dwell in our everyday world implies a heterogeneity prohibiting us from viewing that world as a whole made up of several parts. Further, no transcendental synthesis allows for the construction of this unity or totality.

For Marx the task of philosophy is precisely to destroy the fantasy of a falsely homogeneous and unified world while displaying the multiplicity and heterogeneity of the fields of signification which we inhabit. From this point of view the nostalgia for a falsely unified and homogeneous world – referred to in the German expression *heile Welt* (unharmed world) – must give way to amazement before the multiplicity of worlds in which man can develop simultaneously. The thinker's task is to think this multiplicity as multiplicity.[34] To that end it is not enough to juxtapose compartmentalized worlds. It is necessary to think about the way in which we *pass* from one world to another. Empirical analysis stops at the simple acknowledgement of the co-existence of several worlds: the task of the philosopher is to raise the transcendental question of the conditions of possibility of these transitions, e.g. from the relatively private world of the family to the 'public' world of the political project. Expressed in ethical terms, the renunciation of the nostalgia for a unitary world corresponds to the ancient virtue of 'magnanimity'.[35] Expressed in more metaphysical terms, it corresponds to wonder before the 'richness of being'.[36]

This thesis seems to me to call for a least two critical remarks. First, up to what point can we say that it is faithful to the Husserlian description of the lifeworld? Because Marx himself refers to *Erfahrung und Urteil* (Chapter 7) let us go back to the part (Chapters 6–10) of that work where Husserl reveals the mainlines of the phenomenological justification of the original *doxa*. In Chapter 7 Husserl assigns to genetic phenomenology the essential task of showing that the phenomenological concept of experience must be broadened to include the 'prepredicative consciousness of experience' (*vorprädikatives Erfahrungsbewußtsein*) which precedes every act of judgment. The correlative of this concept of experience is the world as 'universal ground of belief' (*universaler Glaubensboden*).[37] Prior to all cognitive activity objects are already there for us pregiven in simple certainty (*in schlichter Gewissheit vorgegeben*). This pregivenness introduces passivity and a fundamental affection into the structure of experience. Nevertheless Husserl does not hesitate to describe the reign of the 'original doxa' (*Urdoxa*) in terms of unity and totality. It is because we are faced with a 'unity of passive doxa' (*Einheit passiver Doxa*)[38] that pre-predicative experience already presents the holistic form of a world: 'We can also say that an actual *world* always precedes cognitive activity as its universal ground, and this means, first of all, a ground of universal passive belief in being which is presupposed by every particular cognitive oper-ation.'[39] It is a point in favour of Marx's interpretation that Husserl does not say *die Welt* here but rather *eine jeweilige Welt*. Husserl's formulation seems to suggest a plurality of worlds, but it must be emphasized that in this context Husserl does not come to a decision on the status of this plurality.

In contrast, there is no doubt in Husserl's mind that the *Weltbewußtsein in Glaubensbewußtheit* forms a totality:

> It is this *universal ground of belief in a world* which all praxis pre-supposes, not only the praxis of life but also the theoretical praxis of cognition. The being of the world in totality is that which is not first the result of an activity of judgement but which forms the pre-supposition of all judgement[40] . . . the world as a whole is always already pregiven in passive certitude.[41]

If we ask ourselves what the phenomenological sense of this totality is we will find a straight answer to this question in Chapters 8–9: all experience comprises an inner as well as an outer horizon, so that the world becomes the horizon of all possible experience. Moreover it is for this reason that the fundamental structure of the consciousness of world is characterized by a distinctive dialectic of the known and the unknown, of familiarity and strangeness. It is in this very precise context that Husserl introduces the concept of *Lebenswelt*: 'The retrogression to the world of experience is a retrogression to the lifeworld, that is, to the world in which we are always already living and which furnishes the ground for all cognitive per-formance and all scientific determination.'[42] The original sense of this *Lebenswelt* must be recovered from behind 'the garb of ideas' (*Ideenkleid*) in which the exact sciences have clothed original experience.[43] Genetic phenomenology's superiority to science consists in its having understood the necessity of returning to that *lebensweltliche Erfahrung*, not in order to take it as an immediate given, nor in order to contrast it with science's idealization, but in order to recognize there the sedimentations of a long history.[44]

If we compare these Husserlian passages with Marx's theses one differ-ence immediately leaps out: where Husserl accentuates unity and totality Marx maintains that the prelogical relationship with the world has the character neither of unity nor of totality. Another question, taken up only laterally by Marx, but which to my mind takes on a crucial importance, is that of the phenomenological criteria which permit the differentiation of a plurality of worlds. Is it sufficient to let oneself be guided by common sense or sociological distinctions? (Distinctions borrowed from the sociology of types would include world of the family, professional life, political life, public life, etc.) If one were to say that sociological distinctions are sufficient here one would expose phenomenology to the frequently repeated criticism that it is only a transcendental double of empirical psychology. But what use is a phenomenology of the lived social world if it does not tell us anything more than does empirical sociology? Whence the methodological importance of the question: what does the phenomenological concept of 'world' add to the sociological notion of 'environment'? To my knowledge at least three phenomenologists have tried to answer this question. First, I am reminded of the distinctions *Umwelt*, *Mitwelt* and *Selbstwelt* (environing world, shared world, word of the self) which play a crucial role in the early Heidegger's hermeneutics of facticity. Next, I recall its narrative counterpart in Wilhelm Schapp, a version which distinguishes three fundamental forms of 'entanglement' (*Verstrickung*) in histories: personal entanglement (*Eigenverstrickung*); entanglement with others (*Fremdverstrickung*); and collective entanglement (*Wirvestrickung*). But, third, it is without doubt Alfred Schütz who pursues this investigation farthest. Besides the parameters of proximity and distance, Schütz takes into account the temporal parameter thereby permitting the distinctions: the world of contemporaries; the world of predecessors; and the world of successors.[45] It is a matter of regret that while he mentions the works of Schütz in passing Marx does not explore this path of research any further.

Ethics as a force which unifies the plurality of worlds

For Marx the third and final question is whether, in spite of having disqualified the logical concepts of unity and totality and having openly recognized the plurality and richness of lifeworlds, it does not still become necessary to attribute a unitary sense to the concept 'worlds'. If the phenomenological description of lifeworlds shows us that we are continually evolving in a plurality of everyday worlds, that discovery is accompanied by the certitude that this plurality is not chaotic but rather reflects an order which is both internal and transversal. When we speak here of an internal order we mean one which is appropriate for each particular sphere, whether domestic life, professional life, etc. To say that the order is also transversal is to point to its capacity to connect the different lifeworlds to one another.

But how shall we define this unifying trait? In answering this question Marx makes use of the phenomenological notions of 'theme' and 'type'. Here theme refers to the immanent order of each life-praxis. Thus, for example, medical praxis comprises a very large number of 'medical treatments'. But sooner or later the question will arise of the very meaning of life-praxis as such, even if that question can be thematized only with difficulty. The notion of 'type' expresses that non-thematizable aspect: 'We always already sojourn in the meaning of life-praxis as type and it is from it, as from a global meaning, that we understand each everyday world as a world of life-praxis.'[46] Of course this 'typical' unity will never take the form of a logico-systematic totality.

It is at this level that the question arises of the type of unity made possible by ethics. Like religion, ethics could not allow itself to be confined to a specialized world, i.e. a world of specifically religious or moral conduct. Ethics must define a transversal sense, one capable of encompassing every praxis: 'The ethical element [*das Ethische*] claims to penetrate each of the everyday worlds with its demands and from this standpoint to give them a meaning as totality and unity.'[47] This wager on the possibility of a unitary transversal sense straddles the distinction between everyday and non-quotidian worlds, examples of the latter including art, science, philosophy and theology. Moreover, the passage from one world to another is not comparable to a simple change of scenery. As in the case of the composition of a narrative plot where it is necessary to implement a 'synthesis of the heterogeneous' (Paul Ricoeur's phrase) – aligning the events one after the other is not sufficient – so too in the case of ethics. Each passage from one lived world to another requires a work of integration (*verarbeitendes Hereinholen*). This 'integration' – this ethical articulation of heterogeneous worlds – will never be a 'giver of unified meaning' similar to the 'transcendental apperception' of which Kant speaks in the *Critique of Pure Reason*.

Ethics is not alone in finding itself confronted with similar work of integration. Marx finds some equivalents in art, science, philosophy and theology. None of these disciplines can close themselves off in a particular world. On the contrary, each must propose an inclusive interpretation of the world. Very like religion, ethics could not constitute a 'world apart' (*Sonderwelt*) because it has long pervaded the everyday nature of all worlds. What then constitutes its specificity, making it a 'measure' comparable to no other?

On the one hand, being able to sympathize is the measure of all measures. Even if it presents a different face in each of the worlds, it is not absent from any of them. It is clear that the legal expression of compassion would be very different from the compassion expressed by humanitarian organizations. But it would be a serious mistake to contrast the bronze face of justice with the merciful face of charity. Because it is the only measure of ethics, compassion will need to be present just as much in the legal world as in international and domestic relations. On the other hand, its role is to form the minimal unifying character between all these worlds, their diversity notwithstanding. Thus its function is to guarantee the cohesion of a world which is irrevocably plural. The permeation of this measure through all structures is obviously a process which cannot be finished. It is in this sense that Marx can write:

> all that happens in the numerous worlds turns on the question of knowing whether and how the measure of being able to sympathize is active there. In this absolutely precise sense of the term 'measure', it is compassion which measures all behaviour. Thus when all is said and done it is one and the same measure which governs the numerous worlds and which unites them equally in this sense.[48]

On the last page of his book Marx expresses the same conviction in a still more resonant language which perfectly summarizes the core of his thought:

> The measure of being able to sympathize is, in a particular sense, a force immanent in our meaning-experiencing lives. It is the active power in the living performance which liberates all that is *other* and which in this release permeates our meaning-experiencing lives with its force. In fact it permeates equally the connections of experienced meaning and the worlds themselves. In its aura the other appears as other and the many appear as many. It is one and the same light which bathes meaning-experiencing life and the world, and it is one and the same light which unifies the connection of meaning thus experienced and worlds, relating them to one another.[49]

To conclude, I briefly mention some critical questions central to Marx's ethical project. They echo the two texts which provided the point of departure for our reflections. First, anyone who is familiar with the thought of the later Wittgenstein will have difficulty sharing the optimism of the author who calculates that an ethics of compassion appears capable of surmounting the heterogeneity of language games and the corresponding forms of life. Second, as we have seen, Marx tries to found a postmetaphysical ethics. That, however, does not prevent him from taking some of his concepts from the language of metaphysics, starting with the notion of 'principle'. But can we subscribe to the hypothesis which holds that the notion of principle – unlike those of order and law – no longer belongs to metaphysics? Is it not the case that the ethics which Marx tries to establish still remains anchored in the metaphysical tradition?[50] Third, the author tries to found ethics in a phenomenology of ethos, a phenomenology of living in the world. The same notion of habitable world plays an important role in Paul Ricoeur who orders it, however, to the poetic function of metaphor.[51] Perhaps there is a hidden connection between Hölderlin's verse which maintains that man dwells poetically in the world (*dichterisch wohnet der Mensch*) and the verse in which he ponders over the 'measure' appropriate to that same world. From that moment we can wonder whether we need to give greater emphasis than the author has to the necessary complementarity between the ethics whose outline we have just drawn and a poetics of existence.

Notes

1 This essay was given in the form of a paper to a conference given at l'Institut Catholique de Paris on 19 November 1994 on the occasion of the annual congress of l'Association des Professeurs de philosophie des Facultés Catholiques. This conference was transformed into a posthumous homage to Werner Marx (1910–1994) when Marx died two days later on 21 November 1994. An earlier version of this text appeared in the *Revue d'éthique et de théologie morale*, No. 200 (March, 1997), pp. 181–203.

2 Ludwig Wittgenstein, *Tagebücher 1914–1916* in *Schriften* 1 (Frankfurt: 1969), p. 165; translated from the German by G. E. M. Anscombe under the title, Ludwig Wittgenstein, *Notebooks 1914–1916* (Oxford: Basil Blackwell, 1979), pp. 72–3.

3 Edmund Husserl, *Husserliana* XVIII (The Hague: Nijhoff, 1975), pp. 418–19.

4 *The Crisis* can be seen as an historical introduction to the idea of a transcendental phenomenology, a Husserlian equivalent, as it were, of Hegel's *Phenomenology of Spirit*.

5 My inquiry connects with a recent study on the contribution during the present century of phenomenology to the development of moral philosophy. 'Phénoménologie et philosophie morale', in Monique Canto-Sperber (ed.), *Dictionnaire de philosophie morale* (Paris: PUF, 1996), pp. 1120–30.

6 Peter Kemp, *Das Unersetzliche: Eine Technologie-Ethik* (Berlin: Wichern, 1992).

7 Cf. Peter Kemp, *Théorie de l'engagement*: vol. 1 *Pathétique de l'engagement*. vol. 2 *Poétique de l'engagement* (Paris: Editions du Seuil, 1973).

8 Peter Kemp, *Médecine et éthique* (Paris: Editions Tierce, 1987).

9 Peter Kemp, *Das Unersetzliche*, p. 11. Cf. 'Du langage comme sol de croyance', in *L'âge herméneutique de la raison* (Paris: Editions du Cerf, 1985), pp. 125–47.

10 Kemp, *Das Unersetzliche*, p. 15. The 'irreplaceable' plays a role similar in Kemp's thought to that of the 'unjustifiable' in Jean Nabert's moral philosophy.

11 *Ibid.*, p. 14.

12 Werner Marx, *Gibt es auf Erden ein Mass? Grundbestimmungen einer nicht-metaphysischen Ethik* (Hamburg: F. Meiner, 1983). Also, W. Marx, *Ethos und Lebenswelt: Mitleidenkönnen als Maß* (Hamburg: F. Meiner, 1986). There is a detailed presentation and critical discussion of the ideas developed in these two works in Otto Pöggeler, 'Gibt es auf Erden ein Mass?', in *Schritte zu einer hermeneutischen Philosophie* (Freiburg: K. Alber, 1994), pp. 356–88. Pöggeler discusses the precise meaning of Hölderlin's verse on pp. 369–72.

13 Marx, *Ethos und Lebenswelt*, p. 15.

14 *Ibid.*, p. 6.

15 Like Brentano, Husserl and Scheler, Marx proves Hume and Kierkegaard right in their opposition to Spinoza and Kant. And he shares MacIntyre's concern to rehabilitate the notion of virtue while taking issue with the view that the royal road to this rehabilitation is the return pure and simple to the Aristotelian virtues. Marx's inquiry takes place beyond the conflict which sees cognitive ethics confront non-cognitivist ethics (whether the latter is presented as intuitionist in the manner of Scheler or Hartmann, or as emotivist or even decisionist). His problem is to find a third way between Weber's *Zweckrationalität* and a simple return to Aristotelian teleology. And his main objective is to understand the role played by the emotions in the very formation of the virtues. See *Ethos und Lebenswelt*, pp. 8ff.

16 *Ibid.*, p. 9.

17 *Ibid.*, pp. 51–2.

18 *Ibid.*, p. 52.

19 *Ibid.*, p. 52.

20 *Ibid.*, p. 16.

21 Cf. Martin Heidegger, *Gesamtausgabe* Band 20 (Frankfurt am Main: Vittorio Klosterman), pp. 437–8 where Heidegger says 'das moribundus gibt dem sum allerest seinen Sinn' (p. 438).

22 Cf. *Sein und Zeit*, Chap. 30.

23 Cf. Paul Ricoeur, *Soi-même comme un autre* (Paris: Editions du Seuil, 1990), p. 226.

24 Marx, *Ethos und Lebenswelt*, p. 23.

25 *Ibid.*, p. 24.

26 *Ibid.*, p. 28: 'Nur anteilnehmendes Mitsein begründet wahre Intersubjektività'.

27 *Ibid.*, p. 30.

28 *Ibid.*, p. 32.

29 *Ibid.*, p. 43.

30 *Ibid.*, p. 48.

31 Curiously enough, the corresponding social model is the exact picture of the German Democratic Republic, with its *Grundgesetz*, its social security system and the professional code of its civil servants.

32 *Ibid.*, p. 98.

33 *Ibid.*, p. 63.

34 *Ibid.*, p. 94.

35 *Ibid.*, p. 99.

36 *Ibid.*, p. 100.

37 Edmund Husserl, *Experience and Judgment: Investigations in a Genealogy of Logic*, trans. J. S. Churchill and K. Ameriks (London: Routledge, 1973), Chap. 6, p. 27.

38 *Ibid.*, p. 30.

39 *Ibid.*, p. 30.

40 *Ibid.*, p. 30.

41 *Ibid.*, p. 31.

42 *Ibid.*, p. 41.

43 Ibid., p. 45.

44 *Ibid.*, p. 45.

45 Cf. Alfred Schütz, *Strukturen der Lebenswelt*. Regarding ethical states, cf. also *Reflections on the Problem of Relevance* (New Haven: Yale University Press, 1970); trans. from the German, *Das Problem der Relevanz* (Frankfurt am Main: Th. Luckmann, 1971); also *Theory of Relevance* (La Haye, 1978).

46 Schütz, *Strukturen der Lebenswelt*, p. 83.

47 *Ibid.*, p. 86.
48 *Ibid.*, p. 90.
49 *Ibid.*, p. 103.
50 Otto Pöggeler, *op. cit.*, p. 388.
51 Cf. Paul Ricoeur, *La métaphore vive* (Paris: Editions du Seuil, 1975), pp. 359–84; *Du texte à l'action* (Paris: Editions du Seuil, 1985), p. 24.

Part II

DECONSTRUCTION

6

HOSPITALITY, JUSTICE AND RESPONSIBILITY

A dialogue[1] with Jacques Derrida

Q: Allow me to begin with a simple question: after deconstruction, what is to be done? How do we act? Let me try and formulate this more thoroughly.

If there is nothing outside of the text – a much misunderstood phrase – how do we move from the text, understood in the broad sense, to action? If there is a deconstructive logic of undecidability, where an event or an action can be both/and, neither/nor, or in ethical terms both good and evil, neither good nor evil, how do we make a decision on the basis of undecidability? If we take key concepts like 'law', 'truth' and 'lie', and submit them to the subtlety of 100 qualifications and close readings, how can we prevent conscience making cowards of us all?

In a nutshell, how do we discriminate between good and bad actions? How do we decide? How do we know what is the legitimate other that calls us to act and what is the fraud, the impostor?

JD: Your question started with the phrase 'after deconstruction', and I must confess I do not understand what is meant by such a phrase. Deconstruction is not a philosophy or a method, it is not a phase, a period or a moment. It is something which is constantly at work and was at work before what we call 'deconstruction' started, so I cannot periodize. For me there is no 'after' deconstruction – not that I think that deconstruction is immortal – but for what I understand under the name deconstruction, there is no end, no beginning, and no after.

The next step in your question is about deconstruction and ethics, and the relation between text and action. As you well know, what I call the 'text' is not distinct from action or opposed to action. Of course, if you reduce a text to a book or to something that is written on pages, then perhaps there will be a problem with action. Although even a text in the form of a book, in the classical sense of something written on pages, is already something like an action. There is no action, even in the classical sense of the word, no political or ethical action which could be simply dissociated from, or opposed to, discourse. There is no politics without discourse, there is no politics without the book in our culture. So the general frame of the question needs a re-elaboration.

I would include what we call 'action', or 'praxis' or 'politics', within the general space of what I call 'the trace'. Within this general space we have to distinguish between a number of determinate agencies, such as, of course, the book, the text in the narrow sense, and action. Once this has been undertaken the question of 'undecidability' emerges. Many of those who have written about deconstruction understand undecidability as paralysis in face of the power to decide. That is not what I would understand by 'undecidability'. Far from opposing undecidability to decision, I would argue that there would be no decision, in the strong sense of the word, in ethics, in politics, no decision, and thus no responsibility, without the experience of some undecidability. If you don't experience some undecidability, then the decision would simply be the application of a programme, the consequence of a premiss or of a matrix. So a decision has to go through some impossibility in order for it to be a decision. If we knew what to do, if I knew in terms of knowledge what I have to do before the decision, then the decision would not be a decision. It would simply be the application of a rule, the consequence of a premiss, and there would be no problem, there would be no decision. Ethics and politics, therefore, start with undecidability. I am in front of a problem and I know that the two determined solutions are as justifiable as one another. From that point, I have to take responsibility which is heterogeneous to knowledge. If the decision is simply the final moment of a knowing process, it is not a decision. So the decision first of all has to go through a terrible process of undecidability, otherwise it would not be a decision, and it has to be heterogeneous to the space of knowledge. If there is a decision it has to go through undecidability and make a leap beyond the field of theoretical knowledge. So when I say 'I don't know what to do', this is not the negative condition of decision. It is rather the possibility of a decision.

Not knowing what to do does not mean that we have to rely on ignorance and to give up knowledge and consciousness. A decision, of course, must be prepared as far as possible by knowledge, by information, by infinite analysis. At some point, however, for a decision to be made you have to go beyond knowledge, to do something that you don't know, something which does not belong to, or is beyond, the sphere of knowledge. That is why the distinction between good and evil doesn't depend on knowledge; that is why we should not know, in terms of knowledge, what is the distinction between good and evil. To have to make such a distinction, which depends precisely on responsibility, is, I confess, both a terrible and tragic situation in which to find oneself. Without this terrible experience, however, there would be no decision, there would simply be a serene application of a programme of knowledge and then we could delegate decisions to scientists and theoreticians.

Q: So is every decision one of fear and trembling, as in the case of Abraham?

JD: Of course, if there is a decision. That is why Kierkegaard's *Fear and Trembling* is a major text, however we interpret it. It is the moment when the general categories have to be overcome, when I am alone facing a decision. A decision is something terrible.

Now I would not claim that I am sure that there is such a thing as decision. The sentence 'I decide', or 'I made a decision', or 'I assume a responsibility', is a scandal; it's just good conscience. I am never sure that 'I' made a decision in terms of a determinant judgment. It is not a theoretical judgment; I cannot be certain that 'I' made a decision. Not only should I not be certain that I made a good decision, but I shouldn't even be certain that I made a decision. A decision *may* have happened. That is why, as I often say, and it sounds a little provocative, that 'I' never decide, that 'I' never make a decision in my own name, because as soon as I claim that 'I' have made a decision, you can be sure that is wrong. For a decision to be a decision, it must be made by the other in myself, which doesn't exonerate me from responsibility. On the contrary, I am passive in a decision, because as soon I am active, as soon as I know that 'I' am the master of my decision, I am claiming that I know what to do and that everything depends on my knowledge which, in turn, cancels the decision.

At some point, and perhaps you were trying to provoke me, you said that if we practise close reading we will never act. On the contrary, I would assume that political, ethical and juridical responsibility requires a task of infinite close reading. I believe this to be the condition of political responsibility: politicians should read. Now, to read does not mean to spend nights in the library; to read events, to analyse the situation, to criticize the media, to listen to the rhetoric of the demagogues, that's close reading, and it is required more today than ever. So I would urge politicians and citizens to practise close reading in this new sense, and not simply to stay in the library.

In the case of Hamlet, I try to show in *Specters of Marx* that the responsibility in front of the father's call, for it to be a responsibility, demands that choices be made; that is, you cannot remember everything for a fact; you have to filter the heritage and to scrutinize or make a close reading of the call. This means that to inherit, or to keep memory for a finite being implies some selection, some choice, some decision. So the son has to make a decision; even if he wants to be true to the father, or to remember the father, as a finite being he has to select within the heritage and that is again the question of undecidability. Of course, that is the classical interpretation of Hamlet as a victim of undecidability, he doesn't know and he gets paralysed. Nevertheless, if we assume that Hamlet is a figure of paralysis or neurosis because of undecidability, he might be also a paradigm for action: he understands what actions should be and he undergoes the process of undecidability at the beginning.

'How do we know?' was your last question and my answer is simply 'we don't know'! Of course, we have to know as much as possible, but when we make a decision – if we make a decision – we don't know and we shouldn't know. If we know there would be no decision.

Q: Your presentation of 'Two Sources of Religion at the Limits of Mere Reason', in Capri in 1994, uncovers those sources, as far as I understood it, as 'faith' and 'the holy'. In the Book of Job, Job undergoes the loss of this faith and of his experience of the holy as these are conventionally understood. It appears to me that he loses faith and the holy at the first level. Through that, it seems, Job achieves a new experience of the holy beyond all manipulability, as well as a faith in a relationship with an other, in this case a 'You' to whom he now adheres for the sake of the 'You' alone. I would like to ask whether you find in Job any echoes of your own articulation of the religious?

JD: First of all, how could we find an echo in Job, but also how could we not find an echo? Let me improvise with reference to Levinas who mentions Job at some points.

While teaching Levinas on the theme of 'hospitality' recently I made reference to Job in the following situation. As you know, in *Totality and Infinity* Levinas describes the ethical relationship as religious; religion and ethics imply a face to face: you alone face to face with the absolute other, the infinite other, and this face to face (*visage*) is the original ethics. This is described as a dual situation: you and I. Levinas, however, has to take into account 'the third one': when the third appears, and when the demand of the third appears, then the call for justice appears also. But Levinas insists on the fact that the third one does not appear after the other two as someone else – one, two and then three – but is already involved in the face to face relation as a call for justice. At this point we encounter a terrible situation: in order to be just, by taking into account the third one, I have to betray in some way my pure asymmetrical – but dual – relation with the other. This is followed by a complaint in Levinas, a complaint which sounds very much like Job's complaint: 'What should I have to do with justice, because justice is unjust?' For Levinas justice implies comparison, rationality; that is, because the third one is like the second other, I have to compare, I have to use concepts, I have to refer to resemblance, everything which implies ontology in the Greek sense and is divorced from ethics in the Levinasian sense. So I have to go back to philosophy, to Greek philosophy, in order to be just. There is a cry in many passages in Levinas: 'What do I have to do with justice? Why justice?' There is some impatience with justice because justice is unjust. Nevertheless we cannot, we should not, avoid justice.

So what does Job say? He feels that he is innocent and he protests against injustice. This is the terrible situation in which the unjust is not simply the contrary of justice, in which decision is not simply the contrary to undecidability. This looks terrible, and negative, and tragic, but it is also a chance, it is the condition of a decision. This terrible situation of two and three which I have just described is not simply a trap, it is a condition of justice. If there is a justice it has to go through this terrible situation where there are two and three: I have a relation to the other in his/her singularity or uniqueness, and at the same time the third one is already in place. The second one is a third one. 'You are a third one', that is the condition of justice.

Q: Since *Glas* you have been working on the notion of what you call 'the gift', or that which escapes the circular motion of spirit or reason in the Hegelian sense. Recently, you have attempted to define more directly the nature of this quite central motif in works such as *Given Time* and *The Gift of Death*, while endeavouring to relate it to themes such as hospitality, community and the political. There seems, in other words, to be a direct relationship between the notion of the gift and many of your current preoccupations. In brief, therefore, could you tell us how you actually go about applying the idea of the gift to the aforementioned notions which are becoming predominant in your work?

JD: In fact it is the same logic which is at work in both cases. How could we relate briefly the gift and hospitality? Of course, it is obvious that hospitality is supposed to consist in giving something, offering something. In the conventional scene of hospitality, the guest gives something in gratitude. So there is this scene of gratitude among hosts and guests. In the same way that I have tried to show that the gift supposes a break with reciprocity, exchange, economy and circular movement, I have also tried to demonstrate that hospitality implies such a break; that is, if I inscribe the gesture of hospitality within a circle in which the guest should give back to the host, then it is not hospitality but conditional hospitality. That is the way hospitality is usually understood in many cultures, such as the Greek and Islamic cultures. The host remains the master in the house, the country, the nation, he controls the threshold, he controls the borders, and when he welcomes the guest he wants to keep the mastery. 'I am the master of the house, the city, the nation' – that is what is implied in this form of conditional hospitality. This conditionality, which is also the conditionality of the gift as exchange, finds a number of examples in the history of our cultures. The one which interests me most, however, is Kant's example in 'Perpetual Peace',[2] in which he advocates universal hospitality as the condition of perpetual peace. To summarize very briefly, he says that peace must be perpetual; if you make peace only provisionally in order to resume the war, this would not be peace but armistice or cease-fire. For a peace really to be a peace, a promise of eternal peace must be at work.

Such a concept of peace implies, therefore, universal hospitality; that is, all the nation–states should guarantee hospitality to the foreigner who comes, but only under certain conditions: first, being a citizen of another nation–state or country, he must behave peaceably in our country; second, he is not granted the right to stay, but only the right to visit. Kant has a number of sharp distinctions about this. I would call this 'conditional hospitality', and I would oppose it to what I call 'unconditional' or 'pure' hospitality, which is without conditions and which does not seek to identify the newcomer, even if he is not a citizen.

Today this is a burning issue: we know that there are numerous what we call 'displaced persons' who are applying for the right of asylum without being citizens, without being identified as citizens. It is not for speculative or ethical reasons that I am interested in unconditional hospitality, but in order to understand and to transform what is going on today in our world.

So unconditional hospitality implies that you don't ask the other, the newcomer, the guest, to give anything back, or even to identify himself or herself. Even if the other deprives you of your mastery or your home, you have to accept this. It is terrible to accept this, but that is the condition of unconditional hospitality: that you give up the mastery of your space, your home, your nation. It is unbearable. If, however, there is pure hospitality it should be pushed to this extreme.

I try to dissociate the concept of this pure hospitality from the concept of 'invitation'. If you are the guest and I invite you, if I am expecting you and am prepared to meet you, then this implies that there is no surprise, everything is in order. For pure hospitality or a pure gift to occur, however, there must be an absolute surprise. The other, like the Messiah, must arrive whenever he or she wants. She may even not arrive. I would oppose, therefore, the traditional and religious concept of 'visitation' to 'invitation': visitation implies the arrival of someone who is not expected, who can show up at any time. If I am unconditionally hospitable I should welcome the visitation, not the invited guest, but the visitor. I must be unprepared, or prepared to be unprepared, for the unexpected arrival of *any* other. Is this possible? I don't know. If, however, there is pure hospitality, or a pure gift, it should consist in this opening without horizon, without horizon of expectation, an opening to the newcomer whoever that may be. It may be terrible because the newcomer may be a good person, or may be the devil; but if you exclude the possibility that the newcomer is coming to destroy your house – if you want to control this and exclude in advance this possibility – there is no hospitality. In this case, you control the borders, you have customs officers, and you have a door, a gate, a key and so on. For unconditional hospitality to take place you have to accept the risk of the other coming and destroying the place, initiating a revolution, stealing everything, or killing everyone. That is the risk of pure hospitality and pure gift, because a pure gift might be terrible too. That is why exchange and controls and conditions try to make a distinction between good and evil. Why did Kant insist on conditional hospitality? Because he knew that without these conditions hospitality could turn into wild war, terrible aggression. Those are the risks involved in pure hospitality, if there is such a thing and I am not sure that there is.

Q: In your early essay, 'Violence and Metaphysics',[3] you consider the question of a phenomenon of the other, and you move on to state that 'no one more than Husserl has been sensitive to the singular and irreducible style of this matrix and to original non-phenomenologization indicated within it'. Would you still agree with this judgment and regard Husserl's account of the other as being of continuing relevance to your own work?

JD: Yes and no. Yes, because I think it is still a very profound lesson that Husserl taught us, and even Levinas. In the fifth *Cartesian Meditation*, Husserl insists that there is no pure intuition of the other *as such*; that is, I have no originary access to the alter-ego *as such*. I should go, as you know, through analogy or appresentation. So the fact that there is no pure phenomenon, or phenomenality, of the other or alter-ego as such is something which I think is irrefutable. Of course, it's a break within phenomenology, with the principle of phenomenology, and it is within the space opened by this break that Levinas found his way. I think this is true, but it doesn't mean that we subscribe to the whole context of Husserl's statement. However, if we take this simple axiom or principle, the principle which betrays the principle of phenomenology, and keep this apart from phenomenology, it is still valid for me. Now you can transport this statement into another context, which Levinas does and which I shall do, too. But when I have to explain pedagogically to students what Levinas has in mind when he speaks of 'the infinity of the other', of the infinite alterity of the other, I refer to Husserl. The other is infinitely other because we never have any access to the other *as such*. That is why he/she is *the* other. This separation, this dissociation is not only a limit, but it is also the condition of the relation to the other, a non-relation as relation. When Levinas speaks of separation, the separation is the condition of the social bond. There is such a non-intuitive relation – I don't know who the other is, I can't be on the other side.

This has been strongly prepared by phenomenology; in Husserl and in Merleau-Ponty the ego is first the origin of the world; that is, there is a zero-point of space and time here. That is what I mean when I say 'I', and in this place 'you' cannot be, it's irreplaceable. I can't be in your zero-point. Even if we agree that we see the same thing, the condition for such an exchange is that the two origins of the world can never coincide. That is why death is the end of the world and birth is the origin of the world. There is an infinite number of origins of the world. So from the point of view of Husserl's fifth *Cartesian Meditation* I remain a strict phenomenologist.

Q: How do you envisage the connection between 'justice', on the one hand, and what you define as 'the moment of strategy, of rhetoric, of ethics and of politics' (*Limited Inc . . .*) which seems to give rise to a process in your work, one which takes the form of the injunction 'one must' assume responsibility?

JD: Let me, very awkwardly, try to approach these difficulties. In your question you located the 'we must' on the side of strategy, politics, ethics. Yes, and no: the 'we must' has no process; it is foreign to the process. When I feel that 'I must', on the one hand, of course, I enter a process, but in the name of something which doesn't tolerate the process. It's immediate. For instance, I must answer the call of the other: it's something which has to be absolute, unconditional and immediate, that is, foreign to any process.

Now, of course, if I want to be responsible to the 'I must', to the immediate imperative, the unconditional 'I must', then in the name of this just response I have to engage myself in a process; that is, to take into account conditions, strategy, and rhetoric and so on. That is a great dilemma, I have no solution to that. If I told you that I have a solution I would be lying. I think there is no solution, no rules or norms for that.

The response, not the solution, should be invented each time, at each moment in the singular situations. This, of course, doesn't exclude the process, but at some point when I respond, if I want to respond in the name of justice, I have to invent singularly, to sign, so to speak, the response.

Now, you know that I began using the name or the word 'justice' very late in *my* process, and I try to distinguish between 'justice' and 'right' (*le droit*); that is, I try to make a sharp distinction between 'justice' and 'the law' or the 'right'. On the side of the right you would put what you called, a little hastily, politics, ethics, rhetoric (ethics and politics, for me, are also on the other side). Now, when I made this distinction I knew we should not oppose justice to the law, to the history of right. Of course, the history of right can be deconstructed, can be transformed. There is the history of the law, of legal concepts, and because of that the legality can be transformed, deconstructed, criticized, improved. This is an infinite process within the legal space. But this process unfolds itself *in the name of justice*: justice requires the law. You can't simply call for justice without trying to embody justice in the law. So justice is not simply outside the law, it is something which transcends the law, but which, at the same time, requires the law; that is, deconstruction, transformations, revolutions, reformations, improvement, perfectibility – all that is a process. So even if justice is foreign to the process, it nevertheless requires the process, it requires political action, rhetoric, strategies, etc. What is foreign to strategy requires strategy. That is the double-bind which causes the difficulty.

So to repeat, when we talk of this 'we must', of this responsibility, the 'we must' is always foreign to the process. However, in the name of this 'we must' we have to enter the process, and to analyse and to transform infinitely. This is a strange logic indeed. But I would not simply oppose, on the one side, the field of politics, ethics and rhetoric, and, on the other side, justice. We have to pay attention to their heterogeneity, I would insist on that. They are heterogeneous, and because of this one calls for the other: they are indissociable. If I wanted to formalize in a very abstract, empty, or formal way, this situation, I would say that there is at the same time heterogeneity, radical heterogeneity, between two terms, but at the same time the two terms are indissociable. Decision, an ethical or a political responsibility, is absolutely heterogeneous to knowledge. Nevertheless, we have to know as much as possible in order to ground our decision. But even if it is grounded in knowledge, the moment I take a decision it is a leap, I enter a heterogeneous space and that is the condition of responsibility.

This is not only a problem but the *aporia* we have to face constantly. For me, however, the *aporia* is not simply paralysis, but the *aporia* or the *non-way* is the condition of walking: if there was no *aporia* we wouldn't walk, we wouldn't find our way; path-breaking implies *aporia*. This impossibility to find one's way is the condition of ethics.

Q: Richard Rorty has suggested that, in texts such as *The Post Card* and *Glas*, you have entered a whole new literary *genre*. But it seems that *Glas* in particular can be read as a dramatization of the kind of ethical undecidability you have spoken of here today, even if that risks reducing it to the status of an illustration. My question is, how do you look back on *Glas* from the perspective of your current thinking on ethics and undecidability?

JD: I think you are right and Rorty is not. Rorty wants to dissociate in my work philosophy, which is worthless, and literature, which is interesting to him. Of course, this is not the way I view it.

First, let us take the example of *The Post Card*. I hope that this text is not simply a literary piece: I think it is an attempt to blur the borders between literature and philosophy, and to blur the borders in the name of hospitality – that is what hospitality does, blur the border – by writing some sentences, some undecidable sentences, which put in question the limits of what one calls philosophy, science, literature. I try to do this performatively, so to speak. This gesture, to the extent that it is successful,

73

does not belong to philosophy, to literature, nor to any *genre*. However presumptuous it might sound thus, I think this text does not belong to these fields called philosophy or literature.

Going back to *Glas*, it is certainly not a literary piece, no more than *The Post Card*, however literary it might be in some respects. Nevertheless, I wouldn't call it, and this was your word, a 'dramatization' of philosophical or theoretical issues that I would then have put on stage. Perhaps there may be some truth in this, but essentially I think it is something else, a way of asking questions about the borders by using the examples of Genet and Hegel. So there are quite a lot of problems, political, ethical, and psychoanalytical, which are addressed in this book, but with the final aim of writing a text, of producing some signature, some unique idiom. It is a text which constantly asks the question of signature: of Hegel's signature – Genet's signature, what does it mean to sign and to seal, and a host of related questions. But to make of this elaboration of the question of signature, to make a signature, this is almost nothing. What is a signature? It is just something to be deciphered, to be read, whatever consequences that may have. It is very ambitious to go beyond the borders of philosophy and literature, but also very modest. It is just a signature, just one among others: Genet, Hegel, and mine countersigning theirs.

Q: Deconstruction is concerned with a critique of centres of control, as was the work of Michel Foucault. As a method, what can deconstruction offer to advance our ethical understanding of power beyond the analysis already proposed by Foucault?

JD: I don't know. But I don't think deconstruction 'offers' anything *as* deconstruction. That is sometimes what I am charged with: saying nothing, not offering any content or any full proposition. I have never 'proposed' anything, and that is perhaps the essential poverty of my work. I never offered anything in terms of 'this is what you have to know' or 'this is what you have to do'. So deconstruction is a poor thing from that point of view.

Now, perhaps using the strategy of deconstruction, you may for yourself understand, not what power is, but what powers may be in such and such a context. Of course, if I wanted to justify at any cost what I am doing, I would say that everything that I do is concerned with the question of power everywhere. The question of power is so pervasive, however, that I could not isolate the place where I deal with *just* the question of power.

What interests me in what Foucault says about power is not the claim that everything is power, or will to power, in society, but his proposition or assumption that there is no such thing as '*the* Power', and that today power is in fact dispersed and not concentrated in the form of the state. There are rather only micro-powers. This is a more useful approach, that is, not to rely on a homogeneous and centralized concept of power. From that point of view, I think this is the condition of a new politics, a new approach to politics. I think this is very necessary and useful.

Nevertheless, my concern will be this one: of course we have to pay attention to micro-powers, to invisible or new forms of power, larger or smaller than the state, or foreign to the logic of the state. We should not, however, forget the state: the state is still very strong, the logic of the state is still very strong. It is today undergoing an unprecedented process. What one calls 'globalization' or *mondialization*, the constitution of new powers in the form of capitalistic corporations, which are stronger than states and do not depend on states, relativizes the authority of states. Nevertheless, the international law, everything which rules the market today, is in the hands of so-called sovereign states; the international law, the United Nations, GATT and so on are today dependent on states. So the question of the state is not behind us. We have to pay attention to the two logics: on the one hand the deconstruction of the state, and on the other hand the survival of the state.

I want to say that the state has both good aspects and bad aspects, and I mention among its bad aspects repression and authority. However, if we want to resist *some* forces in the world, economic forces for example, perhaps the good old state might be useful! So I am not for or against the state. It depends on the situation: in some contexts I am for the state, and in other contexts I am against the state, and I want to retain the right to decide depending on the context.

Q: When I read your work and that of Gilles Deleuze, I sense certain similar motivations, concerns and even passions behind the writings of you both; for example, I sense that I am being alerted to the dangers of totalitarianism, and that both of you are attempting to think through the ethical problem of difference. Could you tell me where you think your philosophy and your approach to philosophy diverges from that of Gilles Deleuze?

JD: This is a very necessary and difficult question and one that I have been asking myself for a long time. No doubt you are right, we are very close in many respects: attention to difference, opposition to Hegel and dialectics, reference to Nietzsche. As to the content of our work, we say the same thing, apparently; it is indeed very close. But the process, the style, the idiom, the strategy are so different, so different in fact that you cannot even locate *a* difference, it's another language, it is more foreign to one another than English is to Chinese. Deleuze is more French than I am in many respects, and his relation to the French language, his style, is totally different to mine as you have probably noticed. Ours is a strange relationship, but one founded on deep friendship: he is the only one in France that never attacked me, and for that I am very grateful!

If I wanted to go a little further and try to identify some philosophical difference, I would call it philosophy *as such*; that is, he considered himself a philosopher, and when he wanted to dissociate himself from all his friends of the same generation who were against philosophy and who tried to demarcate themselves from philosophy, he would say: 'I am a philosopher, I am happy with philosophy and I want to continue to be a philosopher.' This happiness I did not share with him, although I am interested in philosophy as you well know! Nevertheless, I wouldn't call what I am doing 'philosophy', but he would call it 'philosophy' and he would be happy with this appellation.

There would perhaps be another way of summarizing a possible difference: he constantly came back to what he called 'immanence', a philosophy of immanence. Transcendence for him was something which should have no place in philosophy. I resist, however, this 'immanentism', unless that is I have misunderstood what he meant by 'immanence'. Of course, Deleuze was very attentive to transcendence or heterogeneity, to difference, but within what he called 'the one', 'the universality of being'. Here there might be a difference.

Moreover, even in the reading of authors whom we both admire and love there are differences. Take the case of Artaud: Deleuze took seriously what Artaud said about 'the organless body' (*le corps sans organes*). Both he and Guattari believed in the *corps sans organes*. I must say, however, that although I admire Artaud, I think that is Artaud's mythology, his metaphysics. There is no such thing as a *corps sans organes*. Deleuze, therefore, is interested in something full, something undifferentiated. I would not read Artaud in the same way. That is one of the possible comparisons.

Q: May I start by saying that I have great difficulty with your philosophical position: I am alarmed, and yet pleased, that you now think it possible to talk about ethical issues and, in particular, truth – a truth which seems to be objective, or which can be objectively verified with reference to facts. Ethics seems to me to be a form of metalanguage which calls not for deconstruction but reconstruction. This is so because ethics talks about moral experience, which I think is concerned with codes of behaviour. Can you confirm for me that with your recent work you have begun this process of reconstruction? If so, is it correct to assume that we can juxtapose an 'early Derrida' to a 'late Derrida', the latter having abandoned deconstruction?

Lastly, I am not convinced of the merits of your privileging absence over presence, of difference over unity, as you attempt – if this is what you are doing – to overcome Hegel. In particular, I am not satisfied with your assertion that discourse, knowledge, and therefore moral practice, is a process of endless *différance*: what has been called 'hallucinatory thinking'. Perhaps you can help me with this?

JD: You said at the beginning that you have some difficulty reading me – this I can confirm! First of all, deconstruction is not opposed to reconstruction. Furthermore, I have always insisted that deconstruction is not destruction, is not annihilation, is not negative. As soon as you realize that deconstruction is not something negative, you cannot simply oppose it to reconstruction. How could you reconstruct anything without deconstruction?

What I say about truth would require many precautions and implies a long itinerary. Nevertheless, I never confuse truth with fact, truth is not a fact. Truth has nothing to do with a fact; truth is the quality of a statement, a judgment or an intuition related to something which you might call a fact, but truth is not reality. The distinction between truth and reality is absolutely elementary, as is the distinction between truth and veracity; that is, to say something true does not mean that you say something real. You may say something true without being sincere, you may lie by telling the truth. So there is a distinction between veracity, truth and fact, which must be taken seriously.

Turning to the subject of 'endless difference': it is commonplace today to understand *différance* with an 'a' as simply postponement which neutralizes decision. This is something which, had some attention been paid to the text in the beginning, could have been overcome. If *différance* was simply infinite postponement, it would be nothing. If I played on the 'a' of *différance*, it is in order to keep in a single word two logics: one of the delay, the detour, which implies a process, a strategy or a postponement; and difference with an 'e', which implies heterogeneity, alterity and so on. Now, because there is alterity and the other, for example, this cannot wait. There is an unconditional commandment, so to speak, not to wait, and it is because there is this possibility of postponing that we can and we must make decisions. If there was no possibility of delay, there would be no urgency either. *Différance*, therefore, is not opposed to ethics and politics, but is their condition: on the one hand, it is the condition of history, of process, strategy, delay, postponement, mediation, and, on the other hand, because there is an absolute difference or an irreducible heterogeneity, there is the urge to act and respond immediately and to face political and ethical responsibilities.

So this is far from being hallucinatory thinking, although I am very interested in hallucinations and I think this is a serious problem. If I am interested in spectrality, and if I think the concept of spectrality difficult to overcome, it is because I think some hallucination is irreducible, even here now. But is there a better way of overcoming hallucination than to pay attention to the other? For me the other is 'the real thing', and reference to the other is what breaks with hallucination, if such a break is possible. In order to respect the transcendence or the heterogeneity of the other, we have to pay attention. Sometimes, however, attention is not

77

sufficient to surmount hallucination. But in order to overcome hallucination we have to pay attention to the other, that is, to listen to the other and to closely read the other. Reading, in the broad sense which I attribute to this word, is an ethical and political responsibility. In attempting to overcome hallucinations we must decipher and interpret the other by reading. We cannot be sure that we are not hallucinating by saying simply 'I see' ('I see' is, after all, just what the hallucinating person says). No, in order to check that you are not hallucinating you have to read in a certain way. I have no rule for that. Who can decide what counts as the end of hallucination? It is difficult, and I have difficulties with my own work also.

Q: Several commentators have criticized you for becoming ultimately a relativist, primarily a cognitive relativist, but as a consequence also an ethical relativist, in your emphasis on the question of undecidability – or what I would call indeterminacy of meaning. One such commentator is Putnam, who says strangely enough that both Quine and Derrida arrive at the same point, namely indeterminacy of meaning. Quine has a way of avoiding relativism because he can appeal to the crude behaviourist notion that he has, but Derrida has no resource for getting out of the relativist dilemma. Do you think, first, that this is a misunderstanding of your work; and, second, what is your position on relativism?

JD: If I wanted to be brutal I would say yes, this is a radical misunderstanding. I am shocked by the debate around this question of relativism. What is relativism? Are you a relativist simply because you say, for instance, that the other is the other, and that every other is other than the other? If I want to pay attention to the singularity of the other, the singularity of the situation, the singularity of language, is that relativism? If I say that there is the English and the French language and I have to pay attention to these differences, is the attention paid to these differences relativism? No, relativism is a doctrine which has its own history in which there are only points of view with no absolute necessity, or no references to absolutes. That is the opposite to what I have to say. Relativism is, in classical philosophy, a way of referring to the absolute and denying it; it states that there are only cultures and that there is no pure science or truth. I have never said such a thing. Neither have I ever used the word relativism.

To take the case of Sokal: here is a man who wants to charge a number of, mostly French, people, including me, with being relativists, with threatening science, with threatening everything which shouldn't be threatened. How does he handle this regarding myself? He took a sentence which I improvised at a conference thirty years ago, the only time I referred to science in the strict sense. I was responding to a question from Hyppolite in 1966, in which he asked what was the relation between what I said in my paper 'Structure, Sign and Play', and the constant in Einsteinian relativity. In my answer, referring to what I had said, I quoted Hyppolite's reference to the constant, and this man now charges me with being a relativist and contesting science. This is totally arbitrary. This is relativism: someone, who because he is a scientist, presumes to say anything. I take into account differences, but I am no relativist.

If I say that there are two zero points here and there, and that you cannot reduce the difference, and if this is interpreted as being relativism then I am a relativist, and who is not? This, of course, does not mean that I deny scientificity: indeed I ask in [the Introduction to Husserl's] *The Origin of Geometry*, how is it possible that from perception we constitute ideal objects and a community of truth? So this charge against me amounts to obscurantism, and is issued by people who don't read. My concern would be this: what is their interest and motivation, what do they want?

In the same way, I never said that there is indeterminacy of meaning. I think there are interpretations which determine the meaning, and there are some undecidabilities, but undecidability is not indeterminacy. Undecidability is the competition between two determined possibilities or options, two determined duties. There is no indeterminacy at all; a word in a text is always determined. When I say that there is nothing outside the text, I mean there is nothing outside the context, everything is determined. Now, because there are contexts and singularities, there are movements, processes and transformations, and for transformations to occur something has to be determined, something is determinable. Determinability is not indeterminacy; to take into account determinability you must assume that what is determinable is still undetermined regarding the coming determination, but it is not undetermined. Let me take an example: if I say I have to make a decision and I shall tell you what that decision is tomorrow. This is determinable. Of course, what I shall do tomorrow is undetermined, but this indeterminacy is not an empty something. Everything is totally determined. There is, however, the future, what is to come, and I would say there is indeterminacy of the coming of the future. But that is not relativity of meaning.

Usually they charge me with saying that the text means anything, a charge made even in academic circles, not only in the media. If I were saying such a stupid thing, why would that be of any interest? Who would be interested in that, starting with me? There must be something else. Why are they anxious about their own interpretation of what I say? They are anxious that a text *may* call for interpretation, that there may be some complication in a text. I would say that a text is complicated, there are many meanings struggling with one another, there are tensions, there are over-determinations, there are equivocations; but this doesn't mean that there is indeterminacy. On the contrary, there is too much determinacy. That is the problem. So these charges really have to be interpreted.

Q: Professor Derrida, in relation to your discussion of painting in both *The Truth in Painting* and *Memoirs of the Blind*, how do you think painting can lead us toward a new vision or another kind of faith?

JD: If we refer to faith, it is to the extent that we don't see. Faith is needed when perception is lacking; when I see something I don't need to have faith in it. For example, I don't see the other, I don't see what he or she has in mind, or whether he or she wants to deceive me. So I have to trust the other, that is faith. Faith is blind.

How to relate this question to the question of painting? On the one hand, are we entitled to say that a painting gives you something to be *seen*? Why should a painting show me something better than I perceive it? On the other hand, there is a concept of the truth in painting that would make you think that you see the real thing in a better way through a painting than in reality, that it gives you the truth which is not the reality. In that case, according to a very profound tradition, which I try to analyse in *Memoirs of the Blind* rather than in *The Truth in Painting*, it is through some blindness that visibility would be restored. In the Bible you have the blindness of the flesh which is the condition for the revelation of spiritual visibility. You constantly have this rhetoric of visibility, sensible or intelligible visibility.

So does painting belong to the sphere of sensual visibility, or to revelation, or another order of visibility? Visibility is not visible; the visibility of something, what makes something visible, is not visible. Plato told us that the Good, as the condition of visibility, is invisible; the transparency which makes things visible is not visible, the element of visibility is not visible. There is no opposition between the visible and visibility. So, once again, let us ask, does painting offer us the visible or visibility? I would say the visible *is* invisible.

Q: Professor Derrida, I am interested in the continuity of your thinking because I do not think that there is anything like the *Kehre* or Heideggerian turning in your thought. I would like you to comment, therefore, on your relationship to a certain aspect of Husserl whom you discuss in your early work, namely the *epoché*. Husserl recommends in his radical revision of philosophical practice that we should involve ourselves in *epoché*, which for him means to suspend what he terms the 'natural attitude' through a process of bracketing or parenthesizing – terms, I believe, which are rather similar to some of the deconstructive strategies which you employ; in particular, Husserl talks of 'undecidability', meaning that the very notion of putting things in brackets can make some things undecidable. I was wondering if the notion of undecidability in your work has its source in Husserl, and whether you see deconstruction as essentially a radicalization of Husserl's *epoché*.

JD: First of all, I am grateful that you don't want to cut me in two; I do wish to be cut, but in more than two places! It is true that for me Husserl's work, and precisely the notion of *epoché*, has been and still is a major indispensable gesture. In everything I try to say and write *epoché* is implied. I would say that I am constantly trying to practise this whenever I am thinking and writing. I think it is the condition for thinking and speaking. This does not mean that I think the *epoché* is the last word. I do have questions about it, but I think that the suspension of the thesis, of the judgment, and the attention paid to phenomenality is the elementary and indispensable condition of every step that I take. So it is correct to say that I am true to Husserl from this point of view.

The word, if not the concept, 'undecidability' comes not from Husserl but from Gödel, whose notion of 'indecidables' I came across when writing the Introduction to *The Origin of Geometry*. Now, of course, what I mean by 'undecidability' does not correspond to Gödel's 'indecidables', but the word comes from here and I try to displace the word in other fields. Even at the time when I wrote this first text on Husserl, there was, on the one hand, a certain passage referring to Gödel's discourse on undecidability, but throughout the Introduction, the logic of undecidability was at work without the name or the noun. It was only when I began to take some distance from Husserl that I developed the logic of undecidability, which is not compatible, I would argue, with the strictest practice of phenomenology. On the one hand, I drew undecidability from some interest in Husserl, but, on the other hand, I was interested in undecidability to the extent that I was taking a distance from Husserl. When, in reply to a previous question, I said that it was thanks to Husserl that we can formulate the alterity of the alter-ego, I was implying that he sought to interrupt the principle of principles (the *ego cogito*). This is the moment of undecidability in Husserl.

Levinas says at some point that when phenomenology addresses the question of the other it interrupts itself. What does that mean? Is it possible to interrupt yourself? That is what undecidability means and that is what my relation to Husserl is founded on, self-interruption. Levinas meant by this that it is in order to describe the things in themselves that we have to abandon the principle of intuition; it is because the other is *the* other that I must describe my relation to him/her ethically and not in a purely phenomenological fashion. But I do this in the name of phenomenology: in order to be a phenomenologist to the end, I have to interrupt phenomenology. That is what is meant by self-interruption, which is another name for *différance*. Just as there would be no responsibility or decision without some self-interruption, neither would there be any hospitality; as master and host, the self, in welcoming the other, must interrupt or divide himself or herself. This division is the condition of hospitality.

Q: Professor Derrida, could you comment on the relationship between your work on deconstruction and that of Martin Heidegger?

JD: This is a huge question. When I first used the word 'deconstruction' I referred explicitly to Heidegger; that is, I explicitly referred the uses of the French word *déconstruction* to the German word *Destruktion*. This is the heritage which I acknowledged.

There are, however, differences. Allow me to summarize them. I totally subscribe to or accept what Heidegger means by *Destruktion*, which he describes in a very positive fashion as a way of listening to the heritage. You understand the tradition by simply 'reappropriating' the heritage, by listening to it. I think this is necessary and I would not object to such a strategy.

Now, what I called and what I practised as 'deconstruction' was contextualized in a very different way; it had to do, initially, with the hegemony of structuralism, or with the logocentric models in linguisticism, itself the model for the human sciences in France at the time. In fact, the entire tradition of logocentrism was the target, and I thought I could find in Heidegger himself some logocentric assumptions. So, from that point of view, deconstruction was inherited from Heidegger and sometimes directed against Heidegger with different points of application. Since I was born, brought up, and trained in a context that was so different from Heidegger's, the texts I was reading and the issues I was addressing were quite different. From that perspective, despite the debt and proximity, what I have done is something else; mine is another idiom, another language. Nevertheless, I am still trying to understand Heidegger and to read him. He is one of the thinkers whom I am constantly unable to understand. He still poses a real challenge today. Although I have been teaching Heidegger for thirty years now, his work is still absolutely provocative and new. I would not say this about many others.

Q: Is there a logic of ethical testimony at work in deconstruction?

JD: Yes, it is absolutely central to it. Testimony, which implies faith or promise, governs the entire social space. I would say that theoretical knowledge is circumscribed within this testimonial space. It is only by reference to the possibility of testimony that deconstruction can begin to ask questions concerning knowledge and meaning.

Q: Do you have an absolute definition of the 'human being'?

JD: There can be no acontextual definition of a human being.

Notes

1 Our thanks to the following for contributing to this dialogue: Brendan Purcell, Tim Mooney, Morag Patrick, Liberato Santoro, Aengus Collins, Dermot Moran, Maria Baghramian, Paul Hussain, Tom Dwyer, Aislinn O'Donnell and Fiona Biggiero.
2 Immanuel Kant, 'To Perpetual Peace: A Philosophical Sketch', in *Perpetual Peace and Other Essays on Politics, History, and Morals*, trans. Ted Humphrey (Hackett, 1983).
3 Jacques Derrida, 'Violence and Metaphysics', in *Writing and Difference*, trans. Alan Bass (London: Routledge, 1990).

7

REASON, HISTORY, AND A LITTLE MADNESS
Towards an ethics of the kingdom[1]

John D. Caputo

Questioning philosophy and its ethics

Ethics, venerable philosophical discourse though it be, is for me questionable in the extreme, questionable to the point that I have, God help me, taken a stand against ethics.[2] If ethics is the land of law and universalizability, of rule and normativity, be they natural laws or deontological duties, rules of pure reason or matters of moral feeling, the issue of the Form of the Good or only of utilitarian advantage, then, alas, I must say – *hier stehe ich* – I am against ethics. Ethics is for me highly questionable. To rewrite ever so slightly the saying of a famous man, ethics is something to be deconstructed, while obligation in itself, if there is such a thing, is not deconstructible. For obligation transpires in a realm of radical singularity, where every hair on our head, every tear, has been counted. Obligation – the unconditional hospitality owed to the other – is the ethical beyond ethics, the ethical without ethics, the hyper-ethical, the fine point of the ethical soul, the very ethicality of ethics, but always without and against ethics. For ethics stops short with the law or rule while everything that exists is a singularity of which the coarse lens of the law cannot quite catch sight.

To question philosophy and its ethics, which are in love with law and universality, is not to jettison them altogether, but to let them be rocked by a shock or trauma of something other, to expose them to a view from somewhere else, where things are seen otherwise than with philosophical eyes, where, from a strictly philosophical point of view, things may even seem a little mad. That is why I propose here that we turn to the pages of the New Testament, not in order to undertake a confessional defense of Christianity but, as Levinas might say, in order to read a "good book" (no capitals) from which we might learn a thing or two about ethics, a book which continually holds "ethics" in question. Suppose, then, *per impossibile*, we ask the New Testament to philosophize, to say something to philosophical reason with the aim of questioning philosophy and its ethics. I am not here recommending the violence of taking a work of rich religious imagination and faith and turning it into a rational, philosophical, treatise. I actually have in mind the very opposite violence, *viz.* a hermeneutical violence that would let philosophical reason itself be shocked by the blow of an Aramaic imagination, that would let philosophy be exposed to a site outside philosophy, to what Levinas and Derrida call the "other" of reason and philosophy, where odd and even slightly mad things happen. I propose we do this with the best of intentions and for the good of philosophy, as a way of renewing philosophical ethics, of letting reason and ethics breathe the air of pre-philosophical sources, which is the air that gives it life. I have no wish to undermine reason, or to replace reason with faith; my intent is rather to enlarge the horizons of reason and ethics, to loosen them up, to make them a little more porous and deconstructible, to ferment them with a little dash of divine madness – all of which, I hope to show, is very reasonable and highly ethical, or meta-ethical, or hyperethical. Even if it looks a little impossible.

The impossible

Like a man strolling down a familiar street, philosophy moves with ease within certain settled and well-established distinctions – like the distinctions between presence and representation, reality and image, necessity and contingency, truth and fiction, and – this is what particularly interests me here – the possible and the impossible. But very interesting writers like Nietzsche, Derrida, and Foucault have made a name for themselves showing, to the scandal of (a self-proclaimed and self-congratulatory) "reason," how representation precedes presence, images structure reality, truths are fictions that have taken hold, and how the possible is quite pedestrian and boring while everything we truly desire is impossible, the impossible being what we love most of all. Stampeded by the success of these analyses, philosophers of a more classical frame of mind have come to think that the time is out of joint and a destructive anarchy has been unleashed upon the land. Derrida, impudent and impish to the end, rejoins that being out of joint is just what makes justice possible for those who are enjoined and in bind, that a strategic dose of anarchy is just what opens things up if you happen to be at the bottom end of a hierarchy.

In the essay that follows I raise the question of the "world" in which the New Testament transpires, and by pursuing a kind of phenomenology of its sense of lived "temporality" I hope to gain some insight into its ethics. In accord with the demand of phenomenology, I begin by suspending our most commonplace assumptions, our most unexamined beliefs about time and ethics – putting our commonplace beliefs about these matters into question in order to let the ethical world of the New Testament appear. I suspend the most classical *aporia* that besets us when we open up this book, *viz.* the interminable debate about whether the events portrayed here really happened or are artifices of historical imagination, whether they confirm our faith or are themselves the products of Christian faith. It is only by suspending that debate, which turns on the most classical and modernist distinction between fact and fiction, presence and representation, by adopting a frame of mind that suspects any such settled distinction, that we are allowed to read this book.

The New Testament is a book in which the impossible is around us, in which the most amazing things keep happening: limbs are healed, the dead get up and walk, the blind see, a few loaves feed thousands, water is either walked upon or changed into wine (in either case an improvement), the skies open up and heavenly voices address us, and, above all, hearts change. This change of heart is, I humbly proffer, the point of it all and the heart of its ethics. In short, this is a world of *meta-noia*, a "metanoetic" world, of marvelous metamorphoses. In comparison with this metanoetic world, the commonplace world of regularized and steady patterns, whose map philosophy wants to draw by means of its table of categories, the world of settled distinctions between the real and the unreal, the possible and the impossible, the true and the fictitious, is – well, I am trying to be polite – a little boring. The New Testament is a book filled with what recent French philosophy calls "events," things that come along (*venir*) and break out (*é*), breaking over our heads with unanticipated surprise. For the "event" is what we did not see coming, a very singular and un-classifiable happening that took us by surprise, that shattered the horizon of what we thought was possible, that brings us up short and leaves us lost for words (never fear). There is, on almost every page of this book, what Derrida calls "l'invention de l'autre," the in-coming of the other, of what we did not see coming, opening us up to the coming of something wholly other – like Levinas, Derrida too speaks of the *tout autre* – something that is none of our doing, that delimits our subjective autonomy. The name of God, the power of God, the kingdom of God, in this book, are names for the impossible, for the incoming of the other. "God" is the name that leaps to our lips when what we need is something new and transformingly other, something *tout autre*, which is why this eventually became a name for God.

The New Testament is a book whose odd logic should fascinate writers, like Gilles Deleuze for example, who want to delimit the logic of sense in order to let other, more paradoxical, logics loose. Deleuze is interested in the paradoxical logic of Lewis Carroll's *Alice in Wonderland* and *Through the Looking Glass*, which was used to depict a world of pure becoming in which things show themselves capable of complete reversals: Alice could grow larger and then smaller, and effects could precede their causes.

Unhappily, Deleuze opposes this wondrous world to the name of God, which he takes to be wholly confined by and within a metaphysics of permanence – the substantial "personal self," he says, "requires God and the world in general."[3] But even a casual reading of the New Testament reveals quite the opposite – that those who trust in the regularities of nature and the predictability of human behavior are confounded by the amazing and transforming power of God. The one thing the New Testament seems most clearly not to embrace is the static ousiology of the Greeks.

In what follows I explore in particular the extraordinary "temporality" of the world in which God reigns, in which, beyond any paradox Lewis Carroll imagined or Alice underwent, the past itself is wiped away. By God's power, the past, what happened, is made not to have happened, so that something new begins today. That is what is called "forgiveness," a notion which it is very difficult for philosophical ethics, which runs on standard time and a balance of payments, to think. *Metanoia* is a reversal of which neither Lewis Carroll nor Gilles Deleuze has taken account and it is as a contribution to study of a general metanoetics and a very questioning ethics that I offer here an exploration of the temporality of this highly metanoetic world and its marvelously metanoetic ethics.

I begin by asking, in the hope of delivering a loving blow to philosophy, reason and its ethics, and with the very best of intentions, what can philosophy learn about ethics if it is made to listen to the sapiential sayings about the "kingdom," which may look a little mad to philosophy? To answer this question, let me start by asking another: what is the temporality of what the New Testament calls "the kingdom of God" and what does it tell us about what philosophy calls "ethics"?

The hermeneutics of Christian facticity

In raising a question like this I am repeating a project undertaken by Heidegger in his first Freiburg lectures. Heidegger's earliest work on the path of thought that led up to *Being and Time* took the form of a "hermeneutics of facticity," that is, a retrieval of the factical experience of life that he found embedded both in Aristotle's ethics and in the New Testament. Heidegger's aim was to read past or read through Aristotle's *Metaphysics*, which dominated the scholastic approach to Aristotle, down into the concrete life-experience from which Aristotle's metaphysical categories arose, which he located in the *Nicomachean Ethics*. This was the first form taken by Heidegger's famous *Destruktion* of the tradition. That is today well known. What is less well known is that this project was in fact a dual project, the other leg of which was a parallel retrieval or *Destruktion* of Christian theology down into its founding life-experiences. This took the form of a hermeneutics of the life world of the earliest Christian communities, a hermeneutic phenomenology of early Christian historic- ality, as this is recorded for us in the New Testament.[4]

Heidegger's attention was drawn to the letters of Paul rather than to the Synoptic Gospels, and in particular to the apocalyptic expectation of the early Christians, their belief that, having warned "this generation" about the imminent end of the world, Jesus would soon come again, on a cloud, to judge the living and the dead. In a course entitled "Introduction to the Phenomenology of Religion," given in 1920–21, Heidegger singles out Paul's two letters to the Thessalonians, the first of which is the oldest docu- ment in the New Testament, antedating the Synoptic Gospels, as his texts for explicating the experience of time and history among the early New Testament communities. In this letter Paul answers two questions put to him by the community at Thessalonia on the coming of the Lord, the first concerning those who die before Christ comes again, and the second con- cerning the timing of the *parousia* or second coming of the Lord.

In answer to the first question, Paul assures the Thessalonians that those who have died before the *parousia* do not suffer a disadvantage compared to those who will still be alive. For when the trumpet sounds and an arch- angel announces in a loud voice that the Lord is coming all will be made equal. First the dead will rise and then those who are still alive will be lifted up to a cloud to join them and together they will all meet the Lord in the air (1 Thessalonians 4: 13–18).

Heidegger is – understandably – more interested in the second question, about the "when?" Heidegger emphasizes the fact that for Paul Christian life, "becoming Christian," is a struggle, a matter of fighting the good fight, of running a good race (Galatians 5: 7), of forgetting what is behind and straining toward what is ahead, pressing on toward the goal and win- ning the prize (Philippians 3: 13–14). Becoming Christian is a battle waged in fear and trembling (Philippians 2: 12), a war with legalistic Jews and unbelieving Greeks, which is repaid with distress and persecution, scars and imprisonment, tribulation and suffering. Christian life is a matter of "standing firm" in the faith, bloodied but unbowed, enduring everything, holding up and holding out until the *parousia*.

That means, Heidegger argues, that for Paul the relation to the "when" of the *parousia* is not a matter of an objectivistic calculation, of making one's best estimate about the length of time until then. It is not a matter of an objective "when" in an objective time, but of a *how,* of how to live until then, how to hold out and hang tough. Paul spells out this existential–phenomenological "when" by telling the Thessalonians not to worry about "times and seasons" (*chronoi kai kairoi*) – not to try to pre- dict the *parousia* as if one were forecasting the weather, because it belongs to the very essence of the *parousia* ". . . that the day of the Lord will come like a thief in the night. When people say, 'There is peace and security,' then will sudden destruction come upon them" (1 Thessalonians 5: 1–3).[5]

Those who ignore the fact that becoming Christian is constant struggle, who are lulled into a false sense of security by the distractions and comfort of everydayness, will be taken by surprise. "But you are not in the darkness, brethren, for that day to surprise you like a thief" (1 Thessalonians 5: 4). The eyes of the Thessalonians are open; they are in the light, and they understand the incessant vigilance that Christian life requires, to stay always awake, always sober, always ready. So Paul tells them to put on the breastplate of faith and the helmet of hope, and enjoins them to be ready (5: 8). The question of the "when" is not a question of making a good estimate in terms of days, months, or years, but the existential question of being ready. Never mind *when*; be ready, "battle-ready,"[6] vigilant, on the alert. It is not a question of calculating calendar time but of standing ready all the time, "all alone before God."

Heidegger comments, "Christian religiosity lives temporality as such."[7] The factical sense of life of the Thessalonians is shot through, from beginning to end, with time and temporality, with a sense of the radical contingency and facticity of time and history, with the trembling of time and history. They stand ready for the trumpet's call whenever it sounds, day or night, now or later. Time and history are transfixed with urgency, pushed to an extreme of tension, radically energized by an apocalyptic sense which demands complete existential vigilance.

What I propose here is a variation on the Heideggerian project, one which will be effected by shifting our attention from Paul to the synoptics, from Paul's missionary preaching to the sayings attributed to Jesus, from the early Christian expectation of the end of time to the reports of Jesus' instructions about living in time, from the coming *parousia* of which Paul spoke to the *basileia tou theou* in the preaching of Jesus. Heidegger's project clearly reflects the state of the art of New Testament research in the 1920s – his students were impressed at how well he knew the literature[8] – whose tone had been set by Albert Schweitzer's *The Quest of the Historical Jesus* (1906). Schweitzer held that Jesus was an "eschatological prophet" whose notion that the kingdom of God was about to be realized was in fact a prophetic declaration of the end of time.

Apocalyptic anxiety is well suited to Heidegger's interests. Like Kierkegaard, Heidegger was very much taken with the tempestuous and volatile figure of Paul and with the Pauline thematics of anxiety, freedom, and the moment of transforming conversion in faith. Both Heidegger and Kierkegaard were taken with the Pauline struggle, fighting the good fight, putting on the breastplate of hope and the helmet of faith, the Church militant that forged ahead, pressing towards the goal, free, anguished, projected upon the future in fear and trembling. In Paul and Luther, Kierkegaard and Heidegger, the existential individual looks into the abyss of freedom and possibility, and swoons with anxiety. In such a view of Christian life, one finds a conception of factical life as toiling and troubling about one's daily bread (*sorgen um das "tägliche Brot"*),[9] fighting the good fight for bread and faith, in short, as *Sorge*.

The upshot of the Kierkegaardian–Heideggerian analysis is a twofold emphasis on the priority of battle, struggle, difficulty, disturbance, and anxious care (*Sorge*), on the one hand, and the privileging of the future, of the prize up ahead, the goal to be won, the coming *parousia*, the *vita ventura*, the *vita futura*, on the other hand. For the Church militant, eternity is up ahead and it must be earned, unlike the eternity of the Greeks, which is back behind us and has to be recollected. All of this amounted to a theory of temporality and historicity that was tuned to anxiety and the future.[10]

What Heidegger did not try, what he shows little interest in, is an interpretation that is guided not by Paul's letters but by the synoptics, and not by the evolving faith of the later Christian communities but by the synoptic tradition of the sayings of Jesus, one result of which would be to break with the apocalypticism which Heidegger interprets – brilliantly and existentially – but which he simply assumes. For if it is clear that the later Christian communities held apocalyptic beliefs, it is now rather widely agreed that this was not the case for Jesus himself, that in Jesus' own sayings the kingdom of God is upon us, within us, here and now.[11] Jesus was not alarming us about something that was approaching which we cannot foresee and which may strike like a thief in the night. Rather he was calming us with something that had already happened to us but which we do not appreciate. If this is so, then the early Christian sense of temporality and its conception of life – what philosophy is accustomed to call "ethics" – are quite different from, and not nearly as militant and masculinist, as anxious, agitated, and heroic, as Heidegger makes out.

What is the "temporality of the kingdom," the experience of time that is embedded in sayings about the kingdom of God attributed to Jesus, and what does this say about its "ethics"? In responding to this question, I will make a suggestion or two about the sorts of philosophical category we require in order to interpret this distinctively Christian temporality.

I hope to show – to the scandal of authors on both sides of the divide between religion and "postmodernism" – that such categories bear a greater likeness to the categories we find in what is nowadays called "postmodern" philosophy than to the classical "ousiological" categories of onto-theo-logic. Then, I will shift from temporality to historicality and draw out the implications of this analysis for the question of ethics and history, once again with the aim of showing that ethical reason can profit from a little dash of divine madness.

The temporality of the kingdom

The "kingdom of God" refers not to a place or locale or region but to a reign or rule, a power, a holding sway in which God holds sway rather than the human will or even Satan. Far from referring to some heavenly or future place, the kingdom of God refers to human life, here and now. The kingdom of God is a human life in which God rules. Accordingly, it represents a certain temporalizing, a way of being in time, or, to use Heidegger's expression, a certain "how," the traits of which can be gleaned from a few famous kingdom sayings.

Against anxiety

I begin with the famous discourse – *pace* Paul, Luther, Kierkegaard, and Heidegger – *against* anxiety:

> Therefore I tell you, do not be anxious [*merimnate*] about your life, what you shall eat or what you shall drink, nor about your body, what you put on. Is not life more than food, and the body more than clothing? Look at the birds of the air: they neither sow nor reap nor gather into barns, and yet your heavenly Father feeds them. Are you not of more value than they? And which of you by being anxious can add one cubit to his span of life?
>
> (Matthew 6: 25–27)

If Kierkegaard and Heidegger cultivated a sense of temporality precisely out of anxiety about the future, there is an interesting, quite contrary, temporality in Jesus' discourse *against* anxiety. Do not worry; do not waste time worrying about tomorrow. The day is always time enough. The future is not our doing, not under our control, nothing we can master or provide for, and there is no way to shore ourselves up against the future. The future is God's; it is under his rule (*basileia*), not ours. Trust God, and do not worry. If a man gathers a great harvest and thinks himself secure for the future, he is a fool, for this night God will require his soul of him (Luke 12: 16–20). Live without anxiety for the future, live with freedom from concern; trust the future to take care of itself, because the future is God's business and God will provide: "Therefore, do not be anxious for tomorrow [*aurion*], for tomorrow will be anxious for itself. Let the day's own trouble be sufficient for the day" (Matthew 6: 34). Let the day's own time be sufficient for itself, its troubles and its gifts. Let the day be time enough, all the time you need. Today is its own time, all the time there is, all the time one needs to be concerned with. When tomorrow comes, tomorrow will be today; in the meantime, let tomorrow worry about itself. Today is the day of the Lord.

91

Do not be anxious about tomorrow or today; do not be anxious at all, but trust God's rule. Anxiety frets about what is coming next, about how we will get through tomorrow, for even anxiety grants that we will get through today. Anxiety is like a leak in time, a seepage, which drains the day of its time, of its sufficiency, which robs us of time and today, which exposes us to ghosts and specters. (That is why, as Kierkegaard points out, when the object of anxiety is finally realized, we are always relieved, because what we were worried about turns out not to be as bad as the anxiety itself; even so, the worst things that happen to us are unforeseen.)

Let time be; let it be without anxiety, without a care for what time brings. For the measure of time is life. Time is life. The merit of today is that today gives life and life is all we need. Today, we have life and that is what we need. Anxiety on the other hand turns us away from life and turns us toward other needs. Anxiety is anxious about this or that, but life is always greater than this or that. What we have – life, bodily life – is greater than what we are anxious about not having, which we think we need for life and the body. Behold the birds of the air; let your time and your life and your bodily being in time be like the birds of the air who neither sow nor reap nor make stores for the future, for whom the day is always time enough.

Anxiety does not expand life, or lengthen life, or enrich life. Anxiety cannot add an inch to our stature, or a day to our time. On the contrary, it takes time away, drains the life out of time, and makes life a day shorter. Anxiety takes time and life away; it de-temporalizes and de-vitalizes. Anxiety causes a man to fret foolishly about what he shall wear while humorously forgetting that he is already alive, today. Such a man has much to learn about life and time from the lilies of the field which take no care about what they wear:

> And why are you anxious about clothing? Consider the lilies of the field, how they grow; they neither toil nor spin; yet I tell you, even Solomon in all his glory was not arrayed like one of these. But if God so clothes the grass of the field, which today is alive and tomorrow is thrown into the oven, will he not much more clothe you?
>
> (Matthew 6: 28–30)

This all sounds a little mad, like a "mad economics," without foresight or long-range planning.[12] A time without anxiety, a time ruled by God, not by human care, is not a time without a future, not a time that is only present, for that would not be time at all, but eternity. In time, the present is always a future that has become present, whereas eternity is a present that never was a future. To live in time is to be exposed to the future, either anxiously, which means that God does not rule over that time, or trustfully, entrusting time to God's rule. What has been lifted in the king-dom is not time, but anxiety; what has been lifted is not the future, but the weight of the future, or responsibility for the future. The weight that is lifted is the heavy burden of shouldering the future, mastering the unknown. Human beings are not the lords of the future, not where God rules. The future is God's domain, God's rule. The future remains, but without anxiety – open and free. Let the future come.

What time and life ask of us, which looks a little mad, is to let go. Do not be an "oligopistologist" (Matthew 6: 30), one who takes nothing for granted, who has little trust in the future, who wants a method to master the future and subdue its uncertainty, who will not let go. Let go. Trust God's rule.

> And do not seek what you are to eat and what you are to drink, nor be of anxious mind. For all the nations of the world seek these things; and your Father knows that you need them. Instead, seek his kingdom, and these things shall be yours as well.
>
> (Luke 12: 29–31)

Let God rule within you for God knows what you need and these things will be added on to you (*prostethesetai*), given to you as an addition, so long as you do not treat them as matters coming under your rule instead of God's. Do not try anxiously to provide for yourself, to foresee what is coming and to begin to make provisions. The father sees what you need; there is nothing for you to foresee. Today is all the time there is and all the time you need worry about, and do not worry about even that.

Instructions to the disciples

We find exactly the same sense of temporality in the instructions that according to parts of the synoptic tradition Jesus gave his disciples con-cerning their conduct when they travel. If you go on a journey to preach the word, take nothing with you. Do not bring along heavy stores for the journey; do not provide for the journey; do not be anxious. Accept no wages for your labors, take no bread or money with you, wear sandals but do not bring along an extra tunic (Mark 6: 8–9). Once again, this looks a little mad. But each day is its own time and God will provide for his children, who must be itinerants and mendicants, like birds and lilies. Do not try to foresee; God will do the seeing and see to your needs. Do not worry about your needs, even when you do not fare as well as the birds or the foxes: "Foxes have holes, and birds of the air have nests; but the Son of Man has nowhere to lay his head" (Matthew 18: 20). Still, do not worry.

93

Recent scholarship has pointed out the comparison of these instructions to like practices among contemporary Hellenistic Cynics.[13] Despite the pejorative connotation of the name today, the Cynics bear a striking resemblance to the earliest followers of Jesus: they were itinerants who lived like the birds of the air, who scolded society for its falsity, who said outrageous things to shock the establishment, and set out on journeys with the barest of provisions. But the singular difference between the Cynics and the followers of Jesus was that the Cynics went nowhere without their knapsacks, which contained a little food and the few things necessary for life. The Cynics stressed their independence, their self-sufficiency, which they achieved by reducing their needs to the minimal point at which they could provide for themselves; they needed nothing because they wanted nothing that they could not provide for themselves. The followers of Jesus on the other hand took nothing with them, not even a knapsack for the day's food. But they did this not in order to show their independence but because they trusted that their needs would be provided for by those who would receive them in the next town, by the brethren, which means by God's rule: "Whenever you enter a town and they receive you, eat what is set before you; heal the sick in it and say to them, 'the kingdom of God has come near to you'" (Luke 10: 8). For the very hospitality, the very kindness with which the brethren receive one another, means that there God's rule holds sway: the hospitality is the holding sway of God's rule. The kingdom has drawn near (*enggiken*); it is not off in a distant place. It reigns here, now, in this hospitality.

Time belongs to God's rule; God is the lord of time. The right way to be in time is to trust God, about tomorrow, about today, from day to day, from moment to moment, because time is God's rule, not man's. Time is God's. We are not our own, but God's, and time is God's, and God's time is today. God: today.

Nearness

The same temporality is encountered again in those sayings that tell us the kingdom of God is near, at hand, not off at some distant point in time. The coming of the kingdom is not a matter of prediction or prophesying some coming event, something off in a dark and unknown future. The coming of the kingdom has nothing to do with reading signs: "The kingdom of God is not coming with signs to be observed; nor will they say, 'Lo, here it is!' or 'There!' for behold, the kingdom of God is in the midst of you" (Luke 17: 20–21).

Entos humon: inside you, within you, already, now. The kingdom is something we are already in, or rather something already in us. The time of the kingdom is today, now, already. We should live not by looking for signs, which are outward and exterior, but from within, from the presence within us of God's rule and God's power: "But if it is by the finger of God that I cast out devils, then the kingdom of God has come upon you" (Luke 11: 20). Here, already, in Jesus, who heals tormented minds, God rules now, in Jesus who says that the kingdom is upon us. The finger of God, God's rule, God's power, has come over us (*ephthasen eph humas*), over-taken us, come upon us.

At this point we need to be careful. Jesus is not recorded as saying that the kingdom is "always already" within us, that it has always and already been there, and that we need simply awaken to what we have all along possessed. Were that the case, then the kingdom would be a matter of "recollection," of *anamnesis*, and the *metanoia* which would be a kind of Platonic conversion, a turning that recovers what we have always possessed but have lately forgotten. That, as Kierkegaard rightly insisted, is a Greek view of things that is essentially at odds with the biblical experi-ence. Jesus says that the kingdom has come upon us, not that it has always been within us. The temporality of the kingdom is not the temporality of the *always already* (*immer schon*), but of something that is happening *now*, that has begun to happen today. It is a prophetic conception that God's rule has come over us (*ephthasen*), and therefore an essentially *historical* conception – and not a Greco-ontological theory about the make-up of the human soul. The proclamation of "God's rule" is not a theory about human *ousia*, about the being of the soul, but the announce-ment of an historical event, of God's intervention in history, that the time of God's rule has now begun. Not *ousia*, but *parousia*, and *parousia* now.

Daily bread

Again, the ancient words of the Lord's Prayer ring with the same sense of temporality. When we pray, what should we say? Say *abba*, father, in the most familiar sense, not a severe and distant father, a forbidding, uncon-scious law that prohibits and says no, but *abba*, a near and loving, gift-giving father, providing, sustaining, close at hand, here, now. Say *abba*, may your rule, your *basileia*, come, and provide us each day (*epiousion*) with the bread that we need for today (*semeron*) (Matthew 6: 11). Today's bread is all the bread we need and ask for, for when tomorrow comes, it will be today. Let your rule come each day, day by day, for that is what the kingdom is, the rule of the day, the rule that holds sway today. The time of the kingdom is today. The kingdom lasts but for a day, but that day is every day, and it starts today. The kingdom is "hemeral" (*hemera*), for the day, ephemeral (*ephemera*) even, for the day only, where each day is enough, a great deal really, for it always is today (*semera*). The kingdom is hemeral, ephemeral, semeral. Do not pray for enough bread to last well into the future. Pray to be like the birds and the lilies, like day-lilies (*hemer-acostis*) that blossom for a day, for the day, for today. Do not build great barns in order to store up great reserves of bread against the future, for if tonight our soul is required of us, what good will all that bread be? Do not worry about tomorrow; ask only for the bread that you need today, even if that sounds a little mad, and the father, who knows what you need before you ask, will give it to you. Say father (*abba*), give (*dos*) us today, give us the gift of the day. May your rule come to pass today. May the rule of the day be given.

Forgiveness

Give us the bread we need today and we will not fret over tomorrow *and* (*kai*), the prayer goes on, forgive us the debts we owe, as indeed we forgive the debts that are owed to us (Matthew 6: 12). That introduces an important temporal shift. From the point of view of the temporality of the kingdom, forgiveness is the complementary operation, the temporal counterpart, to the alleviation of anxiety. For the thrust of the kingdom sayings that we have examined so far have to do with relieving anxiety, with dismissing the future: forget tomorrow, forget what you have no memory of yet. But the prayer continues: forgive us the debts we owe as indeed (*hos kai*), since and to the extent that, we have forgiven the debts that are owed to us, thus signifying a reciprocal dismissing. Forgiveness is aimed at dismissing the past. Forget the past. Dismiss our past just insofar as we have dismissed the past of others. Just as we give up providing for the future on our own and let God's providential rule do the providing, so do we give up holding on to the past. We ask the father to forget our past as we forget the past of others. Forget the past; forget the future; the kingdom's rule is now, today.

Hannah Arendt captured a great deal of the spirit and power of these texts in *The Human Condition*. Jesus, she said, was the master of forgiveness, a genius who discovered "the role of forgiveness in the realm of human affairs."[14] For just as the future, which we cannot master or program or plan, is unpredictable, so the past is irreversible. If our redemption from the future is to live without anxiety, the only redemption from the past is forgiveness. What Jesus saw, Arendt says, is the need for

> . . . forgiving, dismissing, in order to make it possible for life to go on by constantly releasing men from what they have done unknowingly. Only through this constant mutual release from what they do can men remain free agents, only by constant willingness to change their minds and start again can they be trusted with so great a power as that to begin something new.[15]

Forgiveness keeps the net of social relationships open and makes possible what Arendt calls "natality," the fresh, natal, initiating power of a new action, new beginnings, new starts. Each day is a new day, a renewal of the day, a new gift. Today is always new. Today you can begin again. Forgiveness is the opposite of vengeance, of getting even, of retribution – which means to cling to the past. Resentment, Nietzsche said, is the will's ill-will expressed toward the past. Vengeance and resentment chain us to the past, forcing us to go over it again and again, pulling the strings of the social net into an ever-tighter knot, whereas forgiveness releases and sets free.

When God holds sway, the past is dismissed. Where God rules, the past does not. If we are slaves to the past, we can expect the future to look like the past. But the work of forgiveness always comes as a surprise. When God rules, our responses are startling and unpredicted, amazingly free from the past and, one might be tempted to say, a little mad: "To him who strikes you on the cheek, offer the other also; and from him who takes away your coat, do not withhold even your shirt. Give to every one who begs from you; and of him who takes away your goods do not ask them again" (Luke 6: 29–30). And just as you do not react in the usual way, by the same token, do things without expecting the usual, predictable, results: "And if you lend to those from whom you hope to receive, what credit is that to you? . . . lend, expecting nothing in return" (Luke 6: 33–35). If you expect a return, that is a sane and sound economy, not the mad economy of the kingdom, where you must expect nothing in return, where the circle of giving in order to get back must be torn up.[16] Break the cycle of injuring and getting even, do not try to balance the books of the past, to even accounts with the past, to get even with your debtors. Dismiss your debtors, forget the past, and forgive the man who offends you. Release him – and release the past.

Today is the day on which a man may change his mind, may undergo a change of heart (*metanoia*), may make a new start; and, if that happens, do not block it off, do not stop it. If your brother has a change of heart (*metanoese*), forgive him, dismiss and release him (*aphes auto*). If he trespasses against you seven times in the course of the day and seven times says to you, "I have had a change of heart," then – mad as it may seem – release him, let him go. Dismiss it, forget it, and let go.[17]

What is the temporality of forgiveness? It has an interesting quality, a rather startling and even mad one for us philosophers, for in it the past acquires a kind of annihilability. The past is over (*vorbei*); forget it; wipe it away. Release from what has happened the man who offends you. If a man asks for forgiveness, we say, if we are forgiving, "forget it – it never happened." That is what forgiveness requires: that we reach the point where it never happened. Otherwise we hold on to it – we retain the past – and we hold it over the man. The man knows we have something "on him," and he is not free. He cannot start all over again. We will not give him an open space or a new start, and we block off the *metanoia*.

One of the most interesting metaphysical replays of what I take to be a very biblical experience of time is found in the debate of Peter Damiens about whether God could change past time, whether he could make the past not to be, that is, transform something that happened into something that had not happened.[18] This speculation moved in exactly the opposite direction of that entertained by the Greeks, who wondered whether something which has already happened in the past becomes necessary. The medievals, by contrast, wondered whether the past could be wiped away, whether, e.g., God could restore lost virginity. Could God make a sinful man sinless? Could God simply wipe away the past, erase the data of the past, delete it? I am not interested in the details of the argument, the question of the logical coherence of the suggestion – for such a time must indeed look quite mad, quite impossible, to ethical and philosophical reason. I am interested in the biblical sense of time that prompts the question. This is the time of forgiveness, the time of the kingdom, the time over which God, not man, rules, not even necessity itself. Might even time's inexorable necessity, its irreversibility, bend before God's rule, not in a machismo show of God's mighty prowess, but in order to clear away the debris of the past, to make for a fresh start and a new beginning, to clear away the space of today? Today is the day which the Lord has made. Today is a gift and so the medieval philosopher asks whether today can be a pure gift, free from the weight of the past.

The kingdom sayings tell us that the kingdom is a kingdom for today, and that today is an open space, free from anxiety about tomorrow, on the one hand, and free from recrimination against the past, on the other hand. Today is a gift. Let the kingdom come today; give us today our daily bread, i.e., give us today; get us through this day. Today is a gift to be received freely, graciously, like the birds of the air, like the lilies of the field. For if you, who are not perfectly good, "know how to give good gifts to your children, how much more will your father who is in heaven give good things to those who ask him!" (Matthew 7: 11). Do not let today be a way of being bound to the past, or an occasion of being anxious over the future. That would destroy the good gift from the father, the gift of today; it would drain the day out of today, drain the time out of the time that is given.[19] That would drive us out of the kingdom; or rather, it would drive the kingdom out of us, for the kingdom has already come and is within us, here, now. Time is not ours, but God's.

The presencing of the kingdom

What is the temporality of the kingdom? What is the temporal sense in those kingdom sayings attributed to Jesus, where the kingdom of God is not a future event but a way to live and be which has already begun in the present?

In contrast to the temporality that Heidegger derived from Pauline apocalypticism, it is not a futurally oriented temporality, full of anxiety about what is coming next, of fear and trembling at the uncertainty of the time. On the contrary, the coming of the kingdom lays anxiety to rest, for the rule of God, which is in the midst of us, sustains us. Rather than something futural, this is a *presential* time, a time of presencing, which lets today be today. By trusting oneself to God's rule, the day is not drained of its time. Today is not sacrificed to tomorrow, spent in making oneself safe and secure against tomorrow. It is a temporality of trust, of trusting oneself to God's rule, and in so doing to time and the day.

This is hardly the ecstatic futural temporality of authentic *Dasein*. If there is a Heideggerian parallel at all, it is much more like what the later Heidegger, in his more meditative – even more Japanese moments – in dialogue with the mystical poet Angelus Silesius, the versifier of the mystical writings of Meister Eckhart, called the "whiling" – the *weil* and *dieweilen* – of things. By this, Heidegger meant a process in which one suspends calculative thought, for calculation is bent on justification, on rendering a reason for a being, which is always sought in some other being, farther up or down the causal chain.[20] But in the experience of "whiling," this discursive–ratiocinative thinking is suspended precisely in order to experience things "in themselves," in their own "presencing" or presential emergence, in their phenomenological upsurge, their rising up and falling back in and out of presence. Just so, in the sapiential eschatology of the kingdom sayings, the power of the experience of the kingdom is to suspend or lift projective planning for the future, our human anxiety about what is coming next, on the one hand, and a recriminatory, vengeful, cleaving to the past, on the other hand. The result is to experience the day in its own "day-ing," if I may say so, its own "hemerality" or diurnality, its own coming to be and passing away, letting the day "while" for a while. This letting be is essentially a letting go, a letting go of human self-sufficiency, human *Selbstständigkeit*, which would deny the very meaning of the kingdom, which means God's rule, not ours. In the kingdom, time can be experienced authentically only by taking time as God's gift and trusting ourselves to time's granting, which is God's rule.

By letting go of our own self-possession, by opening ourselves to God's rule, we release the day from the chain of time in which it is caught up. The temporality that is opposed to the kingdom is a bound time, a time in which today is dragged back into the past by recrimination or wrenched forward into the future by worry. The temporality of the kingdom, on the other hand, is free, open, unbound, unchained, a day or time that is savored, experienced, lived for itself, in its own upsurge.

Such a presential time, then, has nothing to do with the famous "metaphysics of presence" of which Heidegger and Derrida are expressly critical. For the presencing in question is transitory and fragile, like the grasses of which Jesus speaks that today are here and tomorrow are thrown into the oven. The time of the kingdom is not *ousiological* time, the time of *ousia*, in which things have their own substantiality and essentiality, their own *Selbständigkeit*. Ousiology is foundationalism, a philosophy of self-security, of building up stores against the future, whereas in the kingdom there is no self-certainty or self-securing. One falls back, not upon one's own resources, but upon God's rule. The presential or sapiential time of the kingdom is not ousiological but "epiousiological" (*epiousion*: Matthew 6: 11), granted from day to day, like a gift, fleeting, fragile, diurnal. Not *ousia*, which proclaims the subsistence of being, of one's own being, but *epi-ousia*, that strange word in the New Testament which means what we need in order to survive today, what is addressed to life's needs.[21] In the kingdom, things do not have their own independence, their own ability to fend for themselves. Both human and non-human beings can be what they are only by ceasing to assert their own self-subsistence and self-reliance and letting God rule; their being and time are from God, a trace of which is perhaps detectable in St Thomas's notion of a *potentia obedientialis* in his otherwise highly ousiological account of things. Far from asserting the primacy of ousiological presence, far from asserting a kingdom or rule of *ousia*, sapiential time can be experienced only by letting go of human rule and letting go of the self-sufficiency of the natural order, by letting God rule, entrusting oneself to the epiousiological rule of God. It is not precisely nature which feeds the birds of the air or clothes the lilies of the field, but God. God rules in nature as he rules in human life. God rules over *physis* and *polis*, over bread and time, over *ousia* and *epiousia*.

So, however attached Christian philosophy has been to the classical onto-theo-logical tradition, the New Testament shows little interest in the metaphysics of *ousia* or in the time that measures the motions of *ousia*. The kingdom runs on non-standard time, a time that has nothing to do with the standard conceptions of time that have dominated Western philosophy from Aristotle to Husserl. The time of the kingdom is neither a line nor a circle, but a new beginning, a fresh start – now. It is not a sequence of now-points that measure motion in terms of before and after, as in Aristotle. It is not a progressively accumulating, self-completing, time, as in Hegel's philosophy of history. It seems to be the opposite of Husserl's protentional–retentional process, which is organized around the attempt to stretch the now out into the future and to hold on to what has lapsed. It is not the agitated time of ecstatic existential temporality in Kierkegaard and *Being and Time*. It does not turn on a conception of *Erinerrung*, in which one gathers together what has all along been in travail, groaning for birth over a gradual process of inner development and growth, as in Hegel. It does not invoke a Heideggerian notion of *Andenken*, in which the task is to recall the archi-beginning which has fallen into a gradually escalating history of oblivion, as in the later Heidegger.

The time of the kingdom is a more profoundly simple time, a free time, both freedom and freeing, that has been disconnected from the chain of nows, from anxiety and recrimination, protention and retention, anticipation and recollection. By trusting God's rule one breaks the chain of time and frees up the day, letting the day come-to-presence, tearing up the chain of time, freeing it from the circulation of debts and anxieties, letting the day be a "gift." Forget what is owed to you in the past; forget what you owe to the future; tear up the chain of time and take today as a gift, let us say a free gift, a free as opposed to a bound time, an open or released time.[22] In it, something new and freeing has begun now which is now with us and frees us from the past and future.

I would say that such a time is better thought in terms of the categories of "event" and "gift," both of which characterize the work of recent French thinkers, both Catholic – Jean-Luc Marion[23] – and non-Catholic – Levinas, Derrida, Lyotard, and Deleuze. An event (*événement*) is a certain "happening" which is "linked" but not bound causally to antecedence and consequence, not bound by efficient causality to the past or by teleological causality to the future, but is taken for itself, in its own singularity. The event has a certain free-floatingness, an innocence; it is a happening over which we have no mastery, in which things happen to us, overtake and overcome us, as when we say that the rule of God has come over us. Events have the quality of a "gift" that is given us – give (*dos*) us this day – where the grace of being human is to be gracious, to take time without anxiety or revenge, with a kind of sapiential grace, with a letting be that is grateful, with a gratitude that lets be. A gift is a gift for Derrida when it is removed from the circle or circulation of giving and paying back (remuneration, retribution), of action and proportionate reaction, when we let the gift be.

Reason, history – and a little divine madness

What do these profoundly sapiential sayings, which refer principally to the conduct of personal life, have to do with a view of historical life? What do the kingdom sayings tell us, if by "today," "tomorrow," and "yesterday" we have in mind the movements not of personal time but of historical time?

If, in the kingdom, time is God's rule, not ours, what does that mean for historicality? John Dominic Crossan wrote some years ago:

It is here suggested that the basic attack of Jesus is on an idolatry of time. . . . The one who plans, projects, and programs a future, even and especially if one covers the denial of finitude by calling it God's future disclosed or disclosable to oneself, is in idolatry against the sovereign freedom of God's advent to create one's time and establish one's historicity. This is the central challenge of Jesus. The geographers tell us we do not live on firm earth but on giant moving plates whose grinding passage and tortured depths give us earthquake and volcano. Jesus tells us that we do not live in firm time but on giant shifting epochs whose transitions and changes are the eschatological advent of God. It is the view of time as man's future that Jesus opposed in the name of time as God's present, not as eternity beyond us but as advent within us. Jesus simply took the commandment seriously: keep time holy![24]

History is God's present, not man's future. The historical event is God's advent. But what does this mean? The kingdom sayings we have examined suggest a posture that is free and open, ripe with a sense of the possible, extricated from a need for revenge, freed up from anxiety on the one hand and recrimination on the other. They contain a powerful enjoinder to keep "today" open, where today is the name of the contemporary historical setting, and to keep it free from the idolatry of time, which means the idolatry of the human-all-too-human.

The kingdom sayings suggest a view of history in terms of what Hannah Arendt called the "natality" of "action," the present as the possibility of a fresh start. They tell us to forget the past, to dismiss past trespasses, to let the present be the occasion of a new beginning, let each day be the first. Give us this day, today, and let us start over, and make something new. Dare we allow ourselves to imagine what today, our historical situation today, would be like, if we could break the cycle of recrimination by which it is vitiated? Is not the logic of nationalist violence that plagues us today in large part a logic of paying back and is it not caught up in a *regressus ad infinitum* that refuses to let go of the past? Does it not belong to the very essence of the logic of violence that there is always already a prior, older, past offense that requires retribution, that there is no originally innocent party? Is not every horror against the innocent – from the innocents of Sarajevo to the innocents of the West Bank to the innocents of Northern Ireland, innocents everywhere – justified in the name of the retribution of past offenses, of redressing offenses which have themselves been justified in exactly the same way, which leads to infinite regress, to infinite retribution? And whenever human beings are able to dismiss the past and start over again, is that not what we mean by God's advent, by the surpassing of this human, all-too-human, logic of vengeance, by the surprise of being overtaken by something more than human, by something a little unbelievable? Do we not say that here, in every great work of peace-making – when the Berlin Wall falls, when the reign of Soviet terror collapses, when racial harmony is achieved in Georgia or Pennsylvania, when Arab and Jew, or white and black, join hands, when the lamb lies down with the lion – ethical reason has prevailed. But, then, do we not add, as a little supplement, "it is a dream," "it is hard to believe," "it is impossible," "it is a miracle"? Does that not mean that something else has intervened and lifted the moment up, tearing it out of the circle of past and future and freeing it up, something that is a little more than reason and more than human, a little impossible,[25] a little mad?

By the same token, when we speak of tomorrow in historical terms, do we not require a sense of the openness of the historical field, of the radical reconfigurability of human affairs, the sense of trust in the future that the kingdom sayings enjoin? Do we not need to do what is possible today, to alleviate misery today, to let life flourish today, without succumbing to anxiety about tomorrow? For if we look ahead and try to predict what will happen, we will lose hope. Our hope for tomorrow – is that not a hope against hope, a mad hope, not quite, not merely, a human hope? Is that hope not God's rule among us, God's advent, beginning today? God's rule in time, beginning today, and coming tomorrow. *Viens, oui, oui!*[26]

Ethical reason? Does that not require a little dash of divine madness?

Notes

1 This essay, which is a revised version of "Reason, History, and a Little Madness: Towards a Hermeneutics of Christian Temporality," is reprinted with the permission of the American Catholic Philosophical Association and first appeared in *Proceedings of the American Catholic Philosophical Association*, vol. 68: *Reason in History*, ed. Thérèse-Anne Druart (Washington, DC, 1995), pp. 27–44.

2 See John D. Caputo, *Against Ethics: Contributions to a Poetics of Obligation with Constant Reference to Deconstruction* (Bloomington: Indiana University Press, 1993). For some comments on this text, see Richard Kearney, *Poetics of Modernity* (Atlantic Highlands: Humanities Press, 1995), pp. 206 and 246, *n* 3.

3 Gilles Deleuze, *The Logic of Sense*, trans. Mark Lester with Charles Stivale, ed. Constantin V. Boundas (New York: Columbia University Press, 1990), pp. 2–3 and throughout.

4 Martin Heidegger, *Gesamtausgabe*, vol. 60: *Phänomenologie des religiösen Lebens* (Frankfurt: Klostermann, 1995). See Theodore Kisiel, *The Genesis of Heidegger's* Being and Time (Berkeley: University of California Press, 1993), ch. 4, "The Religion Courses (1920–21)." Kisiel also reports (p. 529, *n* 5) that Heidegger had read a piece by Dilthey some years earlier in which Dilthey claimed that the historical consciousness of the West was a Christian heritage, that it was Christian interest in the theology of salvation history that laid the foundation for historical consciousness and for the philosophy of history itself.

5 All citations from the New Testament are from the Revised Standard Version in *The New Oxford Annotated Bible with Apocrypha* (New York: Oxford University Press, 1973).

6 Kisiel, *The Genesis*, p. 186.

7 Heidegger, *Gesamtausgabe* 60, p. 104.

8 Kisiel, *The Genesis*, p. 193.

9 Martin Heidegger, *Gesamtausgabe*, vol. 61: *Phänomenologische Interpretationen zu Aristoteles: Einführung in die phänomenologische Forschung* (Frankfurt: Klostermann, 1985), p. 90.

10 Søren Kierkegaard, *The Concept of Anxiety*, trans. R. Thomte (Princeton: Princeton University Press, 1980), pp. 81–93.

11 For a nice overview of the various understandings of "eschatology," see John Dominic Crossan, *The Historical Jesus: The Life of a Mediterranean Jewish Peasant* (San Francisco: Harper & Row, 1991), pp. 265–302.

12 On a "mad economy" of time, see Jacques Derrida, *Given Time, I: Counterfeit Money*, trans. Peggy Kamuf (Chicago: University of Chicago Press, 1992).

13 See F. Gerald Downing, *Christ and the Cynics: Jesus and Other Radical Preachers in First Century Tradition*, JSOT Manuals 4 (Sheffield: Sheffield Academic Press, JSOT Press, 1988).

14 Hannah Arendt, *The Human Condition* (Chicago: University of Chicago Press, 1958), p. 238.

15 *Ibid.*, p. 240.

16 Derrida, *Given Time*, p. 9.

17 See Arendt's wonderful commentary on Luke 17: 3–4 in *The Human Condition*, p. 240, *n* 78.

18 For a good account of this, with the appropriate references, see Robert McArthur and Michael Slattery, "Peter Damiens and undoing the past," *Philosophical Studies*, 25 (1974): 137–141.

19 For a remarkable development of the notion of "given time" and the "pure gift," see Derrida, *Given Time*, ch. 1.

20 Martin Heidegger, *The Principle of Reason*, trans. R. Lilly (Bloomington: Indiana University Press, 1991), pp. 32–40.

21 For something about the oddity of the word *epiousios*, which, if it is constructed out of *epi* and *ousia*, seems to mean "what is directed to the needs of life," see Gerhard Kittel, *Theological Dictionary of the New Testament*, trans. and ed. G. W. Bromiley (Grand Rapids: Eerdmans Publishing Co., 1991), pp. 590–599. For help with this word, I thank my colleague David Marshall.

22 See Derrida, *Given Time*, p. 9.

23 See Jean-Luc Marion, *God Without Being*, trans. Thomas Carlson (Chicago: University of Chicago Press, 1991), ch. 6.

24 John Dominic Crossan, *In Parables: The Challenge of the Historical Jesus* (San Francisco: Harper & Row, 1973), p. 35.

25 The motif of "*the* impossible" is at the heart of a great deal of Derrida's work, including *Given Time* where the "pure gift," the "impossible" fruit of a "mad economy," is what we "desire," and *The Gift of Death*, trans. David Wills (Chicago: University of Chicago Press, 1995), where it is elaborated in the form of a reading of the story of Abraham and Isaac. In just the same way, "justice," which is not deconstructible, is called the "impossible," the object of our desire, something that occurs in the madness of the instant that tears up time. This connects what I am saying about "time" with the question of "justice" and "hospitality" in Derrida. On justice, see "The Force of Law: The 'Mystical Foundations of Authority,'" in *Deconstruction and the Possibility of Justice*, ed. Drucilla Cornell *et al.* (New York: Routledge, 1992), pp. 3–29; on hospitality, see *Adieu: à Emmanuel Levinas* (Paris: Galilée, 1997). The biblical motifs in Derrida are not accidental; they have made their way into deconstruction by way of Levinas.

26 Jacques Derrida, *Parages* (Paris: Galilée, 1986), p. 116. I have elaborated this motif of the "viens, oui, oui," which he sometimes calls the "messianic," along with that of *the* impossible, in Derrida's work in *The Prayers and Tears of Jacques Derrida* (Bloomington: Indiana University Press, 1997).

8

THE EXPERIENCE OF THE ETHICAL

David Wood

The importance of concepts to ethical life is not too difficult to grasp. We owe to concepts like "justice," "rights," "duty," "virtue," "good," "responsibility," and "obligation" our very capacity for ethical judgement. And yet the work of clarifying and codifying the scope and significance of these terms is the source of another danger – the calculation of our responsibility, in which the ethical as an openness to the incalculable is extinguished.

In his "Letter on Humanism,"[1] Heidegger tries to revive ethics as *ethos*, as abode or dwelling, and, in an example which is truly exemplary, he interprets Heraclitus' location of the gods in his hearth as his way of thinking "dwelling" as the preservation of the unfamiliar in the familiar.

In "Eating Well,"[2] Derrida describes the "subject" as the principle of calculation, and it is for this reason that Heidegger's displacement of a certain *topos* of subject-hood in his essay "Language"[3] is presented in terms of a transformation of our dwelling in relation to language. Heidegger writes:

> Language speaks. Man speaks *in that* he responds to language. . . .
> It is not a matter here of stating a new view of language. What is important is learning *to live in the speaking of language. To do so* we need *to examine constantly* whether and to what extent we are capable of what genuinely belongs to responding . . .[4]

What we call the activity of a subject (speaking) is conditional on something else – something more "middle voice" than a passivity.[5] But it is important to realize that "conditional on" does not mean limited by, or undermined by, quite the opposite. Heidegger is rethinking authenticity here, not in terms of some restrictive sense of "mineness," but in terms of an openness (or responsiveness) to an Other (language). The idea of responding to language is of course a strange one, employing a term

105

(response) that would normally make sense in communicative *interaction* to illuminate a certain productive dependence.

What is at stake here is the way language *gives*, provides, supplies ways of thinking, seeing, being which we do not individually invent, but we do create from, and to which we do have to take up an attitude. To live in the speaking of language suggests maintaining the tension between given form and appropriating response. And it is important that Heidegger speaks of "examining constantly" how far we measure up to the challenge of such a relationship. All this suggests a picture of what it is to be a subject in which the subject is "constantly involved in relating itself to itself" (Kierkegaard). And, again, as Kierkegaard put it, we cannot adequately understand this self-relationship without recognizing a constitutive role for a mediating third term, what in *Sickness Unto Death* he terms a "Power."

The structure of Heidegger's argument here is identical to Kierkegaard's in *Sickness Unto Death*. Kierkegaard claims we cannot understand the kind of despair in which, instead of giving up, we carry on "desperately" (as we might say), without positing a constitutive role for such a power. Kierkegaard is starting off from an experience and insisting on certain transcendental conditions for its possibility. Rather than being a proof of God's existence, this is a demonstration of the role played by a certain deep structure of relatedness in making possible the experience we are undergoing. In Heidegger's case, the experience in question is not despair but another breakdown, the experience of being unable to find the right word.

Both Heidegger and Kierkegaard were here endorsing (what would become) the "implication" of Derrida's account of the subject (and of experience) – that we need to sever the subject's link to naive self-presence, though not the idea itself. Of course, the need for vigilance that Heidegger stresses when he describes our changed relation to language arises again and at another level when Derrida (in conversation with Jean-Luc Nancy, as we have seen) argues for the importance of not becoming too free with the old metaphysical language. My claim, however, is that true vigilance would lead us to conclusions a little different from those of Derrida.

I

First I wish to take this issue of response, dependence, and essential relationality – played out, as I have suggested, in both Kierkegaard and Heidegger – and compare their claims to an important remark from Wittgenstein's *Notebooks*. He writes: "we have the feeling that we are dependent on an alien will. *Be that as it may*, we *are* at any rate, in a certain sense, dependent, and that on which we depend we can call God."[6] Wittgenstein *begins* here with an experience – a *feeling*. It is not a feeling in the sense of a twinge or a tweak. It is after all "a feeling that . . ." – it has propositional content – and it involves complex concepts, such as "alien will." Wittgenstein then takes this experience and reflects on it ("Be that as it may . . .") and performs a phenomenological *epoché* on it – bracketing out any reference to specific other entities. He leaves himself with "a certain sense of dependence," and then reinvents a pole for this dependence in the shape of God.

Of course Heidegger could locate this same dependence in our relation to language. Wittgenstein's sophistication comes in his self-conscious witnessing to the "naming of God," in which the name and the projected entity are drawn back to the experience of dependence which gives rise to them. But while it explains the move to God, it does not necessitate it. After all – and he seems to admit as much – we could call it fate, or even chance. *What difference does it make what we call it?* Here I want to recall another remark of Wittgenstein, this time actually *on* Heidegger and Kierkegaard, which deals with a quite specific experience and says something extraordinary about it:

> I can readily think what Heidegger means by Being and Dread. Man has the impulse to run up against the limits of language. Think, for example, of the *astonishment* that anything exists. This astonishment cannot be expressed in the form of a question, and there is also no answer to it. Everything which we feel like saying can *a priori* only be nonsense. Nevertheless, we do run up against the limits of language. This running up against Kierkegaard also recognized, and even designated in a quite similar way (as running up against Paradox). This running up against the limits of language is *ethics*.
>
> (December 30, 1929)[7]

The *experience* in question – "the astonishment that anything exists" – is, of course, not just any experience: it is one of *the* fundamental philosophical experiences. And the degree to which philosophers find, or do not find, ways of sustaining the power of this experience is a good indicator of their philosophical seriousness. Consider now what Wittgenstein says next. For, despite the fact that for such a serious thinker as Leibniz "why is there anything rather than nothing?" was a deep and central question, Wittgenstein says that this experience of astonishment "cannot be expressed in the form of a question." This seems plain wrong – I have just done it, and so did Leibniz, and Heidegger, and many others. The clue to what Wittgenstein means comes in the second clause – "there is also no answer to it." It is the logical force of this clause that is doing the work: because there is no answer, and could be none, what looks like a question is not one really. But what does it mean to say that this "running up against the limits of language is ethics"? And what does "nonsense" mean here? There is a straightforward sense which would link paradox, etc., with the ethical; but there is also much at stake in how one works through the ethical implications.

Heidegger's "Language speaks, man speaks insofar as he responds to language,"[8] and numerous other remarks of his, are essentially creative distortions of language. The point of these distortions is to break up the habitual grammatical reinforcement of our sense of the subject as an active autonomous agent working on the passive world. And the point of that, as we have seen, is ethical – the transformation of an *ethos*, of a way of being in the world, the way we understand our relation to language. That is the point of those references to passivity, endurance, suffering, responding, etc.

The explicit references Wittgenstein makes are to Heidegger's discussions of Being and Dread in *Being and Time*, or just possibly Heidegger's inaugural lecture "What is Metaphysics?" (1929). Given that for Heidegger "[d]read reveals nothing,"[9] and "[n]othing is neither an object nor anything that 'is' at all. Nothing occurs neither by itself nor apart from what is as some sort of adjunct,"[10] we can read Wittgenstein's references to ethics and nonsense as some sort of response (*avant la lettre*) to Carnap's response to Heidegger in his essay "The Overcoming of Metaphysics . . ."[11] which focuses precisely on what Carnap thinks are the logical howlers in Heidegger's references to nothing. Wittgenstein is *reminding* him (and now us) that there is more at stake. This more, of course, is that Heidegger is not making logical blunders, but is trying to analyze, or respond to, an experience. "Only in the clear night of Dread's nothingness is what is as such revealed in all its original overtness: that it is and is not nothing." The experience is that of recognizing that things exist – a variant of astonishment, in other words. Here we might say that, from the point of view of ethics, what is at stake is, first, the preservation of that potential for transformation of *ethos* that comes from acknowledging that things exist (and might not) – here God is someone to thank – it is perhaps not unconnected that Heidegger writes of thinking as thanking in his book *What Is Called Thinking?*.[12] The world of the grateful man lights up in ways in which the ungrateful man's does not. (Think of the significance of grace at mealtimes.) But there is a second ethical resonance in our very willingness to stay with our experience, to honour it, to ponder it. And if phenomenology has an ethical dimension, it is not its alleged foundationalism, or its search for essential intuition, it is this patience with *experience*.

If, after Hegel, the movement from *naive* awareness to reflection might be called an experience, then what I am seeking to record here is an experience with experience. Experience is a thick and fuzzy concept, being not only a central player in so many philosophical schemes and arguments, but also mediating in so many ways between philosophy and its many other related disciplines (religion, literature, common sense, politics, and science). And, as our understanding of experience develops, the *Methodenstreit* between phenomenology, hermeneutics, and deconstruction is increasingly exposed as a mock-battle. Moreover, these *mediations* are not ones in which dutiful experience reports back its foreign findings to the throne of philosophy, but rather ones that confuse, disrupt, and disturb any and every demarcation between philosophy and non-philosophy. Labeling experiences "religious" or "mystical" ought always to be an issue for philosophy. Experiences do not herd obediently into these categories, and when philosophy thinks they do, something vital has been lost. Wittgenstein's discussion of the experience of the world as a bounded whole, or of the feeling of dependence, might already have come to be seen as exotic, but along with wonder, the astonishment that anything exists, the anxiety that everything is falling apart, the worry that there might be no certainty, many of what are called "religious experiences" are the milk and honey of philosophy. And the same obviously applies to what we call "the everyday," which not only supplies us with the *language* we play with, and sometimes try to regiment as philosophers, but, if the truth be told, with the intelligibility of most if not all of those critical practices by which we seek to transcend the everyday.

Experience, then, both as a *concept* and as an *openness* is a condition for philosophy's productive intercourse with what lies outside of itself – and indeed that very experience of separation and our overcoming of that separation is itself "experience"! If negotiation with alterity is the locus of the ethical, "experience" is the essentially contested marker of that site.

The way in which experience provides philosophy with conduits to other disciplines, other areas of culture, is distinctively and importantly marked in literature and the arts more generally. This is not surprising, because the objects and performances in question exist for no other purpose than to be experienced. The real challenge to philosophy lies in how to access the *complexity* of the experiences involved – which are in no way restricted to supplying natural knowledge – and how to assess their *significance* (e.g. is the coherence of art a *substitute* or a *beacon* for the realization of such unity in the real world?). The challenge that art has always posed to philosophy is how to handle, without compartmentalizing, the force and complexity of aesthetic experience. The link between the teleology of art and that of nature in Kant's third critique is a sign of this challenge, and, without adjudicating on Kant's various accounts of experience, it is clear that a *version* of his concern is still central, namely that which would try to distinguish, in every experience, between what was supplied by the object and what was supplied by the experiencing subject. I say a *version* of this because, after Hegel and his successors, it is clear that there is a category missing from this account, namely that of language and culture, the ways in which the coherence of our experiences is made possible by shared social practices and their symbolic mediation and interruption. If that *was not an issue*, there would be no crisis of modernism, no problem of nihilism. And it is clearly not just a problem for our experience of art, but is one equally for our experience of social life, our relations with others, our sense of political community, etc.

As for such accounts of experience as we think we need in order to make sense of scientific knowledge, the revolutionary origin of these models (science's appearing on the scene as the scourge of religious consensus) made it easy to ignore that this symbolic and social dimension permeates even scientific experience. Habermas' discussion of validity claims and consensus and the ideal speech community is a recognition of this, and Husserl's account of the ideal community of scholars working in harmony is another. But of course the downside of recognizing this third dimension (subject–object and language) is that it may be that *experience* presupposes a certain *actual* or *ideal* "form of life," or a coherence in the public use of language, that no longer obtains. If the "transcendental" conditions of the possibilities of experience may be thought to overlap with social, political, symbolic and linguistic ones, and if these are in principle historically fragile, then it is not impossible that experience may have disappeared, ceased to be possible.

II

However this is *not* so, and how and why it is not so demands a renewal of philosophy, one to which deconstruction makes a singular contribution. And we can find in the movement of Derrida's writings an exemplary *development* of the problematic of experience; deconstruction "itself" and, indeed, the concept of "responsibility," to which Jacques Derrida has recently given so much weight, are each nothing *other* than experience regained. Deconstruction is, if you like, the experience of experience.

An immediate, false, and nonetheless plausible misreading of the development of experience in Derrida's writing would go like this: that the early Derrida identifies *experience* with (self-)presence, with the central myth of phenomenology, which we have to get away from if we want to get anywhere: "As for the concept of experience it belongs to the history of metaphysics, and we can only use it under erasure. 'Experience' has always designated the relationship with a presence."[13] The later Derrida talks, apparently freely, about "the experience of aporia," "an interminable experience," "the (impossible) experience of death," "the experience of the non-passage," "the experience of mourning," and *even* "the experience of what is called deconstruction."[14] If experience here has anything like the dynamic Hegelian sense of a productive undergoing, then we can see how it is that each of these phrases, the "experience of X," will have an objective and a *subjective* genitive sense, the same bivalence that will so easily allow so many of those inversions beloved of Blanchot, such as experience of impossibility: the impossibility of experience.

I will show presently something of the "dialectical" development which Hegel's account of experience has suffered in the transition to Blanchot (and Derrida) I am plotting here. But before doing that I want to explain just why this account of the revaluation of experience in deconstruction is mistaken. And there is much at stake here – not least the relationship between deconstruction and phenomenology. We know, of course, that Derrida's treatment of Husserl extends beyond *Of Grammatology* to (the Introduction to) *The Origin of Geometry* to *Speech and Phenomena* and some other short essays,[15] but the general argument seems to me to be the same throughout, and surprisingly Hegelian it is too. There is a truth of experience, let us call it presence, that presence does not know – that presence (self-presence) involves a constitutive differentiation, a bifurcation, and/or a relation to the other, one that it is not only not aware of, but of which it may *be* the non-awareness (as when we say that love is blind, and mean that love is made possible by a certain objective idealization).

Suppose we think of presence as self-presence, self-awareness, or what Derrida calls "auto-affection." We may think of this as simple identity, or as a *relation* capable of a certain development and complexity as when Kierkegaard shows that *despair* rests on a self that relates itself to itself.[16] Derrida writes: "Auto-affection is a universal structure of experience . . . this possibility – another name for 'life' – is a general structure articulated by the history of life, and leading to complex and hierarchical operations."[17]

And how is this "life" lived? "Speech and the consciousness of speech – that is to say consciousness simply as self-presence – are the phenomena of an auto-affection *lived as suppression of difference*."[18] Later he writes: "Auto-affection constitutes the same as it divides the same. Privation of presence is the condition of experience, that is to say, *presence*?"[19] Presence is experience (is differentiated, articulated, etc.) but does not know it. And of course the implication is not merely that it is *not itself* reflective, but that philosophy, when it does reflect on presence, swallows its story of undivided innocence. And it is hard to see why one could not apply to this the words that Hegel used to describe the movement of experience: "This new object contains the annihilation of the first; it is the experience constituted through that first object."[20]

These allusions first to Husserl and now to Hegel's concept of experience may seem wild. Am I going to make Derrida into one kind of phenomenologist after another? I do think that Derrida is a radical phenomenologist. And to keep the record straight I will briefly quote the crucial move Derrida makes. After talking about how far transcendental phenomenology "belongs to metaphysics," he speaks (nonetheless) of the need to come to terms with the forces of rupture:

In the original temporalization and the movement of relationship with the outside, *as Husserl actually describes them* [emphasis added] non-presentation or depresentation is as "originary" as presentation. *That is why a thought of the trace can no more break with a transcendental phenomenology than be reduced to it.*[21]

Husserl then actually *gives* us the material with which to bring about a deconstructive interruption of his own evidence. That he does not himself effect this interruption can be put down to his commitment to working with a certain *telos* of ideality for which, in a Nietzschean vein, Derrida will supply a further account:

Here idealization is the movement by which sensory exteriority, that which affects me or serves me as signifier, submits itself to my power of repetition, to what thence forward appears to me as my spontaneity and escapes me less and less.[22]

I will not comment on the parallels with Hegel's account of experience here. During the same period Derrida described deconstruction as infinitely close to but absolutely distinct from dialectic.[23] And his claim about the trace shows why and how. Compare the idea of *Aufhebung* (both overcoming and preserving) with the idea that the thought of "the trace can no more break with than be reduced to" – it is the same thought inside-out.

In sum, the apparent contrast between Derrida's early and later remarks about experience may be more apparent than real. What *is* true is that he no longer seems to use the word experience "under erasure." There has been a kind of mutation in the presumption built into references to experience. If "speech" or our consciousness of speech is, as he claimed, the "suppression of difference," *that it is so* is not merely a truth discovered by theory, by reflection. Rather it is testified to by "the experience of writing," "the experience of mourning," "the experience of the impossible." In other words, Derrida is appropriating "experience" in a way that strongly resembles Hegel, for a process productive of a certain kind of insight. To Derrida's claim that there has never been any "perception," we might add there has never *not* been experience!

But the use of this word is not without its strategic risks, risks of which Derrida is always acutely aware. Consider, for example, (i) the connection between the ideal of "experience" and that of the human "subject" (it is hard to imagine the one without the other), and (ii) his discussion with Jean-Luc Nancy[24] on the admissibility of retaining the word "subject." Nancy[25] says he does not understand how Derrida can retain this word "subject" without enormous misunderstandings. And Derrida admits the danger of "reintroducing" precisely what is in question.

So we *might* suppose that he ought to be just as wary, just as cautious, about "experience." We need only to turn for a moment to Blanchot to see why. In *The Writing of the Disaster*,[26] Blanchot repeatedly locates – I will not say explains – "disaster" in terms of a *break* with "experience," with the very possibility of experience. Blanchot writes of subjectivity as exile from the realm of "experience." He talks of "the disaster, unexperienced . . . what escapes the possibility of experience," and he writes of a kind of passivity which "escapes our power to test it, to try or experience it, and as interrupting our reason, our speech, our experience." Whatever Blanchot means by "(the) disaster," he insists on a kind of allergic relation between disaster and experience, as if they occupied or structured the space of thought differently. Surely, were Derrida listening to Blanchot, he would not be so free with experience. But let us keep reading Blanchot. He writes:

> There is suffering, there would be suffering, but no longer any "I" suffering, and this suffering does not make itself known in the present. It is not born into the present (still less is it experienced in the present)![27]

The moments at which the word "experience" erupts in a text are often highly significant, but we do not restrict ourselves to tracking this word. When Blanchot mentions *suffering*, for example, that too is experience. In fact, when we dissect what he says about suffering, we see it is exemplary of the way in which "experience" can itself undergo a transformation, an "experience."

For a Hegelian or a Christian, "suffering" would be instructive. I would be deepened by the recognition of my vulnerability, my dependence, perhaps my mortality, by the recognition of the limits of autonomous selfhood. Undergoing suffering might put a certain sense of self or subject in question, but only in the transition to a deeper sense. For Blanchot, suffering is an experience that demands, that forces, a suspension of self. The "I" that suffers is not thinking, synthesizing, making present. And, in a more Levinasian tone, Blanchot goes on to write of "the neighbour . . . opening me to the radical passivity of the self," and of "subjectivity as wounded, blamed, and persecuted exposure."[28]

These moves lead to a kind of ambivalence, especially in Blanchot, but also in Derrida's writing, between the recognition that concepts like "experience" and "subject" are instruments it is vital for us to preserve, even in their own transformation, and a sense that we need to effect or record a radical break with traditional metaphysical thought – an abyssal exposure of the *loss* of meaning, of any unity of experience, and of the very idea of the subject.

I will argue that the sense that both Blanchot and Derrida have of a kind of abyssal alternative to dialectic is itself in need of a certain deconstruction – that the idea of absolute loss is a kind of dialectical misunderstanding. It is a recognition of the interminability of dialectic – of the instability of any unity, of the incompleteness of mourning – which is an important second-order truth about the teleology of thought. But it must never then spin free; there can be no independent "abyssal" realm. The experience of the impossible is nothing but the recognition of the impossibility of a certain *closure* of experience. In other words, abyssal thought is directly predicated on the value of *closure*. Without the effort at closure, without the necessary failure of such closure (such determination of meaning, such completeness of identity, etc.), there is no abyss. The abyss is derivative from the experience that it undermines. So abyssal thinking is essentially differentiated from (and hence *dependent on*) that recuperative negation which it refuses. That the fate of abyssal thought is tied up with that of recuperative negation would not be at all surprising if one saw it as something like a recognition of the limits of that recuperation. It is, however, a recognition that cashes out, not as a new graspable truth, but as a *way*. I will argue presently that all this comes to a certain problematic fruition in Derrida's account of *responsibility*.

III

Thinking of ethos in terms of dwelling is an ontological short-circuit of the hermeneutic arc from interpretation to action, but it points to a certain character of human comportment. The import of many of Derrida's worries about Heidegger's repeated affirmation of the value of ownness, the proper, etc. is at the very least, to question whether Heidegger has fully released himself from the grip of a recuperative teleology. But it is precisely Heidegger's reading of Heraclitus in which dwelling means locating the unfamiliar (the gods) within the familiar (the hearth) that disrupts this line of questioning. The unfamiliar is interruption as well as deepening. It is by following out such threads that we can eventually come to see Derrida's "responsibility" as a way or a reworking, a reinscribing, a repeating of Heidegger's account of ethos.

The unfamiliar appears as the interruption of experience, in the sense both of experience as interruption and of the interruption of a more domesticated sense of experience. I shall now allow Derrida's own acknowledgement of this moment to emerge through a tracing of the course of "trembling" through Kierkegaard.

The extraordinary virtue of Kierkegaard's philosophical thinking lies in his willingness to think the religious in terms of a certain mediated structure of subjectivity. This is not a simple displacement – probably an unending task, or *work* of experience, a kind of labour of the negative. But this passion for truth, for the deinstitutionalization and dereification of thought, must ultimately derealize God "himself." One could interpret the ambivalent importance of faith as a sign of such a consequence. Kierkegaard repeatedly says that objective thought concerns itself with the *what*, the subjective with the *how*,[29] and when he speaks of silence we discover it takes the form of "indirect communication" where he emphasizes an "artistic *manner*." The knight of faith is a man (or woman) who returns to the finite – but always gets the infinite out of it. The ground structure of his dispositions has changed. To the extent that he is successful, Kierkegaard translates religious belief into complexly mediated and motivated ways of being and acting in the world. In this sense, at least, the religious is ultimately ethical.[30] The infinite is nothing but a certain kind of consideration brought to bear on action and thought. When Heidegger writes (as we have seen) that "nothing occurs neither by itself nor 'apart from' what is, as a sort of adjunct,"[31] he is making a similar claim. We avoid confusion, ultimately, if we understand "nothing," and "being," as *modal* determinations of what-there-is, as *how* we can best see, grasp, understand what is. I am trying here to generalize the force of Kierkegaard's "how" as a recursively applicable way of dealing with such objectifying projections as will continue to emerge. What I am saying here is not too different from Heidegger when he talks of "examining constantly" the adequacy of our "response to language."[32]

There is no doubt that Derrida recognizes what I would call the phenomenological imperative – of staying with the experience, of acknowledging experience. For example, in *The Gift of Death*, Derrida writes:

> As different as dread and fear, anxiety, terror, panic, or anguish remain from one another, they have already begun in the trembling, and what has provoked them continues, and threatens to continue, to make us tremble.[33]

Or again: "In as much as it tends to undo both seeing and knowing, trembling is indeed an experience of secrecy or of mystery."[34]

Derrida introduced the term *trembling* as far back as *Of Grammatology* (making "the value of presence *tremble*"), and I understand him to mean by it an experience in which the forces of difference constitutive of any and every identity or presence are activated and acknowledged. "Trembling" in this context might be thought in terms borrowed from Husserl as a kind of re-activation of difference. But, after Wittgenstein, to say that this coming up against the limits is ethical is surely to say that what is at stake in interpreting this experience, in "appropriating" it, is the formation of certain dispositions, ways of remembering, bearing witness to, honoring the implications of these limits. In *The Gift of Death*[35] "trembling" has come to mark the recognition of human frailty and

115

finitude by contrast to an infinite and inaccessible God. And in each case, we could say that "trembling" is the experience of what escapes and perhaps subverts presence. Here the "coming up against the limits of language" that Wittgenstein calls ethics, and his witnessing of an inexorable "dependency," both point in the same direction. If, as Heidegger would have us do, we think ethics as *ethos* or dwelling, it suggests that the experience of "trembling," when interpreted or (ex-)appropriated, would have to be translated into certain complex dispositions, ways of remembering, bearing witness to, honoring, acknowledging the significance of such an experience.

These dispositions are complex because their very enactment involves a renunciation of a certain model of fulfillment and success. And, in Derrida's writing, as in Heidegger's, there is a tension between the *terms* on which and with which we come to face alterity, and the complex ways of proceeding and "dwelling" (however problematized) into which these terms must be translated.

IV

There is perhaps a change in the experience of the negative in the twentieth century. Is what I have called the loss of the law of the recuperability of loss just a logical discovery, a discovery of flaws in the dialectic? Or is it something else?

If mourning is the working through of loss, then at best we are mourning mourning, working through the loss of the ability to work things through. But, of course, if confidence in the structure of working through has evaporated, then perhaps we cannot be consoled with even this meta-mourning.

The story of this loss of dialectical confidence is not just a logical discovery – some flaw in the idea of absolute knowledge, or salvation, or emancipation, but also a historical and cultural crisis, of which the Holocaust is the most potent sign, the indigestible experience, the experience that stops history in its tracks. What we think of as the displacement or deconstruction of the subject is the attempt to come to terms with the *failure* of that cultural formation – the autonomous individual – and to establish in its place a mode of being in the world that would recognize suffering, passivity, paradox, and loss. However, there is a danger in this, that of replacing one ideological or cultural formation (the autonomous individual) by another (the traumatized individual). The great achievement of the latter is to have brought back into the ethical domain some of the structures and economy of the religious, without the ontological baggage. But the trauma is being suffered *by* a certain cultural fiction of autonomy. In other words, there is a strange dialectical logic to this experience of trauma, and our task now is to translate traumatic loss into *ways* of going on.

Derrida's recent discussions of responsibility reintroduce words like *infinite* and *absolute* – infinite responsibility, absolute singularity, absolute other – in ways that constantly threaten to cross the line between a *modal* truth and a renewed mystification, between recursive reminders and impossible prescription. The battle against good conscience is unending, not because duty calls us to an infinite task which we must fall short of, but because there is no finite response that exhausts our responsibility. Responsibility is not quantifiably (or even unquantifiably) *large* and, therefore, not a basis for guilt through failure to live up to it. It is rather a recursive modality, an always renewable openness.[36]

Derrida writes of "an obligation to the other others I don't know, the billions of my fellows (. . . and animals)."[37] He asks me how I can justify feeding *my* cat every morning, *and* allowing all the other cats in the world to starve. But the Good Samaritan for cats does not go searching for starving cats (or indeed starving anything or everything else), but would feed *any* hungry being that came along, and insists that every and any boundary of concern that one establishes is permeable. Openness does not require that one leaves the door open, but that one is always willing to open the door. Responsibility then is the experience of that openness.[38]

If the argument of this essay is sound, the return of the centrality of experience to philosophy has made possible a reconfiguration of the ethical. Experience regained no longer shelters within conceptuality, or within the classical conception of the subject, but plots their limits, and in time breaks open each and every complacent demarcation. The ethical bearing of experience so understood is not, however, an infinite exposure but a way of comporting ourselves in our necessarily finite engagements, one in which the boundaries we necessarily set up are, as Heidegger put it, "examined constantly." Derrida's "responsibility" inherits this legacy.

Notes

1 "Letter on Humanism," in *Martin Heidegger: Basic Writings*, ed. David Farrell Krell, London: Routledge & Kegan Paul, 1978.
2 "'Eating Well,' or the Calculation of the Subject," Jean-Luc Nancy interview with Jacques Derrida, in Derrida's *Points . . . Interviews 1974–1994*, Stanford: Stanford University Press, 1995.
3 In *Poetry, Language, Thought*, New York: Harper & Row, 1971 (referred to as PLT hereafter).
4 PLT, p. 210.
5 See here the brilliant work of John Llewelyn, for example *The Middle Voice of Ecological Conscience*, London: Macmillan, 1991.
6 *Notebooks 1914–1916*, Oxford: Basil Blackwell, 1961, p. 73.

7 Quoted in *Heidegger and Modern Philosophy*, ed. Michael Murray, New Haven: Yale, 1978, p. 80.
8 From "Language" in PLT, p. 189.
9 "What is Metaphysics?," trans. R.F.C. Hull and Alan Crick in Martin Heidegger, *Existence and Being*, ed. Werner Brock, Chicago: Henry Regnery, 1949, p. 336 (WM hereafter).
10 WM, p. 340.
11 Rudolph Carnap, "The Overcoming of Metaphysics through the Logical Analysis of Language" [1931], in *Logical Positivism*, ed. A.J. Ayer, New York: Free Press, 1951.
12 *What Is Called Thinking?* [1954], trans. Fred D. Wieck and J. Glenn Gray, New York: Harper, 1968.
13 *Of Grammatology* [1967], trans. Gayatri Spivak, Baltimore: Johns Hopkins University Press, 1976 (hereafter OG), pp. 60–1.
14 "Sauf le nom," in *On the Name*, ed. Thomas Dutoit, trans. David Wood, John P. Leavy and Ian McLeod, Stanford: Stanford University Press, p. 43.
15 See for example, "'Genesis and Structure' and Phenomenology [1959]", in *Writing and Difference*, trans. Alan Bass, Chicago: University of Chicago Press, 1978; and "Form and Meaning: A Note on the Phenomenology of Language [1967]", in *Speech and Phenomena*, trans. David Allison, Evanston: Northwestern University Press, 1973.
16 See Kierkegaard, *The Sickness Unto Death*, trans. Walter Lowrie, New York: Doubleday Anchor, 1954.
17 OG, p. 165.
18 OG, p. 165.
19 OG, p. 166.
20 Introduction to *Phenomenology of the Spirit*, trans. A.V. Miller, London: Oxford University Press, para. 14.
21 OG, p. 62.
22 OG, p. 166.
23 See his *Positions* [1972], trans. Alan Bass, Chicago: University of Chicago Press, 1981.
24 "'Eating Well,' or the Calculation of the Subject," see note 2 above.
25 His use of the word "experience" in *The Experience of Freedom* deserves a separate treatment. See Jean-Luc Nancy, *The Experience of Freedom* [1988], trans. Bridget McDonald, Stanford: Stanford University Press, 1993.
26 *The Writing of the Disaster* [1980], trans. Ann Smock, Lincoln and London: University of Nebraska Press, 1986 (hereafter WD).
27 OG, p. 15.
28 WD, p. 24.
29 See his *Concluding Unscientific Postscript*, trans. David Swenson and Walter Lowrie, Princeton: Princeton University Press, 1941, pp. 178ff.
30 For a fuller treatment, see my "Kierkegaard, God and the Economy of Thought," in *The Kierkegaard Reader*, ed. Jane Chamberlain and Jonathan Ree, Oxford: Blackwell, 1997.
31 WM, p. 340.
32 The need for this constant re-examination is intimately tied up with the fact that at a certain point we run out of rules for the application of rules, and yet there is still something to be said, albeit of a different order.
33 *The Gift of Death*, trans. David Wills, Chicago: University of Chicago Press, 1995, p. 53.
34 *Ibid.* p. 54.

35 *Ibid.*
36 The logic of my argument is not dissimilar to the common objection to Descartes' universal doubt. The fact that we can doubt anything does not mean we can doubt everything.
37 *The Gift of Death*, p. 69.
38 Compare here Derrida's discussion of our various "double duties" and the impossibility of choosing between them, his account of the need to go through the "undecidable," each of which emphasizes the need to remember in each decision the struggle in which it is grounded, which is already an antidote to any hyperbolic quantification of our obligations. In this connection, see my "Responsibility Reinscribed (and How)," in *Responsibilities of Deconstruction, PLI: Warwick Journal of Philosophy*, ed. Jonathon Dronsfield and Nick Midgley, vol. 6, Summer 1997.

9

THE ETHICS OF EXCLUSION
Incorporating the Continent

Simon Glendinning

It was a Cambridge affair. At the meeting of the University Congregation in March 1992 an objection to one of the nominations for the degree of *doctor honoris causa* was lodged by the audible cry of 'non placet'. A ballot of the Regent House was organised, fly-sheets were circulated and signed. On a Saturday in the middle of May over five hundred members attended the Senate House to register their opinion, voting by personal signature. The ballot was secret, but as members waited for the result it mattered where you stood and with whom you stood. Younger fellows were aware, some painfully aware, that older eyes were watching.

It was a Cambridge affair, yet, as the Regent House was deciding whether or not to award an honorary degree to the French philosopher Jacques Derrida, it was never simply or solely so. Derrida's candidacy (and the fact that his proposal came from *outside* the Philosophy Faculty) had aroused strong feelings within the University, and the ensuing rumpus attracted wide interest from both the national and international media. Academic opposition to *politicians* receiving such degrees was rare but at least familiar enough. But a philosopher? What was this smoke from the ivory towers? 'Dons Ditch Deconstructionist' might have looked good, if only the lexical background had a circulation approximating that of the newspapers. In fact the event was such that it was not only journalists who sought simplicity where there is none. From the start it was academics ('*certain* academics' as Derrida carefully but pointedly stressed later[1]) who most dramatically violated the very standards of intellectual responsibility in whose name the *non placet* had been voiced.

The terms of criticism were by no means new. Indeed, for the 'non placeters' the 'Derrida affair' was playing out a familiar drama of British letters in its relation to 'Continental' contacts. As Nicholas Denyer put it, for Derrida's opponents this was just another case where a French thinker was being 'acclaimed by many British intellectuals in spite of reservations among their philosophically educated compatriots' (*ibid.*, p. 103). While the image of a 'fissure' (*ibid.*) within the British intellectual culture is apt, it is, I think, secondary to and largely explained by the fact that the same image informs the dominant picture of the contemporary *philosophical* culture in general, a fissure which Denyer's observation implicitly affirms. That is, one might turn the tables here and emphasise that those 'British' (or more presicely 'analytical') philosophers who opposed Derrida were not the first roundly to condemn the work of their 'Continental' colleagues, and to do so in much the same terms.

The template for the Cambridge criticism was, as I hope to show in this essay, well prepared for: the assumption of a wide gulf between 'analytical' and 'Continental' philosophy was already a commonplace. Thus, however personal and personally offensive they may have seemed, the fly-sheets' suggestions that, for example, Derrida's work could 'deprive the mind of its defences' and 'undermine the fundamental grounds which provide . . . for intellectual inquiry' (*ibid.*, p. 101) were not unique to the case. In what we will see is actually far too common a trait to be dismissed as an occasional shortcoming on the part of the 'analytical' critics of what it calls 'Continental' philosophy, a litany of charges was brought against Derrida *without citing a single supporting quote or reference*. Now, if they were justified these charges *would* seriously question the University's wisdom in conferring on Derrida a degree of any sort. *If* it was right to call his work 'stupid and ridiculous' (*ibid.*, p. 108) or 'degenerate' in virtue of 'its contempt for argumentative rigour' and its 'barbarous neologisms and idiotic word-play' (*ibid.*, p. 109), then, yes, it would be understandable if one despaired of one's supposedly intelligent colleagues and their 'appetite for known falsehood' (*ibid.*, p. 104) and the 'non placet' should have been cheered to the rafters of the Senate House.

But there was good reason why the 'non placeters' did not quote from Derrida's work. There was good reason why the standards of scholarship and rigour they were claiming to defend were not, in this case, brought to bear. For all its risks and difficulties (no one ever claimed that Derrida is an easy and obvious thinker), as anyone who has made the effort to read his work discovers soon enough, there is not a single line in his work to support their principal claims.

The 'affair' soon spread beyond Cambridge, and beyond merely 'British' philosophical assessments. A letter was sent to *The Times*, signed by nineteen 'analytical' philosophers outside the UK, including W.V.O. Quine. It repeated many of the charges of the 'non placeters'. It also repeated the basic dereliction of scholarly duty: not a sentence was cited, no references were made, no analyses of argument or lines of criticism from Derrida's 'voluminous writings' (*The Cambridge Review*, p. 139) were pursued. Two words in the letter *were* placed between quotation marks, suggesting Derrida as their source: it was claimed that Derrida's writings 'seem to consist in no small part of elaborate jokes and the puns "logical phallusies" and the like',[2] but, as Derrida himself emphasised, this is a phrase which he has 'never written' (*ibid.*, p. 132). Is it not a very serious deception to pass off as the work of a charlatan what is, in fact, specious invention?

As I have indicated, Derrida is not the first 'Continental' philosopher to have found himself on the receiving end of this kind of attack. I hope that the following examination will help to explain how the Cambridge affair over a degree of *doctor honoris causa* can be seen as a particularly clear case, *not* of what Denyer calls 'reservations' among those who received their philosophical education in Britain, but of the construction of a gulf between what 'we' (analytical philosophers) so seriously do and 'they' (Continental philosophers) so unfortunately do – the construction of a gulf which has led again and again to a tendency to condemn as obscurantist and mystifying works of philosophy which, in fact, have not been seriously read at all.

I

It is unlikely that anyone working in philosophy today would find it difficult to produce a list of recognisable practitioners of Continental philosophy. Yet is it certain that to this category there corresponds an identifiable philosophical movement, approach, style, school or tradition? What holds together the authors named on such lists under this title? My supposition, explored in what follows, is that one will not find out by reading their work. As the name itself should indicate, the forces which brought about a collection of authors and texts under this title do not lie inside that collection. By the time that it became possible to speak of Continental philosophy, and to mean something other than philosophy being done in a certain geographical location, the locus of such forces was itself assuming the name, indeed was naming itself, analytical or analytic philosophy.

Of course, the idea that Continental philosophy emerges as a fruitfully distinguishable philosophical category from within analytical philosophy does not, just like that, confer any problematic status upon it. However, in what follows I will argue that at issue here has not been the identification, as it were *en passant*, of a distinctive philosophical approach, but exclusions of a strictly non-logical and ethically indefensible character. Continental philosophy, as a category, is, I will suggest, part of analytical philosophy in a strong sense: it has been constructed as the defining 'not-part' of analytical philosophy. In psychoanalysis this would be called 'incorporation'; i.e., where something is represented and retained 'within' but *as* an excluded outside, *as* a foreign body which is impossible to assimilate and which must be rejected. This essay thus comprises a sketch for an investigation of Continental philosophy as the incorporated other of analytical philosophy.

It will be important to stress that in recent years, and in significant respects, the English-speaking philosophical culture has become less concerned with, less shaped by, the idea of a philosophical rift. Nevertheless, even today labelling an author as a Continental philosopher can never be a wholly value-free gesture or merely geographical determination. On the contrary, the current use of this label carries with it the burden of an evaluative accent which has suggested not only that the author is doing work of a supposedly distinctive kind but also of an *inferior* quality. It is an abiding legacy of the rise of the movement which has called itself 'analytical philosophy' that what it has called 'Continental philosophy' has been so positioned as to represent all that is 'arbitrary, pretentious and soul-destroying' in philosophy, wherever it is written.[3]

This profoundly negative evaluation is, I think, now (or, for the moment, still) part of the grammar of 'Continental philosophy'. Continental philosophy is, as it were, *given* to analytical philosophy as beyond the pale. It involves a kind of failure of inheritance, an abandonment of the 'accepted standards of clarity and rigour' which should characterise properly philosophical inquiry.[4] Thus, *in so far as* one affirms that 'What one does' is analytical philosophy, then Continental philosophy will be not only What one (*qua* analytical philosopher) *does not do*, but What *ought not to be done* if one wants to think seriously within the central channels of the Western philosophical tradition.

I have no doubt that this view is deeply embedded in and tied up with national, political and religious currents which, for the most part, simply do not appear *as such* within the texts of mainstream analytical philosophy. And in what follows I will try to at least open the debate to these issues. However, I am equally convinced that this idea of philosophical division is not without a classically philosophical significance. To the question What is Continental philosophy? I will answer: it is the false personification, by (self-styled) analytical philosophy, of a possibility which is internal to, and which threatens, *all* philosophizing; the possibility of being empty. Now, as a *false* personification, I take it that the historical emergence of this category betrays misunderstanding. I also think it betrays injustice. I would like to be reasonably self-conscious about establishing this. That is, I would like this work to be part of a drift of thinking in which this injustice is removed.

II

The kind of tendency I want to explore finds one of its most dramatic and spectacular expressions in R.M. Hare's lecture, 'A School for Philosophers', 'given at a number of German centres in the summer of 1957'.[5] Hare does not think of the philosophical landscape in terms of a distinction between analytical and Continental philosophy. But he definitely thinks of it as *philosophically* divided. In his lecture, the 'two different ways' in which 'the same subject' is studied, ways concerning which 'one might be forgiven for thinking . . . are really two quite different subjects' (p. 107), are labelled primarily nationally, as British and German philosophy. This lexicon may have the virtue of avoiding the 'strange cross-classification' of analytical and Continental philosophy.[6] But Hare's distinction is not without at least two major complications of its own. First, he virtually identifies British philosophy with work being done at 'the older British universities' and especially Oxford;[7] and, second, he can hardly be said to identify 'German philosophy' with anything at all. He does speak of 'a typical German philosopher' and refers to 'huge volumes' and 'long obscure books' which nobody in Oxford will read, and which, as E.W.F. Tomlin noted in a rejoinder, 'seems to be tilting at German productions'.[8] But no examples or samples of such works are cited or referred to anywhere in the lecture.[9] As we shall see, Hare's argument is seriously compromised by this vagueness. Indeed, I will suggest that the distinction he insists upon *lives* on being free-floating.

Hare's essay begins with a brief presentation of the merits for philosophy of the Oxford tutorial system. In such a system, he stresses, a student of philosophy will be taught 'how to think more clearly and to the point' (p. 108); taught, that is, 'to express his thought clearly to himself and to others; to make distinctions where there are distinctions to be made, and thus avoid unnecessary confusion – and not to use long words (or short ones) without being able to explain what they mean' (p. 108). These points are intended to introduce us to the basic characteristics of Oxford – and by implication British – philosophy generally. For British philosophy, Hare insists, is guided by the intellectual virtues it teaches; *viz.*, 'clarity, relevance and brevity' (p. 112). Such virtues will then ensure that arguments between 'British philosophers' can circulate and develop through the defence and refutation of work with what he calls 'an unambiguously stated thesis' (p. 112). This, according to Hare, is the central characteristic and great strength of British philosophical analysis.

The unambiguously stated thesis of Hare's paper is that British and German philosophy is 'the same subject studied in two different ways'. The unstated, less clear, but certainly no less unambiguous thesis is that the German philosophical way is the *wrong* philosophical way. Supposing, as is in fact constantly invited, the contrast to the British way is, even when unstated as such, the German way, then the latter enjoys the 'delights of erecting, in solitary thought, imposing edifices – of writing huge volumes which only a handful of people will ever understand' (p. 110); and the typical author of such 'long or difficult books' (p. 113) or 'monstrous philosophical edifices' (p. 115) likes, Hare suggests, to 'collect a private coterie to listen to him' (p. 111); and he will not be averse to 'the turning of philosophy into *mystique*' (p. 110) or to producing 'verbiage' disguised as 'serious metaphysical inquiry' (p. 115). In short, according to Hare, the 'typical German philosopher' thrives on and finds 'uplifting' approaches and styles of thought characterized by 'ambiguities and evasions and rhetoric', i.e., precisely those characteristics which 'British philosophers' regard 'as the mark of a philosopher who has not learnt his craft' (pp. 112–13).

A grave nod. But who are these German metaphysicians who 'have chosen to ignore [the] important developments [made by Vienna Circle positivism] and carry on in their old ways as if nothing had happened' (p. 117)? The trouble is not merely that we are not told (there are, as we know, usual suspects in this game) but that not one example of the 'German way' is presented as an illustration. Thus the idea of philosophical division remains a kind of air-castle or, lest we forget certain developments, at least unverified. Some striking home truths are revealed on this point in a passage where Hare discusses the British philosopher's conception of his duty as a philosopher:

> We do not think it is a *duty* to write books; still less do we think it a duty to read more than a few of the books which others write – for we know that, given our heavy load of teaching, to read more than the essential books would take us away from more important things. Our duty is to discuss philosophy with our colleagues and to teach our pupils to do the same – books and articles are an unconsidered by-product of this process; their content is generally quite familiar from verbal discussion years before they get published. We find out which 'the essential books' are by each reading a very few and telling the others about them. The result is that, if one wants a book to be read by one's colleagues it will have to be short, clear and to the point. . . . The certain way to obscurity, on the other hand, is to write long obscure books. Nobody will ever read them.
>
> (Hare 1960: 114)

He later adds that British philosophers 'find it hard to discuss philosophy with, *or to read the books of*, people who do not even seem worried about convincing the sceptic that their philosophical propositions mean something' (p. 115, my italics). Thus, what Hare calls the 'essential books', books, that is, which will in fact be read by Oxford philosophers with any seriousness whatsoever, will prove, in practice, to be their own alone. So much for avoiding 'coteries'. What can one conclude here but that the very idea of a *philosophical* division within the European philosophical culture must, at least in part, *live* on being free-floating? Indeed, it is arguable that that idea can survive only for as long as the thinkers and themes which are not part of what has called itself 'the analytical

SIMON GLENDINNING

movement' are not only supposed not worth reading but, in fact, *are not seriously read.*[10]

Since Hare's account is developed in ways which force him to slip from the standards of 'rigour and honesty and clarity' which, rightly, he upholds for philosophy generally (p. 120), he cannot have properly or satisfactorily demonstrated his unambiguously stated thesis. But perhaps he has succeeded in showing something else: namely, that 'the rise of the analytical movement' has at times relied on its self-authorised defenders failing to be 'an example of the virtues' which, officially at least, they were 'seeking to inculcate' (p. 116).

If this is so, then how are we to understand the division in the current philosophical culture? Perhaps what needs explaining is not 'What distinguishes analytical philosophy from Continental philosophy?', but how there came to be heirs of philosophy who came to call themselves 'analytical philosophers' and who, in doing so, cut themselves off, supposing themselves to be a world apart, from the rest of the Western philosophical community.

III

As I stated earlier, while I am not convinced that there is a *philosophical* rift in contemporary philosophy, I do not suppose the rift-stricken reality to have no philosophical significance at all. Put bluntly, I believe that the modern category of 'Continental philosophy' is best thought of as a recurrence, in determinate historical circumstances, of a figuration which has, since ancient Greek times, permeated and haunted the Western philosophical imagination in general: namely, that of the Sophist. I want to suggest why this may provide a crucial key to understanding the contemporary philosophical culture.

Between the 1850s and 1950s the Universities of Oxford and Cambridge underwent a transformation so deep and so profound as almost to defy summary.[11] From fairly decadent clerical institutions in which inertia was endemic, the Universities became more or less what they still are today: great centres of learning, staffed by-and-large by full-time *career academics*. University philosophy could not but be touched by these changes. Indeed, by the end of the Second World War, the (hand-in-hand) professionalisation and development of philosophy in England had become so pronounced that the (now almost exclusively young) academic personnel began to talk of a 'revolution in philosophy'. A history of this revolution was also emerging. And, while its focus was essentially national, it told of the emphatic rejection of specifically *foreign* ideas.

Geoffrey Warnock's 1958 assessment of the development of English philosophy since 1900 presents the classic insider's view of these developments.[12] It is an exuberant and confident book. As Warnock saw it, the

126

philosophical culture in which he was working could now, as never before, 'be seen to work' and thus had gained genuine 'intellectual respectability' (pp. 55–56). In short, it had earned a place in the transformed academic culture. At the heart of Warnock's account of this revolution is an image which, to this day, is a central part of analytical philosophy's self-conception, but which, it must be emphasised, would not have been recognised in Britain only a quarter of a century earlier. According to Warnock, 'most philosophy written in English [in this century] has been, for better or worse, and I shall not here say which [but see below], something vastly unlike most philosophy in other languages' (Preface, p. v). This vast difference, is, of course, the philosophical rift with which we are now familiar. But what is so important about Warnock's account for our purposes is that the basic target of his critical obloquy lies not abroad, on the Continent, 'over there', but at home, in Britain, 'over here'. For there was, in Warnock's view, a crucial and singular exception to the rift-stricken state of affairs: namely, in the closing decades of the nineteenth century when British philosophy was dominated by Idealism. It is with this movement that the new history begins for, in large measure, in the post-Great-War era, it was against (what were now seen as) the absurd 'metaphysical pretensions' of that movement that the revolution was directed.

In marked contrast to his treatment of the British philosophers whom he considers 'most important', Warnock does not actually present or discuss any of the British Idealists' writings. Instead, he considers it 'enough' to characterise them simply as advancing 'highly and ambitiously metaphysical' claims about 'Reality' (p. 3). For a reading of their thoughts Warnock substitutes an attack on what he calls their 'characteristic manner of writing', confidently castigating their 'highly coloured rhetorical dress' (p. 6). In what is, rhetorically speaking, a rather thin veneer of objectivity, we are informed that a reader 'attached to the presently prevailing mode, and with the courage of his convictions . . . might well find the style of the Idealists almost unbearable' (p. 6). Bosanquet, for example, 'wrote sometimes with an air of vague high seriousness, in which the serious intent was almost completely muffled by the vagueness. And in the writings of the lesser men solemnity and unclarity seem to rise not seldom to the pitch of actual fraud' (p. 6). Similarly, Bradley's 'opinions' depended for their 'persuasive force' not on 'the relatively unimportant trappings of argument' but the 'artifice of their presentation' (p. 7).

What is so striking about such a dubious, and frankly indefensible, form of unsupported criticism is how closely it resembles Hare's portrait of 'German philosophy' examined earlier. And this, I suggest, is no accident. For, as Warnock revealingly notes at one point, behind the 'vivid, violent, and lofty imprecision' of this species of 'British philosophy' lay 'German influences'. And these influences were, he states, 'very much an alien import' (p. 9).

The 'alien' status here is finely balanced between a national and a philosophical movement. And it will stay that way. In this irreducibly polysemic voice Warnock declares that the philosophical movement of Idealism in Britain was never *really* British anyway. Indeed, British philosophy was, he suggests, not long occupied with such 'strange things' before it freed itself from what the Idealists had called 'the main stream of *European* thought' and returned to what Warnock called 'the main stream of *British* thought' (p. 9).

The British Isles are, of course, part of Europe (some might say the 'not-part'), but 'the mainland of Europe, as distinguished from the British Isles', *that* is the Continent.[13] At home, Warnock later reflected, the 'real campaign was already over' by 1948.[14] Henceforth, what English philosophy had for some time designated as 'Continental philosophy' takes on its distinctive modern guise; figured as 'exotic', 'alien', 'strange', 'vague', 'rhetorical' and 'literary'. Henceforth, it was 'Continental influences' which were frowned upon and, where at all possible, to be avoided.

But were they avoided? Or *could* they be? It is simply undeniable that some of the most powerful and pervasive influences on English-language philosophy in the twentieth century have been, precisely, 'Continental' in origin. Think, for example, of Bolzano, Brentano, Peano, Cantor, Frege, Popper, the Vienna Circle and, of course, Wittgenstein. So the picture of British philosophy coming home is never going to be, cannot be, convincing. Moreover, even its self-imposed insularity has never completely stopped analytical philosophers from engaging with writers in the supposedly 'Continental' camp.[15] In fact, recent developments in the teaching of philosophy at British universities (particularly outside 'the older universities') suggests that the rift-seeking rhetoric of the post-War period is now on the decline. This is nicely illustrated by the Warwick University Philosophy Department. Warwick today has one of the most wide-ranging and adventurous syllabuses in Britain, but as recently as 1972 it was otherwise. In its prospectus of that year it made the following statement:

> The courses at Warwick are those which would be recognised in universities throughout the English-speaking world, and we would expect our graduates to be equipped to deal with the kinds of discussions going on in the graduate schools of Oxford, Harvard or Canberra. They would, however, be in some difficulty in the Sorbonne, the University of Moscow, or a Zen Buddhist monastery. You should apply to the latter institutions, rather than to ourselves, if you have no desire to study within the broad tradition represented by such writers as Russell, Wittgenstein, Carnap, Popper, Quine, Ryle, Ayer, Austin and Strawson.[16]

The selection of unthinkables, the Sorbonne, Moscow and Zen, are of course (by now familiar) caricatures, but nevertheless they accurately reflect the kind of work which was – which, it was thought, *must* – be excluded by professional philosophy.

It should now be clear why 'Continental philosophy' became the tag for that which must be excluded. But what perhaps remains unclear is analytical philosophy's *emphasis* on it. As I have indicated, I think that this can be explained. Derrida was surely right to say, in the context of his notoriously acrimonious exchange with Searle, that 'no one will be astonished when I observe that [the Sophists] haunt our present debate'.[17] For this is the very image of that incorporation which is philosophy's own, the very image of that which is *philosophically foreign to philosophy*, that which threatens philosophy from within, and so *must* be excluded. In virtue of the particular circumstances of its emergence, English-language philosophy in the post-War decades identified that philosophically 'foreign' thinking as that mode of nationally 'foreign' philosophy which had by the 1950s been almost completely 'expelled' by the revolution. Thus 'Continental philosophy' became the insider's own outsider, and was represented in a convincing but free-floating history of a philosophical rift in contemporary philosophy. But, as we have seen, this has not been a well-told tale. This is not *simply* because work identified as 'Continental philosophy' is not so very different to, and possesses qualities supposedly definitive of, its 'analytical' relation (although I would strongly suggest that, as Dummett found in his reading of Husserl,[18] this is normally the case) but, more importantly, because the very process or becoming of the designation and distinction involved a *false personification* of philosophy's own *interminable possibility*: the possibility of failure most famously figured as Sophistry. Sadly its effect occasioned the realisation of just that possibility: at defining moments analytical philosophy has been able to fail as philosophy. This, I believe, is what happens when analytical philosophers condemn thinkers as irrational and obscurantist without taking the trouble to read and argue with them.

The personification of an internal possibility as an 'expelled' (and literally) foreign body gave analytical philosophy the false assurance that it was, essentially, 'healthy' philosophy. Ironically, then, its very sense of health, the confidence in its certain possession of 'rigour and honesty and clarity', lives off an essentially non-logical and fundamentally ethical–political exclusion. Perhaps it will not survive for too much longer. Perhaps what is needed is a more open mind. A more open *Mind*. Now there's a thought.[19]

Notes

1 *The Cambridge Review*, ed. R. Morse and S. Collini, Vol. 113, No. 2318, Oct. 1992, Cambridge: CUP, p. 131. Page references to the 'Cambridge–Derrida affair' that follow are from the articles collected in this number of *The Cambridge Review*.

2 Barry Smith et al., 'Derrida Degree: A Question of Honour', *The Times* (London), Saturday 9 May 1992.

3 J. Passmore, *A Hundred Years of Philosophy*, Harmondsworth: Penguin, second edition, 1978, p. 467.

4 B. Smith et al., 'Derrida Degree'.

5 Reprinted in *Ratio*, Vol. II, No. 2, 1960. Another classic example from this period which should be noted here is Gilbert Ryle's essay 'Phenomenology versus *The Concept of Mind*' (reprinted in G. Ryle, *Collected Papers*, London: Hutchinson, 1971) presented to a conference entitled 'La Philosophie Analytique' in Royaumont, France, in 1958. The very title of Ryle's contribution reflects the assumption of, and perhaps desire for, confrontation and division. Indeed, throughout his presentation Ryle was determined to affirm a 'wide gulf' between 'Anglo-Saxon and Continental philosophy' (p. 182). The sentence which concludes his opening discussion of Husserl's work indicates, however, how uncertain this scene of division really is: 'This *caricature* of Husserl's phenomenology is intended to show up by contrast some of the predominant features of recent philosophy and in particular of the philosophy of mind in the English-speaking world' (p. 181; emphasis added). The factual and philosophical distortions involved in Ryle's distinction are neatly addressed by Ray Monk in his recent essay 'Bertrand Russell's Brainchild' (*Radical Philosophy*, No. 78, 1996). Yet it is not only in retrospect that the non-logical, ethical-political, character of Ryle's gulf-seeking is evident. One of the participants at Royaumont was Maurice Merleau-Ponty. In discussion he stated that, like others present, he was not convinced by Ryle's talk of a 'wide gulf': 'I have also had the impression, while listening to Mr Ryle, that what he was saying was not so strange to us, and that the distance, if there is a distance, is one that he puts between us rather than one I find there' (M. Merleau-Ponty, *Texts and Dialogues*, ed. H. Silverman and J. Barry, London: Humanities Press, 1992, p. 65).

6 As Bernard Williams puts it, the current distinction is 'rather as though one divided cars into front-wheel drive and Japanese' (B. Williams, 'Contemporary Philosophy: A Second Look', in *The Blackwell Companion to Philosophy*, ed. N. Bunin and E.P. Tsui-James, Oxford: Blackwell, 1996, p. 25).

7 Hare does note, however (and correctly I think), that 'the tone of British philosophy is at present set by Oxford' (p. 113).

8 *Ratio*, Vol. III, No. 1, 1960, p. 5.

9 There is one name mentioned, that of Husserl. But one has to question its value as 'evidence' for anything whatsoever: 'My wife has a cousin who studied philosophy under Husserl at Freiburg. I have heard him say that, when he first went to see the great man, Husserl produced about six bound volumes and said: "Here are my books; come back in a year's time"' (p. 107).

10 In this regard I think it is notable that when Michael Dummett (finally) explored Husserl's work in some detail he found that this supposedly alien thought was not, in fact, so very different to Frege's: 'At the very beginning of the century, say at the time Husserl published the *Logical Investigations*, there wasn't yet phenomenology as a school. There wasn't yet analytic philosophy

as a school. There were lots of currents there and you would have to put Frege and Husserl quite close together' ('An Anti-Realist Perspective on Language, Thought, Logic and the History of Analytical Philosophy': an interview with Michael Dummett by Fabrice Pataut, *Philosophical Investigations*, Vol. 19, No. 1, p. 14).

11 For some of the details see, for example, A. Engel, 'Emerging Concepts of the Academic Profession at Oxford 1800–1854', in *The University in Society*, Vol. I: *Oxford and Cambridge from the Fourteenth to the Early Nineteenth Century*, ed. L. Stone, Oxford: OUP, 1975; J.W. Adamson, *English Education 1789–1902*, Chap. XV, Cambridge: CUP, 1964; W.A. Pantin, *Oxford Life in Oxford Archives*, Chap. IV, Oxford: Clarendon Press, 1972; N. Allington and N. O'Saughnessy, *Light, Liberty and Learning*, The Education Unit, 1992.

12 G. Warnock, *English Philosophy Since 1900*, Oxford: OUP, 1958.

13 *Oxford English Dictionary*.

14 G.J. Warnock, 'Gilbert Ryle's Editorship', *Mind*, Vol. LXXXV, 1976, p. 51.

15 A full list of such engagements would be, I think, surprisingly long. However, it perhaps needs saying that such interest as has been shown has tended to be more or less marginal and more or less distanced. The revival of, and the style of the revival of, Kant studies led by P.F. Strawson is a good example of such distancing. John McDowell's recent use of Kant and Gadamer in *Mind and World* illustrates a more contemporary, and, in important ways, far less fraught relationship. That this is so is perhaps nicely picked up by the fact that Crispin Wright does not consider McDowell's book to be a work of analytical philosophy at all (see C. Wright, review of *Mind and World*, in the *European Journal of Philosophy*, Vol. 4, No. 2, August 1996, pp. 235–53.)

16 Cited in S. Sayers, *Reality and Reason*, Oxford: Blackwell, 1985, pp. 185–6.

17 J. Derrida, *Limited Inc . . .*, Evanston: Northwestern University Press, 1988, p. 42.

18 See note 10 above.

19 J.N. Findlay complained that, in its centenary number, *Mind* had simply become 'the organ of [the analytic] school' ('*Mind* under the Editorship of David Hamlyn', *Mind*, Vol. LXXXV, 1976, p. 60). He hoped that it would gradually revert to 'the catholicity of coverage' which had characterized it in earlier decades, but saw no sign of this (*ibid.*). The current editor of *Mind*, Mark Sainsbury, has suggested to me in a private communication that the journal 'has been said to be getting narrower rather than broader' in recent years. He states, however, that he 'would bend over backwards to try to discern the value of a submission emerging from a different tradition rather than dogmatically dismiss what is strange'.

Part III

CRITICAL THEORY

10

THREE NORMATIVE MODELS
OF DEMOCRACY
Liberal, republican, procedural[1]

Jürgen Habermas

I would like to sketch a proceduralist view of democracy and deliberative politics which differs in relevant respects from both the liberal and the republican paradigm. Let me remind you of the opposite feature of these two established models. I will then introduce a new proceduralist conception by way of a critique of the 'ethical overload' of the republican view. The last part of the essay further elaborates the three normative models of democracy by comparing their corresponding images of state and society.

The two received views of democratic politics

According to the 'liberal' or Lockean view, the democratic process accomplishes the task of programming the government in the interests of society, where the government is represented as an apparatus of public administration, and society as a market-structured network of interactions among private persons. Here politics (in the sense of the citizens' political will-formation) has the function of bundling together and pushing private interests against a government apparatus specialising in the administrative employment of political power for collective goals. On the 'republican' view, however, politics involves more than this mediating function; it is rather constitutive of the process of society as a whole. 'Politics' is conceived as the reflective form of substantial ethical life, namely as the medium in which the members of somehow solitary communities become aware of their dependence on one another and, acting with full deliberation as citizens, further shape and develop existing relations of reciprocal recognition into an association of free and equal consociates under law. With this, the liberal architectonic of government and society undergoes an important change: in addition to the hierarchical regulations of the state and the decentralised regulations of the market – that is, besides administrative power and individual personal interests – *solidarity* and the orientation to the common good appear as a *third source* of social integration. In fact, this horizontal political will-formation aimed at mutual understanding or communicatively achieved consensus is even supposed to enjoy priority, both in a genetic and a normative sense. An autonomous basis in civil society, a basis independent of public administration and market-mediated private commerce, is assumed as a precondition for the praxis of civic self-determination. This basis preserves political communication from being swallowed up by the government apparatus or assimilated to market structures. In the republican conception, the political public sphere acquires, along with its base in civil society, a strategic significance. These competing approaches yield two contrasting images of the citizen.

According to the liberal view, the citizens' status is determined primarily according to negative rights they have *vis-à-vis* the state and other citizens. As bearers of these rights they enjoy the protection of the government, as long as they pursue their private interests within the boundaries drawn by the legal statutes – and this includes protection against government interventions. Political rights, such as voting rights and free speech, have not only the same structure as but a similar meaning to civil rights that provide a space within which legal subjects are released from external compulsion. They give citizens the opportunity to assert their private interests in such a way that, by means of elections, the composition of parliamentary bodies, and the formation of a government, these interests are finally aggregated into a political will that makes an impact on the administration.

According to the republican view, the status of citizens is not determined by the model of negative liberties to which these citizens can lay claim *as* private persons. Rather, political rights – pre-eminently rights of political participation and communication – are positive liberties. They guarantee not freedom from external compulsion but the possibility of participation in a common praxis, through the exercise of which citizens can first make themselves into what they want to be – politically autonomous authors of a community of free and equal persons. To this extent, the political process does not just serve to keep government activity under the surveillance of citizens who have already acquired a prior social autonomy in the exercise of their private rights and pre-political liberties. Just as little does it act as a hinge between state and society, for administrative authority is not at all an autochthonous authority; it is not something given. Rather, this authority emerges from the citizens' power produced communicatively in the praxis of self-legislation, and it finds its legitimation in the fact that it protects by institutionalising public liberty. So, the state's *raison d'être* does not lie primarily in the protection of equal private rights but in the guarantee of an inclusive opinion – and will-formation in which free and equal citizens reach an understanding on which goals and norms lie in the equal interest of all.

The polemic against the classical conception of the legal person as bearer of private rights reveals a controversy about the concept of law itself. While in the liberal view the point of a legal order is to make it possible to determine in each case which individuals are entitled to which rights, in the republican view these 'subjective' rights owe their existence to an 'objective' legal order that both enables and guarantees the integrity of an autonomous life in common based on mutual respect: 'For republicans rights ultimately are nothing but determinations of the prevailing political will, while for liberals some rights are always grounded in a higher law of . . . reason.'[2]

Finally, the different ways of conceptualising the roles of citizen and of law express a deeper disagreement about the *nature of the political process*. In the liberal view, the political process of opinion- and will-formation in the public sphere and in parliament is determined by the competition of strategically acting collectivities trying to maintain or acquire positions of power. Success is measured by the citizens' approval, quantified as votes, of persons and programmes. In their choices at the polls, voters give expression to their preferences. Their voting decisions have the same structure as the acts of choice made by participants in a market. They license access to the positions of power that political parties fight over in the same success-oriented attitude.

According to the republican view, the political opinion- and will-formation occurring in the public sphere and in parliament obeys not the structures of market processes but the obstinate structures of a public communication orientated to mutual understanding. For politics, in the sense of a praxis of civic self-legislation, the paradigm is not the market dialogue. This dialogic conception imagines politics as contestation over questions of value and not simple questions of preference.

Proceduralist vs communitarian views of politics

The republican model as compared to the liberal one has the advantage that it preserves the original meaning of democracy in terms of the institutionalisation of a public use of reason jointly exercised by autonomous citizens. This model accounts for the communicative conditions that confer legitimating force on political opinion- and will-formation. These are precisely the conditions under which the political process can be presumed to generate reasonable results. A contest for power, if represented according to the liberal model of market competition, is determined by the political values and interests that are at best aggregated with equal weight in the political process; politics loses all reference to the normative core of the public use of reason. The republican trust in the force of political discourses stands in contrast to the liberal scepticism about reason. Such discourses are meant to allow one to discuss value orientations and interpretations of needs and wants, and then to change these in an *insightful way*.

But contemporary republicans tend to give this public communication a communitarian reading. It is precisely this move towards an *ethical constriction* of *political discourse* that I call into question. Politics may not be assimilated to a hermeneutical process of self-explication of a shared form of life or collective identity. Political questions may not be reduced to the types of ethical question where we, as members of a community, ask ourselves who we are and who we would like to be. In its communitarian interpretation the republican model is too idealistic, even within the limits of a purely normative analysis. On this reading, the democratic process is dependent on the virtues of citizens devoted to the public weal. This explanation of virtue had already led Rousseau to split the citizen oriented to the common good from the private man, who cannot be ethically overburdened. The unanimity of the political legislature was supposed to be secured in advance by a substantive ethical consensus. In contrast, a discourse-theory interpretation insists on the fact that democratic will-formation does not draw its legitimating force from a previous convergence of settled ethical convictions, but from both the communicative presuppositions that allow the better arguments to come into play in various forms of deliberation, and from the procedures that secure fair bargaining processes. Discourse theory breaks with a purely ethical conception of civic autonomy.

According to the communitarian view, there is a necessary connection between the deliberative conception of democracy and the reference to a concrete, substantively integrated, ethical community. Otherwise one could not explain, in this view, how the citizens' orientation to the common good would be at all possible. The individual, so the argument goes, can become aware of her co-membership in a collective form of life, and therewith become aware of a prior social bond, only in a practice exercised with others in common. The individual can get a clear sense of commonalties and differences, and hence a sense of who she is and who she would like to be, only in the public exchange with others who owe their identities to the same traditions and similar formation processes. This assimilation of political discourses to the clarification of a collective ethical self-understanding does not sit well with the function of the legislative processes they issue in. Legal statutes no doubt also contain teleological elements. But these involve more than just the hermeneutic explication of shared value orientations. By their very structure laws are determined by the question of which norms citizens want to adopt for regulating their living together. To be sure, discourses aimed at achieving self-understanding are also important for politics – I refer here to discourses in which the participants want to get a clear understanding of themselves as members of a specific nation, as members of a locale or a state, as inhabitants of a region, etc.; in which they want to determine which traditions they will continue; in which they strive to determine how they will treat each other, and how they will treat minorities and marginal groups: in short, discourses in which they want to be clear about the kind of society they want to live in. But these questions are subordinate to moral questions, being connected with pragmatic questions. Moral questions, in the narrow sense of the Kantian tradition, are questions of justice. The question having *priority* in legislative politics concerns how a matter can be regulated in the equal interest of all. The making of norms is primarily a justice issue and is gauged by principles that state what is equally good for all. And, unlike ethical questions, questions of justice are not related from the outset to a specific collective and its form of life. The politically enacted law of a concrete legal community must, if it is to be legitimate, be at least compatible with moral tenets that claim universal validity going beyond the legal community.

Moreover, compromises make up the bulk of political processes. Under conditions of religious, cultural and societal pluralism, politically relevant goals are often selected by interests and value orientations that are by no means constitutive of the identity of the community at large, hence for the whole of an intersubjectively shared form of life. The political interests and values that stand in conflict with each other without prospects of consensus are in need of a balancing that cannot be achieved through ethical discourses – even if the outcomes of bargaining processes are subject to the proviso that they must not violate a culture's agreed-upon basic values. The required balance of competing interests comes about as a compromise between parties that may rely on mutual threats. A legitimate kind of bargaining certainly depends on a prior regulation of fair terms for achieving results, terms which are acceptable for all parties on the basis of their differing preferences. While the debates on such regulations should assume the forms of practical discourse that neutralise power, bargaining itself well allows for strategic interactions. The deliberative mode of legislative practice is not just intended to ensure the ethical validity of laws. Rather, one can understand the complex validity claims of legal norms as the claim, on the one hand, to compromise competing interests in a manner compatible with the common good and, on the other hand, to bring universalistic principles of justice into the horizon of the specific form of life of a particular community.

In contrast to the ethical constriction of political discourse, the concept of deliberative politics acquires empirical reference only when we take account of the multiplicity of communicative forms of rational political will-formation. It is not discourse of an ethical type that could grant on its own the democratic genesis of law. Instead, deliberative politics should be conceived as a syndrome that depends on a network of fairly regulated bargaining processes and of various forms of argumentation, including pragmatic, ethical and moral discourses, each of which relies on different communicative presuppositions and procedures. In legislative politics the supply of information and the rational choice of strategies are interwoven with the balancing of interests, with the achievement of ethical self-understanding and the articulation of strong preferences, with moral justi-fication and tests of legal coherence. Thus 'dialogical' and 'instrumental' politics, the two ideal-types which Frank Michelman has opposed in a polarising fashion, do in fact interpenetrate in the medium of deliberations of various kinds.

Three images of state and society

If we start from this proceduralist conception of deliberative politics, this reading of democracy has implications for the concept of society. Both the liberal and the republican model presuppose a view of society as centred in the state – be it the state as guardian of a market-society or the state as the self-conscious institutionalisation of an ethical community.

According to the *liberal view*, the democratic process takes place exclu-sively in the form of compromises between competing interests. Fairness is supposed to be granted by the general and equal right to vote, the represen-tative composition of parliamentary bodies, by decision rules, and so on. Such rules are ultimately justified in terms of liberal basic rights. According to the *republican view*, democratic will-formation takes place in the form of an ethical–political discourse; here deliberation can rely on a culturally established background consensus shared by the citizenry. Discourse theory takes elements from both sides and integrates these into the concept of an ideal procedure for deliberation and decision-making. Weaving together pragmatic considerations, compromises, discourses of self-understanding and justice, this democratic procedure grounds the pre-sumption that reasonable or fair results are obtained. According to this proceduralist view, practical reason withdraws from universal human rights, or from the concrete ethical substance of a specific community, into the rules of discourse and forms of argumentation. In the final ana-lysis, the normative content arises from the very structure of communica-tive actions. These descriptions of the democratic process set the stage for different conceptualisations of state and society.

According to the republican view, the citizens' political opinion- and will-formation form the medium through which society constitutes itself as a political whole. Society is, from the very start, political society – *societas civilis*. Hence democracy becomes equivalent to the political self-organisation of society as a whole. This leads to a polemical *understand-ing of politics directed against the state apparatus*. In Hannah Arendt's political writings one can see where republican argumentation directs its salvos: in opposition to the privatism of a depoliticised population and in opposition to the acquisition of the legitimation through entrenched parties, the public sphere should be revitalised to the point where a regenerated citizenry can, through the forms of a decentralised self-governance, appropriate (once again) the power of pseudo-independent state agencies. From this perspective, society would finally develop into a political totality.

Whereas the separation of the state apparatus from society elicits a polemical reaction from the republican side, according to the liberal view it cannot be eliminated but only bridged by the democratic process. The regulated balancing of power and interests has need of constitutional channelling, of course. The democratic will-formation of self-interested citizens is laden with comparatively weak normative expectations. The constitution is supposed to tame the state apparatus through normative constraints (such as basic rights, separation of powers, etc.) and to force it, through the competition of political parties on the one hand and that between government and opposition on the other, to take adequate account of competing interests and value orientations. This *state-centred understanding of politics* can forgo the unrealistic assumption of a citizenry capable of collective action. Its focus is not so much the input of a rational political will-formation but the output of sensible and affective administrative accomplishments. Liberal argumentation aims its salvos against the potential disturbance of an administrative power that interferes with the spontaneous forces of self-regulating society. The liberal model hinges, not on the democratic self-determination of deliberating citizens, but on the legal institutionalisation of an economic society that is supposed to guarantee an essentially non-political common good by the satisfaction of private preferences.

Discourse theory invests the democratic process with normative connotations stronger than those found in the liberal model but weaker than those of the republican model. Once again, it takes elements from both sides and fits them together in a new way. In agreement with republicanism, it gives centre stage to the process of political opinion- and will-formation, but without understanding the constitution as something secondary; rather it conceives the principles of the constitutional state as a consistent answer to the questions of how the demanding communicative forms of a democratic opinion- and will-formation can be institutionalised. Discourse theory has the success of deliberative politics depend not on a collective acting citizenry but on the institutionalisation of the corresponding procedures and conditions of communication. Proceduralised popular sovereignty and a political system tied in to the peripheral networks of the political public sphere go hand-in-hand with the image of a *decentred society*. This concept of democracy no longer needs to operate with the notion of a social whole centred in the state and imagined as a goal-oriented subject writ large. Just as little does it represent the whole in a system of constitutional norms

141

mechanically regulating the interplay of powers and interests in accordance with the market model.

Discourse theory altogether jettisons certain premisses of the *philosophy of consciousness*. These premisses either invite us to ascribe the praxis of civic self-determination to one encompassing macro-subject or they have us apply the rule of law to many isolated private subjects. The former approach views the citizenry as a collective actor that reflects the whole and acts for it; in the latter, individual actors function as dependent variables in system processes that move along blindly. Discourse theory works instead with the *higher level intersubjectivity* of communication processes that flow through both the parliamentary bodies and the informal networks of the public sphere. Within and without the parliamentary complex, these subjectless forms of communication constitute arenas in which a more or less rational opinion- and will-formation can take place.

Informal public opinion-formation generates 'influence'; influence is transformed into 'communicative power' through the channels of political elections; and communicative power is again transformed into 'administrative power' through legislation. As in the liberal model, the boundaries between 'state' and 'society' are respected; but in this case, civil society provides the social basis of autonomous public spheres that remain as distinct from the economic system as from the administration. This understanding of democracy suggests a new balance between the three resources of money, administrative power and solidarity, from which modern societies meet their need for integration. The normative implications are obvious: the integrative force of 'solidarity', which can no longer be drawn solely from sources of communicative action, should develop through widely expanded and differentiated public spheres as well as through legally institutionalised procedures of democratic deliberation and decision-making. It should gain the strength to hold its own against the two other mechanisms of social integration – money and administrative power. This view has implications for how one understands legitimation and popular sovereignty.

On the liberal view, democratic will-formation has the exclusive function of *legitimating* the existence of political power. Election results are the licence to assume governmental power, whereas the government must justify the use of power to the public. On the republican view, democratic will-formation has the significantly stronger function of *constituting* society as a political community and keeping the memory of this founding act alive with each election. The government is not only empowered to exercise a largely open mandate, but also programmatically committed to carry out certain policies. It remains bound to a self-governing political community. Discourse theory brings a third idea into play: the procedures and communicative presuppositions of democratic opinion- and will-formation function as the most important sluices for the discursive rationalisation of the decisions of an administration constrained by law and statute.

Rationalisation means more than mere legitimation but less than the constitution of political power. The power available to the administration changes its aggregate conditions as soon as it emerges from a public use of reason and a communicative power which do not just monitor the exercise of political power in a belated manner but more or less programme it as well. Notwithstanding this discursive rationalisation, only the administrative system itself can 'act'. The administration is a subsystem specialised for collectively binding decisions, whereas the communicative structures of the public sphere comprise a far-flung network of sensors that in the first place react to the pressure of society-wide problematics and stimulate influential opinions. The public opinion that is worked up via democratic procedures into communicative power cannot 'rule' of itself, but can only point the use of administrative power in specific directions.

The concept of *popular sovereignty* stems from the republican appropriation and revelation of the early modern notion of sovereignty initially associated with absolutist regimes. The state, which monopolises all the means for a legitimate implementation of force, is seen as an overpowering concentrate of power – as the Leviathan. This idea was transferred by Rousseau to the will of the united people. He refused the strength of the Leviathian, with its classical idea of the self-rule of free and equal citizens, and combined it with his modern concept of autonomy. Despite this sublimation, the concept of sovereignty remains bound to the notion of an embodiment in the assembled, physically present, people. According to the republican view, the people are the bearers of a sovereignty that in principle cannot be delegated: in their sovereign character the people cannot have others represent them. Liberalism opposes this with the more realistic view that in the constitutional state any authority originating from the people is exercised only 'by means of elections and voting and by specific legislative, executive, and judicial organs'.[3]

These two views would exhaust the alternatives only if we had to conceive state and society in terms of the whole and its parts – where the whole is constituted either by a sovereign citizenry or by a constitution. To the discourse theory of democracy corresponds, however, the image of a decentred society. To be sure, with the political public sphere the proceduralist model sets off an arena for the detection, identification and interpretation of those problems that affect society as a whole. But the 'self' of the self-organising legal community here disappears in the subjectless forms of communication that regulate the flow of deliberations in such a way that their fallible results enjoy the presupposition of rationality. This is not to denounce the intuition connected with the idea of popular sovereignty but to interpret it in intersubjective terms. Popular sovereignty, even if it becomes anonymous, retreats into democratic procedures and the legal implications of their demanding communicative presuppositions only in order to make itself felt as communicatively generated power.

Strictly speaking, this communicative power springs from the interactions between legally institutionalised will-formation and culturally mobilised publics. The latter for their part find a basis in the associations of civil society quite distinct from both state and economy alike.

Read in procedural terms, the idea of popular sovereignty refers to a context that, while enabling the self-organisation of a legal community, is not at the disposal of the citizens' will in any way. Deliberation is certainly supposed to provide the medium for a more or less conscious integration of the *legal community*; but this mode does not extend to the whole of society in which the political system is *embedded* as only one among several sub-systems. Even in its own proceduralist self-understanding, deliberative politics remains a component of a complex society which, as a whole, resists the normative approach practised in legal theory. In this regard, the discourse-theory reading of democracy has a point of contact with a detached sociological approach that considers the political system neither as the peak nor the centre, nor even as the formative model, of society in general, but as just one action system among others. On the other hand, politics must still be able to communicate, through the medium of law, with all the other legitimately ordered spheres of action, however these happen to be structured and steered.

Notes

1 This essay is a version of a paper originally published in *Constellations*, Vol. 1, No. 1, 1994.
2 F.I. Michelman in *Florida Law Review*, Vol. 41, 1989, pp. 446f.
3 Cf. *The Basic Law of the Federal Republic of Germany*, Article 20, section 2.

11

THE PROBLEM OF JUSTICE IN A MULTICULTURAL SOCIETY

The response of discourse ethics

Karl-Otto Apel

Globalization and multiculturalism as a moral problem

It seems to me that *globalization*, i.e. planetary intertwinement of human relations on the levels of technology, economics and politics, in our day is an indisputable fact. And, in my opinion, it is an historically irreversible fact as well. This does not mean that those people are wrong who point to very problematical aspects of the recent development of *globalization*, especially with regard to the global order of the market-led economy, which – notwithstanding its efficiency – seems to result in a growing polarization between the rich and the poor.[1] However, as it seems to me, there is no reasonable option towards a turn or roll back of the techno-logical, economical and political development of globalization. There is only the serious problem of how to deal with, i.e. to respond to, the challenge of globalization on the levels of culture, morality and a morally inspired reorganization of law.

One of the most comprehensive and important aspects of the *secondary globalization* that is required in our day seems to consist in the organiza-tion of human relationships in the way of a *multicultural society*. The indispensability of such an order on the global level – on the level of *cosmopolitan law* – seems to be evident and incontestable;[2] but the cosmo-politan order of law for the peaceful coexistence and cooperation of all the different ethnic and religious communities, I suggest, must also become the paradigm of the organization of all constitutional states; rather than, for example, the *nationalistic* demand for ethnic purge or the fanatic call for unification in the sense of religious fundamentalism.

However, the conception of *multiculturalism* in our day still meets with enraged resistance not only from the side of extreme nationalism or funda-mentalism but also from the side of the inhabitants of national states, in the traditional European sense. These people simply are afraid of multi-culturalism. In most cases they do not properly understand the term *multi-culturalism*, since they are not accustomed to the possible separation between the *national state* in the sense of an ethnic or ethnico-religious tradition and a constitutional state that might even demand *constitutional patriotism* on a level above one's belonging to an ethnico-religious tradi-tion, as is the case in the United States of America.

In this context, it is especially important to reflect on the fact that it was *Europa* that in modern times, through the colonialism and imperialism of its maritime powers, and later through its technological and economical superiority, initiated the *globalization* process. Hence, it is primarily Europa and its transatlantic filiations, especially the United States, that are now confronted with the task of preventing the imminent 'clash of cultures' that could come about through the reactions of the *non-Occidental* cul-tures and the poor of the Third World against the effects of globalization, i.e. the present world system of technological, economic and political power.[3]

In this situation, it seems to me, it is a special task of philosophy to make understandable and to ground or justify by principles the conception of multiculturalism which today has to be accepted as an indispensable part of the response to globalization on the level of culture, morality and law. How can philosophy fulfil this task? In what follows I will try to answer this question from the point of view of a transcendental-pragmatic dis-course ethics.

The complementarity structure of the moral problem of multiculturalism: a preliminary suggestion

In order to win juridico-moral access to our problem, let me start this inquiry by considering talk of the 'right to one's own culture' which is used with regard to people belonging to minorities. In my opinion, this talk may be understood as referring to a fundamental human right. The reason for this lies in the fact that one cannot recognize the *identity* of a person without simultaneously recognizing him or her as belonging to a particular socio-cultural form of life. Thus far (to that extent) the recogni-tion of a person in this case is not a matter of respecting the *universalized other* as such but rather a matter of recognizing the *concrete other* in one of his or her particular but not accidental properties. Nevertheless, talk of someone's '*right* to his own culture' points to the fact that what is at stake here is not only a matter of respecting the *pluralism* of particular cul-tural traditions but also – at the same time – respecting a *right* that befits *all* human persons as such. To that extent it is a *universal norm of justice* that has to be recognized. This universal norm obviously has even to set limits (or impose constraints) to the acknowledgement of the pluralism of

146

cultural values. For justice, in conjunction with co-responsibility, belongs to the universally valid moral condition of the coexistence and cooperation of different cultures in the face of the common problems of humankind.

On the basis of these initial considerations, I already arrive at the conclusion that, from a *moral* perspective, the conception of a multicultural society has to be conceived as grounded by a principle of *complementarity*: what has to be recognized here is the complementarity of polar-opposite values which must presuppose each other but cannot be reduced to each other: *viz.*, on the one hand, the *pluralism* of belonging to different sociocultural forms of life and their different value traditions and, on the other hand, the *universalism* of fundamental norms of justice and of co-responsibility concerning the solution of common problems of humanity.

This looks quite promising as a lead-in to our problem of the ethical treatment of multiculturalism, but on the sophisticated level of today's professional philosophy, great and apparently unsolvable problems here arise with regard to our quest for a satisfactory mediation of *universalism* and *particularism*.

The aporetics of the theory of intercultural justice in contemporary philosophy

In order to get an impression of these difficulties let us look at the discussion between the 'liberals' and the 'communitarians', which originated in the USA but in the meantime has become international at least in the Western world.[4] I cannot display here the whole concern and all the different – not always coherent – arguments of both sides.[5] But I will, for the purposes of my topic, select and typically reconstruct one central argument of the *communitarians* and the reaction to it by the *liberals*, which was, in my opinion, aporetical. I will start with some preliminary considerations.

I have pointed out already that the conception of the constitutional state on the basis of a multicultural society must unite two contrary aspects: acknowledgement of the particularity and plurality of cultural traditions, on the one hand, and respect for a unitary law and its moral foundation, on the other hand. These two aspects have to be related to each other in such a way that no contradiction is constituted, but rather a relationship of complementarity. But how should we conceive of this, if we must suppose that not only the unitary constitution (of law) has to correspond to the unitary moral norm of justice but that each of the many different cultural traditions in its order of strong values implies the moral value of justice as well?

In order to avoid a contradiction, I will try to distinguish (differentiate) between two perspectives on our problem: the *deontological perspective of norms* that are universally valid for all coexisting forms of life, on the one hand, and *the teleological perspective of an authentic evaluation* of

147

the situational circumstances within the context of an individual or collective ethic of the good life, on the other hand.[6] And, in order to conceive as possible the realization and stabilization of an order of law for all citizens of a constitutional state, I will – along with John Rawls – assign priority to the deontic 'right' for all to the 'good' of the comprehensive views of strong values of the different cultural traditions.[7] I am prepared to accept that this conception of the relationship between different perspectives is a presupposition of a *complementaristic solution* to our problem; but precisely at this point, I must introduce the main argument of the *communitarians*, in order not to make things too easy for myself.

The communitarians – e.g. Charles Taylor, Michael Sandel and Alasdair MacIntyre – have well understood and taken into account the insights of hermeneutical phenomenology – those of Martin Heidegger and Hans-Georg Gadamer, for instance – concerning the *a priori* of 'facticity' and 'historicity' of our 'being-in-the-world', and our corresponding 'pre-understanding' of the world, as well as the insights of the later Wittgenstein and his followers concerning the 'interwovenness' of 'language games' and 'life forms'. And, in the case of Taylor,[8] these insights have been integrated with the older insights of Hegel concerning the dependence of all material values of morality on the 'substantial ethos' (*Sittlichkeit*) of the 'objective spirit', as it is historically realized. Now, from these presuppositions, which are widely accepted today, the following thesis seems to result with considerable plausibility.

All normatively relevant conceptions of morality that have a motivational significance, and which to that extent can determine someone's project of the good life and personal identity, are conditioned by the 'substantial ethos' (*Sittlichkeit*) of a community tradition which constitutes the *a priori of facticity* of a concrete pre-understanding of the world. This conviction suggests that even the fundamental norms of a deontological ethics of justice and their claim to universal validity can owe their meaning content, and thus their ethical substance, only to a particular community tradition of morality. Apart from this genealogical dependence, they must lose – so it appears – their motivational impact and be reduced to an abstract powerless (impotent) 'ought', of the kind attributed by Hegel to Kant's 'categorical imperative'.

Now, if this holds good, then also the ethos of *positive freedom*, that is, of political participation of the citizens in a republic or democracy, and so also even the fundamental norm of justice, which lies at the basis of the constitution, must be motivated by the substantial ethos of a community tradition; and the appeal to abstract, universally valid, rights of all citizens as human beings can be conceived – it seems – only as an expression of purely *negative freedom* of individuals who can be motivated – let's say, in the sense of Hobbes – only by their strategically rational self-interest;

hence they cannot be motivated towards a commitment to the common good. So much for the main argument of the *communitarians*.

When we apply this argument to the problem of the constitution of a multicultural society in the world of today, we are confronted, so it appears, with a disastrous difficulty: the complementaristic conception of the relationship between the universally valid 'right' and the 'good' of the 'comprehensive views' of the particular traditions of cultures seems to dissolve itself. On the communitarian presuppositions, it can at best be conceived of as itself being a *value* deriving from a substantial synthesis of value traditions. This synthesis has to be thought of as comprehensive to the extent that it is able also keep up with and satisfy the demand of universally valid justice.

I understand that the communitarian and quasi-Hegelian synthesis of 'strong values' of the Occidental tradition in Taylor's monumental work, *The Sources of the Self. The Making of Modern Identity*, has to be interpreted in this way. This work presents itself as a retrospective reconstruction and synthesis of the 'concrete general' (in Hegel's sense) of Occidental morality (*Sittlichkeit*) which as such, i.e. as a *historical totality*, covers or comprises also the claim to universally valid justice.

However, the *aporia* of this quasi-Hegelian synthesis, in my opinion, is the following: with regard to the present world situation, a retrospective–hermeneutic synthesis of the Occidental values *à la* Taylor cannot equate itself with an *interculturally neutral* conception of justice on the presupposition of an actual plurality of different value-traditions with equal rights. For, with regard to the non-Occidental value-traditions, the comprehensive synthesis of Occidental value traditions has the same structure as any particular value tradition of a given socio-cultural life form.

For, we cannot expect today that the Occidental value synthesis could once more, as Hegel suggested, *integrate* the value traditions of the non-Occidental cultures – say of China, India and the Islamic world – as being just pre-stages of the Occidental tradition. Hence it follows that Taylor's quasi-Hegelian synthesis cannot *integrate* but only *compete with* the non-Occidental value-traditions in our present world situation; that is, in the context of a multicultural society existing on the global scale.

The reason for this *aporia* of Taylor's quasi-Hegelian synthesis, in my opinion, consists in its lack of a philosophical *basis* for its conception of interculturally neutral justice. Even *justice*, we have to remember, on communitarian presuppositions, can be conceived of only as a strong value-claim on behalf of a cultural tradition. If this were correct, then, on communitarian presuppositions, the only possible alternative to Taylor's quasi-Hegelian value-synthesis is *culture-specific value relativism*. This latter position, which is widely accepted today, must renounce – together with the Hegelian claim to an all-embracing synthesis of culture – any possibility of a universal validity of intercultural justice.

When one considers the political realities that characterize the world of today, one can find, even in liberal democracies, many examples of naive strategical versions of the culture-centric claim of sticking to a community-bound value tradition. The practical consequence of this position in most cases is the public suggestion of an assimilation of the foreigners or the minorities to the dominant life-form.

But what about the response of the 'liberals' to these problems, which in the Anglo-Saxon world were, at least implicitly, put on the agenda by the communitarian movement (whereas in old Europe there were prefigurations of *historicism–relativism* already in the nineteenth century, not to speak of the nationalistic, later rationalistic, or even totalitarianistic, versions of a militant communitarianism)? It is deeply significant, I suggest, that some prominent liberals among today's philosophers seem to be so much impressed by the arguments of the communitarians (and other historicists) that they have almost given up the traditional universalism of the liberal tradition – the tradition of *human rights*.

I will, in the present context, deal only with two prominent thinkers, John Rawls and Richard Rorty, of whom the first for a long time was considered to be the foremost contemporary representative of a *universalistic* philosophy of justice. But I will approach Rawls via Rorty, who also calls himself a 'liberal', but gave a provocative interpretation of the later work of Rawls in the spirit of a relativistic version of communitarianism.[9]

In his essay 'The Priority of Democracy to Philosophy' (1991), which is a comment on Rawls' essay 'Justice as Fairness: Political Not Metaphysical' (1985),[10] Rorty starts from the tenet of political liberalism that, with regard to the claims of philosophy, the democratic constitutional state has to take a neutral stand with regard to all claims of religious confessions and other value-traditions. One is neither urged nor entitled to judge the truth of 'comprehensive views', to use Rawls' terminology. However, from this supposition, which in my opinion is quite correct, Rorty draws the eccentric conclusion that a philosophical foundation or justification of the political position of the liberal constitutional state is not meaningful: it is neither needed nor is it possible. From the philosophical neutrality of the liberal democratic state it follows, on Rorty's account, that philosophers who confess to being democrats must suppose that the cultural tradition belonging to the institutions of the liberal–democratic states of the West, especially of the USA, is the 'contingent' but nevertheless solely possible *basis of consent* for all discussion on political questions.

This means that philosophers should not try to defend democracy and its neutrality towards comprehensive world views against possible opponents of this tradition by appeal to independent, universally valid philosophical arguments; although they may, on Rorty's account, very well try to 'persuasively'[11] propagate the Western democratic tradition, including even its 'utopia'. But in the case of a confrontation with opponents who do not share the presuppositions of the democratic tradition – Rorty mentions Nietzsche and Loyola, but he could equally well have thought of Khomeini, Mao Tse Tung, or the presidents of Singapore, Malaysia and Indonesia – 'persuasion' could arrive at its limit. In such a case, Rorty suggests, Westerners should think as follows:

> . . . we heirs of the enlightenment think of enemies of liberal democracy like Nietzsche or Loyola as, to use Rawls' word, 'mad'. . . . They are not crazy because they have mistaken the historical nature of human beings. They are crazy because the limits of sanity are set by what *we* can take seriously. This, in turn, is determined by our upbringing, our historical situation.
>
> (pp. 187–8)

To make clear what he means, we can refer to what Rorty had stated a little earlier in this 1991 paper: we should not resort to universally valid human rights ('because this would be an attempt to enjoy the benefits of metaphysics without assuming the appropriate responsibilities'); but

> we shall still need something to distinguish the sort of individual conscience we respect from the sort we condemn as 'fanatical'. This can only be something relatively local and ethnocentric – the tradition of a particular community, the consensus of a particular culture. According to this view, what counts as rational or as fanatical is relative to the group to which we think it necessary to justify ourselves – to the body of shared belief that determines the reference of the word 'we'.
>
> (pp. 176f)

In my opinion, it is difficult to find arguments in contemporary Western philosophy that outdo Rorty's arguments in making it easy for fundamentalists and nationalists of all stripes to defend their culture-centrism or ethno-centrism against the Western idea of liberal democracy and human rights. What Rorty in fact shows is that historicism–relativism, reducing itself to culture-centrism through proclaiming one's own tradition to be the sole basis of consent for an intercultural dialogue, quickly reduces *ad absurdum* that liberalism to which it is allegedly connected.

In the context of political *praxis*, it is bound to lead to a position which is at least incompatible with the establishment of a multicultural society – be it on the cosmopolitan or on the regional level of human coexistence under a commonly acknowledged law of justice.

I will not continue here to quarrel with the position of Rorty; but I will come back to the fact that Rorty in the paper from which I quoted – 'The Priority of Democracy to Philosophy' – claims to interpret the position of the later Rawls. It is his own 'thoroughly historicist and anti-universalist' attitude that Rorty ascribes to Rawls as well. For his purposes of a 'political theory of justice', Rorty suggests, Rawls does not need 'Socratism', i.e. the idea that anybody who is willing to listen to reason – to hear all the arguments – can be brought around to the truth, because 'the human self has a center (a divine spark, or a truth-tracking faculty called "reason") and . . . argumentation will, given time and patience, penetrate to this center. . . . We are free to see the self centerless, as a historical contingency all the way through' (Rorty 1991: 188). Hence, on Rorty's account, Rawls 'can be content with a notion of the human self as a centerless web of historically conditioned beliefs and desires', and therefore he can assume as well that democratic agreement about justice 'should lead to whatever intersubjective reflective equilibrium may be obtainable, given the contingent make-up of the sujects in question' (*ibid*. 191).

Contrary to my first reaction on reading Rorty's paper, I am today inclined to think that Rorty's hermeneutic pretension is not completely extravagant. Hence I will try in what follows to reconstruct, in the light of Rorty's perspective, the development of Rawls' own interpretation of his 'theory of justice', taking the risk of giving a very selective and simplified account.

Already, in the original version of Rawls' *Theory of Justice* of 1971, I found an unsolved problem of foundation. For the proper foundation of his theory was not provided, as Rawls himself pointed out several times later, by the 'rational choice' (in the sense of the theory of decision and games) of the parties concluding the contract in the 'original position'. (This indeed would have implied that the whole theory of justice had failed from the outset by being subject to the Hobbesian *aporia*, that the 'sense of justice' cannot be derived from the calculated strategical self-interest of those who conclude a contract.[12]) The foundation of Rawls' theory was rather contained in those presuppositions that Rawls himself – in his later so called 'Kantian constructivism'[13] – invested from the outset, as he imposed certain constraints on the 'original position' (such as the 'veil of ignorance' concerning the social position of the voters in the order of justice to be chosen): constraints that were to compel the original voters to imagine themselves in the situation of each possible citizen and thus, as free and equal voters, to take a choice that would be strategically 'rational' and, at the same time, 'reasonable' in the sense of exemplifying 'justice as fairness'.

(The problem of intercultural justice in a multicultural society was also taken into account by this conception in so far as Rawls supposed that the strategical rationality, once released and reasonably restricted, could also refer to the chances of the different, possibly even incommensurable, 'comprehensive doctrines' of the good within the society being established.)

However, what about the foundation of Rawls' idea of 'reasonableness', i.e. of justice as fairness, that was invested in the constraints on the 'original position'? This ultimate foundation of his theory Rawls could provide only through recourse to the 'reflective equilibrium' to be reached by a procedure of mutual correction between the philosopher's 'sense of justice' and the 'common sense of justice' (that would even include that of the voters in the 'original position').[14]

With his suggestion Rawls took recourse, I suggest, to a device that is in fact unavoidable in every case of meaning explication concerning concepts that have not yet been defined. To that extent, there is a close affinity between Rawls' concept of 'reflective equilibrium' and the 'circle of understanding' of the Continental philosophy of 'hermeneutics', in the sense of Dilthey, Heidegger and Gadamer. But in our context, where the universalistic counterweight – *viz.* intercultural justice – to the hermeneutic interpretation of one's own particular cultural tradition is searched for, an ultimate foundation for justice achieved by recourse to the 'common sense' is too weak. It cannot mobilize the resistance of an independent yard-stick against the impact of one's own cultural tradition which anyway enjoys genetic priority in one's pre-understanding of the life world. This fact – i.e. the tendency at least to fall victim to historicism-relativism – has been attested by the development of Rawls' self-interpretation in a way similar to that of the philosophies of Dilthey, Heidegger and Gadamer, as Rorty has correctly stated. Let me try to show this.

In his paper of 1985 – 'Justice as Fairness: Political not Metaphysical' – Rawls adopts the following self-interpretation:

> The essential point is this: as a practical matter no *general moral conception* can provide the basis for a public conception of justice in a modern democratic society. The social and historical conditions of such a society have their origins in the wars of religion following the Reformation and the development of the principle of toleration, and in the growth of constitutional government and the institutions of large market economies. These conditions profoundly affect the requirements of a workable conception of political justice: such a conception must allow for a diversity of doctrines and a plurality of conflicting and indeed *incommensurable conceptions of the good* affirmed by the members of existing democratic societies.
>
> (p. 225, emphasis added)

At this point, Rawls obviously disputes – in a way similar to Rorty's – that a *political* theory of justice can have its *basis* (i.e. the foundation of its validity) in a 'philosophical' conception of 'morality'. Instead, he has recourse only to the *historical genesis* of the conditions of the modern democratic societies of the West. The former universalistic thesis of the *priority of the right to the good* of the different value-traditions is still maintained, in a sense, but it has taken the form of a *political–pragmatic* suggestion, as a *necessary condition* to be fulfilled with regard to the plurality of different conceptions of the good in a given society. Apart from this function, there is no longer any sense of an *autonomous foundation* for a universally valid conception of justice.

But on these novel conditions, where have we to find the *legitimizing criterion* for the politically applicable conception of justice?

Rawls seems to give an answer to this question by his conception of 'overlapping consensus', which is central to his theory of 'political liberalism'.[15] This conception seems to constitute an equivalent of his conception of the 'reflective equilibrium' on the level of a purely *political* 'theory of justice'.[16] In order to quickly expose the point of this conception, I will quote a characteristic passage from Rawls' 'Answer to Habermas':[17]

> I think of justice as fairness as working out a liberal conception of justice for a democratic regime, and one that might be endorsed, so it is hoped, by all reasonable comprehensive doctrines that exist in a democracy regulated by it [or some similar view. . . .] The *central idea* is that political liberalism moves within the category of the *political* and leaves philosophy as it is.

But how, on these conditions, have we to conceive of the normative relationship between the *conception* of justice to be endorsed by all different comprehensive doctrines 'of the good' and the content of these doctrines themselves? Rawls' answer to this question reads:

> It [the political conception of justice] can be formulated independently of any particular comprehensive doctrine, religious, philosophical, or moral. While we suppose that it may be derived from, or supported by, or otherwise related to one or more comprehensive doctrines (indeed we hope it can be thus related to many such doctrines), it is not presented as depending upon, or as presupposing, any such view.

I understand that by this answer is expressed the point of the relationship between the conception of 'political justice' and the conception of the 'overlapping consensus' of the different 'comprehensive views' in a multicultural society. The novel point of the highly sophisticated conception seems to lie in the postulate that the freestanding 'theory of justice' should at the same time be independent of any 'comprehensive doctrine' of the good and derivable from as many of them as possible.

But, if this interpretation is correct, then, from my perspective, the crucial question to address to Rawls' theory of 'political liberalism' is this: can this theory still – like the *Theory of Justice* of 1971 – be understood as the basis for a complementaristic conception of the relationship between the universally valid 'right' and the culture-dependent 'good'? And can it, to that extent, provide the basis for the realization of justice in a *multi-cultural* society?

Presumably, Rawls would at present – in a way similar to Rorty's – refuse (repudiate) talk of a 'philosophical basis' or 'foundation', or he would resort to the conception of 'reflective equilibrium', but restricting this to the persons as citizens in a democratic society.[18] But even if we suspend the question of how Rawls could argue for a (hypothetical) conception of *justice as fairness*, not only independently of any 'comprehensive doctrine' of the good but also without any recourse to a *moral-*philosophical foundation, we are still left with the following question concerning the pragmatic political function of Rawls' novel programme: can it ensure a criterion of intercultural justice (on a regional and, especially, a global level) by replacing the basis of an autonomous philosophical foundation with just a striving for a *factual* 'overlapping consensus' among the competing 'comprehensive views': a factual consensus as broad as possible?

I do not doubt that by following the Rawlsian device, we may – through persuasion and negotiations – reach pragmatically successful compromises on the level of *politics*. But can this method normatively guarantee that an agreement – say among conflicting parties – is not reached at the cost of others, who cannot take part in the agreement but nevertheless are affected by it – that is, by its effects? In other words: Can the principle of the 'overlapping consensus' replace a philosophical *principle of universalization*, as that was proposed by Kant as a *moral* basis for justice?

I do not think so. An 'overlapping consensus' in the Rawlsian sense would be just a *political* device that has emancipated itself from philosophy through paying the price of delivering itself to *factual* conditions of time and power. Therefore, in contradistinction to a moral–philosophical principle, it cannot function as a 'regulative principle' in the Kantian sense, i.e. as a principle that can be used even as a yard-stick for trying to change the direction of the political conditions towards ensuring *intercultural justice*. Let me try to elucidate this through an example.

In the ancient world, during the time of Plato and later during that of the Christian apostle Paul, that is, still within the Roman Empire, which was based on a multicultural society comprising many different religious and metaphysical value traditions, there was no *overlapping consensus* attainable concerning the injustice of *slavery*. Still later, in the sixteenth century, in the famous controversy between the scholastic theologian Sepulveda and Bartholome de Las Casas about the just and Christian treatment of the Indians in the Spanish colonies, Sepulveda could appeal to the ancient 'overlapping consensus' and the arguments of Aristotle in favour of slavery. Would such a discrepancy between the results of an 'overlapping consensus' and the *regulative and universalizable principle of moral philosophy* be excluded in our present world?

I do not think so. Rawls himself obviously has come to believe that today, at the global level, an 'overlapping consensus' on, for example, the rightness of the politico-juridical principle of 'democracy' – i.e., as I understand it, of the liberty and equality of all citizens with regard to participation in legislation – cannot be attained. It is not surprising, therefore, that Rawls has recently construed a novel version of his 'theory of justice' (under the title 'The Law of Peoples') in which he dispenses with the principle of *liberal democracy* in favour of the demand of a 'well-ordered society' ('liberal' or 'hierarchical').[19]

Of course, there are other possibly *unjust* aspects of what has been, or can at present be, reached by way of an 'overlapping consensus' on the global scale. The most relevant examples may be the exclusion of the poor of the Third World and the very insufficient consideration of future generations by the international agreements underlying the present globalization of the capitalist order of market forces.

On the whole, one may say that the development of Rawls' philosophy follows the tendency to replace the moral-philosophical theory of justice which was inspired by Kant with a conception of political pragmatism. As representatives of pragmatist liberalism, Rawls and Rorty have obviously given up the possibility of a philosophical foundation for a moral theory of justice, because they have come to believe – thus far alongside the communitarians – that each type of moral philosophy, as well as metaphysics and theology, must belong to the culture-dependent 'comprehensive doctrines of the good' and therefore cannot be interculturally neutral, i.e. *impartial*. (The difference – if it is one – between Rorty and Rawls now seems to lie only in the fact that Rorty, being an 'ironical sceptic', has given up every mediation through philosophical arguments between (conflicting) culture-dependent 'comprehensive views'; whereas Rawls makes the attempt – original of its kind – to transform his former *complementaristic* philosophy of the priority of the right to the good into pragmatic political advice for the context-relative attainment of a factual intercultural consensus, as broad as possible, about acceptable norms of justice.

Now the question is: have we to be content with this solution, if we want to avoid culture- or tradition-dependent dogmatism?

Transcendental pragmatic discourse ethics as a basis for resolving problems of multiculturalism

As I indicated at the beginning of this essay, my reconstruction of the aporetics of the debate between the communitarians and the liberals concerning political justice was only to set the stage for the introduction of my own attempt at a solution to the moral problems of multiculturalism. I confine myself here to introducing the approach of *discourse ethics* through an attempted refutation of the main (historical) assumptions shared by Rorty and Rawls with the communitarians.

The first assumption of this kind obviously consists in the supposition that a sufficient concept of justice as fairness is somehow available in the Western tradition without a need for a philosophical foundation of its normative criteria. The second assumption, internally connected with the first, consists in the conviction that every possible *philosophical foundation* of justice must be related to a culture-dependent 'comprehensive doctrine of the good', and to that extent cannot be interculturally neutral or impartial.

My main argument against the *first* assumption, I have already suggested indirectly in the preceding discussion. It amounts to the following thesis: a moral-philosophical foundation of justice as fairness cannot simply be dispensed with, as is shown by the price the later Rawls has to pay for doing so. For the substitution of the search for an 'overlapping consensus' in the place of a philosophical foundation of a *universalizable principle* cannot provide a regulative principle for preventing an unjust solution at the cost of excluded parties and for changing the direction of the political conditions towards a fundamental norm of justice. Precisely such a principle, however, is needed today in the face of the globalization of all moral-political problems, e.g. in the case of the discussion about *human rights* on a global scale, or, tied up with this discussion, in the case of conferences about *the global economic order* or an adequate ecological policy.

Now, the desired principle of justice (and co-responsibility) can indeed be grounded, I suggest, by the transcendental pragmatic foundation of discourse ethics. This foundation – and this is my response to the *second* assumption shared by Rawls, Rorty and the communitarians – is neither a *comprehensive doctrine of the good* in the sense of metaphysics or theology, nor is it a foundation the validity of which is dependent on a particular cultural perspective, but it is *strictly impartial* with regard to all different cultural traditions as well as personal worldviews.

How can this thesis be defended against the widely shared conviction concerning the *culture-dependence* of any philosophical foundation of justice?

In order to prepare my answer, let me first recall the difficulties. If and when one follows the insights of *hermeneutic* phenomenology concerning the *a priori* of pre-understanding the life world, which is tied up with the *a priori* of belonging always already to a community of speech and cultural tradition, then it is indeed plausible to assume that with regard to ethics also, i.e. to all valuations of something as good or bad, we are under the sway of a particular cultural tradition. (This, by the way, does not preclude the possibility that our value-judgements differ, nay even conflict, in

157

particular cases. For not only are our individual experiences different but our pertinent community traditions – especially in the case of complex high cultures – are by no means as homogeneous as is sometimes suggested by communitarians. Nevertheless, at least the negative thesis of the *non-independence* of our value-judgements in respect of particular cultural traditions can hardly be contested.)

However, what about this very insight, available on the level of philosophy, which provokes the further insight that there may be conflicts between the different but coexisting cultural value-traditions? And what about the insight, immediately tied up with the preceding one, that there is a problem of *intercultural justice* that has to be solved in an impartial way? Of course, even these reflexive insights could be reached within the frame of a particular cultural tradition – in our Occidental tradition, first through the Greek enlightenment, but approximated in the other philosophical traditions of the 'axis-time' (K. Jaspers) as well;[20] and these insights could even become conventional in the post-Enlightenment tradition of our culture. But does this mean – as for example MacIntyre suggests – that they have proved to be culture-dependent not only by their *genesis* but with regard to their *validity*?

The problem we are dealing with here becomes even clearer when we consider the philosophical *principle of justice* that suggests itself on the level of a reflexive comparison of the different, or even the conflicting, value-traditions in a multicultural society. I mean the principle, already suggested in the preceding, that all just solutions must be acceptable not only to those parties who are present and influential at the level of factual agreements but by all people who might be affected by the effects of our solutions. This principle, I think, would lose its sense, if its validity were to be dependent on just one or some of the conflicting cultural traditions in question. But then how can we otherwise provide a philosophical foundation for our principle? Have we to take recourse to religion or dogmatic metaphysics? Something else is not left, according to the opinion of most philosophers today, if one sticks to demanding a foundation of principles.

We have now reached the point of apparent advicelessness in contemporary philosophy. In my opinion, this 'a-poria' is brought about by the fact that the dominant directions of contemporary philosophy do not know any longer how to conceive of a *transcendental* foundation of principles that would not be *metaphysical*. And, at this point, one has to concede that Kant himself never managed to elucidate and clearly stick to the distinction between critical 'transcendental' philosophy and 'dogmatic metaphysics' which, after all, he suggested. This holds true, especially with regard to ethics.[21]

I can, at this point, only very briefly point to the *transcendental pragmatic* way of an ultimate foundation for ethics. My main thesis, in this context, is the following: the principle of justice I have formulated already – namely the principle of the acceptability of the consequences of our problem solution for all affected people – has its rational foundation in this non-empirical 'fact of reason' (Kant): the principle has by necessity always already[22] been acknowledged by everyone who argues – about whatever topic – with regard to his relationship to all the members of a (potentially unlimited) discourse community. This reflexively uncircumventible fact of acknowledgement is not an appeal to a metaphysical axiom (which would itself stand in need of further grounding or would be stated dogmatically), but it could be confirmed through the following test of transcendental pragmatic grounding: who seriously argues cannot deny – on pain of a performative self-contradiction – that he or she presupposes already, together with his or her claim to truth as intersubjective validity, the validity of certain moral claims and duties with regard to all possible discourse partners. Among these fundamental claims and duties are at least the following two, which are internally connected: the equal rights of all possible discourse partners and the equal co-responsibility of all for the discovery and solution of morally relevant problems.

This ultimate foundation of discourse ethics holds, of course, also with regard to the discursive treatment of moral problems within the context of a multicultural society: for example, with regard to the foundation and the juridical codification of human rights and their relationship to the values and value-hierarchies of the different cultural traditions. And here it shows itself that it simply is not true that the participants in such a discourse are completely determined by or, as it were, immersed in the culture-bound pre-understanding of the life-world. The current analysis of this 'pre-understanding', which is usually inspired by Heidegger, Gadamer or Wittgenstein, is incomplete, on my account. It does not reflect on the conditions of the possibility and validity of the philosophical discourse *about* (the *a priori* of) the culture-dependent pre-understanding of the life-world.[23] Hence it does not reflect either on the fact that the transcendental basis of the uncontestable kernel of human rights that are not culture-dependent is to be found in the moral conditions of the discussion about human rights.

Of course, by this transcendental foundation only the methodological point of departure for a discourse on human rights is provided. This discourse itself, say on a global scale, has to take into account the different needs of the different cultures (e.g. their state of development) in view of a differentiated explication and evaluation of the different rights. This means, for instance, that an appropriate assessment, acceptable for all affected parties, of the relationship between the political rights of liberty and participation may turn out (to be) different for different regional contexts.

159

This last example shows already that we must not assume that the concrete solutions of the morally and juridically relevant problems of a multicultural society could be reached through a philosophical deduction of material norms from the transcendentally grounded principles. This device of classical rationalism would go completely against the spirit of discourse ethics. The methodological point of discourse ethics is rather a *procedural* one in so far as the principle of justice and co-responsibility is only a regulative idea for the practical discourses – to be opened again and again – between the representatives of the different cultures and life-forms and the different constitutional states.

At the *global* level, we may think here of the many conferences on questions concerning humanity, say about nourishment of the poor, policies of population or reproduction, female rights, ecological protection measures, the distribution of financial burdens between the industrial and developmental countries, etc. At the *regional* level, we may think of the public discourses surrounding the legislation of democratic states, say about the rights of foreigners, especially of asylumseekers, on abortion, euthanasia, the application of gene technology etc.

In all of these discussions today, deep-rooted differences, and possibly conflicts, between different cultural traditions come into play. And we cannot expect always to reach solutions of the problems through discursive consent. But, according to the fundamental procedural norms of discourse ethics, it has to be demanded that, even in cases of persistent dissent, we try at least to reach a discursive consent about the reasons of the dissent and its unresolvability in order to facilitate juridical compromises. For this purpose, in a multicultural society permanent efforts of communicative understanding – also in the *hermeneutic* sense – between the different traditions of 'strong values' (Taylor) are required.[24]

Examples of the problems of deep-rooted value differences in a multicultural society are in particular provided by family relationships. Thus, on my estimation we cannot for instance reach moral consensus, at present, with regard to the question of *polygamy* in discourses between Muslims and Christians, or with regard to abortion between most Catholics and most atheistic liberals. But, concerning the latter case, it seems to me that a rational consensus is attainable concerning the reason for the unresolvable dissent, at present, which lies primarily in the different assessments and evaluations of the human status and hence the right to life of the foetus in comparison with the right to liberty of choice of the mother.

By these intimations, I have just pointed to a means of settling intercultural conflicts by discourse. And, as one knows, at this point a philosopher usually – not only for lack of time – has to break off.

Notes

1 Cf. H.-P. Martin and H. Schumann, *Die Globalisierungsfalle. Der Angriff auf Demokratie und Wohlstand*, Reinbeck bei Hamburg: Rowohlt, 4 1996. Cf. further the contributions to R. Fornet-Betancourt (ed.), *Armut im Spannungsfeld zwischen Globalisierung und dem Recht auf eigene Kultur*, Aachen: Augustinus-Buchhandlung, 1997.

2 Cf. the contributions to the bicentennial of Kant's essay 'Zum ewigen Frieden', in M. Lutz-Bachmann and J. Bohman (eds), *Frieden durch Recht*, Frankfurt am Main: Suhrkamp, 1996 (Engl. transl. *Perpetual Peace: Essays on Kant's Cosmopolitan Ideal*, Boston: MIT Press, 1977) and in R. Merkel and R. Wittmann (eds), *Zum ewigen Frieden*, Frankfurt am Main: Suhrkamp, 1996.

3 Before Huntington, it was A.J. Toynbee – in his *Civilization on Trial*, Oxford: Oxford University Press 1948, Ch. 11 – who already expected a counter-reaction from the non-Occidental civilizations to the European-made globalization. For a Latin-American perspective see E. Dussel: *Von der Erfindung Amerikas zur Entdeckung des Anderen. Ein Projekt der Transmoderne*, Düsseldorf: Patmos-Verlag, 1993.

4 See D. Bell, *Communitarianism and its Critics*, Oxford, 1993; D. Rasmussen (ed.), *Universalism vs Communitarianism*, Cambridge, Mass., 1990; M. Brumlik and H. Brunkhorst (eds), *Gemeinschaft und Gerechtigkeit*, Frankfurt am Main: Fischer, 1993; R. Forst, *Kontexte der Gerechtigkeit. Politische Philosophie jenseits von Liberalismus und Kommunitarismus*, Frankfurt am Main: Suhrkamp, 1994.

5 See K.-O. Apel, 'Das Anliegen des anglo-amerikanischen "Kommunitarismus" in der Sicht der Diskursethik', in M. Brumlik and H. Brunkhorst (eds), 1993, 149–72.

6 See J. Habermas, 'Vom pragmatischen, ethischen und moralischen Gebrauch der praktischen Vernunft', in *Erläterungen zur Diskursethik*, Frankfurt am Main: Suhrkamp, 1991, 100–18.

7 Cf. J. Rawls, *A Theory of Justice*, Cambridge, Mass.: Harvard University Press, 1971, §§6 and 68.

8 Cf. C. Taylor, *The Sources of the Self. The Making of Modern Identity*, Cambridge, Mass.: Harvard University Press, 1989.

9 See in particular R. Rorty, 'The Priority of Democracy to Philosophy', in *Objectivity, Relativism and Truth*, Cambridge: Cambridge University Press, 1991, 175–96. Cf. my critical comment in K.-O. Apel, *Diskurs und Verantwortung. Das Problem des Übergangs zur postkonventionellen Moral*, Frankfurt am Main: Suhrkamp, 1988, 398ff.

10 In *Philosophy and Public Affairs*, 14, 3 (1985).

11 Rorty intentionally applies the key words of the Occidental tradition of rhetoric – 'persuasion', 'persuasive', etc. – in their notorious ambiguity of meaning (which e.g. in German can easily be resolved through the distinction between 'überzeugen' and 'überreden'). Thereby, he, so it seems, tries to avoid the admission that philosophical discourse, in contra-distinction to rhetorical suggestions and strategical offers in bargainings, must rely on a constitutive relationship to validity claims and to arguments and reasons for their redemption.

12 Cf. K.-O. Apel, 'Normative Ethics and Strategical Rationality. The Philosophical Problem of Political Ethics', in *Graduate Faculty Philosophical Journal*, 9, 1 (1982), New York: New School for Social Research, repr. in R. Schürmann (ed.), *The Public Realm. Essays on Discursive Types of Political Philosophy*, State University of New York Press, 1989, 107–31.

13 Cf. J. Rawls, 'Kantian Constructivism in Moral Theory. The Dewey Lectures', in *The Journal of Philosophy*, LXXVII, 9 (1980).

14 Cf. J. Rawls (1971), §§4 and 9.

15 See J. Rawls, *Political Liberalism*, New York: Columbia University Press, 1993.

16 Against this interpretation it has been objected that Rawls, by his conception of the 'overlapping consensus', wants only to give an explanation of the possible stability of an order of justice in a pluralistic society, whereas he presupposes already the moral-philosophical foundation of the 'freestanding' political theory of justice (cf. e.g. R. Forst, *Kontexted der Gerechtigkeit*, Frankfurt am Main: Suhrkamp, 1994, 265–89). I think that this objection is correct from the point of view of the foundation that Rawls should have given. But the later Rawls himself has never clearly confirmed it, as far as I can see. In his disputation with Habermas (in *The Journal of Philosophy*, XCII, 3 (1995), 133ff.) he has rather discredited Forst's very sympathetic interpretation, which was inspired by Habermas, through the verdict that Habermas', as any other, moral–philosophical foundation of justice is itself also a 'comprehensive doctrine' of the good from which his own 'political' conception must be independent.

17 See *The Journal of Philosophy*, XCII, 3 (1995), 133ff.

18 *Ibid.*, p. 138, in contradistinction to his 'Dewey Lectures' in *The Journal of Philosophy*, LXXVII, 9, where he still presupposed the philosophical conception of 'moral persons'.

19 See J. Rawls, 'The Law of Peoples', in S. Shute and S. Hurley (eds), *On Human Rights. The Oxford Amnesty Lectures*, HarperCollins, 1993. For Rawls, the need for a novel conception of the 'theory of justice' – and hence his dispensing with the principle of 'liberal democracy' – is indeed also a compensation for the 'domestic' restrictions of the original theory. This shows, in my opinion, that it was extremely problematic that Rawls' original conception, like almost all Western theories of political justice, completely abstracted from the foreign relationships of a democracy on a global scale. The later Rawls seems to have realized that this 'domestic' restriction exposes his theory from the outset to the suspicion of ethno- or culture-centrism. But he does not try to correct this through a new start from 'universal first principles having authority in all cases', but prefers to supplement the first theory by suitable adjustments 'to apply to different subjects as they arise in sequence'. The deeper reason for this – hypothetically 'constructive' – method is given for Rawls by the fact that one can no longer – following the philosophical tradition – start out from the presupposition of the universal 'authority of (human) reason' (cf. pp. 45f.).

20 See e.g. H. Roetz, *Confucian Ethics of the Axial Age. A Reconstruction under the Aspect of the Breakthrough Toward Postconventional Thinking*, Albany: State University of New York Press, 1993.

21 Cf. K.-O. Apel, 'Diskursethik als Verantwortungsethik. Eine postmetaphysische Transformation der Ethik Kants', in R. Fornet-Betancourt (ed.), *Ethik und Befreiung*, Aachen: Augustinus-Buchhandlung, 1990, 10–40; repr. in G. Schönrich and Y. Kato (eds), *Kant in der Diskussion der Moderne*, Frankfurt am Main: Suhrkamp, 1996, 326–59.

22 This phrase indicates the necessary transcendental pragmatic deciphering of Kant's talk of a 'fact of reason' as meaning an '*a priori* perfect' to be realized through strict transcendental reflection on argumentation as non-circumventible performance of 'reason'. Without this deciphering, Kant's talk of a 'fact' could in our day be denounced as a metaphysical version of the naturalistic fallacy. Cf. K.-H. Ilting, 'Der naturalistische Fehlschluß bei Kant', in M. Riedel (ed.),

Rehabilitierung der praktischen Philosophie, Freiburg: Rombach, 1972, vol. I, 113–32; but cf. also: D. Henrich, 'Der Begriff der sittlichen Einsicht und Kants Lehre vom Faktum der Vernunft', in D. Henrich *et al.* (eds), *Die Gegenwart der Griechen im neueren Denken*, Festschrift für H.-G. Gadamer, Tübingen, 1960, 77–115.

23 Neither in Wittgenstein nor in Heidegger can a transcendental reflection on the conditions for the possibility of the validity claims of their own discourse be found. Cf. K.-O. Apel, 'Wittgenstein and Heidegger: Language Games and Life Forms', in C. Macann (ed.), *Critical Heidegger*, London: Routledge, 1996, 241–74.

24 Cf. K.-O. Apel, 'Plurality of the Good? The Problem of Affirmative Tolerance in a Multicultural Society from an Ethical Point of View', in L. Gianformaggio and T. Margiotta Broglio (eds), *Tolerance and Law*, in *Ratio Juris*, 1997 (forthcoming).

12

ENLIGHTENMENT AND THE IDEA OF PUBLIC REASON

Thomas McCarthy[1]

In the eighteenth century and since, diverse projects have been announced under the banner of "enlightenment." One of the philosophically most influential was espoused by Kant in "What is Enlightenment?" with the injunction: "Have the courage to use your own understanding!" This has often been connected with his strong notion of rational autonomy and interpreted in individualist terms. But that essay immediately goes on to declare that thinking for oneself is best done not alone but in concert with others, and thence to define enlightenment in terms of the "freedom to make public use of one's reason,"[2] which is the topic of the remainder of the essay. The same interdependence between using one's own reason and reasoning in concert with others is stressed in Kant's account of the maxims of common human understanding in the *Critique of Judgment*: the first maxim, "to think for oneself," is balanced by the second, "to think from the standpoint of everyone else." And it is also central to his account of justice in "Perpetual Peace" and other political writings, where publicity is said to be no less a condition of right than is individual consent. Elsewhere Kant characterizes the public use of reason ideally as open, critical, free of coercion, and subject to the requirements of consistency and coherence. On this reading, Kant's enlightenment project envisioned the gradual extension of the public use of reason, so understood, to all domains of cultural and political life. Is this today a viable project?

After indicating what Kant understood by reason and its public use, I outline some of the problems that have arisen for his conception from the waves of naturalism, historicism, pragmatism, and pluralism in the two centuries since he propounded it. The problems have been accompanied, to be sure, by ongoing revisions of his project and of the idea of reason on which it rests. The most fully developed contemporary reformulation is that of Jürgen Habermas. Analyzing rationality in terms of communication and centering it in the appeal to reasons to gain intersubjective recognition for contestable claims, he ties public reason to the procedures, forums, practices, and institutions in which validity claims are critically tested in various forms of public discourse. Accordingly, his "discourse" approach to questions of truth and justice may be construed as a communications-theoretic reworking of Kant's idea of the public use of reason. With that as my point of departure, and with attention primarily to the claims of "practical reason" – that is, to ethics and politics – I sketch a version of the project of enlightenment which, I hope, is still viable today. This will require a somewhat more pragmatic account of communicative reason than Habermas's own, in order to meet the powerful objections to Kantian idealization, universality, and unity that spring from our growing aware-ness of practice, context, and diversity.

I

The central idea in Kant's conception of enlightenment is that of submit-ting all claims to authority to the free examination of reason:

> Reason depends on this freedom for its very existence. For reason has no dictatorial authority; its verdict is always simply the agree-ment of free citizens, of whom each one must be permitted to express, without let or hindrance, his objections or even his veto.[3]

By this means, authority deriving from reasoned agreement among indi-viduals, each relying on his or her own independent judgment, is gradually to displace authority deriving from tradition, status, office, or might, in both theoretical and practical matters. The form of this public encounter is critique:

> Our age, is in especial degree, the age of criticism [Kritik], and to criticism everything must submit. Religion through its sanctity, and law-giving through its majesty, may seek to exempt themselves from it. But they then awaken just suspicion and cannot claim the same respect which reason accords only to that which has been able to sustain the test of free and open examination.
> (Kant 1961: Axi)

"Nothing," insists Kant, "is so important through its usefulness, nothing so sacred, that it may be exempted from this searching examination, which knows no respect for persons."[4] This holds for reason itself: only through a sustained critique of reason can we ascertain its "lawful claims" and reject all "groundless pretensions" (Axi).

It is fashionable today to dismiss Kant as a thoroughgoing rationalist, thereby ignoring his own trenchant criticisms of rationalist metaphysics and his renunciation of any claim to determinate knowledge of realms beyond experience. In relation to theoretical inquiry, he explained, "ideas of reason" can function only heuristically, as regulative ideas that spur us on to ever-deeper explanations and ever-broader systematizations. The fundamental error of metaphysics is to understand this drive beyond the conditioned, the partial, the imperfect, as if the unconditioned, the totality, the perfect, have been or could be achieved; that is, to mistake what is merely regulative for constitutive.

This deep-rooted tendency of the human mind repeatedly gives rise to speculative illusions that have to be dialectically dispelled by critical inquiry. This is not to say that ideas of reason are meaningless, but only that we cannot grasp them theoretically, or even have determinate knowledge of them. Rather, *we have to think them in relation to practice* – here the practice of empirical–theoretical inquiry. In this sphere they serve to organize, guide, and constrain our thinking by projecting a consistent, coherent, systematic unity of knowledge. However, the synthesis of such unity from the multiplicity and diversity of experience and judgment is never simply given (*gegeben*); it is always and forever a task (*aufgegeben*). I will argue below that a variation on this approach to ideas of reason in terms of their practical significance for the conduct of inquiry is still a useful way to understand our ideas of an independent reality and the truth about it. Here I want only to note that, notwithstanding his restricting of ideas of reason to a regulative employment, Kant regards them as "indispensably necessary"[5] to the proper use of our understanding and any attempt to deny them as condemned to incoherence.

> The mob of sophists raise against reason the usual cry of absurdities and contradictions. . . . Yet it is to the beneficent influences exercised by reason that they owe the possibility of their own self-assertiveness, and indeed that very culture which enables them to blame and condemn what reason requires of them.[6]

Let us turn now from the role of reason in the conduct of inquiry to its role in the conduct of life, that is, to Kant's treatment of ideas of *practical* reason. The main difference here is that these ideas are not merely indirectly but directly practical, that is, they are directly related to action, determining what we ought to do or aim at. In this sense practical reason is said by Kant to function directly as a source of objective, universally valid laws, without the intermediation of experience and understanding that is indispensable to reason's theoretical employment. However, the laws it generates are purely formal in nature, as, paradigmatically, with the categorical imperative. They receive their content only through being situationally applied by moral agents. In this sense, they too are inherently indeterminate and require filling-in with concrete moral experience, deliberation, and judgment in particular moral situations (and, I might add, not necessarily in the ways indicated by Kant's own examples). Thus the idea of duty as action dictated solely by the force of universalizing reason, or the idea of persons as ends in themselves who may not be acted against, the ideal (i.e. idea *in individuo*) of a kingdom of ends as an association of free and equal rational beings under universal laws they give themselves, the idea of right as the maximum freedom of each so far as this is compatible with a like freedom for all under general laws, the idea of an original (social) contract as based in the united (general) will of a people, or the idea of a cosmopolitan society in which rights, justice, and the rule of law are secured internationally – all function only as general constraints upon, and orientations for, action in particular circumstances. In practice they have to be continually contextualized as changing circumstances demand. And like their theoretical counterparts, these practical ideas function as principles of coherent, systematic unity, only now we have to do with the unity of rational beings under common laws which they give to themselves. Thus the "supreme condition of harmony with universal practical reason"[7] combines the first version of the categorical imperative – the idea of acting on reasons or grounds ("maxims") that are "objective," i.e. valid for all rational beings – with the second version – the idea that persons are "objective" ends, i.e. ends for rational agents as such, inasmuch as each rational agent regards herself in this way and thus, by virtue of the first version, must so regard all others – to yield the ideal of a kingdom of ends, "the systematic union of different rational beings through common laws."[8]

Correspondingly, the moral point of view, as an idea of reason combining respect for each's ends with principles valid for all, considers actions and norms in relation "to that legislation through which alone a kingdom of ends is possible."[9] Thus, in both theoretical and practical matters, reason for Kant functions as a capacity for finding or creating unity in diversity, and of doing so non-coercively, with appeal only to the free agreement of individuals thinking for themselves.

If we turn now to Kant's more explicitly political writings, we find the same dual emphasis on individuality and commonality, autonomy and universality, voluntary acknowledgment and intersubjective agreement. Thus, as noted above, in "What is Enlightenment?" the courage to use one's own reason and the freedom to make public use of one's reason are said to be interdependent moments of the enlightenment project. The specific form of public reason Kant has in mind is that of addressing "the entire reading public," be it of a commonwealth or of cosmopolitan society as a whole. But this is only a particular schema, more appropriate perhaps to an age of the incipient print mediation of public affairs, for the general idea of a public discourse addressed to what Chaim Perelman has called the "universal audience." For whether in theoretical or practical matters, the mark of objectivity for Kant is agreement resulting from "universal human reason in which each has his own say."[10] In practice, it is ascertained precisely in and through public debate and criticism: only what stands up to critical–rational scrutiny merits the voluntary acknowledgment of each member of the universal audience.

The social embodiment of this enlightenment ideal is a "moral whole" having the legal–political shape of a "civil society which can administer justice universally."[11] And it is precisely this idea of "a perfectly just civil constitution"[12] that is the most reliable measure of progress in enlightenment. In considering the latter, we should "concentrate our attention on civic constitutions, their laws, and the mutual relations among states,"[13] for it is only in such legal–political frames that "the germs implanted [in us] by nature can be developed fully."[14] As indicated, this holds not only for relationships within particular commonwealths, but for relationships among them. "The problem of establishing a perfect civil constitution is dependent upon the problem of a law-governed external relationship with other states and cannot be solved unless the latter is solved."[15] Thus the overarching goal of Kant's enlightenment project in the legal–political sphere is "a federation of peoples, in which every state, even the smallest, could expect to derive its security and rights."[16] Only the "universal cosmopolitan existence" afforded by such a "civil union of mankind" could serve as a "matrix in which all the original capacities of the human race may develop."[17]

Is something like this Kantian project of enlightenment viable today? There are strong arguments on both sides. The public use of "theoretical" reason has, however imperfectly, been culturally developed and institutionally embodied in the arts and sciences, universities and research institutes, publishing houses and professional journals, and so forth, of the scientific, scholarly, and artistic worlds. And the public use of "practical" reason has, with more mixed results, been developed and embodied in the legal and political practices and institutions of modern democratic societies. The historical failures, especially in the areas of practical reason, are as familiar as the successes. Here, however, I want to focus on philosophical problems with the very conception of reason at the heart of Kant's enlightenment project. To be brief, the naturalism, historicism, pragmatism, and pluralism of the last century-and-a-half has made the detranscendentalization and decentering of Kantian reason unavoidable. The residue of metaphysics in the noumenal–phenomenal split that undergirds it, the dominance of mentalism in the design and execution of its critique, and the subordination of diversity built into its aspiration to unity are no longer tenable. "Pure" reason has had to make fundamental and lasting concessions to the impurities of language and culture, temporality and history, practice and interest, body and desire. More specifically, Kant's notion of using one's own reason, thinking for oneself, has to be tempered with the ineliminable background of what is always already taken for granted in doing so – the preconceptions, prejudgments, and preunderstandings that inform any rational undertaking. His stress on agreement and consensus, especially on the "united will" of a people as the source of the legitimacy of its laws, has to be tempered with acknowledgment of persistent reasonable disagreements in theory and in practice. And his idealized conception of the public use of reason has to be tempered with a heightened awareness of the significance of context and audience in assessing the strength of reasons and the cogency of arguments.

A revealing case in point is Kant's classically rationalist, hierarchical, distinction between conviction and persuasion.[18] Holding something to be true is said to be conviction if it rests on "objective grounds" and is therefore "valid for everyone" possessed of reason. It is said to be persuasion if it has its grounds "only in the special character of the subject," be it an individual or a group. Persuasion is "illusion" if its grounds are taken to be objective, for it has only "private validity." The "touchstone" whereby we determine whether holding something as true is one or the other is "the possibility of communicating it and finding it to be valid for all human reason." Thus, it is only in and through the effort to secure universal agreement that we can "test upon the understanding of others whether those grounds of the judgment which are valid for us have the same effect on the reason of others as on our own." However, in practice we can do this only by attempting to convince particular audiences and holding the discussion open to others. And that means that "subjective" factors – for instance, who is being addressed, where and when, in what connection and for what purpose, against which taken-for-granted background, and so on – will inevitably figure in the processes and outcomes of such communication. What we need here is an account of the interplay between the universal and particular. But that would point toward a conception of reason that escapes Kant's strict dichotomies. And it would require balancing his stress on "systematic unity" with a correlative recognition of irreducible diversity. The question is, whether all this can be done without giving up on Kant's enlightenment project. Can we desublimate and decenter his transcendental-philosophical conception of reason and still make sense of the ideas and ideals at the heart of his project?

A number of thinkers since Kant have essayed affirmative responses to this question. By and large, they have come to agree that examining the nature, scope, and limits of reason calls for modes of inquiry that go beyond the bounds of traditional philosophical analysis. Once we turn our attention from consciousness to culture and society it becomes clear that rational practices, including epistemic practices like researching and theorizing, have to be viewed in their sociocultural contexts if they are to be understood and appraised. From this perspective, the critique of "impure" reason belongs to the study of culture and society, and aspires to practical import. It aims to reform and enhance our self-understanding as rational beings in ways that affect how we live. This sort of practically significant sociohistorical critique of impure reason has been a live option since the time of the Left-Hegelians. Variants of it dominated the philosophical scene in the United States during the heyday of American Pragmatism. I now consider briefly some ideas of its most important contemporary representative, Jürgen Habermas.

II

Habermas shifts the focus of the critique of reason from forms of transcendental consciousness to forms of interpersonal communication. Accordingly, he understands objective validity, both theoretical and practical, in relation to reasoned agreement concerning defeasible claims. The key to communicative rationality is the use of reasons or grounds – the "unforced force" of the better argument – to gain intersubjective recognition for such claims. This leads, on the one side, to a discourse theory of truth and, on the other, to a discourse theory of justice. The enlightenment project then becomes a matter of cultivating suitable forms of theoretical and practical discourse, and of establishing the institutions and practices required to give them social effect. In regard to theoretical discourse, this requires improving the cultural and institutional conditions for empirical research, theoretical inquiry, scholarly activity, and the like. In regard to practical discourse, it requires reforming the cultural and institutional conditions for moral, legal, and political deliberation and strengthening its role in our lives.

Like Kant's transcendental approach, Habermas's communicative approach assigns an indispensable function to ideas of reason, only now they are understood as *pragmatic presuppositions of communication* which are constitutive of basic forms of social practice, and in this sense unavoidable, but which at the same time project a completeness and finality unattainable in practice. They are, as it were, "constitutive idealizations" of rational practices. We shall take a closer look at some of them below. But here it is important to see that this approach is meant to undercut the immanent–transcendent, real–ideal, and fact–norm dichotomies that have plagued Kantianism. Ideas of reason are now firmly located *within* social reality. As *ideal presuppositions* of rational practices, they are *actually effective* in defining social situations and at the same time *contrary to fact* in ways that transcend the limits of those situations. This tension at the core of forms of life reproduced through communicative rationality accounts for the dual – positive – heuristic cum negative – critical – function of ideas of reason, that is, for why they can subserve both constructive and critical undertakings. And because ideal presuppositions shape the *normative* expectations that inform *existing* practices and institutions, they also lie beyond the "is"–"ought" opposition that pervades modern thought. Constitutive idealizations that are already operative in communicative interaction are no more "oughts" set over against what "is" than they are transcendent *as opposed* to immanent, ideal *as opposed to* real, or universal *as opposed to* particular. What we have to grasp in each instance is the *interdependence in practice* of the alleged opposites.

Languages are spoken and understood, and actions are performed and recognized, by particular individuals in particular situations. And that particularity inevitably contributes to the concrete sense that is made of speech and action. Contextual considerations are always at play in the production and interpretation of meaning. But that is only part of the story. Also required to make communication and interaction work are shared general structures that can be repeatedly recontextualized, that is, general patterns of speech and action which are, on the one hand, relatively invariant to different speakers and actors but are also, on the other hand, able to accommodate the contextual variations they introduce. The interdependence of the general and the particular here takes the form of an interplay between structure and context carried out by linguistically and culturally competent agents who orientate to both. Reciprocally imputed, mutually assumed, and socially sanctioned patterns of expectation are interpretively contextualized by participants themselves through on-the-spot interpretations and judgments. Communicatively competent agents are, then, the lifeblood of this dialectic of general and particular. Only through them do general cultural patterns gain the practical determinacy of speech and action in concrete contexts.

It is important to note also that this achievement happens over time. Not only the determination of an utterance or action's sense but also the judgment of its validity – of its truth, say, or of its normative rightness – is a step-by-step process that involves dealing with considerations as they arise. If social interaction is to remain stable in the face of a vast and unpredictable range of potentially relevant considerations, competent agents must routinely adopt a "wait and see" attitude (Garfinkel) toward one another's utterances and actions, for the meaning and validity of the latter are inherently open to clarification, confirmation, contestation, and alteration by the future course of events in general and by how participants notice and deal with what they take to be relevant considerations in particular. For these reasons, among others, mutual understanding and mutual agreement can only be *ongoingly accomplished in ever-changing circumstances for all practical purposes*. Construed in this way, I now want to argue, the temporality, contextuality, and practicality of communicative reason are not opposed to idealization but are dependent upon it, as it is upon them.

Context-transcendence through the projection of ideal validity has long been a function of reason in our philosophical tradition. In connection with theoretical and practical discourse, the normative force of the ideas of truth and justice is supposed to be given full scope and the bounds of the relevant communication community to be expanded without limit. As noted above, in practice rational agreement by all competent judges is not something we can hope to accomplish all at once or once and for all. Rather, we try to establish the rational acceptability of truth or moral rightness claims in particular forums and before particular audiences, and we assume the responsibility as well for defending their validity in other relevant forums and before other relevant audiences. The universal audience for these claims is, then, never more than potential. To raise such a validity claim is, as it were, to issue a promissory note across the expanses of social space and historical time. Whether or not it can be made good always remains to be seen, for any established consensus is open to contestation. In the end, there is no way of determining which is "the better argument" apart from observing how competing arguments fare over time and in various forums; that is to say, how they stand up to the ongoing give-and-take of critical reflective discourse. The redemption of truth and rightness claims, the establishment of their warranted assertability or rational acceptability, is thus an intrinsically temporal and open-ended process. It is just this temporally extended – in principle never-ending – to-and-fro of claims and criticisms, in institutionalized forums, *vis-à-vis* particular audiences claiming to represent the universal audience, that is characteristic of *reason-in-practice*.

The communicative approach thus seeks to take account of the contextual features of language use without renouncing the context-transcending import of the claims of reason. Even if the idealized assumptions made in projecting universal rational agreement never in fact obtain, ideas of reason are not thereby rendered useless or pernicious. One of their salutary functions is precisely to open a space for the critical examination of actually accepted validity claims, and thus to make possible the critical traditions and the institutions of critical discourse in which established warrants are subjected to ongoing scrutiny. Consider for instance the natural sciences. Scientific claims to truth are raised and discussed in culturally and institutionally established forums that hold them open to critical examination over time. Scientists have reflexively to anticipate the critical scrutiny of their work by others who share the cognitive, normative, and evaluative presuppositions of their scientific subcommunity. If they can convince that particular audience, they have reason to expect they could convince other relevant audiences as well, for in virtue of its presumed competence that audience can plausibly stand in for the universal audience of all rational beings competent to judge in the matter. Scientific truth, as the continually revised outcome of this open-ended discourse, can never be more than an ongoing accomplishment. But the discursive process itself makes no sense apart from idealizing assumptions concerning an independent reality. Thus, conflicts of experience and theory are dealt with in ways that themselves presuppose, and thereby reconfirm, the existence of a coherent, unitary reality. They are attributed not to contradictions in the world but to errors or inadequacies on the part of one or more of the parties to the dispute. That is to say, each practitioner is held accountable, and in turn holds others accountable, for treating the objective reality of the world as invariant to discrepant reports. In this way, procedures for resolving conflicts about "what is really there" are themselves based on the very presupposition they are deployed to maintain.

Further, the supposition of the world's objective reality is internally linked to that of its intersubjective availability. Scientists must assume that they are experiencing and reporting the same independent reality. And as the latter is supposed to be unitary and coherent, all the correct accounts of it must add up in the end to one coherent account: *the* truth about the objective world. To claim truth for sentences about the objective world is thus to anticipate corroborative reports from all other competent observers. When they are not forthcoming, scientists must resort to error accounts to explain the discrepancies. And this indicates that the idea of an objective world knowable in common functions not only "constitutively" – that is, as an assumption that actually shapes scientific practices – but "regulatively," that is, as a presupposition that normatively constrains and guides those practices. It is just this sort of constitutive–regulative duality that the conception of ideas of reason as unavoidable idealizing presuppositions of communicative interaction is meant to capture.

This duality, too, is put into practice by the on-the-spot utterances and actions of competent agents, by their situated exercises of practical reason and judgment. Of course, the agents in question are always already socialized agents, and their agency is always already informed by the cultural patterns they take for granted – and, in taking for granted, renew. But, as we saw, general patterns do not determine in advance particular courses of action in particular circumstances. Rather, their inherent and *functionally necessary* indeterminacy attains the practical determinacy of situated speech and action only in and through the interactions of culturally competent agents. Thus communicative interaction presupposes the "accountability" of agents, their ability to engage in practical reasoning of the sorts required for interaction, to offer (typically conventional) accounts of their behavior, and to assess others' accounts of theirs (usually by reference to conventional standards). As practical reasoners, accountable agents are participants in intersubjective processes of assessment, criticism, and justification. They are capable, by and large, of providing publicly defensible accounts of their beliefs and actions, of satisfying interaction partners that they have grounds for believing and doing what they believe and do.

The difference between everyday accountability and rational autonomy – the ability to step back and engage in critical-reflective discourse concerning the justifiability of existing or proposed beliefs and practices – is only a matter of degree. Autonomy of this sort was central to the enlightened mode of rational agency that Kant referred to as *Mündigkeit*, the capacity to think for oneself. As viewed here, it is only a further development of practices and abilities already inculcated in daily life. To be sure, that development is not merely a matter of occasional ingenuity or individual virtuosity. It is based on social, cultural, and psychological conditions that undergo historical change. In modern as compared to traditional societies, conditions are such as to provide increased cultural, institutional and motivational support for reflective modes of argumentation and critique. Forms of expert discourse have developed which are transmitted and elaborated within specialized cultural traditions and embodied in differentiated cultural institutions. Thus, for instance, the scientific enterprise, the legal system, and the institutions of art criticism represent enduring possibilities of discursively thematizing various types of validity claim and of learning from negative experiences with them. These changes in relation to inherited contexts of meaning and validity, established roles and institutions, and received patterns of socialization and individuation are always only a matter of degree and never global in their reach. But they are not without far-reaching effects on processes of cultural reproduction, social integration, and identity formation. They expose the authority of tradition increasingly to discursive questioning, displace particularistic norms and values by more general and abstract ones, and supersede traditionally ascribed identities by identities that have to be formed and reformed in varied and ever-changing circumstances. It is worth noting that this heightening of reflexivity, generality, and individualism is assumed by all of the various participants – post- and anti-modernist, as well as modernist – in the current debates about modernity. They all take for granted the possibility of reflectively questioning received beliefs and values, of gaining critical distance from established norms and roles, and of challenging ascribed individual and group identities.

In consequence of this spread of reflexivity and differentiation, the beliefs, norms, and values that could stand up to criticism and be upheld in open discussion are by no means coextensive with the spectrum of what has historically been believed, prescribed, or valued. But neither are they always uniquely determined. One of the things we have learned about values, for instance, is that reasonable people can reasonably hold different conceptions of the good, that there is no one way of life suited to all individuals and groups, and thus that a pluralistic society within which members can pursue, within limits, their different ideas of the good life is the most reasonable arrangement. Such limits are derivable from the basic principles built into the very idea of seeking reasoned agreement through open discussion, principles that must be observed if such discussion is to be possible. It is precisely those principles that Habermas's account of practical discourse is meant to reconstruct.

III

"Discourse ethics" is a reworking of Kant's conception of practical reason in terms of communicative reason. Roughly speaking, it involves a procedural reformulation of the categorical imperative: rather than each regarding as valid the norms that he or she can will to be universal laws, proposed norms must be submitted to all who are affected by them for purposes of argumentatively testing their claims to validity. The emphasis shifts from what each can will without contradiction to what all can agree to in rational discourse. As with Kant, then, normative validity is tied to rational acceptability; but now the latter is linked from the start to communication processes governed by a principle of universalization, which Habermas formulates as follows: "For a norm to be valid, the consequences and side effects of its general observance for the satisfaction of each person's interests must be acceptable to all."[19] As this formulation indicates, the discourse-ethical approach no longer makes moral-practical rationality depend on bracketing inclinations and interests; rather, it seeks to determine whether their satisfaction evokes general agreement.

Like Kant, Habermas distinguishes the types of practical reasoning and the corresponding types of "ought" proper to questions concerning what is pragmatically expedient, ethically prudent, or morally right. Calculations of rational choice aim at recommendations relevant to the pursuit of contingent purposes in the light of given preferences. When serious questions of value arise, deliberation on who one is and wants to be seeks ethical insight concerning the good life. If issues of justice are involved, fair and impartial consideration of conflicting interests is required to judge what is right or just. And, again like Kant, Habermas regards questions of the last type, rather than specifically ethical questions, to be the domain of theory. (Thus discourse ethics might more properly have been called "discourse morality.") This is not to deny that specifically ethical discourse can be more or less rational, or that it exhibits general structures of its own; but the pluralism and individualism of modern life mean that questions of self-understanding, self-realization, and the good life do not admit of universal answers. But this does not preclude constructing a general theory of a narrower sort, namely a theory of justice. Accordingly, the aim of discourse ethics is solely to reconstruct, in communications-theoretical terms, the moral point of view from which questions of right can be fairly and impartially adjudicated. Its leading principle is that "only those norms may claim to be valid that could meet with the consent of all affected in their role as participants in a practical discourse."[20] Respect for the individual is built into the freedom of each participant in discourse to accept or reject the reasons offered as justifications for norms, and concern for the common good into the requirement that each participant take into account the needs, interests, feelings, and desires of all those affected by the norms under consideration. It is obvious that the actual practice of moral discourse has to rely on norms of individual socialization, cultural reproduction, and social interaction that foster the requisite capacities, motivations, and opportunities.

It is in fact possible to read Habermas's extensive writings on politics and society as a protracted examination of the psychological, cultural, and institutional conditions for and barriers to the implementation of practical discourse in public life. I shall not be concerned here with the details of those discussions but only with the conception of deliberative democracy that serves as their normative frame of reference. That conception applies the idea of justification by appeal to generally acceptable reasons to the deliberations of free and equal citizens in a constitutional democracy. Accordingly, Habermas's model of democratic deliberation envisages an interweave of fair negotiations and pragmatic considerations with ethical and moral discourses, under conditions which warrant a presumption that procedurally correct outcomes will generally be ones with which free and equal citizens could reasonably agree. And he conceives the basic structures of the constitutional state as an ongoing attempt effectively to secure such conditions of rational deliberation not only in official governmental bodies but in the unofficial networks of the public sphere.

Independent public forums, distinct from both the economic system and the state administration, having their locus rather in voluntary associations, social movements, and other venues and processes of communication in civil society, are for Habermas the basis of popular sovereignty. Ideally, the "communicative power" generated by the public use of reason in non-governmental arenas should be translated via legally institutionalized decision-making procedures – for example, electoral and legislative procedures – into the legitimate administrative power of the state. In this model for a deliberative decentering of political power, the multiple and multiform arenas for detecting, defining, and discussing societal problems, and the culturally and politically mobilized publics who use them, serve as the basis for democratic self-government and thus for political authority. Not even constitutional principles are exempt from this public use of reason. Rather, democratic constitutions should be understood as "projects" that are always open, incomplete, and subject to the ongoing exercise of political autonomy. Constitutional traditions have to accommodate not only inherited self-understandings, patterns of value, and interpretations of needs, but conflicts among them and challenges to them. This means that in practice the acceptability of concrete laws, policies, and programs depends not only on basic rights and universal principles, but on particular

histories and changing circumstances. It also means that specific interpretations of the presuppositions and conditions of democratic self-
determination are themselves subject to debate in the public sphere. In this
sense, democratic discourse is reflexively open: participants may thematize
the very activity in which they are engaged. Its institutionalization is at
the same time the institutionalization of possibilities of internal criticism.

In my view, this approach goes a long way toward detranscendentalizing
Kant's conception of practical reason while preserving many of its most
valuable features; but it does not go quite far enough. In particular, as I
have argued elsewhere, it does not give sufficient weight to what Rawls
has called "the fact of reasonable pluralism."[21] In construing political
autonomy as self-legislation through the public use of reason, Habermas
ties the legitimacy of legal norms to what all could agree to in public
deliberations that take the needs and interests of each equally into consideration. Thus Kant's "united will of a people" reappears here in
discourse-theoretical trappings. Kant, despite his insistence on the public use
of reason, could still rely on a kind of "pre-established harmony" among
rational beings, owing to their sharing in the general structures of *Bewusst-
sein überhaupt*. And since all particularities were to be put out of play as
determining factors in the exercise of "pure" reason, what remained was
common to all. But Habermas's conception of practical discourse brings
particularities – in the forms of values, interests, aims, desires, and the
like – back into the picture, and so he owes us a detailed account of the
dialectical interplay between the general and the particular in this domain.

Let us focus for the moment on the implications of value pluralism.
Habermas acknowledges that evaluative perspectives inevitably inform
our conceptions of what is good not only for ourselves or our subgroups,
but for the larger political communities of which we are members. On
what grounds, then, could we expect free and equal citizens with different
and often incompatible value orientations to be able regularly to achieve
consensus on what is in the common good? Under conditions of value
pluralism, even ideally rational discourse need not lead to rational consensus. When it does not, we may resort to procedures like voting and
majority rule. If those procedures are accepted as democratically legitimate
by all parties to the disagreement, the outcomes may likewise be accepted
as legitimate. But then there is no more reason to characterize them as
"reasonable agreements" than as "reasonable disagreements."

What this does, we might say, is shift the level of agreement, strictly so
called, to a higher plane of abstraction, a move which is in fact characteristic of modern legal and political systems generally. That is, the levels at
which pluralistic societies may hope to secure broad agreements amid the
play of social, cultural, and ideological differences might in some cases
range not much further than basic rights, principles, and procedures.
Reflectively rational participants will *themselves* be aware that their

different interpretive and evaluative standpoints are rooted in different traditions, contexts, and experiences; and if they consider the basic institutions and practices of their society to be just, they may regard collective decisions in accord with them as legitimate, even when they disagree substantively with them. In this view, the *de facto* end of public deliberations expresses only a provisional outcome of procedures intended to produce decisions even in the absence of substantive consensus. The for-the-time-being character of any such decision refers not to an ideal limit point of universal convergence on the "one right answer" but to ongoing efforts by minorities rationally to persuade enough of the majority to change the decision. What is normatively central to this model is not the general or united will of a people, in the form of universal rational consensus, but the structures and procedures that secure official and unofficial spaces for the public use of reason and the practically rational character of that public discourse. This includes its degree of openness to criticisms and innovations, particularly when they issue from challenges to established value orientations, self-understandings, worldviews, and the like – for instance, when they are part of the struggles for recognition of oppressed or marginalized groups – but also when they express more routine disagreements that stem from socially, culturally, and biographically rooted differences. Reasonable members will try to speak to these differences when seeking rationally to persuade others to support laws and policies they believe to be in the general interest. They will seek to accommodate some of them in the arrangements they propose. And they will learn to live with all of them in a non-violent manner. Practical rationality in the face of diversity is as much a matter of recognizing, respecting, and accommodating differences as it is of transcending them. Arrangements predicated upon the former are no less practically rational than those predicated upon the latter, and just political arrangements will normally involve both.

These considerations weigh all the more heavily when we turn to the "universal cosmopolitan existence" that Kant envisioned as a "federation of peoples" guaranteeing "perpetual peace." In our framework this would entail establishing the cultural and institutional conditions for what we might call "multicultural cosmopolitan discourse." If there are basic differences in the beliefs and practices of peoples who nevertheless want to live together in peace, and if there is no "view from nowhere" from which to adjudicate those differences, then there is no non-coercive alternative to finding or constructing common ground in communicative interaction. Viewed normatively, that process would turn on the presuppositions of practical discourse discussed above. In particular, it would require overcoming the social, cultural, economic, political, and military asymmetries of the global networks within which cross-cultural encounters are now situated, and empowering presently excluded or subordinated "others" to participate on equal footing in the "conversation of humankind." It is only in the institutions and practices embodying some such cosmopolitan ideal that the enlightenment project could prove to be more than a Eurocentric illusion.

These last remarks are a reminder of the empirical–historical dimensions of the enlightenment project, which have been left entirely to the side of my purely conceptual and normative reflections – not, of course, because they are unimportant or because existing conditions are fine as they are. The reasons are in part occasional: conceptual and normative issues lend themselves more readily to philosophical discussion; and they are in part theoretical: the enlightenment project depends on interpretive and evaluative standpoints that are grounded in ideas of reason. In this latter connection, it is precisely the situation-transcending import of such ideas that is decisive, for the areas of tension between an established order and the ideas of reason it relies upon are just where enlightened social criticism goes to work. Used in this way, ideas of reason take us in a different direction from those metaphysical representations that have so exercised deconstructionist critics – namely, toward the ongoing critical scrutiny of claims to validity made in their name. The tension between the ideal and the real with which they imbue the construction of the social world represents a potential for criticism that agents can draw upon in seeking to transcend and transform the limits of existing situations. This "normative surplus" of meaning, as Habermas once called it, derives precisely from the constitutive–regulative duality of ideas of reason that function as idealizing presuppositions of communicative interaction.[22] And that means that cultural and social changes may sometimes be understood in terms of the further development and institutionalization of specific dimensions of communicative reason.

It is from this perspective as well that the selectivity of actually existing enlightenment processes becomes evident. Many of our problems result, it seems, from a lopsided rationalization of culture and society, from a failure to develop and institutionalize in a balanced way the *diverse* potentials of communicative reason. Forms of instrumental and strategic rationality have instead achieved a cultural hegemony and institutional dominance, while moral and political uses of public reason have been, by comparison, weak and warped. On this reading, the enlightenment project has not failed. But it has taken some disastrous turns. And it remains unfinished.

Notes

1 This is a version of a paper originally published in the *European Journal of Philosophy*, Vol. 3, No. 3, 1995.
2 Immanuel Kant, "An Answer to the Question: 'What is Enlightenment?'," trans. H.B. Nisbet, in Hans Reiss, ed., *Kant. Political Writings*, Cambridge: Cambridge University Press, 1991, p. 55.

3 Immanuel Kant, *Critique of Pure Reason*, trans. N.K. Smith, New York: St. Martin's Press, 1961, A738–9/766–7. Cited according to the standard "A" and "B" pages of the first and second editions.

4 *Ibid.*, A738/B766.

5 *Ibid.*, A644/B672.

6 *Ibid.*, A669/B697.

7 Immanuel Kant, *Foundations of the Metaphysics of Morals*, trans. L.W. Beck, New York: Library of Liberal Arts, 1959, p. 49.

8 *Ibid.*

9 *Ibid.*, p. 52.

10 Immanuel Kant, *Critique of Pure Reason*, A752/B780.

11 Immanuel Kant, "Idea for a Universal History with a Cosmopolitan Purpose," trans. H.B. Nisbet, in Hans Reiss, ed., *Kant. Political Writings*, Cambridge: Cambridge University Press, 1991, p. 45.

12 *Ibid.*, p. 46.

13 *Ibid.*, p. 52.

14 *Ibid.*

15 *Ibid.*, p. 47.

16 *Ibid.*

17 *Ibid.*, p. 51.

18 Immanuel Kant, *Critique of Pure Reason*, A820–1/B848–9.

19 J. Habermas *Moral Consciousness and Communicative Action*, Cambridge, MA: The MIT Press, 1990, p. 197.

20 *Ibid.*

21 T. McCarthy *Ideals and Illusions*, Cambridge, MA: The MIT Press, 1991, pp. 181–99.

22 J. Habermas *Postmetaphysical Thinking*, Cambridge, MA: The MIT Press, 1992, pp. 115–48.

13

PARADIGMS OF PUBLIC REASON

Reflections on ethics and democracy

David M. Rasmussen

The idea of public reason in some form or other has been around for a long time. For modernity it provides a link between the idea of democracy (and the practice thereof) and some kind of ethical or moral component. In a curious way, the debates which dominate the modern discussion of democracy, between liberalism and republicanism, between thick notions of democracy as informed by a specific set of historical practices and thin notions as related to a theory of universality, between reason based on principles of argumentation and reason informed by historical practice have predominated since the beginning of modernity.

Initially, I am inspired by two historical premodern references in this regard: Aristotle's willingness to blend *ethos* and *polis,* and Augustine's radical rejection of that association. There is a debate between these two positions and it is my contention that current debates over democracy are foreshadowed in the respective arguments presented by Augustine and Aristotle. There are, of course, problems with both views. The problem with the Aristotelian view is that it tends to ground the normative status of politics on the basis of certain assumptions about human capacities and just institutions which are, in modernity at least, difficult to justify. The problem with the Augustinian view is that it tends to be too sceptical of having any valid politics at all because of the assumed impossibility of creating a commonwealth (common will) out of an unorganized horde of corrupt individuals. For both, a valid politics required a form of rational justification. But that is as far as the comparison goes. Aristotle is right to the extent that there should be some kind of link between reason, ethics and politics. But Augustine is appropriately suspicious of the attempt by classical culture to place the burden of goodness on the shoulders of potentially corrupt individuals. My point is that there has to be a rational link between ethics or morality and politics. If one defines that link too narrowly, as Aristotle did, one loses the possibility of a critical distance between the political institutions of the day and their potential ethical or moral foundation. If one divorces them as radically as did Augustine, politics, and by implication democracy, disintegrate under the weight of ethical critique. Where does one draw the line regarding a certain optimism about the rational justification of politics and a certain pessimism regarding the potentiality of reason in the light of the failure of human beings and their institutions?

I

Augustine's critique of classical civilization sets the stage for the modern debate on the relationship between reason, ethics and democracy by questioning the very assumption that the human *polis* could have an ethical foundation. Interestingly, the argument hinges on whether or not a valid public will-formation could be established. Augustine's critique questions the validity of public will-formation as advanced by Cicero's interlocutor Scipio in *On the Commonwealth*. Scipio had argued that the basis for the definition of a commonwealth was the 'weal of the people'. In turn, a 'people' was defined as a group or 'multitude' which was 'united in association by a common sense of right and community of interest'. Echoing later arguments regarding private and public autonomy, Augustine argued that there could never be a public autonomy. In his view, a state which would be said to emerge from public will formation would be valid if it emanated from a common sense of right. That would mean that a shared sense of justice would have to be available to a public at large. Augustine argued that there could be no common sense of right and therefore no commonwealth.[1]

Augustine's argument hinges, as he rightly acknowledges, on what one means by the notion of justice. Following Cicero's argument he acknowledges that a state cannot maintain itself without justice. Justice requires a common sense of right.[2]

Of course Augustine, whose radical scepticism undermines the classical notion of the commonwealth, had reasons derived from another source, namely, divine justice – which affected his notions of both corrupt institutions and corrupt individuals. Since, in his view, the Romans were of a sinful nature and worshipped false gods, they could not possibly constitute a commonwealth. Equally, since they formed their institutions under the sign of human corruption, they could not possibly achieve a certain public autonomy which is fundamental for a just society.

Ultimately, Augustine was not interested in giving arguments which would ground a commonwealth. He was much more interested in constructing an account for the fall of Rome, an account which would, in turn, lead classical civilization to the City of God. However, there is a certain truth in his rather devastating critique. On the one hand, for there to be a commonwealth there has to be a valid will-formation, which led Augustine to suggest that the sought-for public will-formation in which the commonwealth is grounded could not be trusted given the human potentiality for evil. Equally, from a modern point of view, Augustine had no mechanism for conceiving of plurality.[3]

Of course, the underlying view of politics and the good life, which Augustine knew only as it was mediated to him through Cicero and forms of Platonism, was stated by Aristotle, on the first page of the first book of the *Nicomachean Ethics*, in his assertion of the primacy of the good.[4] Aristotle's practical philosophy assumed the eminent validity of just institutions and it trusted in the efficacy of practical judgment (*phronesis*). The argument that Aristotle generates, if one could imagine it as an answer to that constructed by Augustine, assumes a certain role for politics in association with the realization of human happiness. Based as it is on the distinction between *oikos* and *polis*, it assumes that the practice of politics opens the way to the realization of freedom experienced in speech and action. The good, then, being the greatest thing to be attained, could be attained only through practical wisdom in the political realm. Hence, as Hannah Arendt[5] has pointed out, it was in the realm of politics, the public realm, that recognition of human freedom was to be attained. Further, given Aristotle's understanding of nature and potentiality driving toward actuality, politics would have a positive, one might even claim a necessary, function.

We could imagine a debate between Aristotle and Augustine over the justification of politics. Aristotle included politics within a rhetoric about the good, which is to say that politics finds its foundation in ethics. To put it another way, the end of ethics is politics because politics is defined as the highest good for human beings. This is to say that politics can be justified teleologically. Practical wisdom, the handmaiden of politics, enables the achievement of the good life through speech and action. Further, politics is based on a certain shared, universal, capacity[6] which could be defined from a modern point of view as public autonomy.[7]

Augustine's scepticism is derived from his doubts about the capacities of individuals in regard to the pursuit of the good and the consequent implications regarding the possibility of there being good institutions. To put it in modern terms, the propensity for evil, both through the inclination of individuals and of the institutions which they build under that inclination, prohibits the possibility of a valid public will-formation. As a consequence there can be no ethical justification for political action. This leads to rather dire consequences for politics. Robbed of its ethical foundation, about which Augustine was appropriately sceptical, politics could be turned over effectively to the realm of instrumentality.[8] To be sure, Augustine's scepticism was rooted in the framework of a certain religious belief structure which required the subordination of political to theological interests. Modernity, under the pressure of a plurality of theological interests, would retain Augustine's scepticism while at the same time articulating politics on a secular ground. Thomas Hobbes was no less cynical than Augustine regarding the attainment of a certain form of the good life in the public realm. In fact, Augustinian cynicism, or, perhaps better, realism, permeates early modernity as it attempts to wrestle with the establishment of a public order. If one were to date the emergence of modernity with the seventeenth-century attempt to ground politics, it appears that this attempt owes more to Augustinian realism regarding human nature and human institutions than it does to Aristotelian optimism regarding the human capacity for politics. Hobbes' rather flat declaration that there 'is no such *Finis ultimus* (utmost ayme,) nor *Summum Bonum,* (greatest Good,) as is spoken in the Books of the old Morall Philosophers'[9] puts him distinctly on Augustine's side as a sceptic regarding the attempt to ground politics in an ethics of the good.

II

Hobbes had a problem, however, which plagued neither Aristotle nor Augustine, namely pluralism. Hobbes, writing during and after the religious wars, was plainly interested in finding a way to mediate, without reference to ethical intention, fundamental interests of potentially opposing parties. Therefore, it was necessary to abstract from the theological–ethical interest of the appropriate parties in order to enable a non-conflictual consensus at the base of the political order.[10] In order to do so he created a quasi-rational narrative argument regarding a 'fictional' contract which was said to exist at the time of the beginning of the political order.[11] In so doing he created what came to be the modern argument for the origin of democracy.[12] As is well known, this argument attempted to derive the political order from the concept of rights.[13] This concept of rights and the rules associated with them came to be regarded as fundamental to the liberal concept of the state.[14] Hobbes speculated that if everyone had the right of self-preservation, which would lead to humankind's condition as a state of war of all against all, then one would be willing to transfer that right to another under certain conditions or rules. These rules would restore the notion of the commonwealth which had been so radically undermined by Augustine. In a peculiar way, Hobbes' definition of will-formation is not unlike that of Augustine in the sense that in order for the state to exist there must be a unity of wills expressed in one will.[15] However, there is a sense in which Hobbes differed radically not only from Augustine but even from Aristotle in his formulation for the existence of the modern commonwealth. From Hobbes' point of view, the validity of public will-formation as it would exist within the commonwealth need not, as Augustine claimed, be granted by the ethical or religious competence of the individuals of whom it was composed. Rather, Hobbes thought power, in some sense supported by reason, would be sufficient to account for the validity of the commonwealth under the principle of sovereignty.[16]

From the point of view of the classical concept of politics and the critique thereof, Hobbes had restored the idea of a commonwealth seemingly devoid of ethical intention, derived from private autonomy. The commonwealth exists to sustain one's private interests, to effectively reduce conflict and, most importantly, to allow the pursuit of a commodious life under conditions of a market society.[17] Of course, there are ethical components, though more or less overlooked, or perhaps one could say underplayed, in Hobbes's theory. In one sense, sovereignty legitimates coercive power, but in another sense we are still left with the question of the 'authorship' of the covenant which has reference to those who originally granted their consent.[18] The point is that those who originally granted their consent had differing ethical points of view. It follows that it would be impossible to resolve the problem of the generation of sovereignty through consensus on the basis of any one ethical point of view. To be sure, consensus cannot be achieved on ethical grounds, because the expression of ethical interest leads to conflict. However, the quandary produced by a multiplicity of ethical interests expressed at an immediate level of direct conflict among plural interests re-emerges at a higher level, namely, at the level of those who legitimated the agreement. In this view, from now on the focus would be on the conditions of the agreement rather than on the ethical interests of the participants and their respective conceptions of the good life which could not be mediated. It would be wrong to argue that Hobbes conceived of political sovereignty merely instrumentally. But the instrumental focus of the theory would be central to its legitimacy. The problem was that legitimacy could not be conceived in solely instrumental terms. Hence, one would have to argue that there was a normative component to the theory. By conceiving the notion of sovereignty in strategic terms Hobbes was able to conceptualize the phenomenon of necessary power through law which would give society its fundamental cohesion. However, what the model lacked was a basis for the normative justification of legitimacy.[19]

III

Hobbes transformed a discourse about ethics and politics into a discourse about power, law and rationality. Hobbes' disdain for discourses about the good derived in part from his view of human nature, which departed from the teleological tendencies then prevalent.[20] As is well known, in the Hobbesian universe matter is always in motion, signifying that there could be no time in which motion would cease. This view undercut the metaphysical assumptions of both Augustine and Aristotle. Hence, there was no possibility of an eternal happiness towards which human subjects could orient themselves. Instead those very subjects, having consented to the rule of the sovereign, would submit to his instrumental control, while he would keep his subjects 'in check by fear'. Sovereignty, however, could not generate its instrumental power out of nothing. Rather, the medium through which sovereignty would express itself would be civil law.

By turning to law Hobbes immediately finds himself involved in a problem of legal legitimation. It is not enough to suggest that law grounds sovereignty. Rather it is necessary to show how law can be legitimated by relationship to the power of the sovereign. As such, the Hobbes who rejected the concept of the good life as the basis for the legitimation of politics turns to the question of the kind of normative sanction which law can give for the stability of the political order. In this view law, when properly understood, is subject to sovereign power. Or, to put it another way, there is a fundamental relationship between the law and the commonwealth.[21] Hobbes goes on to clarify that relationship in a number of ways.

There is a fundamental relationship between law and legislation. The sovereign is not subject to civil law because he is its subject or creator. More importantly, and here Hobbes was fighting the reigning belief of the time, the authority of law cannot be attributed to tradition. Rather, the authority of the law is to be conceived as legitimated by the will of the sovereign.[22] Law in turn has replaced ethics as the source of stability in the modern political order. Ultimately for Hobbes law replaces the kind of stability which had until then been provided by both ethics and tradition. It is fascinating to see Hobbes restore the link between the legitimacy of a political order and the expression of a common will which had been so rudely uncoupled by Augustine through the reconceptualization of the relationship between law, power and reason. Hobbes fully realizes that power alone cannot guarantee the legitimacy of law. Law seeks the authority of reason for its legitimation. Hence, there must be a kind of public reason to which law is privy in order for law to legitimate the stability of the modern order.[23] When he turns to that argument he must confront the authority of the legal tradition in the form of the arguments of the most renowned jurist of the day, Sir Edward Coke.

Put simply, the question about which he enters into debate with Coke regards what gives consistency to legal interpretation, a matter which in turn affects legal legitimacy. Hence, although Hobbes acknowledges universal agreement among the lawyers of the day regarding the proposition that 'Law can never be against Reason', the real issue regards 'whose reason it is'. It is here that Hobbes puts forth a notion of public reason. He rejects the idea that valid legal interpretation can be based on 'private reason' because if legal interpretation were dependent on the use of private reason 'there would be as much contradiction in the Lawes, as there is in the Schooles'.[24] However, beyond the claims of private reason there is a claim which is more traditional and powerful, coming from the realm of *Juris prudentia*, the practical wisdom of judges. No doubt, these claims legitimate law on the basis of a fundamental assumption about ethics, namely, that the interpretation of law functions for the ethics of the good. It is this assumption that Hobbes is most anxious to overcome.

Consistent with his attempt to abstract from the implications of conflict deriving from multiple ethical traditions, Hobbes attempts to overcome the limitations of Coke's position. In order to do so, he must confront the notion of reason central to Coke's jurisprudential argument. Coke had made famous the phrase an '*Artificiall perfection of Reason, gotton by long study, observation and experience*'.[25] Hobbes rebuts this view with a notion of public reason. With what must have been a touch of irony and a dash of humour, Hobbes suggests that long study may 'encrease, and confirm erroneous Sentences' and, having chosen false ground on which to build their arguments, will come to even 'greater ruine' with the sad result that their reasons will remain 'discordant'. Hence, to follow Hobbes, one should dismiss jurisprudence and along with it the 'wisdome of subordinate Judges'. Instead one should turn to the 'Reason of this our Artificiall Man the Common-wealth, and his Command that maketh Law'.[26] Hobbes' reason for this is again quite simple: consistency. The commonwealth consists of 'one Person', which results in the consequence that 'there cannot easily arise any contradiction in the Lawes'.[27] And, more importantly, when contradiction does arise, according to Hobbes, 'the same Reason is able, by interpretation, or alteration, to take it away'.[28] The result should be that those who judge should subordinate their judgment to the Sovereign, which Hobbes defines as the 'Person of the Common-wealth'.[29]

IV

Thus far I have dealt with the two conflicting paradigms of public reason which will, as the premodern heritage of modernity, dominate modern discourses about politics. Both paradigms relate a form of ethics to politics, although with the emergence of modernity that relationship becomes much more complex. The classical paradigm derives politics from ethics. Politics is seen as necessary for the actualization of the good life, i.e., as an end in itself. This paradigm has a double confidence: a confidence in the individual capacity to pursue the good life as well as a confidence in the actuality of good institutions where the good life may be pursued. It assumes that deliberation will result not only in the actualization of human potentiality, but in the creation of good institutions.[30] Finally, although it assumes that there are good laws, it does not need to grant to law a central role within the paradigm because it is not preoccupied with the central issue of power.[31]

Augustine's critique, admittedly directed more at Cicero than at Aristotle, questions, from a theological point of view, the possibility of achieving the good life in a finite political context. Given their propensity for evil, human beings do not have the capacity to generate the basic common will-formation which would be necessary to develop a legitimate commonwealth. At the same time Augustine attempted to undermine the idea of the good life presupposed by Aristotle both on the ground that felicity was not attainable on this earth and on the assumption that there could be no public good available to reason. Thus, he found the belief in human capacity and good human institutions, central to the classical paradigm, both naive and impossible.[32]

The modern liberal paradigm shares a number of critical insights with Augustine's critique of the classical paradigm, albeit for different reasons.[33] It doubts the classic conception of the good, not on the basis of a sinful nature, but on the basis of the absence of a teleological framework necessary for the classical conception of the good. Equally, it agrees with the Augustinian critique of the common will on a practical level, but it reconstructs this idea on a fictional or ideal level in order to retain the idea of legitimacy.[34] This is crucial to the modern liberal paradigm because, on a practical level, given the multitude of practical interests as well as the competition for available goods, conflict is the order of the day. It becomes necessary to construct a fictional account to which the subjects of political society could ideally agree. It should be noted that this is a secular reconstruction of what Augustine perceived as an essentially ideological or theological problem. Hobbes did not give up on the political idea of the commonwealth precisely for secular reasons. On the practical level, political society could be conceived as a war of all against all precisely because a series of ethical and religious commitments to various conceptions of the good life would compete with one another. Hence, the issue of public will-formation would have to be resolved at the fictional level, abstracted from the ethical commitments of political subjects, in order for a society to achieve the necessary consensus to live in peace. It would appear, then, that the classical relationship between ethics and politics would be forever severed. Indeed, it was. However, the normative conditions under which political action would occur would re-emerge as the central question of modern politics. This would mean that Hobbes opened modern politics to the question of radical democracy, even if this was not his original intention.

While the classical paradigm assumed a basic social cohesion guaranteed by a series of good institutions, Hobbes understood the practical necessity of generating social cohesion through the instrument of the sovereign. He turned to law as that which could order society in terms of its ability to secure obedience through coercive power. This led him to argue for the control of the law under the figure of the sovereign. At the same time he understood that this was not a question of coercive power alone but also of reason. Therefore the argument for rational consistency would extend beyond the claims of instrumentality to the issue of the normative status of sovereignty. This seems to be a necessary move in the transition from the classical to the modern liberal paradigm because a diminished understanding of the good has arisen with the emergence of plurality as well as a changing standard of distributive justice with the emergence of a market society. Hence, from a sociological and historical perspective, the turn towards law appears in the absence of ethical standards shared by all participants in a particular culture. When tradition no longer generates the necessary cohesiveness to sustain the integration of the social order, the coercive power of law steps in to fill the gap.[35]

V

I have attempted to follow the changing paradigm of public reason, as it relates to ethics and politics, through the so-called classical and early modern political formations. With the development of the liberal paradigm of public reason the rhetoric changes from the question of the relationship between ethics and politics to that of the relationship between law and politics, with the question of the normative status of politics replacing the more traditional view that politics is a form of the realization of ethical life. As we have seen, although the Hobbesian model attempts to solve the problem of social integration through the instrumental granting of the coercive power of law to the function of sovereignty, the ideal of the commonwealth as the common will of the people lurks behind the facade of instrumentality. Ultimately, even for Hobbes, law cannot be legitimized on the basis of strategic power alone; it requires reason for its justification. To the extent that reason is based on a prior contractual obligation, associated with the mutual consent of political subjects, the legitimation of law will be ever more based on a public notion. The standard interpretation of the liberal paradigm is that it results in the paradoxical and conflictual relationship of autonomous individual rights and social obligations. This formulation can be found in Hobbes and reappears in various ways in modern political theory – in Kant, in Rousseau, in modern constitutions and in the French *Declaration of the Rights of Man and Citizen*. It defines human liberty as the right to do anything, limited only by the potential harm to others. Modern law secures and protects individual liberty by fixing the limits between individuals. However, such a view is not necessarily democratic because, although it maximizes individual liberty, it does not account for public will-formation. To put it another way, Hobbes had already seen the problem when he argued against Coke that law had to appeal to reason in order to justify its consistency. The legitimation process needs to be located in the reason granted to the sovereign.[36]

This restriction of the idea of the modern state to individual autonomy has been taken to mean that there is a deficit within the liberal paradigm regarding public will-formation. Kantian constructivism attempts to repair this deficit by deriving moral autonomy from universal law. Hence, it is from the capacity to fulfil human obligation that Kant deduces autonomous freedom.[37] Autonomous freedom in turn requires a certain public form of regulation. It follows that this capacity, transcendentally conceived, presupposes a certain private use of reason for public means.[38] Rights, so conceived, justify a certain conception of the public, but of a public justified as derived from the attribution of certain private rights derived from a notion of private autonomy.[39]

Against this perceived deficit it would appear fitting to go all the way back to the classical paradigm which, through its distinction between the *oikos* and *polis* and its use of *phronesis*, reconnects *ethos* and *polis*. Certainly this was Hannah Arendt's 'republican' argument against the liberal paradigm which, in the name of economic freedom, sought to reduce the idea of the realization of human freedom to private interest.[40] In this view, freedom was reduced to private liberty, banished from the public realm. Indeed, in accord with the classical idea of *physus*, participation in politics was a necessary ingredient for human fulfilment.[41] From this point of view, what is lacking in the Hobbesian liberal paradigm is precisely a conception of politics. Given the kind of institutional arrangement presupposed by the 'republican' argument, public will-formation would be the natural outcome of continuous expression in public speech and action. The distribution of power in this view would not simply be for the purpose of strategic control, or even 'political domination' in a Weberian sense. Rather, power would be linked to speech and action.[42] Here, as I take it, emerges the fundamental distinction between the republican and the liberal paradigm. Put simply, the republican view links freedom with politics in the sense that the political realm is the condition for the possibility of fully free expression. The liberal view is suspicious of that claim. With its focus on stability, its concern is with the integration of multiple views of human agency, freedom is linked as much with private, apolitical or non-political, expression of human agency as with the protection of that right. What Arendt seems to object to is this turn from a public notion of freedom to a private one, with its consequence that there is no basic need for political participation while there is a right of protection against the potential imposition of the state.[43] It would follow that the republican thesis is that when power shifts from the public to the private it becomes merely instrumental, having severed its link with freedom. Power is now the power of the state from which the individual must be protected.

But the critical question emerges when one asks about the assertion of a comprehensive view of politics. The standard critique of the republican view is that by returning to the classical conception of politics it cannot determine which of a number of conceptions of the good life is the appropriate one within a comprehensive political culture.[44] By emphasizing an ethical conception of politics, it underplays the concept of *right*. Hence, such a view, because of its commitment to a teleological conception of the world, must impose itself on unwilling subjects in the political process. Further, such a view gives up, through its basic optimism regarding human capacities and its fundamental trust in the goodness of human institutions, the necessary critical distance needed for the recognition of possible institutional and human error. By having too closely identified politics with ethics, the republican view inadvertently limits the public realm by restricting the scope of the tolerance necessary to a modern political culture. Hence, the very achievement of a public will-formation is undermined by undercutting the concept of private autonomy.

One hypothesis to be derived from the prior discussion is that there is a certain advantage to be gained for political philosophy by turning towards a philosophy of law. One could claim that by taking over the method of deriving legal consistency from rationality one would be able to resolve potential conflicts on a higher level – on the level of a certain form of idealization. Implicit in this process would be the claim that consistency is to be achieved by enlarging the claims of rationality. Hence, there would be a correlation between four modalities: consistency, idealization, rationality and validity. What remains controversial in appealing to the philosophy of law tradition is the argument for the form of rationality appropriate to the claims of idealization. As early modern philosophy of law illustrates, the conflict of interpretations was present at the outset of any appeal to rationality as indicated by Hobbes' question regarding 'whose reason it is'.

VI

So the question becomes, can a notion of public will-formation be derived from reason alone? Given the problem generated by the republican critique of the liberal paradigm it would appear that one could overcome the deficit of the liberal paradigm by rationally reconstructing an account of public will-formation. If this could be done it would overcome the difficulties implied by the notions of plurality and with its consequent implications for the notion of toleration. What would be needed is a public form of justification: an idea of public will-formation which could be justified by a certain public use of reason. At this point the idea of public will-formation would take on a deliberative or democratic definition. Rights granted to

191

individuals in this context must be grounded in an idea of public will-formation. So conceived, law would be sanctioned beyond its coercive dimension through a justification by those to whom it is applied. To follow the classic liberal formulation, for law to be reasonable it must be, beyond Hobbes, legitimated by reference to a community of the governed. On the one hand this would satisfy the republican ethical critique of liberalism by referring to a certain kind of *ethos*. But it would not collapse politics into ethics because it would not rely solely on one political community for its justification.[45]

Central to this description of a notion in which private rights could be derived from a notion of the public would be the conceptualization of such a community through which public will-formation occurred. One could approach the issue either historically or systematically. Reference to the legitimation of law by and through the governed could be linked to a demand which occurs only with modernity. This is the *historical* issue. The historical condition for justification would be the demand for plurality which emerges in a more radical way with modern society. Hence, the idea of public will-formation must have a democratic or deliberative character.[46] But the issue is also speculative precisely because this demand for toleration and plurality must be incorporated into the rational claims of justification.[47] This is a deontological demand which requires a process of universalization beyond historical immediacy. The claim of rationality with regard to law would have to extend beyond mere logical consistency (Hobbes) to incorporate a universal community of interpreters of the law. One could conceive such an argument transcendentally. Kant's aesthetics, in contradistinction to his ethics and his philosophy of law, provides the example.[48] In order to grant validity to an aesthetic judgment of taste it is necessary to conceive of a universal community of interpreters who would grant to that judgment a certain validity in the same way that the person who makes the judgment does. If one were to make a political judgment analogous to an aesthetic judgment one could say that the precondition for a concept of private autonomy based on rights is the pre-existence of a community of interpreters which grants validity to that right as a necessity. Public will-formation as embodied in a *sensus communis* would be presupposed as a necessary condition for private autonomy. Hence, the deficit in the liberal paradigm, as perceived through the republican critique, would be overcome.

This aesthetic appropriation could be the basis for a moral norm which would involve the universal *acknowledgement* of a certain public precondition. In essence, a private autonomy would be possible only if it were possible to grant it universally, that is, to give an equal possibility to all other members of a community. Hence, the presupposition of any private right would be the acknowledgement of a deliberative process, a public will-formation, which would be the condition for the possibility of having that right. Hence, lurking behind the backs of individual autonomous subjects would be the notion of *reciprocity*. A reciprocal notion of justice would precede any private notion of justice. Such a notion of justice would be grounded in a notion of public will-formation or deliberation.

In this account of public reason three problem areas have been identified. First, regarding the juxtaposition between private rights and public will-formation, I have, in coming to terms with the republican critique of liberalism, shown how reference to private rights presupposes public will-formation and hence a notion of public reason. Second, regarding the normative or ethical component of politics, the consequence of this association of private rights and public will-formation is the assumption that in order for law to exist it is necessary that a certain normative construction be rationally implied. Hence, the reconstruction of the liberal paradigm through the normative idea of reciprocity allows us to answer the republican critique regarding the ethical lacunae of the liberal paradigm. At the same time one does not have to dissolve politics into ethics with the result that only one theory of the good can be chosen in a context where all or most ideas of the good should be tolerated. Third, with regard to the democratic paradigm, this reciprocal notion of reason provides a public basis upon which notions of both private and public can be based. The deficit of the liberal paradigm may be traced to Hobbes' inability to conceive that paradigm democratically. The insight that law must have reference to a realm beyond the mere private judgment of the judge was Hobbes' great contribution. However, sovereignty is not identical with a notion of public will-formation. Hence Hobbes was restricted to a definition of the relationship of politics and law which was essentially instrumental. The result was that law could be conceived only through the lens of power, with the result that politics would be fatally linked to coercion. The possibility, implied by his notion of reason, of democratic conceptions of law and politics escaped his grasp because of his inability to conceive of reason through the idea of reciprocity.

Notes

1 'Therefore, where there is no true justice there can be no "association of men united by a common sense of right", and therefore no people answering to the definition of Scipio, or Cicero. And if there is no people then there is no "weal of the people," but some kind of a mob, not deserving the name of a people. If therefore a commonwealth is the "weal of the people", and if a people does not exist where there is no justice, the irresistible conclusion is that where there is no justice there is no commonwealth' (Augustine, *Concerning the City of God Against the Pagans*, Harmondsworth: Penguin Books, 1972, p. 882).
2 Apparently, Augustine derives his notion of justice from Plato. Hence, justice would be derived from a certain ability to do the right thing. That ability in turn would be derived from the proper order of the soul. A soul which is not properly ruled cannot perform just acts. Hence, in Augustine's theological

view, the Romans could not have achieved justice because they were improperly ruled, both as individuals and as a people. The technical issue here is whether he is using both the Platonic hierarchical notion and the Aristotelian relational notion of justice. If one uses the former it would follow that a corrupt being would not be capable of justice. In any case, the achievement of a certain public will-formation is based on a certain capacity.

3 Certainly, the argument against the Romans was an argument which could not allow for a tolerance of the point of view of the other. The reconstruction of a fundamentally secular argument through the imposition of a theological interpretation would imply that the public will must conform to the divine will, meaning that there could be no legitimate public will-formation in a secular context.

4 'Every art or applied science and every systematic investigation, and similarly every action and choice, seem to aim at some good: the good, therefore, has been defined as that at which all things aim' (Aristotle, *Nicomachean Ethics*, trans. Martin Ostwald, Indianapolis: Bobbs-Merrill, 1962, p. 4).

5 I refer to Hannah Arendt's Heideggerian argument in *The Human Condition* (Chicago: The University of Chicago Press, 1958).

6 The modern rhetoric regarding both individual capacity and public autonomy originates with Aristotle. Regarding capacity he states: 'We observe further that the most honored capacities, such as strategy, household management, and oratory, are contained in politics. Since this science uses the rest of the sciences, and since, moreover, it legislates what people are to do and what they are not to do, its end seems to embrace the ends of the other sciences' (*op. cit.*, p. 4).

7 The argument for public autonomy is based on the priority of the highest good. Having established that 'the end of politics is the good for man', Aristotle can go on to suggest that 'even if the good is the same for the individual and the state, the good of the state clearly is the greater and more perfect thing to attain and to safeguard' (*ibid.*, pp. 4–5). Surely, this is an argument based on assumptions regarding the ethics of the good life. However, it ends on a somewhat utilitarian note: 'The attainment of the good for one man alone is, to be sure, a source of satisfaction; yet to secure it for a nation and for states is nobler and more divine' (*ibid.*).

8 There is one non-instrumental claim which Augustine makes which should not go unnoticed. He holds out for the option that one can define the term 'people' as united not by justice but in relationship to love. 'If one should say, "A people is the association of a multitude of rational beings united by a common agreement on the objects of their love", then it follows that to observe the character of a particular people we must examine the objects of its love' (*op. cit.*, p. 890). It would follow that either the better the object the better the character or, in the case of the Romans, the opposite. Significantly, however, he is willing to let this definition stand on the basis of an alternative definition which would legitimate a characterization of Rome as a commonwealth. 'By this definition of ours, the Roman people is a people and its estate is indubitably a commonwealth' (*ibid.*).

9 Thomas Hobbes, *Leviathan* (ed. C.B. MacPherson, London: Pelikan Books, 1968 [1651]), p. 160.

10 Hobbes had a non-discursive, practical, notion of consensus which attempted to mediate between a plurality of interests based on legitimating power.

11 The term 'fictional' is derived from a notion of language. By generating a narrative about political origins, which later authors would categorize ironically as

without basis in any historical or scientific investigation (see Rousseau, *Second Discourse*), Hobbes clearly attempted to generate a narrative so powerful as to achieve consensus among radically diverse interests. As I shall show later, this fiction was backed by a certain claim of reason.

12 It is only in the sense that Hobbes was able to establish a theoretical framework for the implementation of certain procedural factors that one could say democracy would find its origin in a Hobbesian formulation. However, the very idea that the stability of the public order would emanate from a mediation of private interests into a public will-formation was fundamental to the development of democracy.

13 In Hobbes' view, right is associated with liberty and differs radically from obligation. He states: 'RIGHT, consisteth in liberty to do, or to forbeare; Whereas LAW, determineth and bindeth to one of them: so that Law, and Right, differ as much, as Obligation, and Liberty: which in one and the same manner are inconsistent' (*Leviathan, op. cit.*, p. 189). It is this inconsistency which would preoccupy political theory to the present.

14 The state arises to protect the rights of individuals in so far as those rights can be protected. Hence, the state exists as the condition of the exercise of those individual liberties but also as the limit of the exercise of liberty. To be sure, Hobbes conceived of the state in instrumental terms. However, it can still be argued that the state originates from the exercise of individual liberty even though it is the basis for the limit of that very exercise.

15 Hobbes states that it must be necessary that the people or inhabitants of the social order 'may reduce all their Wills, by plurality of voices, onto one Will . . . as if every man should say to every man, *I Authorize and give up my Right of Governing my selfe, to this Man, or to this Assembly of men, on this condition, that thou give up thy Right to him, and Authorize all his Actions in like manner*. This done, the Multitude so united in one Person is called a COMMON-WEALTH, in latine CIVITAS' (*ibid.*, pp. 227–28).

16 Hobbes has many words for the term 'commonwealth' such as '*Mortall God*' and even 'LEVIATHAN', however, 'SOVERAIGNE' seems to have been his favourite. By such designations, Hobbes was concerned with the mediation of power and not ethical intention. 'For by this Authoritie, given him by every particular man in the Common-Wealth, he hath the use of so much Power and Strength conferred on him, that by terror thereof, he is inabled to forme the wills of them all, to Peace at home, and mutuall ayd against their enemies abroad' (*ibid.*, pp. 227–28).

17 One might note C.B. MacPherson's observation that Hobbes' *Leviathan* would be impossible without the existence of a market society (*ibid.*, pp. 9–70).

18 With the notion of consent Hobbes begins to formulate a notion of public reason. For him there are two ways of attaining sovereign power. One is by what he calls 'Naturall force', which is analogous to a father ruling his children or dominance through war. But the other way to sovereign power is through agreement. He states: 'when men agree amongst themselves, to submit to some Man, or Assembly of men, voluntarily, on confidence to be protected by him against all others. This later, may be called a Political Common-wealth or Commonwealth by *Institution* . . .' (*ibid.*, p. 228).

19 To be sure, Hobbes understood that the problem of conceiving of society from the point of view of its stability, and not from the point of view of shared interests of the good life, would result in a conceptualization which would seek its justification in conformity to regulations which would be sanctioned through methods of coercion. Hence, Hobbes would turn to law and not to a conception

of the good life to justify his interpretation. However, even Hobbes, the one who turned to a discourse about power to resolve the quandaries of modern politics, found that law alone was not enough to sanction power.

20 Hobbes disagreed with Aristotle's view. 'Nor can a man any more live, whose Desires are at an end, than he, whose Senses and Imaginations are at a stand. Felicity is a continuall progresse of the desire, from one object to another; the attaining of the former, being still but the way to the later. The cause whereof is, That the object of mans desire is not to enjoy once only, and for one instant of time; but to assure for ever the way of his future desire' (*ibid.*, p. 160).

21 'Which considered, I define Civill Law in this manner. CIVILL LAW, *Is to every Subject, those Rules, which the Common-Wealth hath Commanded him, by Word, Writing, or other sufficient Sign of the Will, to make use of, for the Distinction of Right, and Wrong; that is to say, of what is contrary and what is not contrary to the Rule*' (*ibid.*, p. 312).

22 'When long Use obtaineth the authority of a Law, it is not the Length of Time that maketh the Authority, but the Will of the Soveraign signified by his silence, (for Silence is sometimes an argument of Consent;) and it is no longer Law, then the Soveraign shall be silent therein' (*ibid.*, p. 313).

23 Hobbes is quite comfortable stating the following: 'all laws have their Authority, and force, from the Will of the Common-wealth' (*ibid.*, pp. 315–16).

24 *Ibid.*, p. 316.

25 *Ibid.*, p. 317.

26 *Ibid.*

27 *Ibid.*

28 *Ibid.*

29 The result of this argument, as some might surmise, is not the abolition of natural law. Hobbes, on the contrary, goes on to legitimate a framework for interpretation which correlates the natural and the civil law. Neither does he undermine the necessity for interpretation on the part of lawyers and judges. Hence one can safely assume that he is quite ready to accommodate interpretation as long as it follows from the normative structure established by the notion of public reason he has put forth.

30 Central to the classical notion of public deliberation is the notion of *physus*. Hence politics in the classical scheme of things becomes a necessary and not a contingent or optional function. Any modern attempt to regain the classical notion of politics will have to deal with this basic metaphysical assumption which requires a very specific philosophical anthropology as well.

31 Here, I do not mean to overlook Aristotle's observations with regard to the centrality of law and constitutions in the latter part of his *Politics*. However, the problem of stability did not occur in the ancient world in the same way as it does in the modern. And even if it had, given his metaphysical commitments, Aristotle would have had to deal with the problem of political integration in accord with the scheme of potentiality and actuality.

32 The point which Augustine inadvertently makes is that a politics which depends on a common will-formation depends on an idea of the good life which in turn presupposes the possibility of there being good, that is non-self-interested, citizens. Here, Augustine, Machiavelli and Hobbes are in agreement. In a sense, the issue is an anthropological one in modernity, in the sense that human capacity becomes the focus of the debate.

33 Certainly Hobbes differs from Augustine on basic theological assumptions. However, Hobbes' more secular anthropology is strikingly similar to Augustine's understanding of humanity tainted by original sin.

34 Hence, in the Hobbesian view, there is a very close association between fiction and reason as well as between narrative and reason.

35 One observation that follows from this is that law replaces traditional claims for social integration based on ethical solidarity. The question remains regarding whether or not law alone provides the basis for social integration. Also, as we shall see later, this anticipates Habermas' view of the law.

36 This would suggest that although Hobbes may be guilty of deriving public liberty from private rights, he is also the first to assert that a form of rational justification must go beyond private rights.

37 Kant states: '*Right* is the limitation of each person's freedom so that it is compatible with the freedom of everyone, insofar as this is possible in accord with a universal law; and *public right* is the totality [*Inbegriff*] of *external laws* that makes such a thoroughgoing compatibility possible' ('On the Proverb: That May be True in Theory, But Is of No Practical Use' [1793], in *Perpetual Peace and Other Essays*, trans. Ted Humphrey, Indianapolis: Hackett Publishing Company, 1983, p. 72). This is generally taken to mean that public autonomy is derived from a concept of private rights. Certainly, Hegel's critique of Kant as well as later critiques of liberalism follow this form of argumentation.

38 In fairness to Kant there is a certain form of public autonomy in the transcendental concept of public rights in the form of publicity. This 'transcendental formula' reads as follows: 'All actions that affect the rights of other men are wrong if their maxim is not consistent with publicity' ('To Perpetual Peace: A Philosophical Sketch' [1795], *ibid.*, p. 135).

39 To the notion of the public based on the reason of the sovereign, in Hobbes, and to the notion of the public or publicity based on the notion of private autonomy, one must also add Montesquieu's notion of democracy being based on a particular public virtue or moral sentiment. He states: 'Virtue in a republic is a most simple thing; it is a love of the republic; it is a sensation, and not a consequence of acquired knowledge, a sensation that may be felt by the meanest as well as by the highest person in the state' (*The Spirit of the Laws* [1750], New York: Hafner, 1949, p. 41). In democracy he thought those particular virtues were love of equality and frugality. Such love produced a 'stronger attachment to the established laws and customs' (*ibid.*, p. 40).

40 Arendt's *The Human Condition* represents a fundamental attempt to overcome the liberal paradigm. In particular, her introduction of the distinction between the private and the public, based on the classical distinction between *oikos* and *polis*, serves as the critical basis for undercutting the modern understanding of the private realm, justified as it is on fundamental economic assumptions (*op. cit.*, pp. 22–77).

41 I think that Arendt, by relying on the classical understanding of speech and action which assumes a certain metaphysical commitment to a notion of political actualization in speech and action, misunderstands the modern distinction between public and private which is based on the need for toleration. Her theory of politics is based on a certain view of *necessary* action for the purposes of human actualization. In the modern world this view can only compete with other views of the good life; it cannot legitimate itself as the sole or only view of political action. In this she shares with her mentor, Heidegger, a certain failure to understand modern politics.

42 To say that power is fundamentally communicative means that there is a link between power and speech. 'Power is what keeps the public realm, the potential space of appearance between acting and speaking men, in existence. . . . Power is always, as we would say, a power potential and not an unchangeable, measurable, and reliable entity like force or strength' (*ibid.*, p. 200).

43 Arne Johan Vetlesen ('Hannah Arendt, Habermas and the Republican Tradition', *Philosophy and Social Criticism*, Vol. 21, No. 1, 1995) catches the distinction effectively when he interprets Arendt in the following way:

> Arendt traces the history of this shift [from the republican to the liberal paradigm] back to the French Revolution. In the wake of the revolutionary events, Robespierre proclaimed that 'Under constitutional rule it is almost enough to protect the individuals against the abuses of public power' (Hannah Arendt, *On Revolution*, New York: Viking, 1963, p.13). Power thereby takes on a new meaning: it no longer denotes what individuals exercise when they meet and act in concert within the public sphere; rather, it denotes what the individuals as citizens are set over against, and against the abuses and excesses of which they rightfully may claim protection. The shift implied as Arendt sees it is a shift from being the subjects exercising power to being the objects affected by the exercise of power.

44 It is this aspect of Arendt's republican view which I find difficult. Here, I limit my account of Arendt to *The Human Condition*. In that work it is her dependence on Heidegger which leads to such a comprehensive view. On this issue I differ with Seyla Benhabib (*The Reluctant Modernism of Hannah Arendt*, Thousand Oaks: Sage, 1996) and Jacques Taminiaux (*La Fille de Thrace et le penseur professionnel: Arendt et Heidegger*, Paris: Payot, 1992), who interpret this work as Arendt's attempt to liberate herself from Heideggerian categories. To be sure, there is some evidence to support this. However, she was one with Heidegger in her belief that a return to a reinterpretation of the classical ideal would function as a kind of 'overcoming' of modern politics. In later works, particularly in her *Lectures on Kant*, she distanced herself more decisively from a Heideggerian politics.

45 The argument against the republican paradigm of public reason would be that the notion of reason required by the return to a single *ethos* would be too strong to allow for a plurality of interests sustained by a plurality of comprehensive views. At the same time, the liberal view would seek to appropriate politics at the normative level. As such it would enable an ethical or moral moment to exist at the deontological level. Of course, the manner in which this ethical or moral reference can be articulated is controversial and remains to be clarified.

46 There is a sense in which one can appropriate the larger *ethos* of modern legal culture through the traditions of constitutional law which they embody. Hence, appropriation of the *ethos* of a culture can be partially attained through a pragmatic or interpretive approach.

47 Historical appropriation is never enough. Modes of rational justification which sustain any pragmatic appropriation must be part of a legitimating argument for the relationship between law and politics.

48 At issue here is the distinction between reflective and determinate judgment. I refer to Kant's justification of the *sensus communis*, the principles of which – when compared to 'common human understanding' – are: '(1) to think for oneself; (2) to think from the standpoint of everyone else; and (3) to think always consistently' (*Critique of Judgment*, Indianapolis: Hackett, 1987; originally published in 1790 in Prussia).

Part IV

PSYCHOANALYSIS

14

IN THE NAME-OF-THE-FATHER
The Law?

William J. Richardson

The Court wants nothing from you. It receives you when you
come and it dismisses you when you go.
                                    (Franz Kafka, *The Trial*)

The scene is the darkened, otherwise empty, cathedral in Prague. Rain is
falling outside. For a moment, there is no other sound:

> The priest had already taken a step or two away from him, but
> [Joseph K.] cried out in a loud voice. "Please wait a moment." "I
> am waiting," said the priest. "Don't you want anything from
> me?" asked K. "No," said the priest. . . . "[But] you are the
> prison chaplain," said K., groping his way nearer to the priest
> again. . . . "That means I belong to the Court," said the priest.
> "So why should I want anything from you? The Court wants
> nothing from you, it receives you when you come and dismisses
> you when you go."[1]

The words are familiar: they come from the penultimate chapter of Franz
Kafka's landmark novel *The Trial*. When the conversation began, it was
clear that the chaplain was aware of the accusation against K. but unaware
of the state of the process. By the end, the chaplain had heard well enough
K.'s protestation of innocence but was equally convinced of the hopeless-
ness of his cause. Condemnation, he knew, was inevitable. Execution of
the verdict would come immediately in the closing chapter.

Precisely on his thirty-first birthday, one year to the day after the process
began, it happened. Toward nine o'clock in the evening, two men in frock
coats showed up at his dwelling, and K., already dressed in black,
appeared to be waiting for them. Through the city streets and out to the
quarry they led him, where they looked for an appropriate place to lay
him on the ground to perform the deed, propping his head against a rock.

Then one drew from a sheath concealed under his cloak a long double-edged butcher's knife that in a grotesque ritual they passed ceremoniously between them over K.'s prone body, as if somehow he were supposed to interrupt them and perform the deed himself. But he "could not completely rise to the occasion." Finally, one of the two grabbed K.'s throat while the other "thrust the knife deep into his heart and turned it there twice." It was dying "like a dog," he whispered, as if the shame of it would outlive him. The pity of it was that he was innocent, or so he claimed to the very end.[2]

This strange tale of guilt, innocence and the Law (concretized here in the Court) that Kafka left unfinished, intending that it be destroyed, was nonetheless published posthumously (in 1925) by his friend Max Brod, and has challenged interpreters ever since. Some, like George Steiner, find in it an echo of Kafka's Judaic heritage:

> Self evidently Franz Kafka meditates on the Law. It is the original mystery and subsequent application of the Law, of legalism and judgment, which are the essential concern of Talmudic questioning. If, in the Judaic perception, the language of the Adamic [myth] was that of love, the grammars of fallen man are those of the legal code. It is the modulation from one to the other, as commentary and commentary on commentary seek to hammer it out, which is one of the centers of *The Trial*.[3]

Others find in it a more Christian cast, where "the grammars of fallen man" include a faint hope of redemption. As he was about to die,

> [K.'s] gaze fell on the top story of the house adjoining the quarry. With a flicker as of a light going up, the casements of a window there suddenly flew open; a human figure, faint and insubstantial at that distance and that height, leaned abruptly forward and stretched both arms still farther. Who was it? A friend? A good man? Someone who sympathized? Someone who wanted to help? Was it one person only? Or was it mankind? Was there help at hand? Were there arguments in his favor that had been overlooked? . . . He raised his hands and spread out all his fingers.[4]

Others, like Eric Heller, find in it a thoroughgoing Gnosticism, while still others find nothing religious in it at all: no more than a remarkably prophetic anticipation of the anonymous brutality of the legal system of the Third Reich.[5] These are matters of literary criticism, however, and are best left to literary critics. Yet Kafka's work belongs to us all, and if one chooses to reflect on "The Paradox of the Law," Kafka's insights into Law and its paradoxes (he was, after all, a trained lawyer) are so evocative and provocative that it seems legitimate to let him supply a congenial heuristic context within which to interrogate the relation between Law and psychoanalysis as this functions in the desiring (i.e., ethical) subject in the work of Freud and Lacan.

To begin, again the essential story: on the morning of his thirtieth birthday, two strangers come to the apartment of Joseph K., a junior bank officer, to notify him that he is under arrest. They refuse to explain the reason for his arrest, saying only that he would be interrogated. They lead him to another room to be confronted by an inspector, but he, likewise, gives no reason – only that the arrest has been ordered by a higher authority. A few days later K. receives a note telling him to report at a certain address the following Sunday for interrogation before the Court, but without saying when. Arriving at the address, he finds only an apparently empty warehouse. Eventually he finds his way to the fifth floor and meets a washerwoman, who seems to expect him, and who directs him to the meeting room, filled with old men wearing badges, and where the judge tells him he is one hour and ten minutes late. He soon harangues the Court on the injustice of its methods and stomps out after refusing to have anything more to do with the process. After waiting a whole week expecting another summons, K. returns to the meeting hall on his own initiative to find only the washerwoman there. She regrets that the Court is not in session but assures him that it was only a lower body anyway; if one were acquitted by this Court it meant little, because a higher Court might very well re-arrest the prisoner on the same charge. Eventually, K.'s uncle recommends hiring an advocate. It turns out that this attorney stays in bed most of the time and, after several months have passed, K. finds that this man has done nothing but think about writing a petition in his name. Finally, in desperation, K. consults the portrait painter to the Court, Titorelli by name. Titorelli tells K. he can hope for little: no one is ever really acquitted and sometimes cases can be prolonged indefinitely.

It is at that point that the bank asks K. to give a tour of the cathedral to a visiting client from Italy, who in fact never shows up – perhaps because of the rain storm that rages outside. It is then, in the darkened, empty cathedral, that K. notices the solemn figure, robed in black, ascend into a pulpit as if to deliver a sermon. "Joseph K.," calls the priest:

> "You are Joseph K.?" said the priest. . . . "You are an accused man. . . . I am the prison chaplain. . . . I had you summoned here. . . . You are held to be guilty. Your case will perhaps never get beyond a lower Court. Your guilt is supposed, for the present, at least, to have been proved." "But I am not guilty," said K.; "it's a mistake. And, if it comes to that, how can any man be called guilty? We are all simply men here, one as much as the other." "That's true," said the priest, "but that's how all guilty men talk."[6]

Guilt, guilt! But guilt for what? Notice that neither the priest nor K. seems to know. More important, K. does not ask – he simply protests his innocence. Soon the priest descends from the pulpit, and the two engage in a conversation that, if not warm, is at least professionally courteous. Finally, the priest, in order to acquaint K. with the nature of the Law, narrates to him, from the writings that serve as preface to the Law, one of Kafka's most famous parables.

Before the Law stands a door-keeper. To this door-keeper there comes a man from the country who begs for admittance to the Law. But the door-keeper says that he cannot admit the man at the moment. The man, on reflection, asks if he will be allowed, then, to enter later. "It is possible," answers the door-keeper, "but not at this moment." Since the door leading into the Law stands open as usual and the doorkeeper steps to one side, the man bends down to peer through the entrance. When the door-keeper sees that, he laughs and says: "If you are so strongly tempted, try to get in without my permission. But note that I am powerful. And I am only the lowest door-keeper. From hall to hall, keepers stand at every door, one more powerful than the other. And the sight of the third man is already more than I can stand." These are difficulties which the man from the country has not expected to meet [think of the tortuous process of a long analysis]; the Law, he thinks, should be accessible to every man and at all times, but when he looks more closely at the door-keeper in his furred robe, with his huge pointed nose and long thin Tartar beard, he decides that he had better wait until he gets permission to enter. The door-keeper gives him a stool and lets him sit down at the side of the door. There he sits waiting for days and years. . . . In the first years he curses his evil fate aloud; later, as he grows old, he only mutters to himself. He grows childish, and since in his prolonged study of the door-keeper he has learned to know even the fleas in his fur collar, he begs the very fleas to help him and to persuade the door-keeper to change his mind. Finally his eyes grow dim and he does not know whether the world is really darkening around him or whether his eyes are deceiving him. But in the darkness he can now perceive a radiance that streams inextinguishably from the door of the Law. Now his life is drawing to a close. Before he dies, all that he has experienced during the whole time of his sojourn condenses in his mind into one question, which he has never yet put to the door-keeper. He beckons the door-keeper, since he can no longer raise his stiffening body. The door-keeper has to bend far down to hear him, for the difference in size between them has increased very much to the man's disadvantage. "What do you want to know now?" asks the door-keeper, "you are insatiable." "Everyone strives to attain the Law," answers the man, "how does it come about, then, that in all these years no one has come seeking admittance but me?" The door-keeper perceives that the man is nearing his end and his hearing is failing, so he bellows in his ear: "No one but you can gain admittance through this door, since this door was intended only for you. I am now going to shut it."[7]

Notice that the Law here remains *the* Law, with an absolute, quasi-transcendent, character. Yet it is not, strictly speaking, something "universal," i.e., equally accessible to all. Access to it is unique to every individual. K. and the chaplain discuss the parable at length, K. maintaining that the door-keeper deceived the man from the country by failing to tell him the truth from the beginning. The chaplain denies deception but adds: "[I]t is not necessary to accept everything as true, one must only accept it as necessary."[8] The Law, then, is not necessarily "true," but it *is* truly necessary. It is at this point that the chaplain turns in frustration to leave, and K. asks: "Don't you want anything more from me?" "No . . . I belong to the Court," comes the answer. "So why should I want anything from you. . . . The [Law/]Court receives you when you come and it dismisses you when you go."[9] There is nothing else to say!

What may be inferred from all this that might clarify the role of the Law from the perspective of psychoanalysis? Without going any further into an easily expandable interpretation of Kafka, I take him to be suggesting that the Law condemning Joseph K., despite his denial of culpability, is neither a civil-socio-political one that could serve as a paradigm for Nazi totalitarianism, nor a religious one (whether Judaic, Christian or Gnostic) that could hold him guilty of some unspecified moral transgression. It is a Law that functions on a level deeper than consciousness can disclose, inscribed in Joseph K.'s being human as such, and it is from this fundamental Law that other laws in one way or other derive their meaning. In psychoanalysis, it is with this Law that the desiring subject must fundamentally deal, it is here that the ethical question is most radically raised. I propose to consider the nature of this Law, first as Freud understands it, then as Lacan understands it, and to conclude with two remarks of my own.

To be sure, the term "law" is used loosely in Freud and has been taken to refer to such generalized phenomena as the "pleasure principle" or his basic theory of sexual development. More fundamentally, however, and more precisely we may take the Law for Freud to be that of the oedipal structure of every human being, whose principal moral injunction is the prohibition of incest. Forced to account for a phenomenon that he had discovered very early in his own self-analysis and confirmed over and over in clinical experience with patients, Freud finally, in good Platonic fashion, fabricated his own myth to explain it. It is the myth of the Father of the primal horde, a myth that, without any scientifically anthropological evidence to justify the hypothesis, has nonetheless become part of the phylogenetic strain. No need to repeat the myth here, certainly, except, perhaps, to underline the consequences for the sons who murder the Father and for the sons upon sons that come after them: incestuous desire remains in the progeny and is only scotched, not killed, by the prohibiting taboo; more important for us, the sons' love/hate/resentment toward the Father abides with remorse for killing him, thus compounding the unconscious burden of guilt, the unpayable debt (*Schuld*) that, in a sort of parody of the religious conception of original sin, passes from generation to generation. How the incest taboo combined with the taboo against killing the totem animal (representing the Father) expanded into a conception of God and into a taboo against fratricide (eventually into the interdiction of murder) – all this belongs to the lore by which Freud, on the basis of the myth, accounts for the origins of both civilization and culture.[10] What historians consider to be the origins of Law, whether they be mythical (e.g., Aeschylus' sixth-century BC account in the *Oresteia*),[11] cultural (e.g., the Code of Hammurabi, dating [we are told] from the eighteenth century BC)[12] or religious (e.g., the Decalogue and the Law of Moses in the Bible's Book of Exodus, dating probably from the twelfth century BC)[13] derive from subsequent (and in kind much different) sources. Whatever is to be said for traditional myths, Freud's construction is a characteristically modern one. "In truth," Lacan remarks later, "this myth is nothing other than something that is inscribed in the clearest of terms in the spiritual reality of our time, namely, the death of God."[14]

An oedipal interpretation of Kafka's work in general and of *The Trial* in particular, given the notoriety of his relationship with the man who begot him, Hermann Kafka, revealed in the famous *Letter to His Father*, is not difficult to make.[15] There the unequal struggle between father and son is manifest from the beginning:

> I was, after all, weighed down by your mere physical presence. I remember, for instance, how we often undressed in the same bathing hut. There was I, skinny, weakly, slight; you strong, tall, broad. Even inside the hut I felt a miserable specimen, and what's more, not only in your eyes but in the eyes of the whole world, for you were for me the measure of all things. But then when we stepped out of the bathing hut before all the people, you holding me by my hand, a little skeleton, unsteady, barefoot on the boards, frightened of the water, incapable of copying your swimming strokes, which you, with the best of intentions, but actually to my profound humiliation, always kept showing me, then I was

frantic with desperation and at such moments all my bad experiences in all spheres fitted magnificently together.[16]

In *The Trial*, to be sure, we do not find the cruelty of *The Judgment*, where a father condemns his son to die,[17] or of *Metamorphosis*,[18] where he mortally wounds the son with an apple, or of *Amerika*,[19] where he brutally exiles the son to an uncertain fate. Nor do we sense the bitterness of the son's desire to kill in return, as in *In the Penal Colony*, where there is question of an exquisitely designed torture instrument that inflicts a slow and agonizing death by stitching the name of the crime in the victim's flesh through a mechanism using needles of steel.[20] In *The Trial*, the father has been abstracted, generalized, and depersonalized into a heartless, anonymous Court of Law that "wants nothing from you. It receives you when you come and it dismisses you when you go." But the import is clear: "My writing was all about you; all I did there, after all, was to bemoan what I could not bemoan upon your breast."[21] Thus, by the time Kafka turned to writing, "I had lost my self-confidence where you were concerned, and in its place had developed a boundless sense of guilt. (In recollection of this boundlessness I once wrote of someone, accurately [e.g., at the end of *The Trial*]: 'He is afraid the shame [of it] will even outlive him.')"[22]

For Kafka, then, the Law that permeated his very being may be thought in Freudian terms as the Law of the oedipal father. The purely sexual aspects of the interpretation (from his relationship with his mother, through the failed attempts at marriage, to the chaplain's reproach in *The Trial* ("you cast about too much for outside help, especially from women"[23])) are perfectly coherent with this hypothesis but cannot be elaborated here. I should add, however, that some critics see in this scenario not only the theme of an oedipal destiny but a certain "existential" quality, according to which the story unfolds as a sequence of choices that K. makes through which who he is is revealed. This suggests that if K. dies "like a dog" that is because he "chose" to not ask the right question in the first place: instead of proclaiming his innocence, he might have faced up to the allegation of his guilt by asking about the reason for it.[24] I shall return to this.

But is the Freudian Law of the oedipal father as exemplified in Franz Kafka *the* Law of *the* Father as Lacan uses that expression in his much celebrated "return to Freud"? Not exactly – there is a difference. After seventeen years of preoccupation with what he came to call the "imaginary" (i.e., image-bound) dimension of the analytic experience, Lacan begins to talk about "Law" only after discovering in the early 1950s how Lévi-Strauss had gone about discovering the "laws" of cultural anthropology by adopting the methods for discovering the "laws" of general linguistics as first proposed in the work of Ferdinand de Saussure and developed by his followers. Thus, in the famous "Rome Discourse" of 1953 (some call it the *magna carta* of his thought), entitled "The Function and Field of Speech and Language in Psychoanalysis,"[25] Lacan observes:

> No one is supposed to be ignorant of the Law; this somewhat humorous formula taken direct from our Code of Justice nevertheless expresses the truth in which our experience is grounded, and which our experience confirms. No man is actually ignorant of it, since the Law of man has been the Law of language since the first words of recognition presided over the first gifts. . . . [T]hese gifts, their act and their objects, their erection into signs, and even their fabrication, were so much a part of speech that they were designated by its name.[26]

The gifts, Lacan claims, involved above all the exchange of women and were governed by the laws of marriage ties that, to subsequent social anthropologists, were discernible in terms of a logic of numerical combinations of which the participants would be totally unconscious.[27]

> The primordial Law is therefore that which in regulating marriage ties superimposes the kingdom of culture on that of a nature abandoned to the Law of mating. The prohibition of incest is merely its subjective pivot. . . . This Law, then, is revealed clearly enough as identical with an order of language.[28]

This is why Lacan can ask (rhetorically): "Isn't it striking that Lévi-Strauss, in suggesting the implication of the structures of language with that part of the social laws that regulate marriage ties and kinship, is already conquering the very terrain in which Freud situates the unconscious?"[29] There in a nutshell is the reason for Lacan's fundamental claim that "the unconscious [discovered by Freud] is structured in the most radical way like a language."[30] Be that as it may, the whole conception is unified under the figure of fatherhood:

> It *is in the name of the father* that we must recognize the support of the symbolic function which, from the dawn of history, has identified his person with the figure of the Law. This conception enables us to distinguish clearly, in the analysis of a case, the unconscious effects of this function from the narcissistic [i.e., imaginary] relations, or even from the real [i.e., actual but nonrepresentable relations that the subject sustains with the image and action of the [concrete] person who embodies it.[31]

Note that the identification of the symbolic function with the notion of "father" is a purely contingent one that *de facto*, as a matter of (at least Western) history, "has identified his person with the figure of the Law."

The Law that is the symbolic function of language, then, is conceived (as early as 1953) in terms of the name "father" – clearly to be distinguished, however, from some imaginary father that one might merely fantasize, or, in Kafka's case, from the actual father, Hermann Kafka, of lived historical experience. This conception of a symbolic order (the term comes from Lévi-Strauss) as identifiable with the name "father" is formalized two years later in Lacan's Seminar on *The Psychoses* (1955–56)[32] and summarized in a briefer essay of 1958.[33] Lacan is examining here the nature of psychosis *à propos* of Freud's analysis of the Schreber case,[34] and proposes to think of the essence of psychosis as a failure to gain access to, or as exclusion from (Lacan uses the Freudian word "foreclosure" [*Verwerfung*] of), the symbolic order. To do this, he explains the normal manner of gaining access to it through the achieving of what he calls the "paternal metaphor."

The word "metaphor" here is obviously a trope of language: let that say he is using it to articulate in purely linguistic terms the initiation of the subject into the symbolic order as an active participant in that Order, in which it has participated passively, of course, since the first moment of its conception. As a trope of language, metaphor signifies the substitution of a signifier for another signifier. In the "paternal metaphor," the substituting signifier is the name "Father," which, as we have seen, designates for Lacan the signifying function as such – the entire symbolic order, understood now as the Law of *the* Father, designating *the* Law of all laws. This much is clear enough. But what signifier does this primordial signifier substitute *for* so that it may be called a "metaphor" in the first place? It substitutes for what is understood to be the signifier of what precedes it in the evolution of the infant (*infans*: non-speaking child) up to the moment when it is sufficiently developed to be able to become a speaking subject, i.e., an active participant in the symbolic order, as subject to the Law of the Father.

The matter is difficult for the uninitiated but, reduced to the simplest terms, it comes to this: the infant's initiation into the active use of language takes place at the moment typified by the discovery of the o-o-o and the a-a-a of the experience of Freud's grandson as described in *Beyond the Pleasure Principle*.[35] This signifies as well the beginning of separation from the mother, which means the loss of her as a counterpart with which, up to that point, the infant has been, at least in some imaginary way, fused. This loss of the mother as imaginary counterpart induces a lack in the infant, a "want" of the mother as an object that has been lost, and this want[ing] of the mother, now lost, becomes the inchoative subject's radical – indeed insatiable (because that object is lost forever) – want[ing], i.e., its desire. What the signifying system (now named "Father," i.e., the Name-of-the-Father) substitutes for, then, is the desire of the mother, the signifier for which, in Lacan's terminology, is the phallus. This means that henceforth the subject's access to the mother, whether as actually another human subject or as lost object, will be possible only through the mediation of language and its signifying chains (Lacan will speak of this in linguistic fashion [to complement his use of "metaphor" here] as the "metonymy" of desire[36]). This moment of induction of the subject into the symbolic order Lacan speaks of as the "splitting" of the subject, i.e., the division in the subject between a conscious dimension of experience as imaginary "ego" and an unconscious dimension where the Other of language, the "subject of the unconscious" (i.e., the unconscious *as* subject), has its say.

Now Lacan also speaks of this entire process of submission by the subject to the symbolic order as the generation of a "debt" with regard to it. Thus in 1953 he tells us: "it is the virtue of the Word [i.e., the whole signifying system] that perpetuates the movement of the Great Debt whose economy Rabelais, in a famous metaphor, extended to the stars themselves."[37] I take this to mean that the Law of the symbolic order for Lacan governs not only the language that humans speak but the entire physical cosmos. It is as if submission to the symbolic order implied an indebtedness: something owed, some kind of lack, that the subject is responsible for paying off, if only by obedience to the Law. The terminology returns in an odd way in 1958 when Lacan is focusing on Freud's tendency to conjoin the themes of the father and death:

> How, indeed, could Freud fail to recognize such an affinity, when the necessity of his reflection led him to link the appearance of the signifier of the Father, as author of the Law, with death, even to the murder of the Father – thus showing that if this murder is the fruitful moment of debt through which the subject binds himself for life to the Law, the symbolic Father is, in so far as he signifies this Law, the dead Father.[38]

I take this to mean that Lacan clearly wants to identify the symbolic order, under the name "Father," with the dead (murdered) Father of the Freudian myth, and somehow to make equivalent the debt of the sons toward their dead Father with the debt of the subject toward the symbolic order. But how is this possible? The debt of murderous sons toward a murdered Father (e.g., the Menendez brothers) is essentially a moral debt. The debt of the subject toward the symbolic order can be only a symbolic (i.e., structural) one, born of the subject's dependence upon this order as a consequence of its ineluctable finitude. It is paid off, I presume, simply by compliance with this Order. Recalling that "debt" in German would be *Schuld*, i.e., "guilt," we are facing here the question of how to evaluate Joseph K.'s debt, i.e., indebtedness to a Law before a Court that accuses him of a guilt of which he is unaware and which he steadfastly denies. What kind of debt is at stake here?

The whole problem of Law is lifted to another level of refinement in Lacan's Seminar VII,[39] four years after the Seminar on *Psychosis*. Here the issue is not a general ethics that is applied to psychoanalytic problems, as business or medical ethics might do for each respective discipline, but the ethics of the process as such: what *ought* it to be/do in order to be true to itself. For Lacan, the task of psychoanalysis is to help the analysand to discern "the relationship between action and the desire that inhabits it":[40]

> If analysis has a meaning, desire is nothing other than that which supports an unconscious theme, the very articulation of that which roots us in a particular destiny, and that destiny demands insistently that the debt be paid, and desire keeps coming back, keeps returning, and situates us once again in a given track, the track of something that is specifically our business.[41]

> And it is because we know better than those who went before how to recognize the nature of desire, which is at the heart of this experience, that a reconsideration of ethics is possible, that a form of ethical judgment is possible, of a kind that gives this question the force of a Last Judgment: Have you acted in conformity with the desire that is in you?[42]

> [That is why], from an analytic point of view, the only thing of which one can be guilty is of having given ground relative to (*céder sur*) one's desire.[43]

So far, so good. But where is the Law in all this? What Law governs desire? The answer is loud and clear: the Law of the symbolic order, for it is to this Law that the subject, through its splitting, submits when initiated into active participation in the functioning of language; it is this Law that through the metonymy of signifying chains mediates the subject's want of the lost object. But the lost object (the imaginary fusion with the mother) is gone – gone forever; it can never be regained through symbolic structures. The *dictio* of language *inter-venes* between desire and its object (the irretrievably lost "fusion" with the mother), making access to the lost object impossible, and it is this impossibility that constitutes the Law's *inter-diction* of incest. It is in this sense that, according to a famous homophony, the "Name" of the Father (*Nom du Père*) and the "No" of the Father (*Non du Père*) are but one.

Whereas for Freud, then, the fundamental human desire is for incest, and the primordial Law constituting both morality and culture is the prohibition of incest,[44] for Lacan the fundamental desire is for the lost object, and the Law that inter-dicts incest is not a moral injunction but the simple fact of structural impossibility: "It is to the extent that the function of the pleasure principle is to make man always search for what he has to find again, but which he never will attain, that one reaches the essence, namely, that sphere or relationship which is known as the Law of the prohibition of incest."[45] As for the specification of this inter-diction in terms of the moral demands of social life, this is the function of what Western culture has come to know as the "ten commandments." Though "in the beginning, at a period that is not so remote in the past, [the ten commandments] were collected by a people that sets itself apart as a chosen people,"[46] they regulate for humanity at large the distance between desire and its lost object, the full "range of what are properly speaking our [characteristically] human actions."[47]

Now, there is an important subtext in the *Ethics of Psychoanalysis* Seminar that involves a confrontation between Kant and the Marquis de Sade. I shall return to it in a moment. For now let it suffice to say that the same confrontation is orchestrated again in an essay entitled "Kant with Sade" (1963),[48] where the essentials of the foregoing analysis are re-articulated: desire, as mediated by the Law, is the "other side of the Law,"[49] for "Law and repressed desire are one and the same thing."[50] And the Law? Still the symbolic order to which the subject is submitted through the initial splitting of the subject: "[T]he bipolarity by which the moral Law institutes itself is nothing other than this splitting of the subject which occurs in any intervention of the signifier. . . . The moral Law has no other principle."[51] Are the Law of the symbolic order and the Law of morality one and the same? Is *that* the paradox of the Law?

All this suggests much to say, but I shall restrict my remarks to two:

1   To identify the symbolic order as such with the Law/Name-of-the-Father presents an obvious difficulty, for it suggests that the Law for Lacan is patriarchical in structure and thereby identifies it with the odious name of "patriarchy." The impression is understandable but misleading, for the Law of symbolic functioning as a structural (i.e., synchronic) phenomenon is clearly to be distinguished from the diachronic concretization of that Law in any given historical culture. If Lacan associates it with the name "Father," it is because, in his view, "from the dawn of history" the Father's person has been identified "with the figure of the Law."[52] But the Law of symbolic functioning prescinds from sexual differentiation: it would be as essential to matriarchal as it would to patriarchal societies, and inevitably instantiated in either. It specifies us all, simply as human beings (Lévi-Strauss); it

makes human communication possible. It should be thought of, I suggest, as *neither* patriarchal *nor* matriarchal but rather as "ambiarchal" or "biarchal" or simply "archal" (understand: *arche*) if we must name it in these terms at all.

2   The second point is more delicate and deals with the relation between the symbolic order as archal Law on one hand and as moral Law on the other, for "the moral Law," we are told in "Kant with Sade," "has no other principle" than the "splitting of the subject which occurs in any intervention of the signifier." This is a hard saying. The essay elaborates a thesis already suggested in the *Ethics of Psychoanalysis* to the effect that the Marquis de Sade, in his novel *Philosophy in the Boudoir* (1795),[53] appearing seven years after Kant's *Critique of Practical Reason* (1788),[54] actually "completes" the former and yields up its "truth."[55] What is meant is that Kant has achieved the great advance of developing an ethics that is grounded not in some metaphysics of the "good" (e.g., *à la* Aristotle) that Kant himself had discredited in the first *Critique*, but in the inferiority of a transcendental subject. This means that the moral Law is determined by pure reason alone, where the universality and necessity of the Law are discerned after the manner of a categorical imperative (e.g., "so act that the maxim of your will could always hold at the same time as a principle of universal Law giving"[56]). Truly moral action must proceed out of respect for the Law and not be contaminated by any lesser motivation, such as desire for secondary gain or some affect, no matter how noble (e.g., compassion, love, remorse). This makes Kantian morality a rather austere business, as we all know, and even Kant admits: "we can see *a priori* that the moral Law as ground of determination of the will, by thwarting our inclinations, cannot help but produce a feeling which can be called pain."[57] Besides the feeling of respect for the Law, pain, too, would be an *a priori* sign of one's compliance with it.

This is the Kantian conception that Sade, for Lacan, "completes" and reveals in its "truth." For Sade, too, has a moral Law that Lacan, in Sade's name, formulates as follows: "I have the right of enjoyment over your body, anyone can say to me, and I will exercise this right, without any limit stopping me in the capriciousness of the exactions that I might have the taste to gratify."[58] It has the generality of Law, after all, for, in Kantian language, "the will is only obligated to dismiss from its practice any reason which is not that of its maxim itself."[59] Moreover, the Law is exemplified by the liturgy of pain that Sade dramatizes with his usual delicacy in *Philosophy in the Boudoir*. The analogy with Kant is evident – but, for Lacan, Sade improves on Kant and "completes" him. How? By making it clear that the "voice" that articulates the Law is not simply some voice from "within" but the voice of the Other, i.e., the symbolic order as archal Law: "The

Sadian maxim, by pronouncing itself from the mouth of the Other, is more honest than appealing to the voice within, since it unmasks the splitting, usually conjured away [in a purely Kantian reading] of the subject."[60] In such a position, Sade yields up "the truth" of Kant's *Critique*.

How one may react to this intriguing sleight of hand is worth a much longer pause than is possible here. I wish merely to reflect momentarily on what it implies about the "moral Law," if this "has no other principle" than the "splitting" by which the subject is submitted to the symbolic order.[61] For it suggests that the Name-of-the-Father, the Law that mediates desire, acknowledges no difference, from a structural point of view, between the rituals of Sadian cruelty and the prescriptions of the ten commandments. And how could it? The Law of language, foundation of both, shines like the sun upon all indifferently.

What price "ethics of psychoanalysis," then? Is it enough to say that "from an analytic point of view, the only thing of which one can be guilty is of having given ground relative to one's desire," when one's desire is simply the "other side" of the Law, since "the Law and repressed desire are one and the same thing"?[62] For "Law" here is the archal Law of the symbolic order, as valid and validating for the Marquis de Sade as for Moses in the desert at Sinai. The symbolic order, I submit, is not simply morally neutral, it is morally empty, and simple insertion into it cannot be the "principle" of any moral Law – i.e., Law that determines what a human being "ought" to be/ do in order to be specifically human – at all. As primordial Law of the symbolic order, the Name-of-the-Father "wants nothing from you. It receives you when you come and it dismisses you when you go." That is all.

Where, then, does that leave us with regard to the nature of Law, once Lacan contextualizes it this way in terms of an eventual ethics of psychoanalysis? How might Joseph K. have dealt with the accusations of the Court if he had sought and found help from a Lacanian analyst? Assuming that Joseph K. represents one version, in fantasy form, of Kafka himself, I shall consider them here as one. My expectation is that the task of trying to help K. become aware of a debt (*Schuld*) of which he is unconscious and whose existence he firmly denies would begin by trying to help him appreciate the difference between the symbolic Father as primordial Law upon which every human being is dependent (and to which, in that sense, every human is indebted) and his actual (real, historical) father, by whom Kafka, at least, was tyrannized and toward whom one might feel (like Kafka) a crushing burden of guilt – *Schuld*). There is a trace of this distinction in *The Trial*, where the tyrannical father of experience has been sanitized into the detached, depersonalized form of the Law as instantiated in the Court – Law/Court that wants nothing from the subject – that receives the subject when it comes and dismisses it when it goes. Such a conception of the Law of the Father gives some sense to the ambiguity of the opening conversation in the cathedral:

"Your guilt is supposed, for the present, at least, to have been proved," [says the priest]. "But I am not guilty," said K.; "it's a mistake, and, if it comes to that, how can any man be called guilty? We are all simply [human beings] here, one as much as the other." "That is true," said the priest, "but that's how all guilty men talk."[63]

The ambiguity turns on the meaning of "guilt" (*Schuld*): a structural indebtedness to the symbolic order grounded ultimately in the finitude of the subject (Lacan's conception) versus a quasi-moral guilt for patricide transmitted by phylogenetic inheritance (Freud's conception) – both of them distinct from any personal guilt of which K. would be consciously aware. In the situation of fact, K. is unconscious of these differences, but it would be the task of analysis to help him appreciate them and understand in what his symbolic (as opposed to imaginary) indebtedness might consist, and how he might deal with it.

I say that the subject's debt to the symbolic order is grounded in finitude. By that I mean that the subject K.-as-Kafka is inducted into a symbolic order that is determined (therefore negatived) in all manner of ways beyond the constrictions imposed by a domineering father in the flesh. The Order is determined for Kafka by such things as the Judaism of his heritage, the political turbulence of his time, the accident of the language available to him to write in (born a Czech, he chose to write in German) – all added to the contingencies of his personal idiosyncratic circumstances (e.g., the frailty of health in an already fragile body). All such determinations would add up to constrictions, i.e., a set of negations that cut the subject off from what it might otherwise have been and for that reason constitute what Lacan calls "castration" – symbolic, of course. At a given moment he even makes his own the language of Heidegger's "ontological guilt," so that Lacan's "symbolic castration" and Heidegger's "Being-unto-death" are thought of as one. The Law of the symbolic order, then, despite its absolute, quasi-transcendent, character is tailor-made to each individual. That would account for the poignancy of the door-keeper's final shout to the dying man from the country: "No one but you could gain admittance through this door, since this door was intended only for you. I am now going to shut it."[64]

How could he have gained admittance? Staying with a Lacanian reading (though this would have been a bit much for a poor man from the country), I submit that it would be through an appropriate awarenes of his desire, for "the Law and repressed desire are one and the same thing." I understand this to mean that desire, as the wanting of the lost object, is, through the splitting of the subject, submitted to a symbolic order that is trammeled by such limitations as we have just seen. Mediated by *this* Law, desire is inevitably a castrated desire. This does not mean, of course, that desire cannot transgress the Law in its pursuit of the lost object, as if there were an "erotics" by which it stretches beyond the Law,[65] but this simply emphasizes the irretrievability of the object as lost. Desire may indeed strive to transgress the Law, but it cannot transcend its own castration.

How does all this pertain to Joseph K.? Obviously the question of his desire was never raised, still less the fact of its castration. He never passed muster before that Last Judgment: "have you acted in conformity with the desire that is in you?" – but then he was never analyzed. To be sure, desire remained alive in him – how else to explain that last flicker of hope on the edge of death when "the casements of a window there suddenly flew open and . . . a human figure . . . leaned abruptly forward and stretched both arms still farther. . . . [And] he [in turn] raised his hands and spread out all his fingers."[66] But it was too late. "The hands of one of the partners were already at K.'s throat." If he felt that he died "like a dog" and that the "shame of it must outlive him," my sense is that the humiliation lay in the dumb passivity of it all – never to have understood and embraced his desire, made his own – even in, especially in – its very castration as Being-unto-death.

To conclude. What has been offered here is an attempt to spell out what I think can be said for an "ethics of psychoanalysis" that addresses the relation between an act and the desire that dwells in it, where this desire is the inverse of the Law of the symbolic order under the guise of Name-of-the-Father. I have in effect said nothing about the symbolic order as a Law of morality. To do so in such fashion as Lacan seems to do, i.e., by making the symbolic order found a moral Law that permits it to smile equally on Moses at Sinai and on the Marquis de Sade, strikes me as gratuitous hyperbolic non-sense. This is all the more grievous, it seems to me, since psychoanalysis does have serious moral issues raised for it that an ethics of psychoanalysis worth its name ought to address. I am thinking, for example, of the Argentinian analyst who reported having once refused to take into analysis a professional torturer, lest the analysis make him a better torturer. Here the problem of desire, both of analyst and of analysand, is posed in all its urgency. Again, when Lacan tells us that from the viewpoint of psychoanalysis, "the only thing one can be guilty of is to give ground relative to one's desire,"[67] are we to take this to mean that there are no constraints whatsoever, constituted, say, by the social fabric of the analysand's life (e.g., by certain indissoluble relations with others), that are to be respected? If such constraints appear to exist, how are they to be assayed? Moreover, how does the analyst reconcile his/her own desire with constraints extrinsic to desire, say, of the civil law, where, in cases of potential violence, civil society may command that the analyst make exception to the demands of professional confidentiality in the interest of the common good? Questions like these cannot be answered by the *ipse dixit* of Lacan about some abstract refusal to compromise desire. Answers will be forthcoming only when we will have thought through, and more carefully than has been done up to now, the full implications of the absolute primacy of the efficacious word in psychoanalysis in conjunction with the liberation of desire.

Finally, if "a reconsideration of ethics is possible, [if] a form of ethical judgment is possible, of a kind that gives this question the force of a Last Judgment: have you acted in conformity with the desire that is in you?," then the subject must be capable of choosing to conform or not conform to, i.e., to give up or not give up on (*céder sur*), its desire. But such a choice implies a consistency in the psychoanalytic subject that makes possible the coherence of the hermeneutic narrative by reason of which it is capable of assuming "responsibility" for such a choice, i.e., "answering for" it over time. For my part I do not yet see how Lacan's manner of conceiving of the split subject – split, that is, between an imaginary ego (which is no more than a distorting reflection of a disorganized subject-to-be that functions on the level of consciousness) and the unconscious subject (i.e., subject of the unconscious/unconscious as subject), which is essentially the symbolic order itself, however individualized in a dynamic idiosyncratic identity – leaves room for an *ethical* subject, i.e., a desire capable of choosing to be true to itself. Only such a subject is the properly human subject. Unless we can account for this specifically human dimension of a responsible subject, every subject must in the end die in an inhuman passivity, the way Joseph K. felt he did, "like a dog."

Notes

1 Franz Kafka, *The Trial*, trans. by Willa and Edwin Muir (New York: Alfred A. Knopf, 1984), 244.
2 *Ibid.*, 245–51.
3 George Steiner, "Introduction," *ibid.*, vii.
4 *Ibid.*, 250–1.
5 See J.P. Stern, "The Law of *The Trial*," in *On Kafka. Semi-Centenary Perspectives*, ed. by Franz Kuna (London: Paul Elek, 1976), 22–41.
6 Kafka, *The Trial*, 231.
7 *Ibid.*, 234–6.
8 *Ibid.*, 242.
9 *Ibid.*, 244.

10 See Sigmund Freud, *Totem and Taboo* (1913), in *The Standard Edition of the Complete Psychological Works of Sigmund Freud*, trans. by James Strachey (London: Hogarth Press, 1968) vol. 13: vii–xv, 1–162.140–6. Cf. *Civilization and its Discontents* (1930), *ibid.*, vol. 21: 57–145. (Hereafter: SE.)

11 Aeschylus, *The Oresteia*, trans. by Robert Fagles (New York: Penguin, 1977), 335–980, and generally.

12 See Rollin Chambliss, *Social Thought from Hanimurabi to Comte* (New York: Dryden, 1954), 13–41.

13 *The New Jerome Biblical Commentary*, ed. by Raymond E. Brown, Joseph A. Fitzmyer, Roland E. Murphy (Englewood Cliffs, NJ: Prentice-Hall, 1990), 1037.

14 Jacques Lacan, *The Seminar of Jacques Lacan. Book VII. The Ethics of Psycho-analysis (1959–1960)*, ed. by Jacques-Alain Miller, trans. by Dennis Porter (New York: W.W. Norton, 1992), 143.

15 Franz Kafka, *Letter to His Father* [1919], trans. by Ernst Kaiser and Eithne Wilkins (New York: Schocken, 1966).

16 *Ibid.*, 19–21.

17 Franz Kafka, *The Judgment*, trans. by Willa and Edwin Muir (New York: Modern Library, 1952). See also Walter H. Stokel, "The Programme of K.'s Court: Oedipal and Existential Meanings of *The Trial*," in *On Kafka. Semi-Centenary Perspectives*, ed. by Franz Kuna (London: Paul Elek, 1976), 1–21.

18 Franz Kafka, *The Metamorphosis*, trans. by Stanley Corngold (New York: Bantam, 1972).

19 Franz Kafka, *Amerika*, trans. by Edwin Muir (New York: New Directions, 1962).

20 See Kafka, *In the Penal Colony* in *Metamorphosis and other essays*, trans. and ed. Malcolm Pauley (London: Penguin, 1992), pp. 127–153.

21 Kafka, *Letter to His Father*, 87.

22 *Ibid.*, 73. Cf. *The Trial*, 251.

23 Kafka, *The Trial*, 232.

24 See Walter H. Sokel, "The Programme of K.'s Court," 1–21.

25 Jacques Lacan, "The Function and Field of Speech and Language in Psycho-analysis," in *Écrits*, trans. by Alan Sheridan (New York: W.W. Norton, 1977), 30–113. Cf. Jacques Lacan, *The Language of the Self. The Function of Language in Psychoanalysis*, trans. by Anthony Wilden (Baltimore, MD: Johns Hopkins University Press, 1968), 3–87. Wilden's translation is always provocative, his notes and commentary still invaluable.

26 *Ibid.*, 61.

27 See *ibid.*, 65–6.

28 *Ibid.*, 66.

29 *Ibid.*, 73.

30 *Ibid.*, 234.

31 *Ibid.*, 67.

32 Jacques Lacan, *The Seminar of Jacques Lacan. Book III. The Psychoses (1955–1956)*, ed. by Jacques-Alain Miller, trans. by Russell Grigg (New York: W.W. Norton, 1993).

33 Jacques Lacan, "On a Question Preliminary to Any Possible Treatment of Psychosis," *Écrits* (1977), 179–225.

34 Sigmund Freud, *Psycho-analytic Notes on an Autobiographical Account of a Case of Paranoia (Dementia Paranoides)* (1911), SE vol. 12: 1–82.

35 Freud, *Beyond the Pleasure Principle*, SE vol. 18: 14–17.

36 Lacan, *Écrits*, 167.

37 *Ibid.*, 67.
38 *Ibid.*, 199.
39 Jacques Lacan, *The Seminar of Jacques Lacan. Book VII. The Ethics of Psychoanalysis.*
40 *Ibid.*, 313.
41 *Ibid.*, 319.
42 *Ibid.*, 314.
43 *Ibid.*, 319.
44 *Ibid.*, 66–7.
45 *Ibid.*, 68.
46 *Ibid.*, 80.
47 See *ibid.*, 68–9. Cf. "We are then brought back chained to the moral law insofar as it is incarnated in a certain number of commandments. I mean the ten commandments, which in the beginning, at a period that is not so remote in the past, were collected by a people that sets itself apart as a chosen people" (*ibid.*, 80).
48 Jacques Lacan, "Kant with Sade," trans. by James B. Swenson, Jr, *October* (1989), 51: 55–104.
49 *Ibid.*, 73.
50 *Ibid.*, 68.
51 *Ibid.*, 59.
52 Lacan, *Écrits*, 67.
53 Marquis de Sade, *The Complete Justine, Philosophy in the Bedroom and Other Writings*, trans. by Richard Seaver and Austryn Wainhouse (New York: Grove, 1965), 177–367. Lacan builds his case on the interlude essay "Yet Another Effort, Frenchmen, If You Would Become Republicans," 296–339.
54 Immanuel Kant, *Critique of Practical Reason*, trans. by Lewis White Beck (New York: Macmillan, 1993 [1956]).
55 Lacan, "Kant with Sade," 55.
56 Kant, *Critique of Practical Reason*, 30.
57 *Ibid.*, 76.
58 *Ibid.*, 58.
59 *Ibid.*, 58–9.
60 *Ibid.*, 59.
61 See *ibid.*, 59.
62 Cf. *ibid.*, 73 and 68.
63 Kafka, *The Trial*, 231.
64 *Ibid.*, 236.
65 See Lacan, *Book VII. The Ethics of Psychoanalysis*, 84.
66 Kafka, *The Trial*, 250–1.
67 Lacan, *The Ethics of Psychoanalysis*, 321.

15

REVOLT TODAY?*

Julia Kristeva

For at least two centuries the initially rich and complex term 'revolt' has assumed a political significance.[1] Today we take it to mean a contesting of already established norms, values and powers. Since the French Revolution political 'revolt' has become a secular version of that negativity which characterizes the attempt of the life of conscience to remain faithful to its underlying logic: revolt is our mysticism, a synonym of 'dignity'.

We notice increasingly that the 'new world order' does not favour revolt. (It is no longer necessary to praise the democratic advantages of this 'new world order', notwithstanding its dangers and impasses in the East.) *Against whom* do we revolt if power and values are either without content or debased? And, more seriously still, who can revolt, if the human being is increasingly reduced to a conglomerate of functions, i.e. if he is not a 'subject' but rather a 'patrimonial individual' endowed not only with financial but also genetic or physiological 'patrimony', an individual who is free only to 'zap' and choose his 'channel'. I have schematized the picture of our actuality in order to underscore something we all feel: not only is *political* revolt finding itself bogged down in compromises between differing courses of actions (differences which we decreasingly perceive over time), but this once essential element of European culture – a doubting and critical culture – is losing its moral and aesthetic capacity. When revolt exists our spectacle-oriented society marginalizes it as one of its tolerated alibis. Alternatively, it is simply submerged and rendered impossible by *distraction*-culture, *performance*-culture, *show*-culture.[2]

At the risk of accentuating my image as a theatrical person given to painting a dark picture of reality, I am anxious to introduce myself to the reader who does not know me by way of my most recent book, a novel entitled *Possessions*.[3] Against the backdrop of a detective story, and in an imaginary city called Santa Barbara which functions as a symbol of the planetary village, we discover the decapitated body of a woman, Gloria Harrison. The victim had been a translator by profession and the mother

* Translated by Eileen Brennan.

220

of a difficult child. The reader will see that several killers are responsible for her death before her final decapitation. I have put much of my own personal experience into this particular example of female and maternal suffering, an image which sums up the difficulties of being a woman. I am the decapitated woman. I am also the investigator who, at the side of Chief Superintendent Northrop Rilsky, leads the police inquiry, and I am another woman, Stéphanie Delacour, a Parisian journalist.

Because inquiry is still possible in the criminal and virtual world of Santa Barbara, what the detective novel says in substance to the reader is: 'you can know'. It is the popular genre where the possibility of questioning is kept alive. Is it not for this reason that we still read detective novels when we have stopped reading everything else? Interrogation is the birth (*degré zéro*) of this aptitude for judgment, our sole defence against the 'banality of evil'. I consider my novel *Possessions*, together with so many others, as a low form of revolt. As for less base forms, we need to ask ourselves whether they really are more effective. Moreover, the world of women allows me to suggest an alternative to the automated and spectacle-driven society which does harm to the culture of revolt. This alternative is quite simply sensitive intimacy (*l'intimé sensible*). Dominated by their sensitivity and their passions, some beings nevertheless continue to ask themselves questions. I am convinced that after so many more or less reasonable and promising plans and slogans, all of them launched by the feminist movement since the 1960s, the arrival of women at the forefront of the social and moral scene will result in the reassertion of the value of *sensitive experience* as an antidote to hair-splitting technical argument. The immense responsibility of women in ensuring the survival of the species – how to safeguard our bodies' freedom while ensuring the optimal conditions for our children's lives – goes hand in hand with this rehabilitation of the sensitive. The novel is the privileged terrain of such an investigation and of its communication to the greatest number. In addition to and beside the culture of the image with its seductiveness, speed, brutality and superficiality there is the culture of words and narration, and the place it reserves for meditation. This latter appears to me to be a variant of minimal revolt. Doubtless it is not much. But are you certain that we have not reached a point of no return from which we would have to *re*-turn to alter things? Such a return would be an infinitesimal *re*-volt designed to protect the life of the mind and the species.

In this way, revolt as return, reversal, displacement, change, constitutes the underlying logic of a certain culture that I would like to rehabilitate before you, and whose acuteness seems to be really threatened today. But let us reconsider once more the meaning of this revolt which appears to me to specify so profoundly the most lively and promising thing our culture possesses.

Similarity and differences with the 'retrospective return'

Ever since Socrates and Plato, and even more explicitly in Christian theology, humankind has been invited to make a 'return'. Some of you still retain its mark if not its observance. The goal of St Augustine's 'repeating' (*redire*), which is based on a retrospective connection to the Creator's being-there-before (*déjà-là*), is a notable example of this. The possibility of questioning his own being, of searching for his own identity ('*se quaerere*': *quaesto mihi factus sum*), is afforded by this ability to *return*, where return is simultaneously *recollection, questioning and thought*.

Yet the development of technique has favoured knowledge of stable values to the detriment of thought as return or research (as 'repeating', as *se quaerere*). Furthermore, the removal of the sacred aura surrounding Christianity and its own intrinsic tendencies towards stabilization or reconciliation in the immutability of being have discredited this 'fight' with the world and with oneself which also characterizes Christian eschatology, that is, when it has not made such battles impossible. As a consequence, the questioning of values has been transformed into *nihilism*, i.e. the rejection of the ancient values in favour of a *cult* of new values the questioning of which is deferred. For the past two centuries, what we have taken to be a 'revolt' or 'rebellion' – particularly in politics and its accompanying ideologies – is more often an abandoning of retrospective questioning in favour of the rejection, pure and simple, of things ancient so that new dogmas might take their place.

When we say 'revolt', or when the media use the world 'revolt', we generally intend neither more nor less than this nihilistic suspension of questioning in favour of supposedly new values which, precisely as 'values', have forgotten to question themselves and for this reason have fundamentally betrayed the meaning of revolt which I am trying to introduce to you. The nihilist is not a man in revolt as we understand this term. It is not possible to offer a detailed account of his development here, but you can find just such a treatment in *Sens et non-sens de la révolte: Pouvoirs et limites de la psychanalyse*.[4] The nihilist in pseudo-revolt is in fact a man reconciled to the stability of new values. But this stability is illusory – it proves to be deadly, totalitarian. I cannot emphasize enough the fact that totalitarianism is the result of a certain fixation on what is precisely revolt's treachery, namely, the suspension of retrospective return, something which amounts to the suspension of thought. Hannah Arendt has already pursued this analysis quite brilliantly.

That being the case, I am trying to find experiences in which this work of *re*-volt persists and is repeated, work which opens up the life of the mind to an infinite recreation, albeit at the cost of errors and impasses. Let us not present a false picture of reality here. It is not enough to revive the permanence of the revolt, blocked otherwise by technique, in order to attain happiness or who knows what serene stability of being. Re-volt exposes the speaking being to an unbearable conflict, the necessary pleasure and morbid impasses of which this century has assumed the fearsome privilege of demonstrating. But it does so quite differently from the nihilist, who is fixed in the celebration of his pure and simple rejection of things 'ancient', or set in the positivity of the 'new' without any prospect of return.

We are nihilists when we renounce re-volt by withdrawing into either 'ancient values' or even 'new' ones which do not turn over onto themselves, i.e. do not question themselves. We are also nihilists when we take up the opposing position of resuming without respite the retrospective return in order to lead it to the frontiers (made explicit in our century) of what can be represented, thought or defended – in short to the point of 'possession'.

The modern re-volt is not a pure and simple renewal of the retrospective connection which founds the heart of hearts of the Christian who is serene in the quest which ends with his or her return to the *summum esse*. While borrowing the path of retroactive questioning modernity leads it to a *conflict which is henceforth irreconcilable* and which, although it has been able to take place on the margins of art or mysticism in early history, never attained either the height or the scope which we record in modernity.

Just as the concept of 'process' distinguishes modern history from ancient history where the latter is based on destiny and the genius of great men, the concept 'self-organization' specifies contemporary history which in this century has become accustomed to intense crises. Similarly, I maintain that the concept of the human being in *re*-volt distinguishes modern person just as easily from the Christian who is reconciled face to face with God (*coram Deo*) as from the nihilist who is his or her enraged but symmetrically reverse side.

Psychoanalysis as re-volt

There is an understanding of 're-volt' available to us which recalls both Freud, who invites us to go back to the diabolical unconscious, and certain contemporary writers who explore borderline states (*états limites*) of the mind. In what way does this understanding of 're-volt' distinguish itself from the retrospective relationship of *tendere esse* with either the 'not yet' (*pas encore*) or the 'no longer there' (*déjà plus*)? Let us venture a first response. This modern *re-volt* can be distinguished from the latter in that the striving towards unity, being or the authority of the law which is always at work in it, is accompanied more than ever by the centrifugal forces of *dissolution* and *dispersion*.

Further, this conflict issues in an enjoyment which is not simply a narcissistic or egoistic caprice of a consumer or spectacle-oriented society. The enjoyment in question is indispensable to keeping the psyche alive,

223

JULIA KRISTEVA

indispensable to that faculty of representation and questioning which specifies our humanity. In this sense, the Freudian discovery of the unconscious –
of the psyche always already a tributary of the Other and the other – has
been the new Archimedean point which constituted the privileged place
where life finds its sense only if it is capable of *revolt*. It is even on
this ground that Freud founded psychoanalysis as an invitation to
anamnesis with the objective of a *renaissance* or, in other words, a psychic
restructuring.

Everyone's singular autonomy comes to pass through the narrative of
free association and in the regenerating *revolt* against and with the ancient
Law (familial prohibitions, superego, ideals, oedipal or narcissistic limits,
etc.). Our bond to the other is renewed in the same way. But Hannah
Arendt, who praised Augustine's palace of the memory, did not understand
this other Freudian 'palace of the memory' which psychoanalysis re-
examines and transforms, engaged as she was in impugning the assumed
status of psychology and psychoanalysis as 'general sciences'.

Rediscovering the meaning of the negative

The modern age, which I shall date (for the purposes of this reflection)
from the time of the French Revolution, has highlighted the *negative* part
of this retrospective return – experience, both personal and collective, has
become an experience of conflict, of contradiction. What philosophy says
in substance – particularly since Hegel – is that Being itself is shaped by
Nothingness. Heidegger and Sartre say the same thing in different ways.
(This co-presence of nothingness in being took the form of a dialectic in
Hegel.)

As early as 1929, when his text *What Is Metaphysics?* was published,
Heidegger knew the difference between the negation internal to judgment
and a nothingness which negates differently from thought. It is in sensation
and anguish that the philosopher is going to search for the nuclear forms of
what he terms a *repulsion* which would be the characteristic trait of mankind, this rejected (*re-jeté*), this thrown (*je-té*) being. *Dasein* is a repulsion;
exstasis is another word for abjection. Have we given enough consideration to this similarity?

In *Being and Nothingness* (1943) Sartre develops this difference between
the negation appropriate for thought and a primordial negating/nothing-
ness. But, rather than emphasizing *re*-pulsion, he lays stress upon freedom
and thus establishes himself as in fact more Hegelian than Heideggerian
in the philosophical sphere as well as in his political anarchism.

If I am rereading these texts today – if I am asking you to reread them –
it is because they evince an extraordinary moment in Western thought. The
moment in question occurs when the 'retrospective return' – i.e. the knowing subject's questioning of itself and its truth – leads to nothing less than a

224

familiarity with psychosis. Because whether it is a question of the negating 'force' (*Kraft*) which lies behind the concept, the disquieting pressure (*poussée*) of which the concept is required to reduce (Hegel), or whether it is the feeling of dissociation or repulsion in Heidegger or even Sartre's 'pre-judicative negation' which goes to sustain his notion of freedom as radical violence, as questioning of every identity, faith and law – all of these advances (*avancées*) stumble over a psychic reality which places consciousness in difficulty and exposes itself to the pulse of being when we propose human realities to them in order to render their logic accessible. The result: an effacing of the subject–object boundaries, drive's assault (*assaut de la pulsion*), and language becoming 'mood' (*Stimmung*), 'memory of being', music of the body and of matter. Heidegger tries to capture this psychosis by retrospectively examining Hölderlin's work. Sartre avoids this psychosis by clinging to a totalizing and translucent consciousness for whom Flaubert ('the family idiot') and Genet ('comedian and martyr') – in the neighbourhood of melancholy and perversion through style and play (*le jeu*) – offer more purchase to reasoning and humanism than does the radical destruction of an Artaud.

I hope to surprise you in defending the idea that the psychoanalytic current inaugurated by Freud belongs to this examination of nothingness and negativity. This psychoanalytic current comprises not only the American psychoanalysis dominated by *ego psychology* but that radical questioning of the psyche which Freud conducts on the borderline between biology and being, the account of which we find in a still enigmatic text, *Die Verneinung* (*Negation*), published in 1925. For the first time in the history of thought, and a few years before *What Is Metaphysics?*, Freud binds the fate of two types of negation: the rejection (*la rejet*) characteristic of drive (*Ausstossung* or *Verwerfung*) and the negativity internal to judgment. He does so by substantially defending the idea that symbol and/or thought are of the order of a negativity which in certain conditions is only a transformation of the rejection (*rejet*) or disconnection (*déliaison*) which he refers to elsewhere as a 'death drive' (*une pulsion de mort*).

The question arises as to the conditions in which the rejecting drive (*la pulsion rejetante*) comes to symbolize negativity? All psychoanalytic research on, for instance, the paternal function (Lacan) or the 'good enough mother' (Winnicott), among others, tries to answer this question. For her part Melanie Klein bases the most original section of her work on the importance of this dissociating–rejecting drivenness (*pulsionnalité*) which precedes the appearance of the unity of the 'I'. This earlier phase is termed schizo-paranoid and it comes before the depressive phase which is productive of symbolism and language. Studies on narcissism, 'borderline' personalities, etc., for their part attempt to go deeper into this form of the psyche, understood as a tributary of the archaic, the driven, the maternal, and beyond to the extra-psychic and right up to biology or being, depending on the school of psychoanalysis in question.

As distinct currents of theoretical enquiry, philosophy and psychoanalysis have been exceptional in modernity in that they have reached this frontier region of the speaking being that is psychosis, and have done so by means of retrospective questioning, that is to say by means of examination or analysis.

The praxis of writing in parallel with philosophy and psychoanalysis, but this time by non-theoretical means which are appropriate to language itself, unravels meaning to the level of sensations and drives, reaches nonsense and taps its pulse in an order no longer 'symbolic' but 'semiotic'. I am thinking of this desemanticization of style by means of ellipses in Mallarmé or by way of polyphonies and portmanteau words in Joyce. Across language, and thanks to a linguistic overcompetence, we obtain a noticeable 'regression', an 'infantile state of language'. The semiotic *chora*, this infralinguistic musicality aimed at by all poetic language, becomes the principal design of modern poetry, an 'experimental psychosis'.[5] By that I mean that it is the work of a subject, but of a subject who puts itself on trial. It is by means of the return to the archaeology of its unity, conducted in the very materials of language and thought, that the subject reaches these daring regions where its unity is negated.

*Re*volt's paradoxical logics

Rebellious thoughts or writings (some of which I have recently examined in the writings of Sartre, Aragon and Barthes) try to find a representation (language, thought, style) for this confrontation with the unity of law, being and the self which mankind attains in pleasure (*la jouissance*). You will not be unaware that this is perceived as an 'evil' by the older standard. Yet, in so far as it is thought, written or represented, this pleasure is a traversing of evil and is, therefore, perhaps the most profound way of avoiding the radical evil which would be the cessation of representation and questioning. The permanence of contradiction, the provisional arrangement of reconciliation, the underscoring of everything that puts to the test the very possibility of unitary sense (e.g. drive, the unspeakable, the feminine, destructiveness, psychosis) is what this rebellious culture investigates.

This shows that in it a genuine transformation of humankind presents itself which stems from the Christian eschatology of retrospection as the path of truth and intimacy (*l'intimité*). This understanding emerges if the Freudian discovery is treated not as a rejection of this tradition but as its deepening to the limits of conscious unity. Only from here does the Freudian path foreshadow a possible transformation of our culture insofar as it initiates another relation to meaning and the One.

Of course, it is not in the world of action but in that of psychic life and its social expressions (writing, thought, art) that this *re*volt is realized which appears to me to indicate the crises as much as the advances of modern humankind. Nevertheless, insofar as it is a matter of the transformation of humankind's relation to meaning, this cultural *re*volt intrinsically concerns the life of the city (*la vie de la cité*) and, consequently, it has profoundly political implications. It raises the question of *another* politics, that of permanent conflict.

You will not be unaware of the attacks, denigrations and marginalizations to which psychoanalysis has been subjected recently. Since its foundation it has been the object of an inevitable 'resistance' inasmuch as it goes against the 'not wanting to know' of human beings who revel in sexual myth rather than confronting truths precisely capable of leading them into *re*volt.

But keeping analysis in the background – as it is today – seems to be due to supplementary causes to an even greater extent than the aforementioned resistance. Modern life conditions with the primacy of technique, image, speed – inducing stress and depression – have a tendency to reduce the psychic space and abolish the faculty of psychic representation. Psychic curiosity gives way before the requirement of a supposed efficiency. The incontestable neurosciences are then ideologically valued and extolled as antidotes to psychic malaises whose existence is gradually disclaimed in favour of their substratum, i.e. the neurological deficiency.

An oversimplified materialism claims to manage without the Freudian dualism which saved a place for initiative, autonomy and the subject's desire. This extremist cognitivism subsumes the heteronomy of psychic representations, on the one hand, and the neural economy, on the other, under the same logic. Then ideological claims of the politically correct type advocate ethnic and sexual differences while impugning rational approaches which nevertheless are alone in permitting us to better define their singularity. In thus denigrating what they term an analytic universalism, these currents swing over from militancy to a sectarian logic. Finally, the too often overcautious politics of psychoanalytic societies, themselves concerned with protecting their clinical purity, or else aggressively ideological if not spiritualistic, contributes towards discrediting this 'Copernican revolution' which Freud introduced in our century and which we realize more and more is the only one not to turn away either from malaises or *re*volts of modernity.

It is perhaps necessary to recall some paradoxical logics of the analytic cure in order to help you grasp the type of intimacy brought to light by the analytic experience and modern art jointly. It goes without saying that they use completely different means. Do you remember the unprecedented 'outside-time' (*Zeitlos*) to which no philosophy had given prominence before Freud and of which he says that it characterizes the unconscious?

Whereas human existence is intrinsically linked to time, the analytic experience reconciles us to this 'outside-time' which belongs to drives and more especially to the death drive (*la pulsion de mort*). As to the analytic interpretation, which differs from every other translation or decoding of signs, it appears as a secular version of 'pardon' – in which I see more than a suspension of judgment, a giving of meaning beyond judgment, at the heart of the transfer/countertransfer. Outside-time, modification of judgment: the analytic experience leads us to the frontiers of thought, and you know that to venture into these regions interests the philosopher as well as the moralist. So true is it that the questioning of thought (what is a thought without time, without judgments?) implies a questioning of judgment and with it of ethics and, finally, a questioning of the social bond. Nevertheless, we can be interested more specifically in the aesthetic or literary variants of the 'outside-time' and pardon – neither more nor less than intimacy (*l'intimité*) which will then appear to us as an experience waiting to be dealt with. Is it not true that the various forms of our intimacy's 'possessions', including the most demonic, the most tragic, possessions, remain our refuge and our resistance faced as we are with a world termed 'virtual' where judgments become blurred when they do not assume an archaic and barbaric form? Now, as it happens, it is in imaginary experience, notably in literature, that this intimacy with its 'outside-time' and its peculiar pardon unfurls.

The imaginary in question

Am I, in short, defending intimate revolt (*la révolte intime*) as the only revolt possible? I am not unaware of the commercial impasses and spectacular stalemates of all the imaginary productions in which our rebellious intimacy expresses itself. There are times when the mystical path – this acceleration of libertarian transformations – lets itself be confined to the care and attention due to pathology, when it is not in spiritualistic or decorative ghettos. Our time is one of these. But faced with the invasion of spectacle we can still ponder over what the imaginary can reawaken in our intimacy (*intimité*) as rebellious potentialities. This is perhaps not yet the time for great works; or perhaps for us as contemporaries they are still invisible. Nevertheless we can safeguard their possibility of appearing by maintaining our intimacy in revolt.

Notes

1 Thus, from the very old forms *wel* and *welu*, indicating an intentional craft-type action resulting in the denomination of technical objects of protection, and covering the meanings of 'return', 'discovering' (*découvrement*), 'circular movement of the planets', the Italian '*volte-face*', 'volume' (i.e., book), the French 'vaudeville' and even the Swedes' 'Volvo', on wheels, are derived.

2 Translator's note: *distraction, performance* and *show* all appear in English in the original French text. The author notes that 'the Anglicisms are apt here'.
3 Julia Kristeva, *Possessions* (Paris: Fayard, 1996).
4 Julia Kristeva, *Sens et non-sens de la révolte: Pouvoirs et limites de la psychanalyse* (Paris: Fayard, 1996).
5 Cf. Julia Kristeva, *La Révolution du langage poétique* (Paris: Le Seuil, 1974).

16

THE ORIGINAL TRAUMATISM
Levinas and psychoanalysis

Simon Critchley

Es gibt gar keine andern als moralische Erlebnisse, selbst nicht
im Bereich der Sinneswarnehmung.
                    (Nietzsche, *Die Fröhliche Wissenschaft*)

Let me begin with a first working hypothesis: the condition of possibility
for the ethical relation to the other, that is, the condition of possibility for
ethical transcendence, communication and beyond that justice, politics
and the whole field of the third party with the specific meanings that
Levinas gives to these terms, is a conception of the subject.[1] Thus, it is
only because there is a *certain disposition towards alterity within the subject, as the structure or pattern of subjectivity,* that there can be an ethical
relation. Levinas writes in the 1968 version of 'Substitution' (to which we
will have more than one occasion to return):

> It is from subjectivity understood as a self, from the excidence and
> dispossession of contraction, whereby the Ego does not appear but
> immolates itself, that the relationship with the other is possible as
> communication and transcendence.[2]

Or again: 'It is through the condition of being a hostage that there can be
pity, compassion, pardon, and proximity in the world – even the little
there is, even the simple "after you sir"' (p. 91).
  So, to make my claim crystal clear, Levinas's account of ethics, understood as the relation to the other irreducible to comprehension and therefore to ontology, finds its condition of possibility in a certain conception
of the subject. In Kantian terms, the ethical relation to the other presupposes a rather odd transcendental deduction of the subject. In other
words, it is only because there is a disposition towards alterity within the
subject – whatever the origin of this disposition might be, which, as we

will see, is the question of trauma – that the subject can be claimed by the other.

Levinas tries to capture this disposition towards alterity within the subject with a series of what he calls 'termes éthiques' or even 'un langage éthique' (p. 92): accusation, persecution, obsession, substitution and hostage. Of course, and this is already a huge issue, this is not what one normally thinks of as an ethical language. A related second working hypothesis announces itself here, namely: the condition of possibility for the ethical relation lies in the deployment or articulation of a certain ethical language. This is already highly curious and would merit separate attention, namely: that Levinas deploys an ethical language which attempts to express what he calls 'the paradox in which phenomenology suddenly finds itself' (p. 92). The *paradox* here is that what this ethical language seeks to thematize is by definition unthematizable: it is a conception of the subject constituted in a relation to alterity that is irreducible to ontology, that is, irreducible to thematization or conceptuality. Levinas's work is a *phenomenology of the unphenomenologizable*, or what he calls the order of the enigma in distinction from that of the phenomenon.

Of course, the claim that Levinas is offering a phenomenology of the unphenomenologizable does not make his work unique, and one thinks both of the late Heidegger's description of his thinking in his final Zähringen seminar in 1973 as the attempt at a 'phenomenology of the inapparent' and of the important recent debates that this has given rise to in France about the alleged theological turn within French phenomenology (Janicaud, Marion, Henry). As Wittgenstein might have said, the ethicality of thought is revealed in its persistent attempt to run up or bump up against the limits of language. The ethical might well be nonsense within the bounds of sense demarcated by the *Tractatus*, but it is important or serious nonsense, and it is arguably the animating intention of Wittgenstein's earlier *and* later work.

Thus, and here I bring together the two hypotheses, *the disposition towards alterity within the subject which is the condition of possibility for the ethical relation to the other is expressed linguistically or articulated philosophically by recourse to an ethical language that has a paradoxical relation to that which it is attempting to thematize*. As so often in the later Levinas, it is a question of trying to *say* that which cannot be *said*, or *proposing* that which cannot be propositionally *stated*, of *enunciating* that which cannot be *enunciated*, and what has to be said, stated or enunciated is subjectivity itself.

In this essay, I want to discuss just one term in this ethical language: *trauma* or 'traumatisme'. Levinas tries to thematize the subject that is, according to me, the condition of possibility for the ethical relation with the notion of trauma. He thinks the subject as trauma – ethics is a traumatology.[3] I would like to interpret this word *trauma*, and its associated ethical language and conception of the subject, in *economic* rather than strictly philosophical terms; that is to say, in relation to the meta-psychology of the second Freudian topography elaborated first in *Beyond the Pleasure Principle*. For Freud, it is the evidence of traumatic neurosis, clinically evidenced in war neurosis, that necessitates the introduction of the repetition compulsion. Now, it is the drive-like or pulsional character of repetition that overrides the pleasure principle and suggests a deeper instinctual function than had the earlier distinction of the ego and sexual drives. Thus, for Freud, there is a direct link between the analysis of trauma and the introduction of the speculative hypothesis of the death-drive, and it is this link that I wish to exploit as I read Levinas.

What is the justification for this economic understanding of Levinas? Well, there is absolutely none really; there is certainly nothing in Levinas's *intentions* to justify this link. However, as is so often the case with Levinas, his *text* is in a most illuminating conflict with his intentions. It is only by reading *against* Levinas's denials and resistances that we might get some insight into what is going on in his text: its latencies, its possi-bilities, its radicalities. Although Levinas includes such terms as obsession, persecution and trauma in his ethical language – not to mention his invoca-tion in one place of 'psychosis' (p. 102) and of the ethical subject as 'une conscience devenue folle' – he does this by specifically refusing and even ridiculing the categories of psychoanalysis. For example – and there are other examples – Levinas begins a conference paper entitled 'La psych-analyse est-elle une histoire juive?' with the confession, 'My embarrassment comes from the fact that I am absolutely outside the area of psychoanalytic research'.[4] For Levinas, psychoanalysis is simply part and parcel of the anti-humanism of the human sciences, which, in criticizing the sovereignty of 'Man', risks losing sight of the holiness of the human (*la sainteté de l'humain*).[5]

I

Before giving a more careful reading of Levinas and trying to make good on my initial hypotheses on the subject and ethical language, I wish to illustrate the tension between Levinas's intention and his text in relation to psychoanalysis with an example.

In the original version of 'Substitution', Levinas asks (p. 82): 'Does con-sciousness exhaust the notion of subjectivity?' That is to say, is the ethical subject a conscious subject? The answer is a resounding 'no'. The whole Levinasian analysis of the subject proceeds from a rigorous distinction between subject and consciousness or between the *le Soi* (the self) and *le Moi* (the ego). Levinas's work, and this is something far too little recog-nized in much of the unduly edifying or fetishizing secondary literature on Levinas, proceeds from the rigorous distinction between consciousness and subjectivity, where 'c'est une question de ramener le moi à soi', a question of leading back the ego of ontology to its meta-ontological subjectivity. For Levinas, it is the reduction of subjectivity to consciousness and the order of representation that defines and dominates modern philosophy. It is necessary to reduce this reduction – such is the sense of Husserlian intentional analysis for Levinas, where what counts is the overflowing of objectivistic, naive thought by a forgotten experience from which it lives; that is to say, the pre-conscious experience of the subject interlocuted by the other.[6] Levinas breaks the thread that ties the subject to the order of consciousness, knowledge, representation and presence. Levinas gives the name 'psychism' to this subject which constitutes itself and maintains itself in a relation to that which escapes representation and presence: the subject of the trace, of a past that has never been present, the immemorial, the anarchic, etc. In brief, consciousness is the belated *nachträglich* effect of the subject as trace, the dissimulating effect of a subjective affect. *Consciousness is the effect of an affect*, and this affect is trauma.

Of course, the Freudian resonances in what I have said thus far will already be apparent, but any possible rapprochement between the Levinasian analysis of the subject and Freudian psychoanalysis is specifically and violently refused by Levinas in the text I am commenting upon. He writes (p. 83) in the 1968 version of 'Substitution',

> But to speak of the hither side of consciousness is not to turn toward the unconscious. The unconscious in its clandestinity, rehearses the game played out in consciousness, namely the search for meaning and truth as the search for the self. While this opening onto the self is certainly occluded and repressed, psychoanalysis still manages to break through and restore self-consciousness. It follows that our study will not be following the way of the unconscious.

It should go without saying that this is a pretty lamentable understanding of Freud. But, provisionally, one can note two things:

1   If Levinas appears to believe that psychoanalysis seeks to restore self-consciousness, then it is interesting to note that he says exactly the opposite – and rightly – in an important text from 1954, 'Le moi et la totalité', where it is claimed that psychoanalysis 'throws a fundamental suspicion on the most indeniable evidence of self-consciousness'.[7]
2   Although Freud arguably always harboured the therapeutic ambition of restoring self-consciousness, an ambition expressed in the famous formula *Wo Es war soll Ich werden*, one should note that there are other ways of returning to the meaning of Freud, and other ways of reading that formula, notably that of Lacan who interprets the

Freudian *Es* as the subject of the unconscious and sees the imperative driving psychoanalysis as to arrive at the place of the subject beyond the imaginary *méconnaissance* of the conscious ego.[8]

However, the tension that interests me has not yet been established. Returning to the passage quoted above on Levinas's refusal of the psychoanalytic concept of the unconscious, what is fascinating here and typical of the relation between Levinas's intentions and his text, is that Levinas's statement that he will not be following the way of the unconscious is flatly contradicted later in a footnote (p. 183) in the 1968 'Substitution' text, just after a couple of key references to trauma.

> Persecution leads back the ego to the self, to the absolute accusative where the Ego is accused of a fault which it neither willed nor committed, and which disturbs its freedom. Persecution is a traumatism – violence par excellence, without warning, without apriori, without the possibility of apology, without logos. Persecution leads back to a resignation without consent and as a result traverses a night of the unconscious. *This is the meaning of the unconscious, the night where the ego comes back to the self under the traumatism of persecution* [*nuit où se fait le retournement de moi à soi sous le traumatisme de la persécution*] – a passivity more passive than all passivity, on the hither side of identity, becoming the responsibility of substitution [emphasis added].[9]

Here is the paradox (or is it a simple contradiction?): in one breath, Levinas writes that he will not follow the psychoanalytic way of the unconscious because it seeks to restore self-consciousness. But, in the next breath, Levinas gives us the meaning of the unconscious conceived as the night when the ego comes back to the self under the traumatism of persecution. So, the concept of the unconscious, the *pierre angulaire* of psychoanalysis, is strategically denied and then reintroduced with a *méconnaissance* that is perhaps too easily understood within a Freudian logic of *Verneinung*.

My question to Levinas has already been announced, but can now be more sharply formulated: what does it mean to think the meaning of the unconscious in terms of the traumatism of persecution? What does it mean to think the subject – the subject of the unconscious – as trauma?

II

In order to approach this question, I will return to my first hypothesis and try to show the central place of the subject in Levinas through a brief overview of the main argument of *Otherwise than Being or Beyond Essence*.[10]

234

Levinas begins his exposition by describing the movement from Husserlian intentional consciousness to a level of preconscious, pre-reflective, sensing or sentience, a movement enacted in the title of the second chapter of the book, 'De l'intentionalité au sentir'. In a gesture that remains methodologically faithful to Heidegger's undermining of the theoretical comportment to the world *(Vorhandenheit)* and the subject–object distinction that supports epistemology and (on Levinas's early reading in his doctoral thesis) Husserlian phenomenology, the movement from intentionality to sensing, or in the language of *Totality and Infinity*, from representation to enjoyment, shows how intentional consciousness is conditioned by *life* (p. 56). But, against Heideggerian *Sorge*, life for Levinas is not a *blosses Leben*. It is sentience, enjoyment and nourishment; it is *jouissance* and *joie de vivre*. Life is love of life and love of what life lives from: the sensible material world. Levinas's work is a reduction of the conscious intentional ego to the pre-conscious sentient subject of *jouissance*. Now, it is precisely this sentient subject of jouissance that is capable of being called into question by the other. The ethical relation, and this is important, takes place at the level of pre-reflective sensibility and not at the level of reflective consciousness. The ethical subject is a sentient subject, not a conscious ego.

So, for Levinas, *the subject is subject*, and the form that this subjection assumes is that of sensibility or sentience. Sensibility is what Levinas often refers to as 'the way' of my subjection, vulnerability and passivity towards the other. The entire argumentative thrust of the exposition in *Otherwise than Being . . .* is to show how subjectivity is founded in *sensibility* (Chapter 2) and to describe sensibility as a *proximity* to the other (Chapter 3), a proximity whose basis is found in *substitution* (Chapter 4), which is the core concept of *Otherwise than Being*. So, if the centre of Levinas's thinking is his conception of the subject, then the central discussion of the subject takes place in the 'Substitution' chapter of *Otherwise than Being*, a discussion that Levinas describes as 'la pièce centrale' (p. ix) or 'le germe du présent ouvrage' (p. 125). However – a final philological qualification – the 'Substitution' chapter was originally presented as the second of two lectures given in Brussels in November 1967; the first was an early draft of 'Language and Proximity', which was published separately in the second edition of *En découvrant l'existence avec Husserl et Heidegger*, elements of which were redrafted in the third chapter of *Otherwise than Being*. The original published version of 'Substitution' appeared in the *Revue Philosophique de Louvain* in October 1968. Although much is missing from the first version of this text, particularly Levinas's qualified endorsement of Kant's ethics, I would say that it is philosophically more concentrated and easier to follow than the 1974 version. So, if the concept of the subject is the key to Levinas's thinking, then the original version of the 'Substitution' chapter might well provide a key to this key.

III

I will now try to analyse this traumatic logic of substitution – a self-lacerating, even masochistic, logic – where I am responsible for the persecution that I undergo, and where I am even responsible for my persecutor. No one can substitute themselves for me, but I am ready to substitute myself for the other, and even die in his or her place.

In the original version of 'Substitution', the first mention of trauma comes after a quotation of *Lamentations*: 'Tendre la joue à celui qui frappe et être rassasié de honte' ('To offer the cheek to the one who strikes him and to be filled with shame' [p. 90]). Thus, the subject is the one that suffers at the hands of the other and is responsible for the suffering that it did not will. I am responsible for the persecution I undergo, for the outrage done to me. It is this situation of the subject being 'absolutely responsible for the persecution I undergo' (p. 90) that Levinas describes with the phrase 'le traumatisme originel'. Thus, the subject is constituted as a subject of persecution, outrage, suffering or whatever, through an original traumatism towards which I am utterly passive. The passage itself and the surrounding text are dramatically expanded in the 1974 version of 'Substitution', and Levinas adds (p. 111):

> A passivity of which the active source is not thematizable. Passivity of traumatism, but of the traumatism that prevents its own representation, the deafening trauma, breaking the thread of consciousness which should have welcomed it in its present: the passivity of persecution. But a passivity that only merits the epithet of complete or absolute if the persecuted is liable to respond to the persecutor.

This 'traumatisme assourdissant', this deafening traumatism (which incidentally recalls the opening lines of Baudelaire's *A une passante*, 'La rue assourdissante', where it refers to the traumatic noisiness of nineteenth-century Paris), is that towards which I relate in a passivity that exceeds representation, i.e. that exceeds the intentional act of consciousness, that cannot be experienced as an object, the noematic correlate of a noesis. Trauma is a 'non-intentional affectivity', it tears into my subjectivity like an explosion, like a bomb that detonates without warning, like a bullet that hits me in the dark, fired from an unseen gun and by an unknown assailant.[11]

Now, it is this absolute passivity towards that which exceeds representation, a non-relating relation of inadequate responsibility towards alterity experienced as persecuting hatred, that is then described in the 1974 version – very suggestively for my concerns – as *transference*: 'Ce transfert . . . est la subjectivité même' ('This transference . . . is subjectivity itself' [p. 111]). Thus, subjectivity would seem to be constituted for Levinas in a transferential relation to an original trauma; that is to say, the subject is constituted – without its knowledge, prior to cognition and recognition – in a relation that exceeds representation, intentionality, symmetry, correspondence, coincidence, equality and reciprocity – to any form of ontology, whether phenomenological or dialectical. The ethical relation might be described as the attempt to imagine a non-dialectical concept of transference, where the other is opaque, reflecting nothing of itself back to the subject. In Lacanian terms, it would seem that the subject is articulated through a relation to the real, through the non-intentional affect of *jouissance*, where the original traumatism of the other is the Thing, *das Ding*. It is only by virtue of such a mechanism of trauma that one might speak of ethics.[12]

Thus, the subject is constituted in a hetero-affection that divides the self and refuses all identification at the level of the ego. Such is the work of trauma, *die Trauma-Arbeit*, the event of an inassumable past, a lost time that can never be *retrouvé*, a non-intentional affectivity that takes place as a subjection to the other, a subject subjected to the point of persecution.

It is at this point, and in order to elaborate critically this concept of the subject as trauma, that a short detour into Freud is necessary.

IV

What is trauma? Trauma is etymologically defined in Larousse as 'blessure', as wounding, as 'violence produite par un agent extérieur agissant mécaniquement'. As such, trauma has a physiological as well as psychical meaning, denoting a violence effected by an external agency, which can be a blow to the head or a broken arm, as much as the emotional shock of bereavement. For Freud, trauma is an economic concept and refers to a massive cathexis of external stimulus that breaches the protective shield of the perceptual-consciousness system or ego. Trauma is shock and complete surprise. In terms of the Freudian model of the psychical apparatus governed by Fechner's constancy principle, trauma is an excess of excitation that disrupts psychical equilibrium and is consequently experienced as unpleasurable. In Lacanian terms, trauma is the subjective affect of contact with the real. It is the opening up of the ego to an exteriority that shatters its economic unity. Recalling Levinas's allusion to a 'deafening traumatism', trauma is like a bomb going off which produces a sudden and violent pain. With the breach in the ego caused by such a trauma, the pleasure principle is momentarily put out of action. However, the ego responds to the cathexis of stimulus caused by the trauma with an equivalent anti-cathexis, by a defensive strategy that seeks to transform the free or mobile energy of the trauma into bound, quiescent, energy. If the defensive strategy succeeds, then the economy of the ego is restored and the pleasure principle resumes its reign.

Thus arises the riddle of traumatic neurosis. Traumatic neurosis is the disorder that arises after the experience of a trauma: a car accident, shell-shock or a terrorist bombing. In clinical terms, the neurosis can manifest itself in a number of ways: in a paroxysm, a severe anxiety attack, a state of profound agitation (compulsive twitching) or sheer mental confusion (shell-shock). What characterizes the symptoms of traumatic neurosis, like the other neuroses, is both their compulsive character – and compulsion is one of the main traits of the unconscious (*com-pulsare* = the constraint of a *pulsion*, a drive) – and their repetitiveness. In traumatic neurosis the original scene of the trauma, its deafening shock, is compulsively and unconsciously repeated in nightmares, insomnia or obsessive (another Levinasian term in 'Substitution') reflection. The subject endlessly attempts to relive that contact with the real that was the origin of the trauma, to repeat that painful *jouissance*. That is to say, the traumatized subject *wants* to suffer, to relive the jouissance of the real, to repeatedly pick at the scab that irritates it.[13]

Thus, the dream of the traumatic neurotic repeats the origin of the trauma. Freud's huge theoretical problem here is the following: if this is true, that is, if there is a repetition compulsion at work in traumatic neuro-sis that repeats the origin of trauma, then how can this fact be consistent with the central thesis of his magnum opus, the *Traumdeutung*, where it is claimed that all dreams are wish-fulfilments and are governed by the pleasure principle? *It cannot*, and it is with the evidence of the repetition compulsion exhibited in traumatic neurosis and fate neurosis that the whole sublime architecture of the *Traumdeutung* and the first Freudian topography begins to fall apart. The move from the first to the second topography is that from *Traumdeutung* to *Trauma-Deutung*.

The dreams of traumatic neurotics are not, then, in obedience to the pleasure principle, but to the repetition compulsion. And not only is this true of traumatic neurosis, it is true of dreams that bring back the traumas of childhood, hence the importance of the Fort/Da game in Freud, where the infant attempts to sublimate the absence of the mother with a game that repeats the trauma of her departure. Thus, the original function of dreams is not the dreamwork *(die Traumarbeit)* that permits the sleeper to sleep on, it is rather the interruption of sleep, *die Trauma-Arbeit*, that is beyond the pleasure principle. Insomnia is the truth of sleep.[14]

In Chapter 5 of *Beyond the Pleasure Principle*, Freud tries to establish the instinctual or 'drive-like' (*Triebhaft*) character of the repetition compul-sion and, *vice versa*, to establish the repetitive character of the drives. Freud's claim is that the representatives or manifestations of the repetition compulsion exhibit a highly *Triebhaft* character, being out of the control of the ego and giving the appearance of a 'daemonic' force at work –

such is fate neurosis. Once Freud has established the *Triebhaft* character of the repetition compulsion, he is then in a position to introduce his central speculative hypothesis, namely that a drive is an inner urge or pressure in organic life to restore an earlier condition. That is to say, a drive is the expression of a *Trägheit*, an inertia, sluggishness or laziness in organic life. It is this speculation about the fundamentally conservative nature of drives – wrapped up in a pseudo-biological phylogenetic myth of origin – that yields the extreme (and extremely Schopenhauerian) conclusion of *Beyond the Pleasure Principle*: 'Das Ziel alles Lebens ist der Tod [the aim of all life is death]'.[15] Thus, death would be the object that would satisfy the aim of the drives.

V

By way of conclusion, I want to use the above Freudian insights to throw some light on what seems to be happening in Levinas. As I have hopefully established, the subject is the key concept in Levinas's work. The subject's affective disposition towards alterity is the condition of possibility for the ethical relation to the other. Ethics does not take place at the level of consciousness or reflection; it rather takes place at the level of sensibility or pre-conscious sentience. The Levinasian ethical subject is a sentient self (*un soi sentant*) before being a thinking ego (*un moi pensant*). The bond with the other is affective.

We have already seen the tension in Levinas's work where – on the one hand – he writes that his analysis of the subject is not going to follow the way of the unconscious because psychoanalysis seeks to restore self-consciousness, but – on the other hand – Levinas gives us the meaning of the unconscious as 'the night where the ego comes back to itself in the traumatism of persecution'. That is to say, Levinas seeks to think the subject at the level of the unconscious in relation to an original traumatism. The subject is constituted through a non-dialectical transference towards an originary traumatism. This is a seemingly strange claim to make, yet my wager is that if it does not go through then the entire Levinasian project is dead in the water.

How does Levinasian ethical subjectivity look from the perspective of the second Freudian topography? In the following way, perhaps: under the effect of the traumatism of persecution, the deafening shock or the violence of trauma, the subject becomes an internally divided or split self, an interiority that is radically non-self-coincidental, a gaping wound that will not heal, a subject lacerated by contact with an original traumatism that produces a scarred interiority inaccessible to consciousness and reflection, a subject that *wants* to repeat compulsively the origin of the trauma, a subject that becomes what Levinas calls a recurrence of the self without identification, a recurrence of trauma that is open to death, or – better – open to the passive movement of dying itself (*le mourir même*), dying as the first opening towards alterity, the impossibility of possibility as the very possibility of the ethical subject.

The Levinasian subject is a traumatized self, a subject that is constituted through a self-relation experienced as a lack, where the self is experienced as the inassumable source of what is lacking from the ego – a subject of melancholia, then. But, this is a *good thing*. It is only because the subject is unconsciously constituted through the trauma of contact with the real that we might have the audacity to speak of goodness, transcendence, compassion, etc.; and, moreover, to speak these terms in relation to the topology of desire and not simply in terms of some pious, reactionary and ultimately nihilistic wish-fulfilment. Without trauma, there would be no ethics in Levinas's particular sense of the word.

In this connection, one might generalize this structure and go so far as to say (although in a provisional and wholly formal manner) that without a relation to trauma, or at least without a relation to that which claims, calls, summons, interrupts or troubles the subject (whether the good beyond being in Plato, the moral law in Kant, or the relation to *das Ding* in Freud), there would be no ethics, neither an ethics of phenomenology, nor an ethics of psychoanalysis. Without a relation to that which summons and challenges the subject, a summons that is experienced as a relation to a Good in a way that exceeds the pleasure principle and any promise of happiness (any *eudaimonism*), there would be no ethics. And without such a relation to ethical experience – an experience that is strictly inassumable and impossible, but which yet heteronomously defines the autonomy of the ethical subject – one could not imagine a politics that would refuse the category of totality. The passage to justice in Levinas – to the third party, the community and politics – passes through or across the theoretical and historical experience of trauma. No democracy without the death drive!

Notes

1 For an exhaustive and exhausting account of the subject in Levinas, see Gérard Bailhache, *Le sujet chez Emmanuel Levinas* (PUF, Paris, 1994).
2 'Substitution', trans. Atterton, Noctor and Critchley in *Emmanuel Levinas. Basic Philosophical Writings*, eds Peperzak, Critchley and Bernasconi (Indiana University Press, Bloomington, 1996), p. 92. Subsequent references to this book are given in the body of text.
3 In this regard, see Elisabeth Weber, *Verfolgung und Trauma* (Passagen Verlag, Vienna, 1990); and Michel Haar, 'L'obsession de l'autre. L'éthique comme traumatisme', *Emmanuel Levinas* (L'Herne, Paris, 1991), pp. 444–53.
4 'Quelques réflexions talmudiques sur le rêve', *La psychanalyse est-elle une histoire juive?* (Seuil, Paris, 1981), p. 114.
5 On the importance of the notion of *la sainteté* in Levinas, see Derrida's remarks in his stunning recent book, *Adieu à Levinas* (Galilée, Paris, 1997), p. 15.

6 Levinas, *Totality and Infinity*, trans. A. Lingis (Duquesne University Press, Pittsburgh, 1969), p. 28.

7 'Le moi et la totalité', in *Entre Nous. Essais sur le penser-à-l'autre* (Grasset, Paris, 1991), pp. 36–7:

> Ce n'est pas la parole seulement que démolissent ainsi la psychanalyse et l'histoire. Elles aboutissent en réalité à la destruction du *je* s'identifiant du dedans. La réflexion du cogito ne peut plus surgir pour assurer la certitude de ce que je suis et à peine pour assurer la certitude de mon existence même. Cette existence tributaire de la reconnaissance par autrui, sans laquelle, insignifiante, elle se saisit comme réalité sans réalité, devient purement phénoménale. La psychanalyse jette une suspicion foncière sur le témoignage le plus irrécusable de la conscience de soi. (. . .) Le *cogito* perd ainsi sa valeur de fondement. On ne peut plus reconstruire la réalité à partir d'éléments qui, indépendants de tout point de vue et indéformables par la conscience, permettent une connaissance philosophique.

8 Lacan, 'La chose freudienne', in *Ècrits* (Seuil, Paris, 1966), pp. 416–18.

9 A similar line of thought is expressed in 'La ruine de la représentation', in *En découvrant l'existence avec Husserl et Heidegger* (Vrin, Paris, 1967), p. 130. Levinas writes:

> Cette découverte de l'implicite qui n'est pas une simple 'déficience' ou 'chute' de l'explicite, apparaît comme monstruosité ou comme merveille dans une histoire des idées où le concept d'actualité coïncidait avec l'état de veille absolue, avec la lucidité de l'intellect. Que cette pensée se trouve tributaire d'une vie anonyme et obscure, de paysages oubliés qu'il faut restituer à l'objet même que la conscience croît pleinement tenir, voilà qui rejoint incontestablement les conceptions modernes de l'inconscient et des profondeurs. Mais, il en résulte non pas nouvelle psychologie seulement. Une nouvelle ontologie commence: l'être se pose non pas seulement comme corrélatif d'une pensée, mais comme fondant déjà la pensée même qui, cependant, le constitue.

10 Levinas, *Otherwise than Being or Beyond Essence*, trans. A. Lingis (Nijhoff, The Hague, 1981). Further references to this work are given in the body of the text.

11 See Andrew Tallon, 'Nonintentional Affectivity, Affective Intentionality, and the Ethical in Levinas's Philosophy', in *Ethics as First Philosophy*, ed. Adriaan Peperzak (Routledge, London and New York, 1995), pp. 107–21.

12 I have in mind Lacan's formula in his commentary on Sade: 'la jouissance est un mal. Freud là-dessus nous guide par la main – elle est un mal parce qu'elle comporte le mal du prochain.' ['Jouissance is suffering. Freud guides us by the hand on this point – it is suffering because it involves or bears itself towards the suffering of the neighbour'] (*L'éthique de la psychanalyse*, Seuil, Paris, 1986, p. 217).

13 Freud writes:

> Das Studium des Traumes dürfen wir als den zuverläsigsten Weg zur Erforschung der seelischen Tiefenvorgäge betrachten. Nun zeigt das Traumleben der traumatischen Neurose den Charakter, das es den Kranken immer wieder in die Situation seines Unfalles zurückführt, aus der er

mit neuem Schrecken erwacht. Darüber verwundert man sich viel zuwenig. (*Psychologie des Unbewussten, Freud-Studienausgabe, Band 3*, Fischer, Frankfurt am Main, 1975, p. 223)

The study of dreams may be considered the most trustworthy method of investigating deep mental processes. Now dreams occurring in traumatic neurosis have the characteristic of repeatedly bringing the patient back into the situation of his accident, a situation from which he wakes up in another fright. This astonishes people far too little. (*On Metapsychology*, Penguin Freud Library, Vol. 11, Penguin, Harmondsworth, 1984, p. 282)

14 Freud writes:

Aber die obenerwänten Träme der Unfallsneurotiker lassen sich nicht mehr unter den Gesichtspunkt der Wunscherfüllung bringen, und ebensowenig die in den Psychoanalysen vorfallended Träume, die uns die Erinnerung der psychischen Traumen der Kindheit wiederbringen. Sie gehorchen vielmehr dem Wiederholungszwang, der in der Analyse allerdings durch den von der 'Suggestion' geförderten Wunsch, das Vergessene und Verdrägte heraufzubeschwören, unterstützt wird. (*op. cit.*, p. 242)

But it is impossible to classify as wish-fulfilments the dreams we have been discussing which occur in traumatic neuroses, or the dreams during psychoanalyses which bring to memory the psychical traumas of childhood. They arise, rather, in obediance to the compulsion to repeat, though it is true that in analysis that compulsion is supported by the wish (which is encouraged by 'suggestion') to conjure up what has been forgotten and repressed. (trans., p. 304)

15 Freud, *op. cit.*, p. 248; trans., p. 311.

Part V

APPLICATIONS

17

SOME ENLIGHTENMENT PROJECTS RECONSIDERED

Alasdair MacIntyre

The Enlightenment is of course an historian's construction. There were several of them, French, Scottish and German, each complex and hetero-geneous. Nonetheless we can identify some major shared themes and pro-jects, each of which claimed and still claims the badge of Enlightenment. There is, first of all, the attempt to define *enlightenment* by drawing a dis-tinction between the unenlightened and the enlightened, unenlightened them and enlightened us. Here the canonical text was and is Kant's *Beant-wortung der Frage: Was ist Aufklärung?* of 1784. And Kant's text has of course had its heirs and successors, most recently Foucault's of 1984, whose title repeats Kant's *Was ist Aufklärung?* ('What is Enlightenment?' in *The Foucault Reader*, ed. P. Rabinow, New York: Pantheon Books, 1984).

Both Kant and Foucault defined Enlightenment as primarily a task, the task of achieving a condition in which human beings think for themselves rather than in accordance with the prescriptions of some authority. For Kant in 1784 such reasoning in the sphere of morality requires the adop-tion of the standpoint of what he took to be universal reason, a standpoint independent of the particularities of kinship and political ties, of one's culture and one's religion. But how is this standpoint to be characterized? About this, widespread disagreement had already been generated by a second major Enlightenment project, that of specifying in detail the nature and content of the moral rules that universal reason requires, a project embodied in what were to become canonical Enlightenment texts by authors as various as Locke, Hume, Smith, Diderot, Bentham, Robespierre, Jefferson and Kant himself, each of these affirming positions incompatible in some respects with those of most or all of the others. And these disagree-ments have proved irresoluble. Does this outcome of the second project damage the first?

Foucault's answer was: Not too much. In his 1984 essay he asserted that the task set by Kant embodies attitudes towards the relationship of past to present, and towards practical enquiry into how we are 'constituted as moral subjects of our own actions' (*op. cit.*, p. 49), that we still need to make our own, but we must now do so without the hope of being able to 'identify the universal structures . . . of all possible moral action' (p. 46). It is instead through investigating our contingency and our particularity that we will become able to test those limits that we must transcend, if we are to become free. Foucault's hope was that such investigation would enable us to disconnect 'the growth of autonomy' from that intensification of power relations 'which had resulted from the technologies of economic production, social regulation and communication' (p. 48). And he thus raised sharp questions about the relationship of the first project of the Enlightenment, that of becoming enlightened, not only to what I have called its second project, that of providing a single set of universal moral prescriptions, compelling to all rational individuals, but also to yet a third major Enlightenment project, that of bringing into being and sustaining a set of social, economic and technological institutions designed to achieve the Enlightenment's moral and political goals. It has of course been a central belief of the Enlightenment's modern heirs that such institutions have by now been brought into being in so-called advanced countries and that they do, substantially even if imperfectly, embody the Enlightenment's aspirations, so that those actual institutions – apart from their imperfections – have a claim to the allegiance of rational individuals, analogous to that which rationally founded moral principles have.

The roll-call of those institutions is a familiar one: representative democracy through which potentially autonomous individuals are portrayed as expressing their political preferences; a legal system purporting to safeguard the rights which individuals need, if they are to be treated as autonomous, including rights to freedom of expression and enquiry; a free-market economy through which individuals are to express their preferences as consumers and investors; an expansion of those technologies which supply the material and organizational means for the gratification of preferences; and a system of public education designed to prepare the young for participation in these institutions. Were it to be the case that the conjoint workings of these institutions systematically achieved and achieves very different outcomes from those expected by the Enlightenment, by in fact frustrating or undermining the autonomy and choices of individuals, how much would *this* matter to the ultimate fate of the Enlightenment's projects?

I

On this reading of the Enlightenment, its first project is presupposed by the other two. So I begin by examining Kant's claims about thinking for oneself. *Aufklärung*, enlightenment, so Kant asserted, is the casting off of

an immaturity which is self-caused insofar as its cause is not lack of intel-
ligence. That immaturity consists in thinking as directed by some other.
Casting it off requires courage, the courage to think for oneself, and Kant
quotes Horace: *Sapere aude!* He goes on to assert that if I have a book
which takes the place of my understanding, if I have a spiritual director
who takes the place of my conscience, or if I have a physician whose
judgment about my dietary regime displaces my own, then, according to
Kant, I have not yet shown this courage. Thinking for oneself is thus con-
trasted with thinking in accordance with the dictates of any authority. But
this is not the only relevant contrast. Statutory rules (*Satzungen* – the
term is used principally of articles of association) and formulas, useful
aids as they may be, often instead act as a substitute for thinking for oneself. So unenlightened thinking is characterized by the indiscriminate and
unintelligent use of and appeal to rules and formulas. How then is the
courageous individual to free her or himself from bondage either to alien
direction or to rules and formulas? Such freedom may not, Kant held, be
possible when one is acting or speaking in some official civic or ecclesiasti-
cal role in which obedience and conformity can be justly required, if that
role-playing is to be effective. But it is possible for someone to achieve the
requisite independence, when that individual instead makes what Kant
calls 'public use' of her or his reason, that use 'which the scholar makes
before the whole reading public'. What does Kant mean by this?

Foucault points out that the verb Kant uses here – '*räsionieren*' – is
characteristically used by him to refer to reasoning which pursues the
goals internal to reasoning: truth, theoretical and practical adequacy and
the like. Those to whom such reasoning is presented are invited to evaluate
it, not instrumentally from the standpoint of their own particular purposes
or interests, but simply *qua* reasoners, in accordance with standards which
are genuinely impersonal, just because they are the standards of reason as
such. I hold myself accountable to other such reasoners in the light of
those standards. I expose my reasoning to their objections, as they expose
theirs to mine. And who, we may ask, could object to this and still claim
the title of 'reasonable' for her or his objection?

The force of this question has seemed to be such that it has been turned
into an argument. Suppose that someone were to advance an objection to
this Enlightenment ideal of public reason. Then, in order for this objection
to be evaluated as a better or worse reason for asserting its conclusion, it
would have to be framed in accordance with these very same standards of
public reason, and its author would thus have implicitly conceded just
what she or he had intended to dispute. So the adherents of Enlightenment
can know, in advance of any particular objections, that this fundamental
position of theirs is immune from refutation.

Yet what this argument ignores is the fact that such public reasoning
always occurs in a local context as part of a set of conversations that

have their own peculiar history. We reason not just in the company of others, but in the company of particular others, with whom at any given time we will share some set of background presuppositions. What makes your theses or my objections to those theses relevant to our shared enquiries always depends upon the specifications of the social and intellectual context of our enquiries and debates. And here the example of Kant's practice is instructive. For in his essay on Enlightenment Kant was himself a scholar making use of reason 'before the whole reading public'. What was that reading public? It was of course one particular, highly specific, reading public.

The journal in which Kant's essay appeared in November 1784 was the *Berlinische Monatsschrift*, edited by J.E. Biester, a librarian in Prussia's Royal Library. In December, 1783, the Berlin pastor and educator J.F. Zöllner had raised the question to which Kant was now supplying an answer – not the first of such answers, since in September 1784 Moses Mendelssohn had contributed his response. The *Berlinische Monatsschrift* was one of a number of such journals in various European countries with an overlapping circulation, so that there had come into being a collective readership not only for those periodicals but for books reviewed or otherwise noticed in them. In some cities local societies brought such readers together. And individual readers engaged in often prolonged intellectual correspondence with those at a distance. So the public which Kant addressed was a network of periodical subscribers, club members and letter-writers, to whose collective conversation he was a major contributor.

What this suggests is twofold: first that *the* reading public at any particular time and place is always some particular, highly specific, reading public with its own stock of shared assumptions, expectations and focus of attention. What is regarded as obvious or taken for granted, what is treated as problematic, which considerations have more weight and which less, which rhetorical modes are acceptable and which not, vary from reading public to reading public. Indeed in some times and places there may be more than one reading public. So that it is not so much humanity in general as some socially particularized 'anyone' whom a scholar making public use of her or his reason addresses, when she or he addresses what she or he takes to be 'the whole reading public'.

Second, reading publics have to be distinguished from other types of public, such as the public that is composed of every member of some particular political society or the public constituted by some other shared interest. How do reading publics relate to such other publics? Kant avoids this question, for he equates considering oneself 'as a member of the whole commonwealth, in fact even of world society', with considering oneself 'in the quality of a scholar who is addressing the true public through his writing'. And at the end of his essay he envisages a spreading of

Enlightenment from the cultures of the arts and the sciences to religion and thereafter to politics, the framing of legislation.

> This free thought gradually acts upon the mind of the people and they gradually become more capable of acting in freedom. Eventually, the government is also influenced by this free thought and thereby it treats the human being, who is now more than a machine, according to his dignity.*

Kant's conclusion provokes questions: Is he right in asserting that it is through one's relationship to this kind of reading public that one comes to think for oneself? What is the relationship between thinking for oneself, however that is understood, and effective action on the basis of such thought? And what is the relationship between thinking for oneself in any one particular sphere – that, say, in which one addresses a particular *reading* public – and thinking and acting for oneself in other spheres of activity? These are questions that Kant did not pursue. Perhaps they were among those whose answers seemed to him and his readers unproblematic. For that reason alone they are worth pursuing.

II

Kant is unquestionably right in this: that thinking for oneself always does require thinking in cooperation with others. Some episodes of thought do of course consist in solitary monologues. But even solitary monologues have to begin from what others have provided, and their conclusions have to be matched against rival conclusions, have to be stated in such a way as to be open to critical and constructive objections advanced by others, and have to be thereby made available for reflective interpretation and reinterpretation by others, so that sometimes one comes to understand only from those others what one means or must have meant. We learn to think better or worse from others, much that is matter for our thought is presented to us by others, and we find ourselves contributing to a complex history of thought in which our debts to our predecessors are payable only to our successors. What distinguishes my thought from my meditative fantasy is in key part the relationship in which that thought stands to the thought of others, a very different relationship from that which holds between my fantasies and the fantasies of others. For, in the case of thought, what I say both to myself and to others and what they say both to themselves and to me has to involve recognition, almost always implicit rather than explicit, of shared standards of truth, of rationality, of logic, standards that are not mine rather than yours or *vice versa*. This kind of relationship to others is an essential and not an accidental characteristic of thought.

We can always enquire therefore about any public, reading or otherwise, how well its practices embody the kinds of relationship that genuine thought requires. And all reading publics have this in common, that they depend upon the art of writing and the dissemination of writing. In the *Phaedrus* Plato warned us about – perhaps not against – those whose relationships depend upon writing. There is of course a well-established interpretation of the *Phaedrus* according to which we are to ascribe the unqualified condemnation of writing as such, which Plato puts in the mouth of the Egyptian King Thamus, to Plato himself. And from this interpretation it is the shortest of steps to Derrida's claim that there is something inherently paradoxical and deconstructive in what he takes to be Plato's use of writing to issue an unqualified condemnation of writing, one endorsed by Socrates who never taught by writing.[1] Yet perhaps the condemnation implied by the argument of the *Phaedrus* is more qualified than the condemnation by Thamus. Perhaps what the *Phaedrus* in fact condemns is one particular kind of writing and all writing only insofar as it approaches the condition of that particular kind, so raising the question of whether and how far the *Phaedrus* itself falls under that condemnation, but not answering it. What *is* condemned is all writing that has become detached from the author who speaks in and through it, so that the author as author cannot be put to the question along with her or his text. Yet must not this be the case with *all* writing when the author is dead? Perhaps not, if someone else is able to stand in the author's place, to supply the needed authorial voice, and to respond to interrogation by others.

The thesis that I am ascribing to Plato, as conveyed by the dialogue rather than by what Thamus or Socrates says in it, is that, if writing is to escape condemnation, it must function as subordinated to and only within the context of spoken dialogue. Texts, on this Platonic view, can play no part in the dialectical and dialogical development of genuine thought except when they are part of the matter of spoken conversation. But, if this view is correct, then the whole notion of a reading public as the type of public required for thought, required for thinking for oneself, is a little more complex than it at first appeared.

Consider the difference between the relationship of Plato's pupils at the Academy, who were able to put Plato to the question about the doctrines of the *Phaedrus*, to Plato, and the relationship of Kant's readers, many of them far distant from Koenigsberg and therefore unable to question Kant, to Kant. Texts such as Kant's serve as matter for genuine thought for their readers only insofar as their reading and the ideas drawn from that reading become part of the dialectical conversation of some group, in which imagination enables someone – perhaps more than one person – to speak on Kant's behalf and others – or on occasion perhaps the same person – to raise objections. So the kind of reading public which provides the context for genuine thought will be a network, not of individuals but of small face-to-face conversational groups who pursue their enquiries systematically and make their reading part of those enquiries. And there certainly were places and periods during the eighteenth and the early nineteenth century in which the Enlightenment's reading public did to greater or lesser degree approximate to that condition – I am thinking here of various societies ranging from those meeting under the auspices of the great Academies in Paris or Berlin or St Petersburg to such bodies as Berlin's *Mittwochsgesellschaft*, a group closely associated with the *Berlinische Monatsschrift*, the Oyster Club in Glasgow, the Rankenian Club in Edinburgh and the Philosophical Society in Aberdeen.[2]

Thinking then is indeed an essentially social activity. But when he wrote of the public use of reason Kant was not engaged in characterizing thinking as such, but rather thinking for oneself, contrasting an immature reliance upon authorities and formulas with mature intellectual activity. What are we to make of *this* contrast? Thinking for oneself is in the first instance a condition for one's being able genuinely to contribute to and to benefit from those exchanges with others through which thinking is carried on. And this precludes the substitution of appeals to authority or to formulas for one's own conclusions, just as Kant contended. But is it the case that any kind of appeal to authority is thereby precluded? What about – to return to Kant's example – my reliance upon my physician's judgment in respect of my diet? She or he after all has the relevant expertise, while I do not. It cannot be a mark of maturity for me to substitute my untrained judgment for her or his trained judgment. (Kant, it is true, did pride himself on having restored himself to health without medical aid, after he became ill at the time of writing the first *Critique*.) But presumably it is not *any* reliance on the superior knowledge of others which is to be condemned, but only a reliance that exempts authority from rational scrutiny and criticism.

All representatives of rationally unfounded authority need of course to inculcate just such an uncritical reliance, attempting to ensure that others argue and enquire only within limits prescribed by them. When they succeed, the result is indeed that those others think, not for themselves, but only as the representatives of authority prescribe. And even legitimate authority will have the same bad effect if it is relied upon uncritically, since such reliance will set the same kind of arbitrary limits to thinking. Note that in both types of case the failure to think for oneself is also a failure in thinking as such. And because all thinking is social, such failures are generally more than failures of individual thinkers, and the only effective remedies for such failures may always involve some change in the social conditions of thought, in those social and institutional frameworks within which rational enquiry is carried on and by which it is sustained.

251

To recognize this involves acknowledging both the truth of Kant's central claim in *Beantwortung der Frage: Was ist Auflkärung?*, and the need to go beyond Kant. Thinking, in any particular time and place, let alone thinking for oneself, always involves thinking with certain particular others, thinking in the context of some particular and specific public, with its own institutional structure. Every such public has its own limitations and failure to recognize such limitations and to examine them critically may well involve a reliance upon them quite as damaging to enquiry as the reliance upon unscrutinized authority. The key question at any particular time and place is then: within what kind of public with what kind of institutionalized structures will we be able to identify the limitations imposed on our particular enquiries as a prelude to transcending those limitations in pursuit of the goods of reason?

The theorists of the European Enlightenment were brilliantly successful for their own time and place in identifying certain types of social institution which could not but frustrate that pursuit, and they did so by their negative critique of the intellectual justifications advanced by the representatives of the established powers of eighteenth-century Europe. It was for them, and it remains for us, crucially important to recognize that the centralizing state powers that had reduced local communities to administered dependence, the landed powers that had systematically encroached upon or abolished customary peasant rights, the imperialist hegemonies that had wiped out the original inhabitants of Prussia, enslaved large parts of the Americas, and conquered Ireland and India, all of these had rested on what was in fact arbitrary power disguised by a set of false legitimating theories and histories: the sixteenth-century French invention of the doctrine of the divine right of kings, the mythologizing genealogies devised for *nouveau riche* landowners by imaginative English heralds, the *ad hoc* theories of property which purported to justify the enclosure by the rich and powerful of hitherto common land, the defences of slave-owning which elicited Vittoria's refutation, the doctrines of ethnic inferiority attacked by Las Casas. Insofar as it was the Enlightenment's project to expose the groundlessness of these pretensions of the ruling and owning classes of the seventeenth and eighteenth centuries, its theorists succeeded both argumentatively and imaginatively, and we are all of us the better for it.

Yet if the institutions of the *ancien régime* and of the post-1688 British oligarchy fail the tests of the Enlightenment, indeed the tests of rationality on any adequate view of it, what about the institutions characteristic of post-Enlightenment modernity? How do those institutions fare, if judged by the same standards?

III

Within what kinds of institutional structure have the moral and political concepts and theories of the Enlightenment been at home? Within what types of discourse in what types of social context have they been able to find effective expression? A salient fact is that for some considerable time now in post-Enlightenment culture moral and political concepts and theories have led a double life, functioning in two distinct and very different ways. They are afforded one kind of expression and exposed to one kind of attention in the contexts of academic life, in university and college teaching and enquiry, and in the professional journals of philosophers and theorists, but receive very different expression in the contexts of modern corporate life, whether governmental or private, contexts constituted by a web of political, legal, economic and social relationships.

Each of these two contexts is constituted by a public or set of publics very different from those to which the concepts and theories of the Enlightenment were first announced and among which they were initially elaborated, as well as from each other. Reading has had a different part to play in each; discussion and debate, too, play very different parts; and the relationship of power and money to argument is not at all in each case the same. Yet both in contemporary academic milieux and in contemporary political, legal and economic life, Enlightenment and post-Enlightenment concepts of utility, of right, of moral rules, of presupposed contractual agreements and shared understandings, are very much at home. And in each they are put to use in formulating and answering such questions as: How is the maximization of my utility to be related to the maximization of the utility of particular sets of others and to the general utility? When the maximization of either my or the general utility requires the infringement of somebody's rights, how are rights to be weighed against utility? Is each right to be weighed in the same way? How more generally is utility to be conceived and how are rights to be understood? When may I legitimately mislead, deceive, or lie to others? When may or should I keep silent when I know that others are lying? By what tacit agreements am I bound? What generally and in such and such types of particular case is required of me, when I have encouraged and relied upon reciprocal relationships with others?

When such questions are posed in academic contexts at the level of philosophy and theory, they receive not only incompatible and rival answers, but incompatible and rival answers each of which has by now been developed in systematic detail. I noted earlier how the great Enlightenment theorists had themselves disagreed both morally and philosophically. Their heirs have, through brilliant and sophisticated feats of argumentation, made it evident that if these disagreements are not interminable, they are such at least that after 200 years no prospect of termination is in sight. Succeeding generations of Kantians, utilitarians, natural rights' theorists and contractarians show no symptoms of genuine convergence.

It is not of course that the partisans of each view do not arrive at conclusions which they themselves are prepared to treat as decisive. It is rather that they have provided us with too many sets of conclusions. And each has been subjected to the most stringent tests that can be administered by a reading public in which face-to-face discussion provides a basis for and reinforces the effects of publication in books and journals. The modern academic philosophical community constitutes a reading public and a conversational public of a high order, in which each participant tests what is proposed to her or him by others and in turn subjects her or his own proposals to criticism by those others. So what we get is not at all what the early protagonists of the Enlightenment expected; what we get is a combination of exactly the right kind of intellectual public with a large absence of decisive outcomes and conclusions.

The contrast in this respect with the areas of political, legal, economic and social life is striking. For within the corporate institutions that dominate government and the economy the needs of practice are such that decisive outcomes and conclusions cannot be avoided, and philosophical or other disagreement cannot be allowed to stand in the way of effective decision-making. All those questions about utility, rights and contrast that remain matters for debate in the academic sphere receive decisive answers every day from the ways in which those who engage in the transactions of political, legal, economic and social life act or fail to act. But in those areas the fact that there is no rationally established and agreed procedure for evaluating the claims of utility against rights or *vice versa* – or, if you like, that there are too many such procedures, but each rationally established and agreed only among its own protagonists – has a quite different significance. For what is unsettlable by argument is settlable by power and money; and, in the social order at large, how rights are assigned and implemented, what weight is accorded to this or that class of rights and what to the maximization of the utility of this individual or this group or people in general, what the consequences of following or failing to follow certain rules are, are questions answered by those who have the power and money to make their answers effective.

One peculiar set of features of distinctively modern social structures will bring out one aspect of this use of power. It is that compartmentalization of social life as a result of which each sphere has its own set of established norms and values as a counterpart to the specialization of its tasks and the professionalization of its occupations. So the activities and experiences of domestic life are understood in terms of one set of norms and values, those of various types of private corporate workplace in terms of somewhat different sets, the arenas of politics and of governmental bureaucracies in terms of yet others, and so on. It is not of course that there is not some degree of overlap. But the differences between these compartmentalized areas are striking, and in each of them there are procedures for arriving at decisions, procedures generally insulated from criticism from any external standpoint.

Consider as an example how the deaths of individuals are valued in different sectors of social life. Premodern societies characteristically have a shared view of the significance of death, and their public rituals express shared beliefs. Modern societies generally have no such shared public view, but teach their members to respond to individual deaths differently in different contexts. (There are of course some widely shared attitudes, one of them expressed in the attempt by the medical profession in the United States to use its technologies to postpone death for as long as possible, an attempt which is a counterpart to the general loss of any conception of what it would be to have completed one's life successfully and so to have reached a point at which it would be the right time for someone to die. But this is the expression of something absent, something negative.) So (all the examples that I use are North American) in the private life of the family or household it is taken to be appropriate to treat the death of a young adult as the kind of loss for which *nothing* can compensate. And this is what is commonly said to and by the recently bereaved. Yet in the world of the automobile industry and the automobile user things are very different. Over quite a number of years the society of the United States has tolerated without strain the deaths of many thousand persons – about 17 in every 100,000 persons die on the roads each year, a significant proportion of them young adults. (The only class of such deaths about which there is any public concern is that due to drunk-driving.) Such deaths were and are treated as an acceptable and unavoidable trade-off for the benefits conferred by the use of automobiles and the flourishing of the automobile industry. The benefits are taken, without any soul-searching, to outweigh the costs. Yet generally if a parent were asked, immediately before or after the death of an adolescent child, what degree of social benefit would outweigh the cost of that child's life and make that death an acceptable occurrence, the question would be thought shocking.

Contrast with both of these two other areas in which questions of compensation for death *are* systematically answered. One socially established measure for the loss incurred by families as a result of accidental deaths for which someone can be held liable is that established by juries. When the victim is a married woman, the sum awarded in recent years may be over a million dollars.[3] But the socially established measure for the loss incurred by the families of police officers killed in the line of duty is very different. What is awarded is a very modest pension and some act of ceremonial recognition. And the same is true of the deaths of soldiers in action. So in each of these social contexts the value assigned to a life and the measure of that value are determined by norms specific to each particular context. There is indeed evidence from time to time of pressure to make measures and judgments more consistent within each particular context, but there seems to be little or no evidence of pressure towards consistency *between* contexts. And so, in each particular context in which different possible courses of action which have potentially fatal consequences for some person or set of persons are evaluated, practical reasoning and decision-making will be guided by different norms.[4] Note that in 1981 an Executive Order by President Reagan resulted in the assignment by various government agencies during the next ten years of a monetary value to a human life. The differences between them are notable, with the values varying from, for example, $8.3 million by the EPA to $650,083 by the FAA.

These and similar facts support a crucial generalization: that the dominant culture of post-Enlightenment modernity lacks any overall agreement, let alone any rationally founded or even rationally debatable agreement, on what it is that would make it rational for an individual to sacrifice her or his life for some other or others or what it is that would make it rational to allow an individual's life to be sacrificed for the sake of some other individual or some group or institution. But this does not mean that within that culture there is no way of arriving at practically effective agreements on the basis of shared norms and values. It is rather that what shared norms and values there are vary from one compartmentalized context to another, within each of which the relationships between rights, duties, utility and presupposed contract are understood in a way that is the outcome of the power relationships which dominate that particular context. Hence practically effective agreements embody conclusions that also vary from one context to another. And, given that there are no generally agreed rational standards available for deciding how competing claims concerning rights, duties, utility and contract are to be adjudicated, it could scarcely be otherwise. (Hence failure to reach agreement in academic moral and political enquiry is not without practical significance. It renders the academic community generally politically impotent except in its provision of services to the private and public corporations.) In this type of social situation reason has no effective way of confronting the contingencies of power and money.

Notice then that it is not just in its inability to provide rationally justifiable and agreed moral values and principles that the Enlightenment and its heirs have failed. The failure of those modern institutions that have been the embodiment of the best social and political hopes of the Enlightenment is quite as striking. And those institutions fail by Enlightenment standards. For they do not provide – in fact they render impossible – the kinds of institutionalized reading, talking and arguing public necessary for effective practical rational thought about just those principles and decisions involved in answering such questions as: 'How is a human life to be valued?' or 'What does accountability in our social relationships require of us?' or 'Whom, if anyone, may I legitimately deceive?' – questions to which we need shared answers. And there is no type of institutional arena in our society in which plain persons – not academic philosophers or academic political theorists – are able to engage together in systematic reasoned debate designed to arrive at a rationally well-founded common mind on these matters, a common mind which might then be given political expression. Indeed the dominant forms of organization of contemporary social life militate against the coming into existence of this type of institutional arena. And so do the dominant modes of what passes for political discourse. We do not have the kinds of reading public necessary to sustain practically effective social thought.

What we have instead in contemporary society are a set of small-scale academic publics within each of which rational discourse *is* carried on, but whose discourse is of such a kind as to have no practical effect on the conduct of social life; and, by contrast, forms of organization in the larger areas of our public life in which effective decisions are taken and policies implemented, but within which for the most part systematic rational discourse cannot be systematically carried on, and within which therefore decisions and policies are by and large outcomes of the distributions of power and money and not of the quality of argument. Within these contexts of academic and public life the same central moral and political concepts of the Enlightenment are at home, but the divorce between them is such that the original projects of the Enlightenment have been frustrated.

Notes

* Immanuel Kant, 'An Answer to the Question: What is Enlightenment?' in *Perpetual Peace and Other Essays on Politics, History, and Morals*, trans. Ted Humphrey, Hackett, 1983. pp. 41–48.

1 Jacques Derrida, *Dissemination*, trans. Barbara Johnson, London: The Athlone Press, 1981.
2 For a discussion of this type of public see J. Habermas, *The Structural Transformation of the Public Sphere*, Cambridge, Mass.: The MIT Press, 1989.
3 'Compiling Data, and Giving Odds, on Jury Awards', *New York Times*, 21 January 1994.
4 See also E.J. Mishan, *Cost Benefit Analysis*, Amsterdam: North Holland, 1969, Chapters 22 and 23; and J. Broome, 'Trying to Value a Life', *Journal of Public Economics* 9(1), 1978: 91–100.

18

QUESTIONING AUTONOMY
The feminist challenge and the challenge for feminism

Maeve Cooke

Within the interpretative horizons of Western modernity, individual autonomy has generally been prized as a valuable attribute of personal identity and hence as a condition of human good. Feminism, however, has taught us to look suspiciously at many of the core values that are part of our modern Western interpretative horizons and to interrogate them from the point of view of their 'masculine bias'. In the first section of this essay, I identify two broad strands of feminist critique of the notion of individual autonomy.[1] I argue that although each of these strands makes an important contribution to debates on self-identity, neither offers compelling reasons for abandoning autonomy as an ideal. Rather, taken together they suggest the need to rethink the notion of autonomy in light of feminist objections. Since these are primarily objections to the normative conceptions of self that underlie traditional interpretations of autonomy, the first challenge for feminism is to provide an account of self-identity that avoids the shortcomings of traditional interpretations.

However, such an account, though an important first step, is not sufficient. What is required in addition is an account of autonomy that identifies the intuitions central to its historical formulations and rethinks them from the point of view of feminist concerns. In the second section I suggest that the metaphor of self-authorship expresses these central intuitions. I propose an interpretation of self-authorship in terms of capacities for responsibility, accountability, independence, purposive rationality and strong evaluation, arguing that the resulting conception is readily compatible with feminist views of the self.

Why *should* autonomy be prized and promoted? In the third section, I argue that making sense of the common perception that autonomy should be valued and encouraged calls for some general account of the fundamental motivations of human beings. I propose an ethical interpretation of human well-being that stresses the individual's capacity to develop and pursue her own conceptions of the good. Such a view of the self as motivated in a fundamental way by the attempt to define itself meaningfully raises the question of ethical validity: of the nonarbitrary basis for the self's subjectively developed assignments of meaning and value. I conclude that feminists (and others) concerned to rethink autonomy should explore its possible ethical dimension and respond to the problems arising from this.

Autonomy: the feminist challenge

Feminist resistance to the ideal of autonomy divides into two main camps.[2] The first camp contains feminists in the fields of moral and political theory, the second contains feminist supporters of poststructuralism and postmodernism. I will deal briefly with each of these in turn.

The challenge by feminist political and moral theory

In the areas of moral and political theory, feminists have long pointed out that the ideal of autonomy as traditionally conceived has been inimical to feminist concerns. In analysing the reasons for this, feminists have criticized the conceptions of subjectivity or self traditionally associated with the ideal. Several feminist critics have drawn attention to the way in which a conception of the self as disembedded underlies both the deontological tradition of moral theory and the contractarian tradition of political theory.[3] As Seyla Benhabib, referring to a formulation by Hobbes, points out, the self is regarded as a mushroom – as though it had sprung up overnight, without history and without connection to other persons.[4] Such a conception of self is unacceptable to feminists for at least two reasons. First, it fails to acknowledge the self's embeddedness as constitutive of its identity. By 'embeddedness' is meant locatedness in contexts of meaning: for instance, in political arrangements, in contexts of history, in networks of relationships with others, in frameworks of 'strong evaluation',[5] and so forth. While emphasis on the self's embeddedness is neither peculiar to feminism nor shared by all feminists, it seems to tie in with many women's experience of self as relational and contextual.[6] Second, conceptions of self as disembedded tend to go hand in hand with ideas of self-identity as self-control and self-ownership. Conceptions of self guided by the ideal of self-control stand accused of denying, or at least minimizing, the importance of bodily and affective–emotional needs and desires; the idea of the self as *disembedded* is thus closely linked with the idea of the self as *disembodied*. This latter idea is unacceptable to feminists on account of its suppression of dimensions of subjectivity that historically have been central to many women's experience both of self and of others; in addition, feminists stress its unwelcome consequences as far as the socialization of the

259

individual is concerned, and with regard to its effects on intersubjective relationships. It is argued that the suppression of bodily and affective–emotional needs and desires gives rise to pathological forms of individual subjectivity, with further undesirable implications for intersubjective relations; it may also produce models of politics that split off the bodily and affective–emotional aspects of human agency from deliberations on law, politics and matters of justice, leading to an arguably problematic privatization of ethical concerns.[7] Conceptions of self guided by the ideal of self-ownership give rise to similarly unwelcome relations between self and self and self and others, and to comparable unwelcome political consequences: they point in the direction of the minimal state, a form of political arrangement regarded by many feminists as destructive of community and the caring values they wish to promote.

To begin with, therefore, feminists have rejected the ideal of autonomy on account of the objectionable conceptions of self on which traditional interpretations of autonomy have relied. What it is important to note here, however, is that what is rejected is not the very ideal of autonomy, but certain historical *interpretations* of it. More precisely, what is rejected are interpretations based on conceptions of self arising from the traditions associated with so-called Enlightenment or modernist thinking. Values closely connected with the ideal of autonomy, such as capacities for critical reflection and for integration of personal experience into a coherent narrative, are not themselves undermined: as a rule, neither the need for critically reflective distance with regard to the contexts of meaning in which selves are embedded, nor the desirability of constructing and accepting responsibility for a coherent life-history oriented towards the right or good is disputed. If it were possible to work out a conception of autonomy that takes account of the self's embeddedness and embodiedness, then this first kind of feminist resistance to the ideal of autonomous agency would probably dissipate.

The challenge by postmodernist–poststructuralist feminism

But feminist challenges to the ideal of autonomy have come also from another direction. Feminists inspired by postmodernism and poststructuralism frequently reject the ideal of autonomy on the grounds that it presupposes a notion of identity that, *qua ideal*, is repressive and exclusionary.[8] The objection here is not (in the first instance) to the particular *interpretations* of self-identity that traditionally have been associated with the ideal of autonomy; rather, what is rejected is the very notion of (self-)identity, for (self-)identity itself is held to imply repressive and exclusionary ideals. According to this viewpoint, to postulate identity of meaning is to effect a closure: a splitting off and exclusion of certain aspects of experience that are perceived as not part of the postulated identity. Thus, for example,

Judith Butler queries the desirability of the category 'women' on the ground that it presumes a set of values or dispositions, thereby becoming normative in character and exclusionary in principle. In addition, Butler appears to find unattractive the ideal of a unified or integrated self implicit in the construction of categories such as 'women'. She argues for a notion of the gendered body as radically performative, a body that constantly invents and reinvents its identity and the unity of its life within multiple contexts of meaning. Butler's bodies are fluid and fragmented rather than fixed and coherent, and are constituted through multiple acts that are expressive of public and social discourse.[9] In a similar vein, Jane Flax objects to the term 'the self': on the one hand, because it effects a closure, necessarily attaching importance to certain attributes of subjectivity and dismissing other ones; on the other hand, because of its implicit assumption that successful subjectivity is unitary, fixed, homogeneous and teleological.[10] Thus, for writers such as Butler and Flax, the notion of autonomy is problematic from two points of view: first, because it postulates an *ideal* of self, thereby effecting a closure; second, because it affirms the value of attributes such as coherence, resolution and unity at the expense of values such as fragmentation, fluidity and multiplicity.

Difficulties with the postmodernist–poststructuralist feminist challenge

There are difficulties with this kind of feminist challenge to the ideal of autonomy. One set of difficulties concerns the possibility of feminist politics. Feminist political action or, more generally, feminist struggles to overcome oppression and disadvantage seem to presuppose some sort of notion of reflective, coherent, responsible and value-directed agency. Both Butler and Flax acknowledge this problem, while disputing that their respective conceptions of subjectivity preclude emancipatory political action. Butler's solution seems to be acceptance of the need for temporary strategic engagement in identity politics. On occasion – but not consistently – she recognizes the *political* necessity of speaking and acting as and for 'women'; even here, however, she insists on the need simultaneously to deconstruct the subject of feminism.[11] Flax attempts to reconcile her postmodern commitments with a commitment to justice and liberatory political activity through appeal to notions such as 'taking responsibility in a meaningful way';[12] she speaks also of 'better or worse ways of being a person'.[13] However, she neither accounts for nor elaborates on these formulations, and they sit uneasily with her conception of fluid and heterogeneous subjectivities. A fundamental problem with the respective approaches of Butler and Flax is that they treat subjectivity purely as a linguistic effect and, in reducing self-identity to the systems of meaning in and through which it is constituted, they leave no room for intentionality. As we shall see, this criticism resurfaces persistently in feminist discussions of poststructuralism and postmodernism; it is one of the main reasons why even feminists favourably disposed to these movements find their positions with regard to emancipatory political action unconvincing.[14]

Another set of difficulties has to do with the capacities and dispositions that postmodernist and poststructuralist feminists regard as valuable. For, notwithstanding their rejection of normative categories, feminists who ally themselves with poststructuralism and postmodernism do not seem to be able to avoid the affirmation of alternative norms. They do not succeed in avoiding normative projections, but merely replace traditional or established normative conceptions of identity with alternative ones. This gives rise to the problem of *why* feminists should prefer the normative models of self-identity advocated by writers such as Butler and Flax to other available models. Connected with this is the question of the status of their critique: as Linda Alcoff points out, poststructuralist critiques of subjectivity must pertain to the construction of *all* subjects, or they pertain to none. In her words: 'Why is a right-wing woman's consciousness constructed via social discourse but a feminist's consciousness not?'[15]

Quite apart from problems of justification, however, it is not clear that feminists do prefer the normative models of self-identity proposed by postmodernist and poststructuralist feminists. Patricia Huntington, for instance, argues that poststructuralist feminists provide too minimalist an account of situated agency, to the extent that they fail to allow equally for women's deliberate involvement in patriarchy and their ability to resist patriarchy. This is because they conflate language and identity, reducing subjectivity to a linguistic effect of the complex knot of signifying practices that comprise its world. They thus deny the possibility of intentional control over personal and social change. Huntington concludes that in leaving women in the position of too great a passivity with regard to the construction of their desires and motives, poststructuralist feminism falls prey to the threat of a stoical acquiescence in the face of oppressive signifying practices. Against this, Huntington argues that feminists need to construct a normative conception of autonomy that takes account of the activities whereby individuals cultivate critical consciousness and assume responsibility for their transformations of self and constructions of identity.[16]

Even feminists sympathetic to postmodernism and poststructuralism admit disquiet with regard to the emphasis on fragmentation and rejection of values such as coherence, reflexivity and directedness.[17] Thus, Susan Bordo associates herself with deconstructionist postmodernism with regard to its critique of disembodied knowledge while voicing reservations concerning its proposed alternative ideals of knowledge and subjectivity.[18] Bordo argues that feminists who insist on the need for vigilant suspicion of all determinate readings of culture, committing themselves to an aesthetic of ceaseless textual play, succumb to a dangerous (counter-)fantasy, the fantasy of escape from human locatedness; a fantasy, moreover, that echoes in disturbing ways the rejected traditional ideals of self as detached and disembodied. She strongly criticizes the 'new, postmodern . . . dream of being *everywhere*';[19] of 'limitless multiple embodiments, allowing one to dance from place to place and from self to self'.[20] Or, again, Patricia Waugh maintains that feminists can learn from postmodernism, but worries about the rejection of 'modernist' ideals of agency. She holds that postmodern celebration of radical fragmentation is a collective psychological response to the recognition that Enlightenment ideals of subjectivity as autonomous self-determination are unattainable. Waugh's thesis here seems to be that the Enlightenment ideal of autonomous agency is unattainable to the extent that it presupposes a self defined without reference to history, God, political arrangements or traditional values. We have already encountered feminist critique of this kind of picture of the self. Waugh argues that in rejecting such a conception of dislocated selfhood, postmodernism all too often succumbs to nihilistic nostalgia: the impossible yearning for the lost (imaginary) object of desire issues in the frustrated smashing of the ideal object.[21] She also points out that for feminists the goals of agency, personal autonomy, self-expression and self-determination can neither be taken for granted nor written off as exhausted.[22]

Allison Weir is another feminist who sets out to straddle both sides of the postmodernist–modernist divide. She argues that feminists need a normative account of self-identity that makes space for postmodernist and poststructuralist insights, in particular concerning the multiplicity and fragmentation of identity and its constitution through exclusionary systems of meaning. But, in the face of postmodernist and poststructuralist antipathy towards certain other dimensions of subjectivity, she reminds us that the capacity and responsibility to define one's meanings are both the privilege and the burden of modern subjects. However, she points out that the increasing need for self-definition is accompanied by an increasing production and differentiation of identity attributes – that is, of possible roles, attachments and affiliations, values, beliefs and so forth – with the result that our identities are increasingly multiple and conflicting. In the same vein, she stresses that struggles to resolve differences and conflicts through an openness to difference are prerequisite for change and the generation of new meanings. Weir's commitment to certain 'Enlightenment' values thus goes hand in hand with an acknowledgement of the truth in postmodernist and poststructuralist accounts of subjectivity.[23] In short, many feminists wish to take on board some of the insights of postmodernism and poststructuralism without wholeheartedly supporting their emphasis on fragmentation, multiplicity and fluidity, and without wanting to reject outright 'modernist' or 'Enlightenment' ideals of agency.[24]

The challenge for feminism

Rethinking the self

The discussion so far suggests that much feminist opposition to the ideal of autonomy can be construed as opposition to traditional interpretations of this ideal. While this may not be true of some feminists who ally themselves with poststructuralism and postmodernism, there is a widespread feeling even among feminists sympathetic to these movements that we should be selective as far as their claims and criticisms are concerned. There is a belief – which I share – that feminists can learn from poststructuralism and postmodernism without throwing overboard all normative ideas connected with the ideal of autonomy. The task facing feminists in this regard is to identify the valuable core of the ideal of autonomy, to use it as a basis for developing a conception of self-identity while avoiding the pitfalls of its traditional interpretations, and to spell out what commitment to this ideal implies.

Any attempt to develop an ideal of autonomy that is acceptable to feminists must take on board the main charges the various strands of feminist critique have levied against its traditional interpretations. As we have seen, these are directed primarily against the notions of self underlying these interpretations. The criticisms I have discussed so far remind us that the self develops its identity as a being located in a plurality of (frequently shifting and conflicting) systems of meaning. We are also reminded that the self is an embodied being, with bodily needs, desires and an affective-emotional constitution that is intimately bound up with its capacities for rational reflection and action. Poststructuralist and postmodernist feminists make the further points that subjectivity is multiple and overdetermined. It is multiple not just in the sense that it develops within multiple contexts, but also in the sense that it is not unitary but heterogeneous. We can take this, to begin with, as a reminder about the interrelation of reason and desire; however, it serves also as a warning about the possible non-transparency of the self. For, as psychoanalytic approaches, from Freud onwards, have taught us, there is good reason to suppose that some dimensions of subjectivity will always resist the individual's attempts to retrieve them rationally. However, the aim of transparency is held to be problematic not only because it is probably unattainable; for it is often seen as repressive in its denial of the importance of the prelinguistic and non-linguistic dimensions of subjectivity.[25] The idea that subjectivity is fully rationally retrievable is thus a potentially repressive fiction, and as such presents a possible danger that feminist attempts to work out a conception of autonomy should bear in mind.

The poststructuralist and postmodernist thesis that subjectivity is overdetermined overlaps with the theses that the self is embedded and embodied, although there are two significant differences in emphasis. First, whereas 'embeddedness' suggests rootedness or fixedness, poststructuralists and postmodernists emphasize the processual, fluid and fragmented character of subjectivity. I have already drawn attention to some feminist unease as regards this emphasis; nonetheless, to the extent that the focus on fragmentation, fluidity and processuality *supplements* rather than undermines the thesis of embeddedness, I see it as providing a fruitful vantage point for discussion of subjectivity. However, the thesis of overdetermination has yet another dimension. As we have seen, poststructuralists and postmodernists tend to regard subjectivity as a linguistic effect: as completely produced by the systems of meaning in which it is formed and over which it has no control. They leave no room for a gap between language and identity, reducing subjectivity to the (multiple) discursive cultural practices in which it is constituted. They thus stand accused of denying the possibility of choice and decision; they cannot account for women's active acceptance of, or resistance towards, prevailing systems of meaning. For this reason, while it is important to acknowledge that subjectivity is constituted in and through various systems of meaning, reduction of subjectivity to these systems of meaning is not useful for feminist theories of self-identity and agency.

An initial specification of a reworked conception of autonomy would thus have to take account of the self's locatedness in multiple, possibly conflicting and shifting, contexts, the bodily and affective–emotional dimensions of subjectivity, the self's capacities for fluidity and fragmentation as well as for critical reflection, coherence, responsibility, and value-directed judgement and action, the possible fundamental non-transparency of subjectivity, and the self's constitution in and through systems of meaning over which it does not have full control. To begin with, therefore, the attempt to work out a conception of autonomy congenial to feminists requires an account of self-identity that avoids the shortcomings of traditional interpretations. I have argued elsewhere that Jürgen Habermas's theory of communicative action provides a potentially useful framework within which the required model of self-identity could be developed.[26] His theory has the advantage that it offers a relational account of the identity of the self without reducing this identity to the intersubjective relationships and contexts of meaning in which the self is located at any given time; furthermore, his theory places value on the self's capacity to distance itself reflectively from its everyday desires, volitions and behaviour while acknowledging the self's non-rational motivations. However, although indispensable, such an account of the self is no more than a starting-point. What is needed, in addition, is an account of autonomy. More precisely, what is required is a conception of autonomy that accommodates core intuitions about autonomous agency, modifying and interpreting them from the point of view of feminist concerns. As we shall see, such a conception of autonomy draws on a normative picture of self-identity that goes beyond the picture elaborated so far.

Rethinking autonomy

Notwithstanding the plurality of ways in which autonomy historically has been interpreted, it seems possible to identify some important intuitions as part of its core. These intuitions are summed up by the idea of self-direction as expressed by the metaphor of self-authorship. The autonomous self is held to be in some sense self-directing: it must be able in some sense to see itself as author of its own life-history and of its constructions of personal identity. The metaphor of self-authorship should not be taken too literally. Although it implies that the self must be able to see itself as making its own life, it should not be interpreted as the view that the autonomous self is the sole origin of its own will, desire and behaviour and has complete control over these. For the view that the self is its own ultimate origin is arguably incoherent. It appears to require that the self's will, desire and behaviour be governable only by itself, whereby the governing self must be some sort of deeper self, that is in turn governed only by its deeper self, and so on *ad infinitum*.[27] The metaphor of self-authorship is therefore suspect when it is taken to imply *self-origination*.[28]

Equally problematic is the view that the self should have *complete* control over its will, desires and behaviour, for it ignores the determining influences of heredity and environment and the various ways in which individual will, desire and behaviour are determined by forces originating outside of the self. Furthermore, it appears to uphold the ideal of the fully transparent self, which, as we have seen, has been called into question by post-Freudian psychoanalytic theory. The metaphor of self-authorship should thus not be construed in a way that denies the determining influences of heredity, environment, contingency, and the prelinguistic and non-linguistic dimensions of human agency. But what *does* it imply? I want to suggest that the metaphor of self-authorship conjures up a picture of the self as *responsible* and *accountable* for its actions, judgements and self-interpretations, as *independent* (that is, objective in its critical assessments of others, the world, society, its own past and present self, and so on), as *purposive–rational* (that is, capable of setting and pursuing goals), and as a *strong evaluator* (that is, capable of selecting goals from diverse options on the basis of strongly evaluative criteria).

Responsibility and *accountability* imply neither that the self is origin of its will, desire and behaviour, nor that it is completely in control of them: these capacities require only that the self can come to see itself as responsible for its judgements, actions and self-interpretations in the sense of being able, if need be, to explain and justify them to others; in giving an account of itself to others, the self acts *as though* its self-definitions and life-history were the product of its conscious deliberation;[29] in postulating the self's ability to reflect critically, construct coherent meanings through reference to normative ideals, and assume responsibility for its assignments of meaning and value, we do not deny that the self is determined by external influences or imply that all dimensions of subjectivity are rationally retrievable. At the same time, the requirements of responsibility and accountability mean that the self must take issue with the external (and internal) forces that influence its life, and query their inevitability and justifiability. Some influencing factors are purely contingent or, possibly, so deeply rooted in culture and biology that the self has no option but to accept them as given; others can be criticized on normative grounds (as exploitative, reifying, alienating, unjust, pathological and so forth), and resisted in various ways and with more or less success. It could be argued that self-authorship is *avoidably* impaired by economic and social disadvantage as well as by social forces of manipulation and control; by contrast, the negative influence of sudden, unexpected, natural occurrences (such as an earthquake or death of a parent) cannot be criticized directly on normative grounds but as a rule must simply be accepted as the starting-point for further action and reflection.

Similarly, the *independence* required by self-authorship does not imply that the self can achieve complete freedom from the influences of environment, heredity, biology and so on. For this reason, the requirement of independence is not bound up with the atomistic and dislocated views of the self rightly criticized by feminist theory since self-authorship does not deny that the self is determined by the historical contexts of meaning and the relationships with others within which it is situated. The metaphor of self-authorship suggests not radical isolation but the need for independence in the sense of objectivity. By objectivity is meant a critically detached, informed and flexible way of engaging with one's surroundings, with other persons and with one's own self-interpretations and life-history.[30] Independence in the sense of objectivity forbids over-reliance on the opinions and judgements of others in one's views of the world, relationships to others, self-definitions and narrative constructions of identity; it also calls for the attempt to free oneself from the pernicious influence of one's own earlier lives.[31]

The *purposive rationality* required by self-authorship is the ability to deliberate about, and sustain, short-term and long-term plans; it should not be misconstrued as single-mindedness or rigidity: the self may justifiably regard itself as author of its life even if it pursues multiple and heterogeneous goals and frequently changes its tastes and opinions. The requirement of purposive rationality can therefore accommodate post-structuralist and postmodernist insistence on the fluidity and heterogeneity of subjectivity; it does, however, imply some degree of internal cohesiveness (a disintegrated self cannot be autonomous), and the ability to set goals and pursue them.

The capacity for *evaluation* demanded by self-authorship is the ability to select from among a range of options those goals that the self judges to be desirable from the point of view of its constructions of self-identity. It thus requires the capacity for reflective self-evaluation that is manifested in the formation of second-order desires and volitions. Drawing on an influential essay by Harry Frankurt,[32] Charles Taylor emphasizes this capacity as one essential to persons, and he uses it as a core element in his view of the modern self. In Taylor's account, the modern self is a strong evaluator, a person who can raise the question: Do I really want to be what I now am? It is someone who is capable of evaluating what it now is and of shaping itself on the basis of this evaluation; in doing so it makes use of the language of evaluative distinctions (in which, for instance, motivations are described as 'lower' or 'base', 'courageous' or 'cowardly', 'clairvoyant' or 'blind', and so on) that is richer and deeper than the language required by a simple weighing of alternatives.[33] It appears from this that strong evaluation demands certain creative powers, dispositions (such as flexibility and open-mindedness) and faculties (such as memory and imagination). We should note that it also has a social–material dimension: if the self is autonomously to select goals on the basis of its strong evaluations, it must have at its disposal certain material goods (such as food, clothing and accommodation) and will receive the upbringing and education that enable the requisite powers, dispositions and faculties to flourish; furthermore, as Joseph Raz points out, we can meaningfully speak of autonomous choice only if sufficiently diverse options are available:[34] if the self can choose only from among trivial options, or if all the choices are potentially horrendous or evil, then strong evaluation is not possible.

Whereas it is possible to object to my interpretation of the metaphor of self-authorship on a number of grounds, the assertion that it is connected with strong evaluation may seem most contentious. Before turning to a fuller discussion of this, however, I would like to make two further points. First of all, the metaphor of self-authorship is applicable in the first instance to an individual life-history rather than to single decisions or episodes within such a life-history; furthermore, it is a matter of degree.[35] Second, the metaphor of self-authorship is central not just to the concept of personal autonomy but to that of public or political autonomy: citizens are held to be politically autonomous to the extent that they see themselves as authors of their own laws. Recently, political theorists such as John Rawls and Habermas have emphasized the internal connection between personal autonomy and political autonomy.[36] As I understand it, the thesis here is that the development of personal autonomy is impeded by lack of public autonomy, and that political autonomy is justified through reference to the value of personal autonomy.[37] For present purposes, the first part of the thesis is most relevant, for it reminds us that the attempt to rework the concept of personal autonomy in light of feminist concerns should not forget how women's possibilities for self-authorship have suffered as a result of their exclusion from public life and of their lack of political power.

As explicated in the foregoing, the metaphor of self-authorship seems readily compatible with the view of the self that emerged from my discussion of feminist theory. It highlights capacities for responsibility, accountability, independence, purposive rationality and strong evaluation without denying the self's locatedness and embodiedness, her affective–emotional constitution, and the fluidity and heterogeneity of subjectivity. However, although it may not pose problems for feminist conceptions of subjectivity or self-identity, my sketch of key ingredients of the concept of autonomy raises questions that pose a challenge for feminist theory (and, indeed, for all attempts to rethink autonomy). These have to do with the connection I proposed between self-authorship and strong evaluation and can be summarized as follows: Is the ethical interpretation of autonomy the most plausible one? If so, what is the nonarbitrary basis for judgements of ethical validity?

The ethical view of autonomy

Autonomy and strong evaluation

The postulated connection between autonomy and strong evaluation has historical roots in an older association of autonomy with virtue and moral validity. Rousseau and Kant, who made major contributions to the modern understanding of autonomy, did not conceive of it simply as self-direction: they connected autonomous self-government with an objectively conceived *moral law*. Rousseau's *Emile* is truly free only when he is virtuous;[38] for Kant, the principle of autonomy declares that 'man is subject only to those laws which are made by himself and yet are universal', moral laws being for Kant universal ones.[39] Although some contemporary writers such as Habermas and Rawls have affirmed the connection between autonomy and moral validity,[40] others link autonomy to validity in a more general, not strictly moral, sense. A common contemporary formulation of individual autonomy is that offered by Charles Taylor, who characterizes it as each person's ability 'to determine for himself or herself a view of the good life'.[41] On this view, autonomy is defined in terms of strong evaluation: evaluative reflection on the kind of person I want to be. It stresses the individual's capacity to work out and pursue her own conceptions of the good. Furthermore, it leaves open the question of whether autonomy requires an orientation towards moral goals, postulating merely an orientation towards ego ideals.[42] I shall refer to this as the ethical view of autonomy. We might say: the ethical view of autonomy is agnostic with regard to the *content* of the strong evaluations and conceptions of the good life that guide the self in its self-definitions and life-history.[43] As we shall see, however, although this view distinguishes between autonomous agency and moral agency, it too presupposes nonarbitrary standards of validity. The fact that the self must work out for itself what is right for it in light of its personal circumstances, desires and volitions does not mean that such strong evaluations are purely subjective. For this reason, this view of autonomy's agnosticism regarding the content of the self's ego ideals should not be confused with other kinds of suspension of evaluative judgement. It should be distinguished, in particular, from the agnosticism of the modern liberal–democratic state concerning the worth of the conceptions of the good life that shape the identities and lives of its individual citizens, and from the self's temporary suspension of judgement in the course of reflective deliberation on the validity of claims.

According to the *liberal–democratic view* of the role of the modern state, the state must abstain from judging or showing preference to the conceptions of the good that motivate some but not all individuals (and social groups) and must, in this sense, practise a kind of ethical agnosticism.[44] But the state's agnosticism in this regard does not mean that individuals, in their day-to-day lives, simply leave open the question of the validity of the ideas of the good that guide them in their self-definitions and projects. To assert this would be to misunderstand what is meant by a conception of the good. Conceptions of the good are developed and held by individuals (and groups) in specific historical situations; moreover, they must be justified through reference to the wills and desires of those individuals (and groups). Nonetheless, despite their context-specificity, they are not reducible to the subjective wills and desires of the individuals (and groups) concerned; rather, they are connected with claims to validity that extend beyond the concrete contexts in which they are developed and have an application.

Ideas of the good are normative demands that both emanate from beyond the self and reach beyond the self: in regarding a given idea as good, the self engages (more or less critically) with already existing horizons of significance;[45] at the same time, it (implicitly or explicitly) raises a claim to validity which supposes that everyone with the requisite information and insight would have to agree with its judgement.[46] A judgement of value that did not have this context-transcending universalist thrust would not be a validity claim. Since the conceptions of the good with which autonomy is linked are held to be validity claims, they have an inherent context-transcending dimension. Although context-specific and subject-related, they are both nonconventional and nonsubjective claims to validity.

Neither autonomy's agnosticism with regard to the content of the self's ego ideals, nor the state's agnosticism with regard to the validity of its citizen's ego ideals, should be confused with the self's *temporary suspension of judgement* in its reflective deliberations on matters of validity. In its reflective deliberations – Habermas speaks of discourses – the self adopts a different attitude towards its conceptions of the good from in its day-to-day behaviour.[47] In its reflective deliberations, the self suspends judgement on the validity of the goals and ideals that motivate it; it relativizes its evaluative judgements in light of the actual or possible objections of others; it acknowledges their essential fallibility and opens itself to the critical opinions of others. This kind of suspension of judgement is always temporary, however. A self who never moved from the level of reflective deliberation would be incapable of even the simplest decision-making and action. The need to act and to make decisions means that, at any given time, the self must take the validity of most of its judgements for granted. Thus, the – more or less conclusive – results of its critical deliberations are fed back into the reservoir of convictions that inform its actions and decisions in everyday life. For this reason, although the self may acknowledge theoretically that its evaluative judgements are essentially fallible and open to the critical objections of others, in its role as participant in everyday action it cannot remain agnostic as to the validity of its subjectively held conceptions of the good but must rather act and make decisions as though they were valid.

From the foregoing it is clear that the postulated connection between autonomy and strong evaluation implies the possibility in principle of finding a rational basis for distinguishing between valid and invalid evaluative judgements. From the perspective of strong evaluators, some modes of defining their identity and living their lives are better than others; furthermore, they see the validity of their evaluative judgements as reducible neither to convention nor to subjective wills and desires but as having a context-transcending universalist dimension.

At least since Nietzsche, however, the attempt to find a rational basis for evaluative judgements has been denounced as illusory and repressive.[48] For Nietzsche and his followers, the claim that evaluative judgements are more than mere psychological or conventional distinctions is erroneous and dangerous. At the very least, therefore, we must acknowledge the difficulties involved in specifying rational criteria for evaluative judgements – particularly under 'postmetaphysical conditions'.[49] This is one reason why some writers have rejected attempts to define autonomy in terms of strong evaluation, that is, to interpret it as an ethical category.[50]

Problems with the ethical view of autonomy

The difficulties involved in specifying rational criteria for evaluative judgements are not the only reason for rejecting the ethical view of autonomy.[51] At least two other objections have initial plausibility. The first objection leaves open the question of whether strong evaluation is constitutive of (modern) human identity while disputing that normative questions of self-identity are relevant to discussion of autonomy. The second objection acknowledges a link between autonomy and a normative picture of human identity, but disputes that strong evaluation is part of this picture.

The first objection rejects attempts to define autonomy through reference to the fundamental motivations of human beings or to normative pictures of self-identity. Bernard Berofsky, for example, insists on the need to separate questions of autonomy from questions concerning self-identity. Berofsky argues forcefully against what he calls the evaluative view of autonomy – the view that the autonomous agent must evaluate the worth of the goals and desires that motivate him.[52] Moreover, he maintains that it is possible to sever the link between autonomy and strong evaluation without committing himself to any view of the self, urging us to separate the conditions of autonomy from the conditions of selfhood.[53]

Although such a position may have certain advantages,[54] it has a serious *dis*advantage that is often not recognized by its proponents. If the question of autonomy is separated from normative questions about human self-identity it becomes difficult to explain why autonomy is regarded as something to be aimed for – as something we encourage in our children and try to develop and promote. Of course, this common perception, which informs the evaluative horizons of Western modernity, may simply be misconceived. For we can distinguish at least three possible perspectives on the question of the value of autonomy: the view that it is inherently evil or undesirable; the view that it is inherently good or desirable; and the view that it has no inherent worth but merely an instrumental value deriving from its connection with other goods held to be valuable. Those who set out to develop a conception of autonomy that leaves aside questions of self-identity are unlikely to hold the first view. The third view requires them to explain autonomy's instrumental value while avoiding reference to any normative picture of human well-being. I cannot see how this is feasible. We can therefore expect those who wish to separate questions of autonomy from questions of self-identity to favour the second view: the position that autonomy is inherently attractive or worthwhile.[55] Against this, I want to argue that autonomy is not inherently desirable or valuable: it merely becomes so in connection with other goods, more precisely, with some kind of picture of the good for human beings. In other words, I regard the third of these perspectives as the most plausible.

It is difficult to see how autonomy could be held to have any inherent worth. The capacities associated with autonomy – for example, independence, and purposive rationality – are not in themselves self-evidently desirable or valuable. We can see this in situations where they are used for purposes that are generally regarded as morally bad. A cold-blooded murderer is not normally admired for the critical detachment and purposive rationality that enable her to carry out her crimes successfully; indeed we tend to see this as making the deed more rather than less morally reprehensible, and shudder at the perversion of human capacities involved. In general, we deplore the capacities associated with autonomy when these are exercised for morally unacceptable purposes. This suggests that the capacities closely associated with autonomy, such as critical detachment and purposive rationality, cannot be assessed independently of the various goals and values an individual pursues over the course of her life-history. The attempt to answer the question of why the capacities associated with autonomy – and thus autonomy itself – are valuable or desirable points in the direction of an account of why some goals are more valuable or desirable than others. An account of this kind amounts to a general account of human motivation, which in turn presupposes a general account of the good for human beings. Such an account might attribute to human beings a fundamental interest in justice, or in obeying the moral law, or in happiness, or in self-preservation, or in beauty, or in working out for themselves a conception of the good life. In every case, however, it amounts to a normative picture of the self as fundamentally motivated by some or other conception of the good life for human beings. It is this normative picture of the self that makes sense of the perception that autonomy should be prized and promoted. It follows from the foregoing that autonomy (and its associated capacities) is not inherently valuable or desirable but is esteemed only to the extent that it enables the self to achieve some good that in turn is seen as fundamentally important for its well-being. This view of autonomy is supported by writers such as Raz who insist that autonomy is valuable only if it is exercised in pursuit of the good,[56] indeed, ultimately, only to the extent that it contributes to personal well-being.[57] I consider this the most convincing perspective on the value of autonomy, and place the onus on those who urge the separation of questions of autonomy from normative questions of self-identity to provide a better one.

The second objection allows a connection between questions of autonomy and normative questions of self-identity but rejects attempts to interpret the latter in terms of strong evaluation. It challenges the view that reflective self-evaluation is an essential part of what is meant by self-identity, even under the historical conditions of Western modernity, thus denying that the modern self is motivated in a fundamental way by questions as to the kind of person it would like to be. It rejects, for example, the picture of modern self-identity constructed by Taylor, according to which the self is motivated in a fundamental way by the attempt to define itself meaningfully, to seek significance in life.[58] As we have seen, Taylor locates the modern self within a horizon of important questions – questions about history, nature, society and God – with which it has to engage critically in working out its own conception of the good[59] and, accordingly, Taylor regards strong evaluation as a fundamental part of modern self-identity. Against Taylor, it could be argued, for example, that the modern self is motivated essentially by a purely subjectively defined self-interest, or by a concern with the moral law, or with convention. Although I cannot do more than mention these objections in the present context, some clarification of Taylor's position may be helpful. We may note, for example, that the picture of modern self-identity articulated by Taylor does not exclude self-interest as an important human motivation, although it does imply that it is not the overriding concern. Nor does it deny the power of moral motivation, although in separating strong evaluation and moral deliberation (in the strict sense of 'moral'[60]) it remains agnostic as to the nature of the normative demands with which the modern self engages. Equally, it does not deny the power of convention, although it associates the modern self with a conception of rationality that requires independent critical reflection on the validity of the norms it encounters.

A full discussion of the strengths and weaknesses of Taylor's picture of the modern self is beyond the scope of this essay. My main point in the present context is that feminist (and other) attempts to rethink autonomy must critically assess such normative pictures of self-identity. I have argued for a connection between autonomy and some general account of human well-being on the grounds that it is difficult otherwise to account for the common perception that autonomy should be prized and promoted. If this argument is accepted, we can see that rethinking autonomy requires more than an account of self-identity that takes account of the feminist critique as outlined above; in addition, it calls for a general account of human well-being. Given feminist suspicion of grand schemas and metaphysical projections of truth, justice, ethical validity and so on, the *formal* nature of Taylor's account of the good for human beings makes it a potentially attractive proposal. At the very least, therefore, the postulated link between autonomy and strong evaluation seems a good starting-point for further critical discussion.

Concluding remarks

In connecting autonomy with strong evaluation we make sense of the modern Western intuition that autonomy is something to be prized and promoted. We account for the value of autonomy by connecting it with a conception of the good life for human beings – more precisely, with the idea that human well-being requires the self to define itself meaningfully through reference to normative conceptions of the good. However, although the link with strong evaluation helps to clarify the status of autonomy, it also gives rise to problems. One of the serious problems it raises is that of finding nonconventional and nonsubjectivist criteria for assessing the strongly evaluative judgements and distinctions that autonomous self-authorship demands.

I see two sets of issues here, each of which poses a challenge for feminist (and other) attempts to rethink the notion of autonomy. The first has to do with the possibility of obtaining any nonarbitrary notions of validity – such as truth, the moral law, or the good – that are reducible neither to the standards of validity prevailing in actual local contexts nor to individual subjective wills and desires. The second has to do with the theoretical and political implications of the postulated connection between autonomy and ethical validity.

The first set of issues raises at least two difficult but important questions. First of all, on a general level, it raises the question of whether a context-transcending notion of validity is conceivable at all without recourse to metaphysical projections. Many contemporary thinkers distance themselves from the ahistorical, foundationalist, absolute and emphatic conceptions of reason, truth and moral validity that have been handed down to us by the philosophical tradition.[61] Habermas refers to this as a 'postmetaphysical impulse' and sees it as one of the most important currents in twentieth-century thinking.[62] Since, as already indicated, many feminists share his suspicion of the grand pretensions and abstract theorizing of Western philosophy, we may expect them to be sympathetic to postmetaphysical thinking. But is it possible to reject traditional, timeless, foundational and substantive conceptions of truth, justice and reason without rejecting the very notion of context-transcending validity? Habermas himself attempts to develop a notion of communicative rationality that is postmetaphysical yet nondefeatist in that it does not reduce reason to the standards of validity that prevail in any given historical context or, indeed, to subjective wills and desires.[63] However, Habermas's specific proposals for 'postmetaphysical' conceptions of truth and justice have been subjected to several kinds of criticism, not least by feminist writers. Feminist critics have focused above all on problems connected with his conception of moral validity (justice), querying what is perceived as its abstractly universal impulse; they have argued that Habermas's theory of moral validity – notwithstanding his relational model of self-identity – disregards the located-ness and embodiedness of concrete selves concerned with matters of justice.[64]

Thus, to begin with, feminists must engage with the problem of finding postmetaphysical conceptions of reason, truth and justice that provide a basis for rational critique of irrationality, error and injustice without running up against their own critique of traditional or 'masculine' accounts of self-identity. Alternatively, or in addition, they must reopen the question of metaphysics. It could be argued that what we need is an account of validity that takes on board the contemporary critique of metaphysical *foundations* while acknowledging the metaphysical dimensions of truth and justice: for instance, truth's imperative character – its power to irrupt into and explode the contexts of our lives and actions.[65]

The general problem of rational critique is connected with one that is more specific: this is the question of whether it is possible to find non-arbitrary standards for adjudicating the individually held evaluative judgements that are part of autonomous agency. For it might be possible, on a general level, to find a rational basis for social critique that would permit, for example, criticism of oppressive social structures and arrangements *and* of unjust laws and policies. However, the critical standards appealed to here would not necessarily be applicable to the validity of strong evaluations or to the validity of the conceptions of the good life that are the reference point for these.[66] Feminists must therefore address also the specific issue of a possible rational basis for individually held evaluative judgements: they must explore the question of 'ethical truth'.

The second set of issues is related to the first. We have seen that autonomous self-authorship involves raising validity claims that are nonsubjectivist and nonconventional. One implication of the postulated connection between autonomy and validity claims is that autonomy thereby acquires an intersubjective dimension. For validity claims are not only context-transcending: they demand for their validity recognition from other persons. Here it is important to distinguish two kinds of intersubjective recognition. First, the self who raises a claim for the validity of his or her evaluative judgements presupposes that the claim, if valid, would be recognized as such by anyone with the requisite information and insight. We might say: ethical validity is connected conceptually with the idea of universal recognition. This kind of intersubjective recognition is primarily cognitive: it expresses the intuition that something, if true, would be agreed to by all under ideal epistemic conditions.[67] It may be fruitful for feminists concerned with autonomy to explore the implications of this implicit reference to intersubjective recognition.

One implication might be its ability to provide a basis for rational critique at both an individual and a social level. Arguably, the conceptual connection between autonomy and intersubjective agreement permits criticism both of certain modes of identity-formation and of the social forces that contribute to the development of such modes. If the validity of ethical judgements is linked to the idea of universal recognition, then no opinion on a given matter can be dismissed as *in principle* wrong or irrelevant. Although, in a given concrete instance, it may turn out that there are good reasons for rejecting the opinions of others with regard to a matter under discussion, the concern with truth requires us, initially at least, to take these opinions seriously. The conceptual connection between ethical validity and universal recognition thus has implications for the possibility of rational critique. The link, if it holds, implies that the individual's development as an autonomous agent is impaired when she suppresses the intersubjective dimension of her evaluative judgements by sealing them off from the critical approbation of others.[68] From this we obtain a basis for criticizing modes of identity formation in which individuals, when working out for themselves their conceptions of the good, deny the relevance in principle of other people's opinions and judgements, thereby withdrawing into an impermeable private space. Furthermore, criticism of this kind of disorder of identity (which is also a failure of autonomy) simultaneously permits criticism of the reifying and alienating social forces that frequently create the need for the individual to retreat from the critical opinions of others.[69] Thus, even a merely conceptual link between autonomy and intersubjective recognition has possible implications for social and political critique.

In addition, however, the intersubjective dimension of evaluative judgements can be given a stronger interpretation, one that goes beyond a mere conceptual connection. On this view, the self seeks public – and possibly even political – recognition for the validity of its evaluative judgements and for the conceptions of the good life on which these evaluations are based. If, for example, homosexuals are permitted to live the lifestyle of their choice only so long as they do so in private or in carefully delimited enclaves, they are denied the public affirmation of identity and of their assignments of meaning and value that is afforded to those who lead conventionally accepted heterosexual lifestyles. The same argument applies to the innovative self-inventions espoused by feminists such as Judith Butler, and to the self-definitions, life-choices and conceptions of the good held by individuals and groups on the margins of society. Arguably, the freedom to have a public identity – and this means a publicly affirmed identity – is fundamental for individual human well-being. It has been said that the 'freedom to have impact on others – to make the "statement" implicit in a public identity – is central to any adequate conception of the self'.[70] If this is so, autonomy has not only an intersubjective dimension: it has an inherently public – and possibly political – dimension that requires further exploration and discussion.

My concern in this essay has been to look at autonomy from the point of view of the challenge to it issued by feminism, and to indicate some ways forward for feminist thinking in this regard. I have tried to show that the notion of autonomy is not necessarily connected with conceptions of self-identity that are unacceptable to feminists, and that it can be interpreted in a way congenial to feminist concerns. However, in my proposed interpretation of autonomy as self-authorship I attribute to it an ethical dimension, thereby introducing to the discussion of autonomy an element that has not, so far, been the focus of feminist debate. While I have defended the ethical view of autonomy as one way of making sense of the common perception that autonomy should be prized and promoted, I acknowledge that nonethical interpretations of autonomy are also possible. I thus call on feminists – and others – concerned to rethink autonomy to engage critically with the ethical view. If, as I believe they should, they favour it as an account of human well-being, they must respond to the further questions it poses. Above all, they must respond to the question of ethical validity and address the problem of obtaining a nonarbitrary basis for evaluating the 'truth' of subjective assignments of meaning and value.

Notes

1 My discussion of the feminist critique of autonomy forms part of a discussion of Habermas and autonomy in Maeve Cooke, 'Habermas, Feminism and the Question of Autonomy', in Peter Dews (ed.), *Habermas: A Critical Reader* (Oxford: Blackwell, 1998).

2 Clearly, this schema cannot do justice to the many variations in the position held within either camp. It may also fail to do justice to the complex positions of 'French' feminists such as Julia Kristeva and Hélène Cixous. Kristeva can be read as proposing an idea of the 'feminine' as an alternative to the 'masculine' symbolic order; Cixous as proposing one that is subversive of it. Arguably, however, Kristeva does not reject the 'masculine' value of autonomy, but sees it as in need of supplementation through the 'feminine' dimensions of subjectivity. Furthermore, although Cixous's notion of the 'feminine' does seem to undermine the ideal of autonomy, it runs into difficulties similar to those encountered by poststructuralist and postmodern critics (see below).

3 See, for example, Susan Moller Okin, 'Reason and Feeling in Thinking about Justice', in Cass Sunstein (ed.), *Feminism and Political Theory* (Chicago: University of Chicago Press, 1990), pp. 15–35; Seyla Benhabib, 'The Generalized and the Concrete Other', in S. Benhabib and D. Cornell (eds), *Feminism as Critique* (Minneapolis: University of Minnesota Press, 1987), pp. 77–95.

4 Benhabib, 'The Generalized and the Concrete Other', p. 84.

5 Here I follow a central thesis of Charles Taylor set forward in his *Philosophical Papers*, vol. 2 (Cambridge: Cambridge University Press, 1985) and *Sources of the Self* (Cambridge: Cambridge University Press, 1989). Cf. also below, esp. pp. 269–270 and 274.

6 Cf. Carol Gilligan, *In a Different Voice* (Cambridge, MA: Harvard University Press, 1982).

7 Cf. Maeve Cooke, 'Are Ethical Conflicts Irreconcilable?', *Philosophy and Social Criticism*, vol. 23, no. 2 (1997): 1–19.

8 This is not true for all feminists who associate themselves with poststructuralism and postmodernism. Drucilla Cornell, for instance, draws heavily on Derridean poststructuralism without wanting to reject normative conceptions of self-identity as such. She argues rather for a particular normative conception of self-identity – one that takes account of difference as an inevitable part of conceptual thought, and that recovers the affective and 'natural' dimensions of moral agency. Cf. D. Cornell, *The Philosophy of the Limit* (New York:

278

Routledge, 1992); also D. Cornell and A. Thurschwell, 'Feminism, Negativity, Intersubjectivity', in Benhabib and Cornell, *Feminism as Critique*, pp. 143–62.

9 Judith Butler, 'Gender Trouble, Feminist Theory and Psychoanalytic Discourse', in L. Nicholson (ed.), *Feminism/Postmodernism* (New York: Routledge, 1990), pp. 324–40.

10 Jane Flax, *Disputed Subjects* (New York: Routledge, 1993), pp. 93ff.

11 Judith Butler, 'Contingent Foundations: Feminism and the Question of Postmodernism', in J. Butler and J. Scott (eds), *Feminists Theorize the Political* (New York: Routledge, 1992), pp. 3–21; here p. 15.

12 Cf. Flax, *Disputed Subjects*, pp. 32, 108, 127.

13 Flax, *Disputed Subjects*, p. 101.

14 See, for example, Linda Alcoff, 'Cultural Feminism versus Poststructuralism: The Identity Crisis in Feminist Theory', in M. Malson *et al.* (eds), *Feminist Theory in Practice and Process* (Chicago: University of Chicago Press, 1989); and Allison Weir, 'Toward a Model of Self-Identity: Habermas and Kristeva', in J. Meehan (ed.), *Feminists Read Habermas* (New York: Routledge, 1995), pp. 263–82.

15 Alcoff, 'Identity Crisis', p. 309.

16 Patricia Huntington, 'Toward a Dialectical Concept of Autonomy', *Philosophy and Social Criticism*, vol. 21, no. 1 (1995): 37–55.

17 To be sure, Flax states explicitly that she is not advocating fragmentation as the only possible or desirable alternative to a false sense of unity (*Disputed Subjects*, p. 102); furthermore, she shows convincingly that 'lacking the ability to sustain coherence, one slides into the endless terror, emptiness, desolate loneliness, and fear of annihilation that pervade borderline subjectivity' (pp. 102–3). What is needed, in her view, are better ways of organizing subjectivities. But it is far from clear on what basis subjectivities are to be organized and how such normatively guided organization of subjectivity fits with her outright rejection of 'Enlightenment' values such as autonomy, self-determination and individuality.

18 Susan Bordo, *Unbearable Weight: Feminism, Western Culture and the Body* (California: University of California Press, 1993), pp. 225ff.

19 Bordo, *Unbearable Weight*, p. 227.

20 Bordo, *Unbearable Weight*, pp. 228f.

21 Patricia Waugh, 'Modernism, Postmodernism, Feminism: Gender and Autonomy Theory', in Waugh (ed.), *Postmodernism. A Reader* (London: Edward Arnold, 1992), pp. 189–204; here pp. 191–92.

22 Waugh, 'Modernism, Postmodernism, Feminism', p. 194.

23 Weir, 'Toward A Model of Self-Identity'.

24 Michèle Barrett, for instance, argues that we need better conceptions of agency and identity than have been available in either (anti-humanist) poststructuralist thought or its (humanist) modernist predecessors. She calls for an imaginative reopening of the issue of humanism (Barrett, 'Words and Things', in Michèle Barrett and Anne Phillips (eds), *Destabilizing Theory*, Cambridge: Polity Press, 1992, pp. 201–19; here p. 216). This call is echoed by Judith Grant who advocates a feminist humanist vision: a new and improved post-Enlightenment humanism (Grant, *Fundamental Feminism*, New York: Routledge, 1993, p. 183).

25 For instance, the aim of full rational retrievability would be seen as repressive according to the model of subjectivity developed by Julia Kristeva, which attaches central importance to the prelinguistic (and essentially nonlinguistic) 'semiotic' realm; cf. J. Kristeva, 'The System and the Speaking Subject', and

other essays, in Toril Moi (ed.), *The Kristeva Reader* (New York: Columbia University Press, 1986).

26 Cooke, 'Habermas, Feminism and the Question of Autonomy'.

27 Susan Wolf makes both these points in her critique of the 'autonomy view' of the self in *Reason within Freedom* (New York, Oxford University Press, 1990), pp. 10–14.

28 Since Wolf (1990) interprets the idea of self-direction only as self-origination, she ends up rejecting the ideal of autonomy completely. Bernard Berofsky's rejection of the view that autonomy is self-direction is also based on an interpretation of self-direction as self-origination; see *Liberation from Self: A Theory of Personal Autonomy* (New York: Cambridge University Press, 1995), pp. 1ff.

29 Cf. Jürgen Habermas, *The Theory of Communicative Action*, vol. 2, trans. by T. McCarthy (Boston: Beacon Press, 1987), p. 99 and *Postmetaphysical Thinking*, trans. by W.M. Hohengarten (Cambridge, MA: MIT Press, 1990), p. 227.

30 Berofsky situates objectivity at the core of his conception of autonomy, defining it as 'an open, informed and flexible response to the materials, structure and constraints of those disciplines, institutions, and enterprises, interaction with which constitutes our life and provides it with meaning' (*Liberation from Self*, p. 181).

31 Berofsky, *Liberation from Self*, p. 2.

32 Harry Frankfurt makes the case for the capacity for second-order reflection and volition in idem, 'Freedom of the Will and the Concept of a Person', reprinted in G. Watson (ed.), *Free Will* (Oxford: Oxford University Press, 1982), pp. 81–95.

33 Cf. C. Taylor, 'Responsibility for Self', reprinted in Watson, *Free Will*, pp. 111–26.

34 Joseph Raz, *The Morality of Freedom* (Oxford: Clarendon Press, 1986), pp. 372ff.

35 Raz (see *Morality of Freedom*, pp. 372f.) focuses on the autonomous life rather than on isolated episodes of autonomous judgement; Berofsky makes a comparable distinction between what he calls dispositional and occurrent autonomy (see *Liberation from Self*, pp. 208f.). Both Berofsky (pp. 31f.) and Raz (pp. 372f.) emphasize that autonomy is a matter of degree.

36 Jürgen Habermas, 'Reconciliation through the Public Use of Reason: Remarks on John Rawls's Political Liberalism', *Journal of Philosophy*, XCII, 3 (1995): 109–31; J. Rawls, 'Reply to Habermas', *Journal of Philosophy*, XCII, 3 (1995): 132–79.

37 Cf. M. Cooke, 'A Space of One's Own: Liberty, Privacy, Identity', *Philosophy and Social Criticism* (forthcoming).

38 J.J. Rousseau, *Emile*, trans. by B. Foxley (London: Dent, 1974), p. 408.

39 Immanuel Kant, *The Moral Law*, trans. and ed. by H.J. Paton (London: Hutchinson, 1948), pp. 94–5.

40 See, for example, Jürgen Habermas, 'Individuation through Socialization', in *Postmetaphysical Thinking*. In his *Theory of Justice* (Oxford: Oxford University Press, 1972), John Rawls underscores the connection between freedom and (moral) reason (cf. pp. 516ff.).

41 Charles Taylor, 'The Politics of Recognition', in Amy Gutmann (ed.), *Multiculturalism and the 'Politics of Recognition'* (Princeton, NJ: Princeton University Press, 1992), p. 57.

42 This distinction relies on a distinction between moral validity and ethical validity of the kind proposed by Habermas (cf., for example, 'On the Employments of Practical Reason' in his *Justification and Application: Remarks on Discourse*

Ethics, trans. by Ciaran Cronin, Cambridge, MA: MIT Press, 1992, pp. 1–17) and Ricoeur (cf. *OneSelf as Another*, trans. by Katherine Blamey, Chicago: University of Chicago Press, 1992, especially Chapter X). On such a view, only universalizable norms and principles can be morally valid; by contrast, claims to ethical validity are always context-specific and relate to individuals and their culture-bound conceptions of the good life.

43 Admittedly, proponents of this view usually insist that ego-ideals may not *infringe against* moral norms and principles.

44 One justification offered for this is the claim that, under the postmetaphysical conditions of modernity, no metastandards are available for adjudicating the worth of competing conceptions of the good.

45 This is the aspect emphasized by Taylor. See, for example, his *Ethics of Authenticity* (Cambridge, MA: Harvard University Press, 1989).

46 Habermas connects validity claims with a number of idealizing suppositions that unavoidably guide participants in communicative action. One such supposition is that a claim, if valid, would command the assent of everyone under ideal epistemic conditions. See M. Cooke, *Language and Reason: A Study of Habermas's Pragmatics* (Cambridge, MA: MIT Press, 1994), especially Chapters 2 and 5.

47 Habermas makes this point with regard to what he calls 'discourses': intersubjective forums for critical reflection in which participants are guided by certain unavoidable presuppositions. (Cf. Jürgen Habermas, 'Rorty's Pragmatic Turn', in M. Cooke (ed.), *On the Pragmatics of Communication*, Cambridge, MA: MIT Press, 1998). For our present purposes, however, we can leave open the question of whether reflective deliberation on conceptions of the good life must satisfy the demanding conditions of discourse.

48 Friedrich Nietzsche, *Beyond Good and Evil*, trans. by R. J. Hollingdale (Harmondsworth: Penguin, 1990). Berofsky, *Liberation from Self* (especially Chapter 5) appears to follow this Nietzschean line.

49 I explain this term in my concluding remarks below.

50 For instance, Berofsky, *Liberation from Self*, pp. 235–36.

51 I return to this problem in my concluding remarks below.

52 Berofsky, *Liberation from Self*, especially Chapter 5.

53 Berofsky, *Liberation from Self*, pp. 236–7.

54 Berofsky argues that it frees us to pursue debates about the self such as that between 'psychological realism' and 'psychological constructivism' without the worry that our views on autonomy are going to be profoundly affected (*ibid.*, pp. 236–7).

55 In fact, they rarely advance this view explicitly or show why the other two positions are misguided. For example, Berofsky appears to address explicitly the question of the value of autonomy (this is the title of his final chapter). However, despite engaging with some feminist criticisms of autonomy, he in fact seems to take its value and desirability as self-evident (see Berofsky, *Liberation from Self*, pp. 239–49).

56 Raz, *Morality of Freedom*, p. 381.

57 Raz, *Morality of Freedom*, pp. 289ff. and 391ff.

58 Taylor constructs this picture most comprehensively in his *Sources of the Self*.

59 Taylor, *Ethics of Authenticity*.

60 See above, note 42.

61 Cf. Richard Rorty, *Philosophy and the Mirror of Nature* (Princeton: Princeton University Press, 1979).

62 Habermas, *Postmetaphysical Thinking*, especially Chapter 1.

63 Cf. Cooke, *Language and Reason*, Chapters 2 and 5.
64 See, for example, Iris Marion Young, 'Impartiality and the Civic Republic', in Benhabib and Cornell (eds), *Feminism as Critique*, pp. 57–76, and Benhabib, *Situating the Self*, especially Part 1. Cf. also Cooke, 'Habermas, Feminism and the Question of Autonomy'.
65 Cf. Peter Dews, 'The Paradigm Shift to Communication and the Question of Subjectivity: Reflections on Habermas, Lacan and Mead', *Revue Internationale de Philosophie*, vol. 4 (1995).
66 Habermas stresses the difference between general social critique and critique of subjectively held evaluative judgements. Whereas his concept of communicative rationality is supposed to provide a basis for the former, it leaves open – and arguably evades – the question of the possible rational basis for the latter.
67 Cf. Hilary Putnam, *Realism and Reason* (Cambridge: Cambridge University Press, 1983), 'Introduction'. Cf. also Habermas, 'Rorty's Pragmatic Turn'.
68 I outline such an argument in Cooke, 'A Space of One's Own'.
69 Cooke, 'A Space of One's Own'.
70 Frank Michelman, 'Law's Republic', *Yale Law Journal*, vol. 97, no. 8 (1988): 1,493–537 (here p. 1,534, quoting Law, 'Homosexuality and the Social Meaning of Gender', *Wisconsin Law Review*, vol. 1, no. 15 (1988).

19

FROM ETHICS TO BIOETHICS

Peter Kemp

Ethics in general

The good life

I consider ethics as a vision of the good life, expressed in stories about our existence and our behaviour towards and together with others in a world of life. As such, it expresses itself in certain ideas about the values of human beings, of human society and of the living nature. In that sense ethics belongs to the self-understanding of every human being. It is our understanding of what counts as highly valuable in personal encounters, in social relationships and in our ties to nature. It is a double vision, of what is and what ought to be, but if we have not already experienced it to some extent and discovered it as a reality, we would never have been able to imagine it as a goal. Conversely, if the good life had already totally realised itself, we would never have the need to speak about ethics. Thus ethics is first of all a vision which shapes us as human beings, as persons able to take our responsibilities for our life with others and with the whole living world.

And this is the reason why ethical conceptions have also been studied as a fundamental field for systematic philosophical reflection. Such a study we also call 'ethics'. Now, if ethics is concerned primarily with visions of the good life, it is fundamentally not a system of rules and norms. But morals as the norms for right action follow from these visions. The ethical vision demands morality with its norms in order to protect and enforce the good by the right. And so moral laws declare some actions harmful for the good life and therefore forbidden, whereas other actions are recommended as beneficial and proper for the expansion of the good. However, laws or moral rules are always secondary in ethics. Truly, the basis for ethics is the imagination of what is good in human beings, society and nature. Norms, obligations and prohibitions are only judgements about right and wrong actions and omissions the aim of which is to protect and promote the basic good.

Thereby some actions such as killing, lying and stealing may be condemned as harmful for the good life, not in any imaginable situation, but most of the time (it may be necessary to lie in order to protect someone, but it does not mean that normally it is right to lie); and some actions such as care for the other, searching for truth and giving gifts are prescribed as right behaviour, perhaps not always, but most of the time (I cannot personally take care of all persons at the same time; it is not always good to speak the truth, and a gift might be more of an obligation for the other than a real support, etc.).

In ethics the ideal is not obedience, but joint creativity; not order, but happiness; and by a 'happy life' one does not intend the narrow egoistic satisfaction of individual needs, but rather the enrichment or protection of life by mutual giving and receiving irrespective of what and how much is given and received in the concrete situation.

Care for the other can be considered as the first and highest virtue before it is also prescribed as a first command. It aims at the enrichment and protection of lives which can be lost, in particular of all living beings who form parts of our own lives, as irreplaceable realities. Moreover, this idea of *irreplaceability* is not only integral to our concept of kinship, but is a key component of an ethical world-vision, which includes all human beings and all species living in nature (by which is meant life-forms which are not by their mere existence a fatal threat to human life, such as the HIV virus). It even concerns the whole eco-sphere as the irreplaceable condition for all living organisms.

We have a name for 'the good' in social life; we call it 'justice'. Justice is the condition for the good life at the level of society. It is equity, fairness and impartiality in judgements about actions and in distributions of goods and services. It follows that in an ethical perspective justice which makes the social life a happy life is more fundamental than are the laws which intend order amongst the citizens.

The concept of 'person'

I have said that ethics is a vision which shapes us as persons who are responsible for our co-existence with other persons and with the whole living world. The question then is how to define the human person and to specify the sense in which the concept of person implies ethics. This is a philosophical question about our own being and about the being of other persons. Our being has an ethical impact by virtue of our actions. Ethics of course concerns our way of acting.

Thus I am a person from the moment I discover myself and understand myself as a will-to-life and at the same time discover others as a condition for expanding the capacities of my own life. A person is then a self-conscious physical being who lives by receiving something from and giving something to other self-conscious physical beings.

My self is my relation to my own will-to-life as an autonomous will. This autonomy supposes on the one hand a separation from others by which I am an individual and not a simple member of a crowd, and on the other hand an association with others by which they recognise my self as autonomous. Thus the self cannot exist without the other. But the other's recognition of me and my recognition of the other must be more than a simple statement of human existence as an entity in the world. What I need to receive from the other is his or her openness towards me by which the other is present to me. And this presence means that he or she who gives him or herself to me is giving something that expresses this fundamental gift of community.

This idea of the person implies that a person needs practical wisdom about what Aristotle called the good life. According to Aristotle this practical wisdom can never be expressed in pure theory, because it is an insight about living that we learn only by practice and by the good example of others. It sets a goal for our lives, but it is not simply a state of pleasure to be reached after long and hard work; rather the goal is the very way of life as such which takes form and develops from day to day in practical relationships and friendships.

Dignity

The person's need of the other person is expressed through the consideration accorded to the dignity of the other. In our culture this dignity implies that the value of the person resides in or is constituted by the human individual as such and not dependent on the power he or she exercises and the property he or she holds. It implies the irreplaceability of every person in such a way that the death of the other is a loss which can never be compensated. No person is just a social function which may be executed by anyone who has the necessary skills and capacity for performing that function. In terms of function no one is indispensable, but as a person each and every one of us is irreplaceable.

In his *Groundwork of the Metaphysic of Morals* (1785) Immanuel Kant expresses this idea of human dignity by the distinction between intrinsic and extrinsic value. He has learned from Adam Smith's economic theory of value that on the market everything has its price (a market price or a fancy price), which means that it has an equivalent. This price is its external or relative value. But no human being capable of reason has an equivalent, and consequently it has no price. This is its intrinsic or absolute value.

Following Kant this idea of a person's intrinsic value was prescribed by a practical imperative present universally in people's morality. The practical imperative says that you must 'act in such a way that you always treat humanity, whether in your own person or in the person of any other, never simply as a means, but always at the same time as an end' (p. 439). By this formulation Kant does not deny that we are obliged and even allowed to treat each other as means for some ends. He does not deny this implication of our existence for one another as bodies. But he claims that there must be limits to this treatment of such a kind that the autonomy of the other is preserved and the intrinsic or absolute value of him or her as a person respected.

His formulation of the practical imperative is brilliant as a prescription of the inviolability and integrity of the person as a living, thinking and feeling being in a scientific–technological time, where many people, fascinated by the advancements of science and technology, believe that the production systems are in themselves the highest value and the individual has value only from its function in the systems where he or she may be replaced at any moment.

Ethics and moral rules

Kant's ethical theory presupposed an idea of the good life; in other words, the imperatives which constitute the moral command or the moral law are derived from a view of personal life. Therefore it is this view of the good life which founds the moral command and not the contrary.

Unfortunately, in general Kant has not been understood in this way. Kantian morality has often been taken as a system of observance of the moral law for its own sake, and founded on purely abstract thinking. He was to some extent himself responsible for this understanding of his insistence that the foundation of good practice must be comparable to the foundation of scientific knowledge, i.e. founded on laws. Thus he claimed that the maxim for human action should be considered as if it were 'a universal law of nature' (p. 421). Consequently he believed that the moral law must be the ground of practice and not the contrary.

But many new ethical questions raised by modern technology demonstrate our inability to answer them without first having recourse to a view of life in narratives about how life succeeds. In particular the questions in bioethics to which I turn in the second part of this essay and which concern the limits to our manipulations of living beings cannot be answered by pure abstract thinking but need visions of life based on experiences of concrete situations in which the questions arise. We have to establish norms which give us the means of generating solutions to these questions. These norms will serve life as long as they are not made absolute or unshakeable. But they oppress life as soon as they are insisted upon in spite of the fact that the old conditions on which they were based no longer exist or have changed radically.

Happiness

But what is the good life? Aristotle was claiming happiness as the goal for his ethics. For him happiness was a way of living well and doing well. It was 'a virtuous activity of the soul' (*Nicomachean Ethics*, 1097b) and not simply a pleasant state. But in our culture the idea of happiness has developed in such a way that it often is incapable of giving direction to our search for the good life. This was the reason why Kant rejected happiness as the end for good action. He considered happiness as merely the satisfaction of all material needs: needs of power, wealth, honour, health, in short 'complete well-being and contentment' (*Groundwork*, p. 393).

But when happiness is understood in this way it is clear that it cannot serve as an end for the ethics of persons who constitute a community with others and therefore must be ready to renounce some material satisfactions in order to care about others. Should we then give up Aristotle's idea of happiness as the goal of all good practice? If not, we must redefine happiness in relation to the deepest need of the person. I mentioned that this need is a reciprocity of giving and receiving something. Thus happiness is more a successful relationship between autonomous human beings than it is the enjoyment of material advantages and benefits.

That does not mean that material welfare is without importance for the good life. But human life does not need luxury in order to be fulfilled. It needs only the interaction of irreplaceable persons who offer themselves and their works to each other and express this attitude by the giving and receiving of gifts, but without considering the size or quantity of the gifts. What counts in that case is only that we are giving gifts, not what gifts we are offering, to each other. Therefore well-being does not in itself imply happiness, but happiness depends on the other person as the source of goodness in our life. The experience of that goodness is the very foundation of all ethics. It gives meaning to the idea of the respect for myself and other persons as irreplaceable.

Towards a universal ethics

However, in the debate with the Kantian model the Aristotelian model should not have the last word in ethics; there remains a dialectic between an Aristotelian experience of the good life and the Kantian plea for normativity – or between wisdom and practical reason – by virtue of the fact that this plea for normativity is fundamentally a claim for universality. This is why Paul Ricoeur in his recent book *Oneself as Another* links together the two conceptions of ethics by showing that the desire for the good life must undergo the test of the norm in terms of a moral judgement, if it is to confirm itself as universally valuable and valid.[1] The claim to universality is grounded in the Kantian idea of the 'good will' which is a will to do through the particular moral act what is good for everybody concerned. On the other hand, as far as the good will tends to do something good for someone, it presupposes an idea of the good life to be realised by moral action.

We may conclude that there can be no normativity without the experience of the good life and our desire to create, conserve and protect it against the irremediable loss of the irreplaceable; but this experience of the good we do not want to lose can only retain strong validity as the ground for all ethics if it can be recognised as such by everyone, i.e. as being a universal value.

Ethics and the rise of bioethics

The term 'bioethics'

It might be useful to recall how the word 'bioethics' first entered the modern debate about ethics. The word bioethics was first applied in 1971 by Van Rensselaer Potter who understood 'bioethical' as the application of biological sciences in order to improve the quality of life. He thought that the study of the nature of human beings and the world could help us to formulate the goals for humankind. Thus, for Potter, bioethics is the 'science for survival'. This use of the word related the term 'bio' to questions that were not only biological, but involved healthcare.

However it seems problematic to consider ethics as an applied science. Ethics may guide and use sciences, but in itself it is a practical view of life, not an area of theoretical knowledge. Indeed, the word came into fashion not as an application of bio-sciences, but as a term for ethics in medicine and the bio-medical sciences. In that sense it is treated in Sissela Bok's consideration of the fundamental principles of bioethics in 1976.

This is also the principal sense of the word in the standard work *Encyclopaedia of Bioethics*.[2] Nevertheless the *Encyclopaedia of Bioethics* does not limit bioethics to medical ethics. The editor, Warren T. Reich, extends the meaning of 'bioethics' to concern for the whole living world, since there are ethical questions which concern living beings (and not only with regard to animal experimentations), but which are not, at least not directly, concerned with the ethics of medicine and medical science, for instance questions about genetic engineering in animal reproduction and plant breeding.

The enlargement of ethics to bioethics

Following both Greek philosophical and Christian theological traditions, the field of ethics includes questions about achieving life in practice and about the practical relationships between persons, i.e. between human beings having acquired full consciousness of their actions. But modern bio-technologies have created new possibilities of manipulating human life in its different stages of development, from the moment of the conception of a fertilised human egg to the adult human being. Therefore the first step has been to enlarge the ethical field to this new domain of possible manipulation.

It is true that in our culture prenatal human life has always been a concern of ethics since the permissibility of abortion has been considered as an ethical question about 'the right to life' of the foetus versus the right of the woman to decide about the development of the foetus in her own body. But the involvement of modern biotechnologies and medical science in the genetic engineering of fertilised eggs, and the research and tests carried out on human embryos and foetuses have created many new questions, most of which concern the insight: all that we are able to do is not to be identified with what we are allowed to do.

However, nearly all the research, testing and manipulation of prenatal human life has been made possible because it has already been done on highly developed animals. This calls our attention to the fact that what now is going on in laboratories using animals as subjects may sooner or later be tried on human beings. It may also remind us that as living beings we are rooted in the living world or in the whole 'family of life' on earth, and there might be limits to what is permissible in our treatment and use of other living beings if we still want to behave with a certain dignity in relation to nature.

It follows that there are ethical questions which have nothing to do with medicine because they concern the relation in general between human action and living nature. This is the reason why a second step in extending ethics beyond its classical field may be taken. This second step in enlarging ethics cannot be avoided in our time when biotechnologies tend to convert all living beings, be they human or nonhuman, into objects for manipulation. This bioethical regard for nature is implicit in all criticism of human exploitation of the living world.

Thus bioethics includes three levels:

1 first the level of persons;
2 then the level of 'potential' persons or prenatal human life; and
3 the level of living beings in general.

The foundation of bioethics

The question which is discussed with the greatest passion today is how we can conceive the foundations of bioethics in its full extent. It might seem plausible that if we extend ethics to mean care of the whole living world, then a scientific foundation of ethics can be claimed since biology and ecology can give us the information about what we have to do in order not to destroy our earth. But the ethics of the environment in question here may envisage only a calculation of what we have to do in order to survive, and this calculation may be very narrow, i.e. concerning only the individual's own survival (perhaps together with some family and friends), or at most may countenance the survival of future generations of *human* beings.

The individual might even prefer to live in 'a hard way' destroying nature to derive very short-term benefits and thereby taking the risk of perishing as a consequence of his or her own behaviour. No science is in a position to tell the individual that this attitude to nature is morally wrong. Thus the norms for behaviour in respect to nature cannot find their ethical foundation in biology or ecology alone. The sciences can say only what will happen if this or that behaviour is practised. They cannot say what *ought* to be done. This can be said only on the basis of our ethical conviction.

It is also to be noted that the ethics of the environment must be distinguished from bioethics. We take care of the environment, of its 'sustainability' (not to pollute it, not to plunder it, etc.), for our own sake and perhaps also for the sake of our children and descendants. The motive for our behaviour is then utilitarian: our action is determined by what we find useful for ourselves and the life we want continued on earth.

To be concerned and to have respect for prenatal and potential human life and for the living nature in general, may have a quite different explanation. It may be founded on the idea of a certain inviolability of living beings which is claimed because the human person has its life roots in nature and the development of a foetus. The concern for nature is then understood and claimed as an extension of the idea of the inviolability of the human person to all living beings. It follows that, considered in this way, bioethics is neither founded in biosciences nor grounded in the ethics of the environment, but in the ethics of persons extended to the whole living world because this world is the home of humanity.

The limits to the manipulation of human life

The ethics of persons requires that a person is never treated simply as a means to an end, but always as an end in itself or as having an intrinsic value. But what we call a prenatal human being (zygote, embryo or foetus) or potential person (newborn baby) is distinguished from a fully adult person by the fact that the former is unable to think distinctions, i.e. that it cannot think at all, and therefore cannot understand itself as a will-to-life, as autonomous, etc. It is life, but life without reflection, without comprehension of itself. Such life, as in animals, is unable to understand its own death or the death of the other. It can avoid death only by instinct, and consequently it can have no fear of death which is not an imminent danger.

This difference means that modern biotechnologies may manipulate premature human life in certain ways without injuring it as a self-consciousness, simply because such self-consciousness does not yet exist. Should we then consider all prenatal life or even the first stages of life after birth as a pure material we can use as we like? Should we be inclined to answer yes to this question we should first be certain that there is no connection between the developed person and the prenatal human being or potential person such that it provides reason for extending respect for persons to the prenatal human life or potential person. But there is such a connection.

A prenatal human being or a potential person is a living being who will develop into an autonomous being if nothing happens to interrupt the normal evolution of its potentialities or to handicap its potentialities. Thus, to hold a prenatal human being or potential person in respect is to express a respect for what is similar to what we have all been prior to becoming aware of ourselves, and this is in a way to hold our own humanity in respect.

Moreover, observations of a foetus' reactions to violent damage indicate that it is able to feel pain from a certain stage in its development. Pain is quite different from suffering which we can define as awareness of a discrepancy between what a person wants to do and what he or she is able to do; pain refers to a feeling stimulating the subject to come out of an unpleasant state, and a pain can be so heavy as to make life unbearable. Therefore we must be opposed to causing pain in a living being for which we have sympathy, such as a prenatal human being or potential person, and we may consider that to cause pain even in an animal is not compatible with human dignity in action.

These are the main reasons for extending respect to embryos and foetuses. Thus we have to take into account that there are both differences and connections between developed persons and prenatal human beings. This is important when modern biotechnologies constrain us to take decisions – eventually in ethical committees composed of doctors, scientists and educators – about whether or not we can permit research, tests and manipulations on prenatal human life, and eventually to what extent we can permit such research.

The differences can be taken as a reason for the permissibility of some biotechnological and medical interference in the organism of a prenatal human being, whereas the connections must imply that we have to determine certain limits to this interference, so that we can still show our respect for the potential human life. Moreover, we must recognise that we can never find clear demarcations in the biological and personal evolution from embryo to foetus, and from foetus to baby and, finally, from baby

291

to autonomous person. We must consider that there is a gradual transition in the development from the prenatal human being via the baby (potential person) to the developed person. This implies that our stipulations of limits to interference on prenatal life must also be gradual, and that there must be still stronger limits to what is permitted in research, testing and manipulation for those developmental stages which guide work undertaken, from genetics to the medical treatment of human patients.

The limits to exploitation of living nature

If we can extend the respect for persons to babies and, further, to prenatal human life, why not extend respect to animals and the whole living world? This respect would be without reason only if we could maintain an absolute cut between human life and life in general. There is indeed a cut, because we use animals as food and we domesticate some animals for the production of our food or purely for our pleasure.

But if all kinds of exploitation and manipulation of animals and of their genetic structures were to be accepted (and such manipulation is possible, even without painful experimentation: genetic engineering, for instance, is not painful for the manipulated being), then in the end living nature will be no more than pure material for our exploitation.

The issue could not be clarified as a problem for humanity for as long as human beings were obliged to fight against nature in order to overcome and harness its forces, limiting their capacities to destroy lives. We have inherited an ethics which considers only the relationships between persons but does not include nature in the relationships countenanced. A certain insensibility towards the living world was the result of that ethical inheritance. Today, however, the biotechnologies at work might transform the whole living world into an enormous laboratory in which all kinds of manipulation takes place. This new perspective and its implications for our social life can open our eyes to the importance of claiming limits to biotechnological manipulation and research.

A final story

Let me finish by telling you of an experience I had ten years ago in a seminar at the Inter-University Centre of Dubrovnik. At the beginning of the meeting several participants declared firmly that there could be a question of bioethics for human beings only. Of course, they had heard of battery-hens and factory calves, but that had given them no trouble. Perhaps they had heard also how it was then possible by genetic engineering to create hens without feathers (to make it impossible for the hens to pluck one another) and cows without paunches (to shorten their long digestion process). But they were convinced that as a cultural being, a human person must oppose nature, fight against it and master it in order to assure a good human society. Thus human beings are allowed to treat all things in nature as material for use in the development of human welfare.

But then someone told of an extreme case of manipulating animals. A participant had been present at an international meeting of veterinary scientists where it had been revealed that experiments were going on in certain laboratories in order to produce pigs without eyes. These pigs were more interested in eating than were normal pigs and they became big and fat more quickly. Indeed, here was the pig of which the food industry has dreamed! It was not claimed that these pigs were already being created, but scientists present at our meeting had no doubt about the real possibility of engineering them.

The fact that this case of producing pigs without eyes was brought into our seminar provoked a new turn in our discussions: no one wanted to undertake the defence of such food production. The idea of creating deliberately blind pigs was considered monstrous by all the participants. The monstrosity does not consist in torture of the pigs or inflicting pain on them (this would have been 'normal' cruelty against animals), but rather consists in the fact that the pigs have been deprived in advance of the gift of sight and are thereby treated as pure means for manipulation.

The story tells us that there seem to be limits to how far we can and are willing to go in transforming the whole of nature into an enormous factory for food production. So it is not only human beings towards whom we may feel that we owe the respect due to their intrinsic value; the same can be said about other living beings. It follows that in ethics we cannot maintain an absolute distinction between animal and human beings which allows us to exclude animals from the field of bioethics. Bioethics is not only medical ethics but an ethics for the entire living world.

Notes

1 Paul Ricoeur, *Soi-même comme un autre*, Paris: Seuil, 1991, p. 238.
2 *Encyclopaedia of Bioethics*, ed. W.T. Reich, Washington, DC: Kennedy Institute, Georgetown University, 1978; revised edn., New York: Free Press, 1995.

INDEX